EUROPEAN STUDIES ON CHRISTIAN ORIGINS

Wonders Never Cease

The Purpose of Narrating Miracle Stories
in the New Testament and
its Religious Environment

EDITED BY
MICHAEL LABAHN
AND
BERT JAN LIETAERT PEERBOLTE

t&t clark

Copyright © Michael Labahn, Bert Jan Lietaert Peerbolte and contributors, 2006
A Continuum imprint

Published by T & T Clark International
The Tower Building, 11 York Road, London SE1 7NX
15 East 26th Street, Suite 1703, New York, NY 10010

www.tandtclark.com

British Library Cataloguing-in-Publication Data
A catalogue record for this book is available from the British Library

Typeset by Free Range Book Design & Production
Printed on acid-free paper in Great Britain by MPG Books Ltd., Bodmin, Cornwall

ISBN 0567080773   (hardback)

CONTENTS

Preface   vii
Abbreviations   ix
List of Contributors   xv

Part I

JACQUES VAN RUITEN
A Miraculous Birth of Isaac in the *Book of Jubilees*?   1

JAN DEN BOEFT
Asclepius' Healings Made Known   20

ULRIKE RIEMER
Miracle Stories and Their Narrative Intent in the Context
of the Ruler Cult of Classical Antiquity   32

MICHAEL BECKER
Miracle Traditions in Early Rabbinic Literature:
Some Questions on their Pragmatics   48

ERKKI KOSKENNIEMI
The Function of the Miracle Stories in Philostratus's
Vita Apollonii Tyanensis   70

Part II

GEERT VAN OYEN
Markan Miracle Stories in Historical Jesus Research,
Redaction Criticism and Narrative Analysis   87

REINHARD VON BENDEMANN
'Many-Coloured Illnesses' (Mark 1.34):
On the Significance of Illnesses in New Testament
Therapy Narratives   100

MICHAEL LABAHN
Fishing for Meaning:
The Miraculous Catch of Fish in John 21   125

MATTI MYLLYKOSKI
Being There:
The Function of the Supernatural in Acts 1–12   146

BERT JAN LIETAERT PEERBOLTE
Paul the Miracle Worker:
Development and Background of Pauline Miracle Stories   180

BEATE KOWALSKI
Eschatological Signs and Their Function in the Revelation
of John   200

Part III

LAUTARO ROIG LANZILLOTTA
Cannibals, Myrmidonians, Sinopeans or Jews?
The Five Versions of *The Acts of Andrew and Matthias*
and Their Source(s)   221

BERND KOLLMANN
Images of Hope:
Towards an Understanding of New Testament Miracle Stories 244

Index of References   265

Index of Authors   281

PREFACE

Wonders never cease, and miracle stories never cease to occupy the students of biblical writings and the literature contemporary to them. Over the past two decades, a number of important works have been published on miracle stories in the New Testament – some of their authors are part of this collection.[1]

Much as these works have contributed to our understanding of miracle stories, there are still many matters unsolved. The present volume focuses on the *purpose* of narrating miracle stories. It discusses evidence of miracles and the narrating of miracle stories from both the New Testament itself and its religious environment. It asks for the literary and religious dynamics of miracle stories and studies different contexts out of which miracle stories originated: why did, why do

---

1. Cf., e.g., S. Alkier, *Wunder und Wirklichkeit in den Briefen des Apostels Paulus: Ein Beitrag zu einem Wunderverständnis jenseits von Entmythologisierung und Rehistorisierung* (WUNT, 134; Tübingen: Mohr Siebeck, 2001); M. Becker, *Wunder und Wundertäter im frührabbinischen Judentum: Studien zum Phänomen und seiner Überlieferung im Horizont von Magie und Dämonismus* (WUNT, II.144; Tübingen: Mohr Siebeck, 2002); W. Cotter, *Miracles in Greco-Roman Antiquity: A Sourcebook for the Study of New Testament Miracle Stories* (New York: Routledge, 1999); M. Hüneburg, *Jesus als Wundertäter in der Logienquelle: Ein Beitrag zur Christologie von Q* (ABG, 4; Leipzig: EVA, 2001); W. Kahl, *New Testament Miracle Stories in their Religious-Historical Setting: A Religionsgeschichtliche Comparison from a Structural Perspective* (FRLANT, 163; Göttingen: Vandenhoeck & Ruprecht, 1994); H. C. Kee, *Miracle in the Early Christian World: A Study in Sociohistorical Method* (New Haven and London: Yale University Press, 1983); H. C. Kee, *Medicine, Miracle and Magic in New Testament Times* (Cambridge: Cambridge University Press, 1986); B. Kollmann, *Jesus und die Christen als Wundertäter: Studien zu Magie, Medizin und Schamanismus in Antike und Christentum* (FRLANT, 170; Göttingen: Vandenhoeck & Ruprecht, 1996); B. Kollmann, *Neutestamentliche Wundergeschichten: Biblisch-theologische Zugänge und Impulse für die Praxis* (UT, 477; Stuttgart: Kohlhammer, 2002); M. Labahn, *Jesus als Lebensspender: Untersuchungen zu einer Geschichte der johanneischen Tradition anhand ihrer Wundergeschichten* (BZNW, 98; Berlin: de Gruyter, 1999); A. M. Reimer, *Miracle and Magic: A Study in the Acts of the Apostles and Life of Apollonius of Tyana* (JSNTSup, 235; London: Sheffield Academic Press, 2002); S. Schreiber, *Paulus als Wundertäter: Redaktionsgeschichtliche Untersuchungen zur Apostelgeschichte und den authentischen Paulusbriefen* (BZNW, 79; Berlin: de Gruyter, 1996).

people narrate miracle stories? This question is highly relevant to our under-standing of the early Christian writings we know as New Testament literature, but also to that of the Jewish and pagan contexts of these writings. Far from offering one all-encompassing theory of the dynamics of narrating miracle stories, the present volume offers a number of case studies.

Since early Christian writings were not written in any form of splendid isolation, but originated from religious and social contexts in which miracle stories appar-ently also played an important part, the present volume starts with a number of contributions which consider these contexts. Part One offers five analyses of the use of miracle stories from pagan or Jewish writings roughly contemporary to the New Testament. Jacques van Ruiten focuses on the miraculous birth of Isaac as described in the *Book of Jubilees*, Jan den Boeft presents an analysis of the reports of miraculous healings by Asclepius, Ulrike Riemer studies the dynamics of miracle stories within the cult of the Roman Emperor, Michael Becker treats miracle stories as found in Rabbinic sources, and Erkki Koskenniemi deals with the descriptions of perhaps the most important pagan miracle worker in antiquity, Apollonius of Tyana.

Part Two focuses on miracle stories in the New Testament: Geert Van Oyen deals with miracles as studied in the quest for the historical Jesus, whereas Reinhard von Bendemann focuses on the medical portrait of illnesses that people are miracu-lously cured from according to the Gospels. Michael Labahn discusses the catch of fish that is reported in John 21, Matti Myllykoski deals with miracles in Acts, and Bert Jan Lietaert Peerbolte presents the case for Paul as a miracle worker. Finally, Beate Kowalski discusses miracles as eschatological signs as described in the Book of Revelation.

The final part consists of two contributions: Lautaro Roig Lanzillotta deals with the *Acts of Andrew and Matthias* and their miracle stories, whereas Bernd Kollmann offers a hermeneutical perspective on New Testament miracle stories.

All but one of these contributions have been presented as papers in two subse-quent meetings of the Early Christianity Seminar of the European Association for Biblical Studies (Berlin 2002 and Copenhagen 2003). It is with pride and honour that we now present their written versions in this series of European Studies on Christian Origins, a series that wants to further the study of the New Testament and early Christianity within its social, religious and historical contexts.

The editors are grateful to all the contributors who submitted their revised papers for this collection and for their co-operation. We give thanks to the organ-isers of both conferences, to the audience and to everyone who contributed to the discussion within the seminars. Our thanks are also due to T & T Clark for accepting the volume at its current length and to all the staff at the Press, especially to Joanna Taylor, Rebecca Mulhearn and Rebecca Vaughan-Williams.

Halle and New Haven, CT – 2005
Michael Labahn and Bert Jan Lietaert Peerbolte

ABBREVIATIONS

AASFDHL	Annales Academiae scientiarum fennicae. Dissertationes humanarum litterarum
AB	Anchor Bible
ABD	*The Anchor Bible Dictionary*
ABo	*Analecta Bollandiana*
ABRL	The Anchor Bible Reference Library
ABG	Arbeiten zur Bibel und ihrer Geschichte
AC	Antike und Christentum
ACW	Ancient Christian Writers
AGAJU	Arbeiten zur Geschichte des antiken Judentums und des Urchristentums
ANCL	Ante-Nicene Christian Library
ANRW	*Aufstieg und Niedergang der römischen Welt*
ANTC	Augsburg New Testament Commentary
BAB	Beck'sche Archäologische Bibliothek
BASStP	Bulletin de l'Académie des Sciences de St. Petersbourg
BBB	Bonner biblische Beiträge
BENT	Beiträge zur Einleitung in das Neue Testament
BETL	Bibliotheca Ephemeridum Theologicarum Lovaniensium
BEvT	Beiträge zur evangelischen Theologie
BFCT	Beiträge zur Förderung christlicher Theologie
BGBE	Beiträge zur Geschichte der biblischen Exegese
BHTh	Beiträge zur historischen Theologie
Bib	*Biblica*
BJS	Brown Judaic Studies
BKAT	Biblischer Kommentar: Altes Testament
BN	*Biblische Notizen*
BSt	Biblische Studien
BTB	*Biblical Theology Bulletin*
BU	Biblische Untersuchungen
BWANT	Beiträge zur Wissenschaft vom Alten und Neuen Testament
BZ	*Biblische Zeitschrift*
BZAW	Beihefte zur ZAW
BZNW	Beihefte zur ZNW
CBET	Contributions to Biblical Exegesis and Theology
CBQ	*Catholic Biblical Quarterly*
CIL	*Corpus Inscriptionum Latinarum*
COT	Commentaar op het Oude Testament
CQ	*Church Quarterly*
CRINT	Compendium rerum iudaicarum ad Novum Testamentum

CSEL	Corpus scriptorum ecclesiasticorum latinorum
Diss.T	Dissertation Theologische Reihe
DJD	Discoveries in the Judean Desert
DK	H. Diels and W. Kranz (eds), *Die Fragmente der Vorsokratiker*
DOS	Dumbarton Oaks Studies
DSD	*Dead Sea Discoveries*
EichM.	Eichstätter Materialien
EKKNT	Evangelisch-Katholischer Kommentar zum Neuen Testament
Eos	*Eos: Commentarii Societatis Philologae Polonorum. Warszawa*
EvT	*Evangelische Theologie*
FC	Fontes Christiani
FDV	Franz-Delitzsch-Vorlesungen
FJB	Frankfurter Judaistische Beiträge
FOTL	The Forms of the Old Testament Literature
FRLANT	Forschungen zur Religion und Literatur des Alten und Neuen Testaments
GTA	Göttinger theologische Arbeiten
HBS	Herders Biblische Studien
HNT	Handbuch zum Neuen Testament
HorSem	*Horae semiticae*
HR	History of Religions
HTKNT	Herders theologischer Kommentar zum Neuen Testament
HTR	*Harvard Theological Review*
HUCA	*Hebrew Union College Annual*
IBS	*Irish Biblical Studies*
ICC	International Critical Commentary
IDB	*Interpretor's Dictionary of the Bible*
IG	*Inscriptiones graecae*
IGUR	*Inscriptiones graecae Urbis Romae*
Int	*Interpretation*
JAC	*Jahrbuch für Antike und Christentum*
JBL	*Journal of Biblical Literature*
JBLMS	*Journal of Biblical Literature*, Monograph Series
JETS	*Journal of the Evangelical Theological Society*
JFSR	*Journal of Feminist Studies in Religion*
JJS	*Journal of Jewish Studies*
JQR	*Jewish Quarterly Review*
JRS	*Journal of Roman Studies*
JSHRZ	Jüdische Schriften aus hellenistisch-römischer Zeit
JSJ	*Journal for the Study of Judaism*
JSJSup	*Journal for the Study of Judaism*, Supplement Series
JSNT	*Journal for the Study of the New Testament*
JSNTSup	*Journal for the Study of the New Testament*, Supplement Series
JSOT	*Journal for the Study of the Old Testament*
JSOTSup	*Journal for the Study of the Old Testament*, Supplement Series
JudChr	Judaica et Christiana

KBANT	Kommentare und Beiträge zum Alten und Neuen Testament
KEK	Kritisch-exegetischer Kommentar zum Alten Testament
KuI	*Kirche und Israel*
KVR	Kleine Vandenhoeck-Reihe
LCL	Loeb Classical Library
LS	*Louvain Studies*
LXX	Septuagint
MAG	*Mitteilungen der Anthropologischen Gesellschaft in Wien*
MGWJ	*Monatsschrift für Geschichte und Wissenschaft des Judentums*
MnSup	Mnemosyne Supplementum
MTS	Marburger Theologische Studien
NBL	*Neues Bibellexikon*
Neot	*Neotestamentica*
NIGTC	New International Greek Testament Commentary
NovT	*Novum Testamentum*
NovTSup	*Novum Testamentum*, Supplement Series
NTD	Das Neue Testament Deutsch
NTS	*New Testament Studies*
ÖAWP	*Österreichische Akademie der Wissenschaften. Philosophisch-historische Klasse*
ÖTbK	Ökumenischer Taschenbuch-kommentar
OGIS	*Orientis graeci inscriptiones selectae*
PaThSt	Paderborner theologische Studien
PG	Patrologiae cursus completus. Series graeca
PGM	*Papyri graecae magicae*
PhS	*Philologische Studiën*
PRES	*Pauly's Real-Encyclopädie der classischen Alterthumswissenschaften. Supplementum*
PRSA	*Problemi e ricerche di storia antica*
PRSt	Perspectives in Religious Studies
PS	*Philologus*, Supplement
PTS	Patristische Texte und Studien
QD	Quaestiones disputatae
RAC	*Reallexikon für Antike und Christentum*
REJ	*Revue des études juives*
RHLR	*Revue d'histoire et de littérature religieuse*
RNT	Regensburger Neues Testament
RT	*Religion and Theology*
RTL	*Revue théologique de Louvain*
RSR	*Recherches de science religieuse*
RVV	Religionsgeschichtliche Versuche und Vorarbeiten
SAM	Studies in Ancient Medicine
SamP	Samaritan Pentateuch
SBAB	Stuttgarter biblische Aufsatzbände
SBB	Stuttgarter biblische Beiträge
SBLDS	SBL Dissertation Series
SBLSCS	SBL Septuagint and Cognate Studies
SBLSP	SBL Seminar Papers
SBLTT	SBL Texts and Translations

SBS	Stuttgarter Bibelstudien
SBWGJWG	Sitzungsberichte der Wissenschaftlichen Gesellschaft an der Johann-Wolfgang-Goethe-Universität Frankfurt am Main
SC	Sources chrétiennes
SFEG	Schriften der Finnischen Exegetischen Gesellschaft
SCHNT	Studia ad corpus hellenisticum Novi Testamenti
SDPI	Schriften des Deutschen Palästina-Instituts
SE	*Studia evangelica*
SFSHJ	South Florida Studies in the History of Judaism
SGFWL	Schriften der Gesellschaft zur Förderung der Westfälischen Landesuniversität zu Münster
SHR	Studies in the History of Religions
SIG	*Sylloge inscriptionum graecarum*
SJLA	Studies in Judaism in Late Antiquity
SNT	Studien zum Neuen Testament
SNTA	Studiorum Novi Testamenti Auxilia
SNTSMS	Society for New Testament Studies Monograph Series
SNTU	Studien zum Neuen Testament und seiner Umwelt
SNTU.A	Studien zum Neuen Testament und seiner Umwelt, Serie A
SNTW	Studies in the New Testament and its World
SPB	Studia postbiblica
SPP	*Studien zur Paläographie und Papyruskunde*
SPS	Sacra pagina Series
SR	*Studies in Religion*
SSAAG	Saarbrücker Studien zur Archäologie und Alten Geschichte
STAC	Studien und Texte zu Antike und Christentum
STAR	Studies in Theology and Religion
SubB	*Subsidia biblica*
StudJ	Studia judaica
SudArch	Sudhoffs Archiv, Zeitschrift für Wissenschaftsgeschichte, Beihefte
SWJT	*Southwestern Journal of Theology*
TANZ	Texte und Arbeiten zum neutestamentlichen Zeitalter
TBN	Themes in Biblical Narrative
TbzA	Tübinger Beiträge zur Altertumswissenschaft
THKNT	Theologischer Handkommentar zum Neuen Testament
TLG	*Thesaurus linguae graecae*
TRu	*Theologische Rundschau*
TRE	*Theologische Realenzyklopädie*
TSAJ	Texte und Studien zum Antiken Judentum
TU	Texte und Untersuchungen
Tusc	Tusculum-Bücherei / Sammlung Tusculum
TvT	*Tijdschrift voor Theologie*
ThWAT	*Theologisches Wörterbuch zum Alten Testament*
ThWNT	*Theologisches Wörterbuch zum Neuen Testament*
TynBul	*Tyndale Bulletin*
UARG NF	Untersuchungen zur allgemeinen Religionsgeschichte. Neue Folge
UT	Urban Taschenbücher

UTB	Uni-Taschenbücher
VC	*Vigiliae christianae*
WBC	Word Biblical Commentary
WdF	Wege der Forschung
WüJb	*Würzburger Jahrbücher*
WMANT	Wissenschaftliche Monographien zum Alten und Neuen Testament
WUNT	Wissenschaftliche Untersuchungen zum Neuen Testament
ZAW	*Zeitschrift für die alttestamentliche Wissenschaft*
ZBKNT	Zürcher Bibelkommentare. Neues Testament
ZNT	*Zeitschrift für Neues Testament*
ZNW	*Zeitschrift für die neutestamentliche Wissenschaft*
ZPE	*Zeitschrift für Papyrologie und Epigraphik*
ZTK	*Zeitschrift für Theologie und Kirche*

LIST OF CONTRIBUTORS

Michael Becker is Lecturer for New Testament at the Ludwig-Maximilian-Universität of Munich, Germany.

Reinhard von Bendemann is Professor for New Testament at the Christian-Albrechts-Universität of Kiel, Germany.

Jan den Boeft is Professor Emeritus of Latin, Amsterdam (Vrije Universiteit), and of Hellenistic Religions, Utrecht University, the Netherlands.

Bernd Kollmann is Professor for New Testament at the University of Siegen, Germany.

Erkki Koskenniemi is Adjunct Professor for New Testament at Joensuu and Åbo Academi and Pastor in Finland.

Beate Kowalski is Terence Albert O'Brien Professor of Biblical Studies at Mary Immaculate College, University of Limerick, Ireland.

Michael Labahn is Wissenschaftlicher Assistent for New Testament at the Martin-Luther-University, Halle-Wittenberg, Germany.

Bert Jan Lietaert Peerbolte is Lecturer for New Testament at Kampen Theological University, the Netherlands, and Research Fellow at Yale Divinity School (2005).

Matti Myllykoski is Research Fellow of the University of Helsinki, Finland.

Ulrike Riemer is 'Lehrbeauftragte' for Classical Philology at the University of Saarland in Saarbrücken, Germany.

Lautaro Roig Lanzillotta is Lecturer and Research Fellow of the Facultad de Filosofía y Letras, University of Córdoba, Spain.

Geert Van Oyen is Professor of New Testament at Utrecht University in the Netherlands.

Jacques van Ruiten is Lecturer for Old Testament, the Rijksuniversiteit Groningen in the Netherlands.

PART I

A MIRACULOUS BIRTH OF ISAAC IN THE *BOOK OF JUBILEES*?

Jacques van Ruiten

The *Book of Jubilees* belongs to the early Jewish era of the New Testament in the broadest sense. It was written at some point in the mid second century BCE[1] and was presented as a revelation to Moses on Mount Sinai. It actually consists of a rewriting and interpretation of the biblical narrative from the creation (Genesis 1) up to the arrival of the people at Mount Sinai (Exodus 19). It influenced the community of Qumran considerably; at least fifteen fragments of *Jubilees* having been discovered among the Dead Sea Scrolls, while also of note is a reference to the book in the *Damascus Document*. 'Therefore, one will impose upon himself to return to the law of Moses, for in it all is defined. And the exact interpretation of their ages about the blindness of Israel in all these matters, behold, it is defined in "The book of the divisions of the periods (ס פ ר מחל קות הע תים) according to their Jubilees and their weeks".' (CD 16.1-4).[2] The discovery of the *Jubilees* fragments in Qumran confirmed the already current hypothesis that the book was originally written in Hebrew.[3] Subsequently it was translated into Greek, and from Greek into Latin and Ethiopic. Only the Ethiopic version, a translation of a translation, is complete, whereas the other texts are only fragments. However, as far as can be verified, the published Hebrew fragments show that the Ethiopic translation is fairly faithful.[4] The *Book of Jubilees* is usually classified as belonging

---

1. It is not the purpose of the present article to deal with the question of dating. For a discussion see K. Berger, *Das Buch der Jubiläen* (JSHRZ, V.3; Gütersloh: Gütersloher Verlag, 1981), pp. 298–300; R. H. Charles, *The* Book of Jubilees *or the Little Genesis. Translated from the Editor's Ethiopic Text* (London: Black, 1902), pp. lvii–lxvi; G. L. Davenport, *The Eschatology of the Book of Jubilees* (SPB, 20; Leiden: Brill, 1971), pp. 10–18; G. W. E. Nickelsburg, *Jewish Literature Between the Bible and the Mishnah. A Historical and Literary Introduction* (Philadelphia: Fortress Press, 1981), p. 78; J. C. VanderKam, *Textual and Historical Studies in the Book of Jubilees* (Missoula: Scholars Press, 1977), pp. 214–85.

2. For the translation see F. García Martínez, E. J. C. Tigchelaar, *The Dead Sea Scrolls. Volume One 1Q1-4Q273* (Leiden: Brill, 1997), p. 565.

3. For the official edition of the copies found in cave 4 of Qumran see J. C. VanderKam, J. T. Milik, 'Jubilees', in H. Attridge *et al.* (eds), *Qumran Cave 4* VIII: *Parabiblical Texts* Part 1 (DJD, 13; Oxford: Clarendon Press, 1994), pp. 1–185. Those from cave 11 are published in F. García Martínez, E. J. C. Tigchelaar, A. S. Van der Woude (eds.), *Qumran Cave 11 11Q2-18, 11Q20-31* (DJD, 23; Oxford: Clarendon Press, 1998), pp. 207–28.

4. J. C. VanderKam, '*Jubilees* and the Hebrew Texts of Genesis-Exodus', *Textus* 14 (1988), pp. 71–86.

to the literary genre of the 'rewritten Bible', in the company of the fragmentarily preserved *Genesis Apocryphon* and the *Liber Antiquitatum Biblicarum* of Pseudo-Philo. The term 'rewritten Bible' was coined by Vermes, who described it as a midrashic insertion of haggadic development into the biblical narrative in order to anticipate questions and solve problems before they arose.[5] The rewritten Bible follows the Scriptures but includes a considerable amount of additions and interpretative developments.[6] According to Nickelsburg, the rewritten Bible is 'very closely related to the biblical texts, expanding and paraphrasing them and implicitly commenting on them'.[7] It follows a sequential, chronological order. Although it makes use of biblical words and phrases, these words and phrases are not set apart by way of quotation formula or lemma but are integrated into a seamless retelling of the biblical story.[8]

My contribution concentrates on the manifestation of God in the story of the miraculous birth of Isaac in the book of Genesis, especially on how this story was transformed in the book of *Jubilees*. In the Old Testament, the birth of Isaac is an extraordinary event 'that manifest[s] divine power', that is a wonder 'to human understanding, and therefore what human beings perceive as signs from God'.[9] In fact, all stories in the Old Testament are based on Israel's understanding of God's continuous sovereignty over the created world and its history. Specific stories about the manifestation of God's miracles and signs are spread throughout the Old Testament,[10] although this text will restrict itself to only one of these stories.

1. The Birth of Isaac in the Book of Genesis
In the book of Genesis, the story of the birth of Isaac is part of the central plot, the storyline of the narratives about the patriarchs and especially of the story of Abraham.[11] It deals with the promise of numerous offspring who would inherit

5.   G. Vermes, 'The Life of Abraham', in G. Vermes, *Scripture and Tradition in Judaism: Haggadic Studies* (SPB, 4; Leiden: Brill, 2nd edn. 1973), pp. 67–126 (95). Cf. also C. Perrot, P. M. Bogaert, *Pseudo-Philon: Les Antiquités Bibliques* II (SC, 230; Paris: Cerf, 1976).

6.   E. Schürer, *The History of the Jewish People in the Age of Jesus Christ (175 B. C. – 135 A. D.)* III.1 (Revised and edited by G. Vermes, F. Millar, M. Goodman; Edinburgh: Clark, 1986), p. 326.

7.   G. W. E. Nickelsburg, 'The Bible Rewritten and Expanded', in M. E. Stone (ed.), *Jewish Writings of the Second Temple Period: Apocrypha, Pseudepigrapha, Qumran Sectarian Writings, Philo, Josephus* (CRINT, II.2; Assen: Van Gorcum, 1984), pp. 89–156 (89).

8.   P. S. Alexander, 'Retelling the Old Testament', in D. A. Carson, H. G. M. Williamson (eds.), *It Is Written: Scripture Citing Scripture. Essays in Honour of Barnabas Lindars* (Cambridge: Cambridge University Press, 1988), pp. 99–121 (116–17).

9.   Cf. D. N. Freedman (ed.), *Eerdmans Dictionary of the Bible* (Grand Rapids, MI: Eerdmans, 2000), pp. 903–4.

10.   *Eerdmans Dictionary*, 903.

11.   For a synchronic study of the plot of the story of Abraham, see, e.g., L. A. Turner, *Announcements of Plot in Genesis* (JSOTSup, 96; Sheffield: JSOT Press, 1996), pp. 51–114. See also E. A. Phillips, 'Incredulity, Faith, and Textual Purposes. Post-Biblical Responses to the Laughter of Abraham and Sarah', in C. A. Evans, J. A. Sanders (eds), *The Function of Scripture*

the promised land. However, this promise continually hangs by a thread. Since the focus here is on the transformation of Genesis in later literature, a description of the biblical text in various Yahwistic, Elohistic and Priestly sources will not be dealt with.[12] For the present purpose, it will be assumed that the genesis of the biblical story was of no interest to the author of *Jubilees*, and consequently, only the intrigue resulting from the final form of the text will be explored.

The main intrigue begins right at the start of the Abraham story. In the closing passage of the primeval history, which also forms the beginning of the Abraham stories (Gen. 11.27-32), it is said that Sarah was Abraham's wife (Gen. 11.29: 'And Abram and Nahor took wives; the name of Abram's wife was Sarai'), and the first thing said about this Sarah is that she was infertile (Gen. 11.30: 'Now Sarai was barren; she had no child'). Stating this fact twice underlines the pivotal role of her barrenness in the story and the hopelessness of the couple's situation.[13] The narrator reveals Sarah's sterility even before God commanded Abraham to leave Mesopotamia.[14] Elsewhere, too, Sarah's infertility is further emphasised: 'Now Sarai, Abram's wife bore him *no children* ... "Behold now, *YHWH has prevented me from bearing children*".' (Gen. 16.1-2). Abraham complains several times about his childlessness: 'O, Lord God, what will you give me, for I continue childless, and the heir of my house is Eliezer of Damascus? ... Behold, you have given *me no* offspring' (Gen. 15.2-3). In apparent contrast with this, time and again God promises Abraham offspring: 'To your descendants I will give this land' (Gen. 12.7; 15.18), 'Your own son shall be your heir' (Gen. 15.4). This offspring will be numerous: 'Look toward heaven, and number the stars, if you are able to number them ... So shall your descendants be' (Gen. 15.5).

Sarah's bareness was the justification for giving her Egyptian slave-girl Hagar to Abraham as a surrogate: 'Now Sarai, Abram's wife, bore him no children. She had an Egyptian slave-girl whose name was Hagar; and Sarai said to Abram: "Behold now, YHWH has prevented me from bearing children; go in to my slave-

in Early Jewish and Christian Tradition (JSNTSup, 154; Sheffield: Sheffield Academic Press, 1998), pp. 22–33 (22–27).

12. For a study of the plot of the Abraham story taking into account the diachronic dimension of the text, see G. W. Coats, *Genesis with an Introduction to Narrative Literature* (FOTL, 1; Grand Rapids, MI: Eerdmans, 1984), pp. 97–175. For a study of the assignment of the text to several sources, see, e.g, J. Van Seters, *Abraham in History and Tradition* (New Haven, CT: Yale University Press, 1975); E. Blum, *Die Komposition der Vätergeschichte* (WMANT, 57; Neukirchen-Vluyn: Neukirchener Verlag, 1984). See also the commentaries on Genesis, e.g., C. Westermann, *Genesis: 2. Teilband. Genesis 12-36* (BKAT, I.2; Neukirchen-Vluyn: Neukirchener Verlag, 1981); H. Seebass, *Genesis II: Vätergeschichte I (11,27-22,24)* (Neukirchen-Vluyn: Neukirchener Verlag, 1997).

13. See, e.g., W. H. Gispen, *Genesis II. Genesis 11:27-25:11* (COT, Kampen: Kok, 1979), p. 20; C. Westermann, *Genesis 2*, p. 159.

14. According to E. A. Phillips, 'Incredulity', pp. 22–23, they had had sufficient years to experience their childless estate, since Abraham was 75 years old (Gen. 12.4) and Sarah 65 when they left Mesopotamia. However, when the Abraham story is read against the background of the story of the forefathers (Gen. 5.1-32; 11.10-32), these ages are not excessively old.

girl; it may be that I shall obtain children by her". And Abram listened to the voice of Sarai … And he went in to Hagar, and she conceived' (Gen. 16.1-2, 4).

After this diversion with Hagar and the ensuing birth of Ishmael, it became clear to Abraham that Ishmael was not the promised child.[15] He should come from Sarah. This is revealed in Genesis 17, where YHWH appears to Abraham at the age of 99 (Gen. 17.1). He repeats his promises about the covenant and stresses the numerous offspring (Gen. 17.2-6). On this occasion Abraham is given his new name and the condition of the covenant, i.e., the duty of circumcision is introduced (Gen. 17.4-14, 23-27). Between the command for circumcision and its actual execution, the promise of a son through Sarah is brought up: 'And God said to Abraham: Your wife Sarai, you shall not call her name Sarai, for Sarah shall be her name. I will bless her, and moreover I will give you a son from her; and I will bless her, and she shall give rise to nations; kings of peoples shall come from her' (Gen. 17.15-16). In response, Abraham falls prostrate, he laughs, and he says to himself: 'Will a son be born to one who is 100 years of age? Will Sarah who is 90 years of age give birth (to a child)'? This could have been the voicing of doubt and disbelief[16] but also of surprise and gratitude.[17] Simultaneously, Abraham expresses his concern for Ishmael ('O, that Ishmael could live in your presence'). God's answer is clear: Sarah would indeed be the mother, his name would be Isaac, and with him God would establish his covenant. As far as Ishmael is concerned, he would be blessed and be made fruitful.

After the circumcision of Abraham and of his household, there was another theophany elaborated through the visit of three men (Gen. 18.1-15). The promise of a child by Sarah was announced again. This story's intended purpose seems to be to communicate the message to Sarah; at any rate, Sarah certainly came to learn of it (v. 10d: 'And Sarah was listening at the tent door behind him'). Furthermore, Sarah laughed when she heard the news. Her laughing seems to imply some sort of doubt and disbelief. She considered herself too old. Subsequently, YHWH spoke to Abraham about his wife's conduct because of its implied denial of the omnipotence of God (18.14a: 'Is anything too hard for YHWH?').

Finally, after the stories about Sodom and Gomorrah (Gen. 18.16–19.38) and Abraham's visit to the king of Gerar, the birth of Isaac is mentioned (Gen. 21. 1-7). The statement is very brief. 'YHWH visited Sarah as he had spoken, and YHWH did for Sarah as he had said. And Sarah conceived, and she gave birth to a son for Abraham in his old age at the time of which God had spoken to him. Abraham called the name of his son who was born to him, whom Sarah bore him, Isaac' (Gen. 21.1-3). Subsequently, the circumcision, Abraham's age and Sarah's reference to her laughing are related.

---

15.   Cf. E. A. Phillips, 'Incredulity', p. 23.

16.   Cf. L. A. Turner, *Announcement*, p. 78; E. A. Phillips, 'Incredulity', pp. 23–24; H. Seebass, *Genesis* II.1, p. 109.

17.   Cf. B. Jacob, *The First Book of the Bible: Genesis* (New York: Ktav, 1974), pp. 112–13. See also J. Calvin, *A Commentary on Genesis* I (trans. J. King; London: Banner of Truth, 1965), p. 460.

To sum up: the promise of offspring from Sarah is threatened by her infertility which is interpreted as 'YHWH has prevented me from bearing children'. From the outset, the Genesis text stresses the infertility of Sarah. At the same time, it stresses Abraham's and Sarah's ages, both with regard to the promises and to the actual birth. However, through YHWH's intervention, the promise would be fulfilled in a set period. God would keep his promise. He would make the impossible possible. The text is not entirely explicit about the nature of this intervention, only stating: 'YHWH visited (פקד) Sarah as he had spoken, and YHWH did (עשׂה) for Sarah as he had said' (Gen. 21.1). This might reflect the more general idea found in ancient teachings that human birth was considered to be a reflection of a divine manifestation – God of Heaven as the ultimate source of fertility. A God who causes, like a father, the seed to sprout. As the creator of heaven and earth, he brings vegetation and animal life into being, and ultimately, has the power of giving birth to human beings.[18]

The expression of doubt engendered by Abraham's and Sarah's old age reveals an interesting point of tension between the Abraham story and the primeval history. Not only did the forefathers die at very old ages, they also each begat their first child at a late age.[19] This is certainly the case for the antediluvian fathers from Adam to Noah. As for the postdiluvian forefathers, even in the MT of Genesis 11, Shem was already a centenarian when his first child was born, while Terah was only 70. The other versions of Genesis (LXX and SamP) add 100 years to the ages of all postdiluvian fathers. Finally, the text does not reveal much more about the purpose of narrating this miracle story than its general plot. It is important that God's promise was fulfilled and that the power of giving birth ultimately came from God. However, the text does not make it explicitly clear why the promise of posterity should go through Sarah.

2. The Birth of Isaac in the *Book of Jubilees*

Attention will now be paid to the transformation of the account of the story of the miraculous birth of Isaac in Genesis into the form found in the *Book of Jubilees*. In terms of my research, the important questions raised by the comparison

18. Cf. W. J. van Bekkum, 'Eve and the Matriarchs: Aspects of Woman Typology in Genesis', in G. P. Luttikhuizen (ed.), *The Creation of Man and Woman: Interpretations of the Biblical Narratives in Jewish and Christian Traditions* (TBN, 3; Leiden: Brill, 2000), pp. 128–39 (129–30).

19. For a study of the chronological problems with regard to the age of the forefathers, see, e.g., J. Skinner, *A Critical and Exegetical Commentary on Genesis* (ICC; Edinburgh, T&T Clark, 1910), pp. 127–39, 231–39; A. Jepsen, 'Zur Chronologie des Priesterkodex', *ZAW* 47 (1929), pp. 251–55; S. J. de Vries, 'Chronology of the Old Testament', *IBD* 1 (1962), pp. 580–99; R. W. Klein, 'Archaic Chronologies and the Textual History of the Old Testament', *HTR* 67 (1974), pp. 255–63; K. Koch, 'Sabbatstruktur der Geschichte: Die sogenannte Zehn-Wochen-Apokalypse (1 Hen 93,1-10; 91, 11-17) und das Ringen um die alttestamentlichen Chronologien in späten Israelitentum', *ZAW* 95 (1983), pp. 403–30; J. Hughes, *Secrets of the Times: Myth and History in Biblical Chronology* (JSOTSup, 66; Sheffield: JSOT Press, 1990); M. Rösel, *Übersetzung als Vollendung der Auslegung: Studien zur Genesis-Septuaginta* (BZAW, 223; Berlin: de Gruyter 1994), pp. 129–44.

of Genesis and *Jubilees* are: *which* elements of the story were preserved, *how* were they preserved and *what* was the function of the story of the miraculous birth of Isaac in this new context? It is striking that, in the first instance, the story is repeatedly abridged, whereas in the latter version the story is expanded. The results of my investigation can be found in the synoptic overviews below. A classification of the similarities and dissimilarities between Genesis and *Jubilees* is also included there. The elements of Genesis which do not occur in *Jubilees* are in SMALL CAPS, and vice versa, i.e., the OMISSIONS and ADDITIONS. The corresponding elements between the two texts, i.e., the verbatim quotation of one or more words of the source text in *Jubilees* are in 'normal script'. The *variations* between Genesis and *Jubilees* are in *italics*, except for additions or omissions. The verbatim quotations and their variants can occur in the same word order or sentence order in *Jubilees* as in Genesis. However, sometimes there is a <u>rearrangement</u> of words and sentences. These elements have been <u>underlined</u>. Within the limitations of this article's context it will not be possible to explore in detail all the various differences between Genesis and *Jubilees* and this text will have to be restricted to those elements relevant to this volume's purpose.

a. *Jubilees* 12.9–11

Sarah occurs for the first time in *Jub.* 12.9, a passage that is incorporated in quite an extensive pericope (*Jub.* 11.14–12.15) containing the rewriting of the closure of the genealogy of Gen. 11.26-32. In the following overall comparison of these texts, the numerous deviations of *Jubilees* from its model text should become evident:

Genesis 11.26-32	*Jubilees 11.14–12.15*
a. Birth of Abram, NAHOR AND HARAN (11.26-27b)	a. Birth of Abram (11.14-15)
	b. STORIES ABOUT ABRAM (11.16–12.8) WITH THE MENTION OF TWO BROTHERS (12.8)
b. <u>Birth of Lot</u> (11.27c)	
c. <u>Death of Haran</u> (11.28)	
d. Marriages of Abram <u>and Nahor</u> (11.29)	c. Marriage of Abram (12.9)
e. BARRENNESS OF SARAI (11.30)	
	d. MARRIAGE OF HARAN and <u>birth of Lot</u> (12.10)
	e. <u>Marriage of Nahor</u> (12.11)
	f. STORY AROUND THE <u>death of Haran</u> (12.12-14)
f. Departure of Terah with Abram, Lot and Sarai from Ur and arrival in Haran (11.31)	g. Departure of Terah and his sons from Ur and arrival in Haran (12.15)
h. DEATH OF TERAH (11.32)	

I have restricted myself here to *Jub.* 12.9-11, which is a rewriting of Gen. 11. 29-30. While the biblical writer seems not to have been interested in Sarah's background, with the exception of the fact that she was infertile, the author of *Jubilees* rewrites the story in a subtle manner. In his rewriting he does not establish her barrenness as a central issue but rather her *descent*, her origin.[20] As can be seen in the synoptic overview, the content and form of the reports of marriage and birth are completely different in both texts:

Genesis 11.29-30	*Jubilees 12.9-11*
	9a DURING THE FORTIETH JUBILEE, IN THE SECOND WEEK, IN ITS SEVENTH YEAR, Abram *married a woman*
29a And Abram <u>and Nahor</u> *took wives*;	whose name was Sarai, THE DAUGHTER OF HIS FATHER,
b the name of Abram's wife was Sarai,	b AND SHE BECAME HIS WIFE.
	10a HIS BROTHER <u>Haran</u> MARRIED A WOMAN IN THE THIRD YEAR OF THE THIRD WEEK,
[cf. Gen. 11.27]	b *<u>and she gave birth to</u>* <u>A SON FOR HIM IN THE SEVENTH YEAR OF THIS WEEK.</u>
	c HE NAMED HIM <u>Lot.</u>
	11a HIS BROTHER <u>NAHOR</u> ALSO GOT MARRIED.
c AND THE NAME OF NAHOR'S WIFE WAS MILCAH, THE DAUGHTER OF HARAN THE FATHER OF MILCAH AND ISCAH.	
30a NOW SARAI WAS BARREN;	
b SHE HAD NO CHILD.	

As far as the report of Abraham and Sarah's marriage is concerned, *Jubilees* omits to mention that Sarah was barren (Gen. 11.30). However, the information about their marriage is at once enlarged upon considerably.[21] In Genesis, the mention is quite brief. In *Jubilees*, a date is provided ('During the fortieth jubilee, in the second week, in its seventh year') and their marriage is taken apart and described more extensively ('Abram married a woman whose name was Sarai ... and she became his wife'), and (most importantly) her descent is mentioned ('the daughter of his father'). In other words, Sarah was Abraham's sister (*Jub.* 12.9). This addition could have been prompted on the one hand by the fact that Abraham called Sarah 'his sister' elsewhere in Genesis – namely, when he visited Pharaoh (Gen. 12.10-20) and the king of Gerar (Gen. 20.1-18).[22] On the other hand, it is

---

20. This aspect of the rewriting of *Jubilees* is stressed emphatically by B. Halpern-Amaru, *The Empowerment of Women in the* Book of Jubilees (JSJSup, 60; Leiden: Brill, 1999), pp. 34–35. She underlines that Sarah is the 'dominant bride', that she is the only woman named and the only one with 'genealogical credentials'.

21.   Cf. B. Halpern-Amaru, *Empowerment*, 35.

22.   It is interesting to note, however, that the author of *Jubilees* does not refer to Sarah as Abraham's sister when they encounter the Pharaoh (*Jub.* 13.13-15), and the visit with the king of Gerar is omitted altogether.

not impossible to imagine that the author of *Jubilees* would have stressed Sarah's excellent provenance. She came from the right family. In the mind of the author she could not have been the daughter of Haran, as could be concluded on the basis of the biblical text: 'Abram and Nahor took wives; the name of Abram's wife was Sarai, and the name of Nahor's wife, Milcah, the daughter of Haran the father of Milcah and Jiscah' (Gen. 11.29). Sarah's father is not mentioned, however, although Milcah's is, and it could be inferred that Sarah was also a daughter of Haran. In early Jewish literature, there are several examples of the identification of Sarah and Jiscah.[23] This was not the case for the author of *Jubilees*, however.

Further changes in the text support the author of *Jubilees's* opinion that Sarah could not have been Haran's daughter. This is a reference to the fact that in the book of Genesis, most items concerning Haran are located *before* the marriages of Abraham and Nahor: his birth, his fathering of Lot and his death (Gen. 11. 26-28). In *Jubilees*, however, the information concerning the marriage of Abraham with Sarah is placed *before* the marriage of Haran (cf. *Jub.* 11.9-10).[24]

Haran's marriage is described in a manner comparable to the marriage of Abraham and Sarah. It is striking, however, that the name of Haran's wife is not recorded, nor, even more importantly, is her *origin*. The marriage report of Nahor, which is quite extensive in Gen. 11.29, where the name of the wife and her origin are mentioned, is very cursorily presented in *Jubilees*: 'His brother Nahor also got married' (*Jub.* 12.11).

Finally, in Genesis the report of the death of Haran, the father of Lot, is quite neutral (cf. Gen. 11.28). In *Jubilees*, however, his death is connected with the fact that he tried to save from fire the idols that Abram tried to burn (cf. *Jub.* 11. 12-14). The report of the death of Terah is not included in *Jubilees*, whereas the extensive description of the events surrounding the death of Haran does serve a clear function. It characterizes Haran as the prototype of the unfaithful, in opposition to the faithful and righteous Abraham. Although both derive from Terah and in that sense are in the line of Shem, the line of the chosen people only continues through Abraham. It is therefore significant that Sarah should also not be defiled by the faithless Haran, that she should come straight from Terah. According to *Jubilees*, it is important that a pure line can be drawn from Abraham and Sarah back to the forefathers, via Terah, Shem, Noah and the other antediluvians, back to Seth and Azura and with them to Adam and Eve. The election of Israel is built into the creation of the world, as can also be illustrated using other passages from the book of *Jubilees*.[25]

---

23.   See *LAB* 23.4; Josephus, *Ant.* 1.151; *Tg. Ps-J.* on Gen. 11.29; *bMeg.* 14a; *bSanh.* 69b; *Gen. Rab.* 38.14. Cf. D. U. Rottzoll, *Rabbinischer Kommentar zum Buch Genesis. Darstellung der Rezeption des Buches Genesis in Mischna und Talmud unter Angabe Targumischer und Midrashischer Paralleltexte* (StudJ, 14; Berlin: de Gruyter, 1994), pp. 201–2; B. H. Halpern-Amaru, *Empowerment*, p. 35, n. 4.

24.   B. Halpern-Amaru, *Empowerment*, p. 35.

25.   See, e.g., *Jub.* 2.20. Cf. B. Schaller, *Gen. 1.2 im antiken Judentum: Untersuchungen über Verwendung und Deutung der Schöpfungsaussagen von Gen 1.2 im antiken Judentum* (Diss. masch.; Göttingen, 1961), p. 63; J. C. VanderKam, 'Genesis 1 in Jubilees 2', *DSD* 1 (1994),

The way in which this marriage is rewritten closely resembles the way in which *Jubilees* rewrote the reports of the marriages of the forefathers. This might hint at a clue to understanding the intention of *Jubilees*, that is, that the author considered the marriage of Abraham and Sarah to be in the same line as that of the forefathers. In this respect it is the establishment of a sibling relationship between Abraham and Sarah. This draws them back to the first generations after Adam and Eve, which were, in the eyes of *Jubilees*, also brother–sister unions.[26]

In conclusion, the main focus in *Jub.* 12.9-11 is on the marriage of Abraham and Sarah. The author of *Jubilees* was not really interested in Abraham's brothers. Only Haran is mentioned at any length in order to provide a contrast to a holy Abraham, and in order to make clear that Sarah was not his daughter. Sarah's infertility was unimportant to the author of *Jubilees*, it was rather her origin that carried weight, going straight back to the creation of the first man and woman. With these few changes to the Genesis text, the author of *Jubilees* completely changes the plot of the story. It is no longer the story of the continuously threatened promise of numerous offspring, it is a story of a pure lineage. By setting the marriage of Abraham and Sarah in the same line as the forefathers, the nature of the miracle, i.e., the conception of children in old age, becomes much less important.

b. *Jubilees* 12.30; 13.18

Nevertheless, although the theme of infertility is much less important, the text of *Jubilees* makes clear that Abraham continues not to have children for considerable time while desiring them very much. This is a reference to *Jub.* 12.30, which is a text without parallel in Genesis. As Abraham is leaving Haran to go to the land of Canaan, his father Terah blesses him. He says to Abraham that if he sees the good land, he should come back and take Terah with him. But he also adds: 'Take Lot, the son of your brother Haran, with you *as your son*'. Despite Lot's dubious birth (his mother is unnamed and her origin unknown), and the problems with his father (idolatry), the author of *Jubilees* seems to confirm that there was a certain affinity between Abraham and Lot. Lot seems to function for Abraham as a sort of surrogate son.

Moreover, in *Jubilees* 13, it is striking that the passage of Gen. 13 about the struggle between the herdsmen of Abraham and those of Lot is left unmentioned. The text states simply: 'Lot separated from him' and then continues 'Lot settled in Sodom' (*Jub.* 13.17). The complete responsibility for the separation of Lot and Abraham is put, in this way, on the shoulders of Lot. Lot is the one who left, Abraham and his herdsmen are not to blame. What becomes of interest now, however, is that *Jubilees* adds Abraham's emotional reaction to his separation from Lot: 'He was *broken-hearted* that his brother's son had separated from him *for he had no children*' (*Jub.* 13.18).

pp. 311–21 (318); L. Doering, 'The Concept of the Sabbath in the Book of Jubilees', in M. Albani, J. Frey, A. Lange (eds.), *Studies in the* Book of Jubilees (TSAJ, 65; Tübingen: Mohr Siebeck, 1997), pp. 179–205 (185–88); J.T.A.G.M. van Ruiten, *Primaeval History Interpreted: The Rewriting of Genesis 1-11 in the* Book of Jubilees (JSJSup, 66; Leiden: Brill, 2000), pp. 49, 57–65.
    26.   Cf. B. Halpern-Amaru, *Empowerment*, pp. 36–37.

Abraham also refers in *Jub.* 14.1-6 to his childlessness. However, this text is quite close to Gen. 15.1-6. The only interesting addition in *Jubilees* with relevance to this text's theme is the addition at the end of v. 2. where *Jubilees* not only reads: 'You have given me no descendants', but adds Abraham's wish: 'Give me descendants'.

c. *Jubilees* 14.21-24

It is important to realise that in the book of *Jubilees* up to the scene with Hagar, the author has not yet provided any clue to the fact that Sarah could not bear children. Furthermore, Abraham is cast as unaware of this fact. As can be seen above, the couple's age is probably of no importance. In the rewriting of the opening to this scene (cf. Gen. 16.1-4, 15-16 and *Jub.* 14.21-24), this attitude is made clear quite neatly:

Genesis 16.1-4, 15, 16	*Jubilees 14.21-24*
	21a ABRAM WAS VERY HAPPY
	b AND TOLD ALL THESE THINGS TO HIS WIFE SARAI.
	c HE BELIEVED THAT HE WOULD HAVE
[ ]	DESCENDANTS.
1a *Sarai, Abram's wife*, bore him no children.	d *She* continued not to have a child.
b SHE HAD AN EGYPTIAN SLAVE-GIRL WHOSE NAME WAS HAGAR;	[ ]
	22a AND SARAI ADVISED HER HUSBAND ABRAM
2a [ ] and *Sarai* said to *Abram*:	b and *she* said to *him*:
b 'BEHOLD NOW, YHWH HAS PREVENTED ME FROM BEARING CHILDREN;	[ ]
c go in to my [ ] slave-girl [ ];	c 'Go in to my EGYPTIAN slave-girl HAGAR;
d Perhaps I will build up [ ] from her'.	d perhaps I will build up DESCENDANTS FOR YOU from her'.
e And Abram listened to the voice of Sarai [ ].	23a And Abram listened to the voice of Sarai, HIS WIFE
	b AND SAID TO HER:
	c 'Do (AS YOU SUGGEST)'.
3a SO, AFTER ABRAM HAD DWELT TEN YEARS IN THE LAND OF CANAAN,	[ ]
b Sarai, ABRAM'S WIFE, took her Egyptian slave-girl Hagar,	d Sarai [ ] took her Egyptian slave-girl Hagar,
c and gave her to her husband Abram *as a wife.*	e and gave her to her husband Abram *to be his wife.*
4a And he went in to *Hagar*,	24a And he went in to *her*,
b and she conceived;	b and she conceived,
[GEN. 16.4c–14]	[ ]

15a And *Hagar* bore ABRAM a son.
b *Abram* called the name OF HIS SON,
WHOM HAGAR BORE, Ishmael [　].
16a *Abram was eighty-six years old*
b WHEN HAGAR BORE ISHMAEL TO ABRAM.

c and *she* gave birth [　] to a son.
d *He* called the name [　] Ishmael IN
THE FIFTH YEAR OF THIS WEEK.
e *That year was the eighty-sixth year in
Abram's life.*
[　]

Abraham was happy with the promise of many offspring and thought that he would achieve this with his wife Sarah. Ultimately, they would have children (cf. *Jub.* 14.21a-c). When she continued to have no children (*Jub.* 14.21d), however, Sarah advised Abraham to try with her slave-girl Hagar (*Jub.* 14.22). It is significant that the phrase 'Behold now, YHWH has prevented me from bearing children' (Gen. 16.2b) is omitted. This indicates that Sarah was not really convinced that she would never bear at all, but that she was wise to protect YHWH's promise by giving Hagar to Abraham. It is interesting to see that Abraham asserts expressly what his wife proposes: 'And Abram listened to the voice of Sarai, his wife and said to her: Do (as you suggest)' (*Jub.* 14.23).

In Genesis, between the conception and the birth there is a passage on Sarah's jealousy of Hagar (Gen. 16.4c-14). This is completely omitted in *Jubilees*. There may have been several reasons for this. It would probably have contradicted the fact of Sarah's decision and Abraham's positive assertion, as described above. In any case, Hagar's role is somewhat reduced by the omission. See also some of the other omissions in this passage (Gen. 16.1b, 15b, 16).[27]

d. *Jubilees* 15.15-22

It is striking that the first announcement of the birth of Isaac runs strikingly parallel to the corresponding announcement in the book of Genesis. *Jub.* 15.15-22 is a near verbatim quotation of Gen. 17.15-22.

Genesis 17.15-22	*Jubilees 15.15-22*
15a And *God* said to Abraham: b 'Your wife Sarai, *you will not call* her name Sarai c for Sarah will be her name.	15a And *the Lord* said to Abraham: b 'Your wife Sarai *will no* LONGER *be called* the name Sarai c for Sarah will be her name.

27.　According to Söllner, the following three narrative themes of Gen. 16.4c-14 are omitted as follows: 1. the arrogance of Hagar (cf. Gen. 16.4); 2. the fact that Abraham puts Hagar under the authority of Sarah, who humiliates her (cf. Gen. 16.6); 3. the tribal proverb (cf. Gen. 16.12). See P. Söllner, 'Ishmael und Isaak – muss der eine den anderen denn immer nur verfolgen? Zum Verhältnis der beiden Abrahamsöhne im Jubiläenbuch', in A. von Dobbeler, K. Erlemann, R. Heiligenthal (eds.), *Religionsgeschichte des Neuen Testaments* (FS K. Berger; Tübingen: Francke, 2000), pp. 357–78 (360–61).

16a I will bless her,
b and MOREOVER I will give you a
son from her;
c and I will bless *her*,
d and *she* shall give rise to nations,
e [ ] kings of *peoples* will come
from *her*'.

16a I will bless her,
b and [ ] I will give you a son
from her;
c and I will bless *him*.
d And *he* will become a nation,
e AND kings of *nations* will come
from *him*'.

17a And Abraham fell prostrate
b and *laughed*,
c He said to himself:
d 'Will a son be born to one who
is 100 years of age?
e Will Sarah who is 90 years of age
give birth (to a child)'?

17a And Abraham fell prostrate
b and *was very happy*.
c He said to himself:
d 'Will a son be born to one who is
100 years of age?
e Will Sarah who is 90 years of age
give birth (to a child)'?

18a And Abraham said *to God*:
b 'O that Ishmael could live in
your presence.'

18a And Abraham said to *the Lord*:
b '*I wish* that Ishmael could live in
your presence'.

19a *God* said:
b '*No*, but Sarah YOUR WIFE will give
birth to a son for you,
c and you will call his name Isaac.
d I will establish my covenant with
him as an eternal covenant [ ]
for his descendants after him.

19a *The Lord* said:
b '*Very well*, but Sarah [ ] will give
birth to a son for you
c and you will call his name Isaac.
d I will establish my covenant with
him as an eternal covenant AND for his
descendants after him.

20a Regarding Ishmael, I have
listened to you.
b [ ] Behold, I will bless him
c and increase him,
d and make him very numerous.
e He will be the father of 12 princes,
f and I will make him into a large
nation.

20a Regarding Ishmael I have listened
to you.
b AND behold, I will bless him,
c and increase him,
d and make him very numerous.
e He will be the father of 12 princes,
f and I will make him into a large
nation.

21a But my covenant I will establish
with Isaac, to whom Sarah will give
birth for you *at this season* next year'.

21a But my covenant I will establish
with Isaac, to whom Sarah will give
birth for you *in these days* next year'.

22a When he had finished speaking
with him,
b *God* went up from Abraham.

22a When he had finished speaking
with him,
b *the Lord* went up from Abraham.

One can barely point to a single addition or omission. Some interesting variations are probably due to the fact the author of *Jubilees* had a *Vorlage* of this text that differed from the MT. The different suffixes in *Jub.* 15.16 should be noted, and the use of 'very well' instead of 'no'. The only remaining thing is *Jub.* 15.17b, which reads: 'and he was very happy' rather than 'and he laughed' (Gen. 17.17b). The same interpretation of the laughter can be found in Josephus and the

Targumim. The laughter and the subsequent question of age is not a sign of doubt and disbelief but of happiness.

e. *Jubilees* 16.1-4

Jubilees 16.1-4 deals with the second annunciation of the birth of a child to Abraham and Sarah and corresponds with Genesis 18.1-15.[28] In contrast to the first announcement, the author of Jubilees has abbreviated the story of Genesis 18 considerably, as can be seen in the following synoptic overview.

Genesis 18.1–15	*Jubilees 16.1–4*
1a [ ] *YHWH* appeared to *him* by the *oaks* of Mamre, b AS HE SAT AT THE DOOR OF HIS TENT IN THE HEAT OF THE DAY.	1a ON THE FIRST OF THE FOURTH MONTH *we* appeared to *Abraham* at the *oak* of Mamre. [ ]
2a HE LIFTED UP HIS EYES b AND LOOKED, c AND BEHOLD, THREE MEN STOOD IN FRONT OF HIM. d WHEN HE SAW THEM, e HE RAN FROM THE TENT DOOR TO MEET THEM, f AND BOWED HIMSELF TO THE EARTH,	
3a AND SAID: b 'MY LORD, IF I HAVE FOUND FAVOR IN YOUR SIGHT, c DO NOT PASS BY YOUR SERVANT.	
4a LET A LITTLE WATER BE BROUGHT, b AND WASH YOUR FEET, c AND REST YOURSELVES UNDER THE TREE,	
5a WHILE I FETCH A MORSEL OF BREAD, b THAT YOU MAY REFRESH YOURSELVES, c AND AFTER THAT YOU MAY PASS ON d – SINCE YOU HAVE COME TO YOUR SERVANT'. e SO THEY SAID: f 'DO AS YOU HAVE SAID'.	
6a AND ABRAHAM HASTENED INTO THE TENT TO SARAH, b AND SAID: c 'MAKE READY QUICKLY THREE MEASURES OF FINE MEAL,	

28.   Cf. J.T.A.G.M. Van Ruiten, 'Lot Versus Abraham: The Interpretation of Genesis 18.1-19.38 in *Jubilees* 16.1-9', in E. Noort, E. J. C. Tigchelaar (eds.), *Sodom's Sin: Genesis 18-19 and its Interpretations* (TBN, 7; Leiden: Brill, 2004), pp. 29–46.

d KNEAD IT,
c AND MAKE CAKES'.

7a AND ABRAHAM RAN TO THE HERD,
b AND TOOK A CALF, TENDER AND GOOD,
c AND GAVE IT TO THE SERVANT,
d WHO HASTENED TO PREPARE IT.

8a THEN HE TOOK CURDS, AND MILK,
AND THE CALF WHICH HE HAD PREPARED,
b AND SET IT BEFORE THEM;
c AND HE STOOD BY THEM UNDER THE
TREE WHILE THEY ATE.

9a *They said to* him: b *We spoke with* him
b 'WHERE IS SARAH YOUR WIFE?'
c AND HE SAID:
d 'SHE IS IN THE TENT'.

10a YHWH SAID:
b 'I WILL SURELY RETURN TO YOU IN
THE SPRING,
c and Sarah *your* wife *shall have* a son'.   c AND TOLD HIM that a child *would be*
d AND SARAH WAS LISTENING AT THE   *given to him* from *his* wife Sarah.
TENT DOOR BEHIND HIM.

11a NOW ABRAHAM AND SARAH WERE
OLD, ADVANCED IN AGE;
b IT HAD CEASED TO BE WITH SARAH
AFTER THE MANNER OF WOMEN.

12a Sarah laughed TO HERSELF, SAYING: 2a Sarah laughed [ ]
b 'AFTER I HAVE GROWN OLD, AND
MY HUSBAND IS OLD,
c SHALL I HAVE PLEASURE?'   b WHEN SHE HEARD THAT WE HAD
     SPOKEN THIS MESSAGE TO ABRAHAM,
13a *And YHWH said to Abraham:*   c *And we chided her.*
b 'WHY DID SARAH LAUGH,   [ ]
c AND SAY:
d 'SHALL I INDEED BEAR A CHILD,
NOW THAT I AM OLD?'

14a IS ANYTHING TOO HARD FOR
YHWH?
b At the appointed time *I* will return
to *you,* IN THE SPRING,
c and *Sarah shall have* a son'.

15a *Sarah* denied, SAYING: d *And* she was afraid
b 'I DID NOT laugh';   e and *she* denied
c *for* she was afraid.   f THAT SHE HAD laughed ABOUT THE

d He said: MESSAGE.
e 'No, but you did laugh'.

                                        3a We told her the name of her
                                        son as it is ordained and written
                                        on the heavenly tablets – Isaac –
                                        4a and (that) when *we* returned to
                                        her at a specific time
                                        b and *she would have conceived*
                                        a son.

The perspective from which the story is told is different. Genesis has an objective narrator who speaks about YHWH, the angels, Abraham and Sarah in the third person. *Jubilees* presents the story of the Angel of the Presence, who dictates the *whole* story of the *Jubilees* to Moses. It presents the acts of the angels themselves in the first person plural. It is clear that the combination of the appearance of YHWH with Abraham's meeting with three men introduces a certain ambiguity to the text of Genesis. Though this tension could point to an interesting genesis of the Genesis text, the author of *Jubilees* apparently chose to remove this ambiguity. In so doing, he identified the three men with the angels. The omission of the theophany and its substitution for the appearance of the angels is remarkable because the author of *Jubilees* often preserved the theophanies in his rendering of Genesis. It shows, I feel, that this author was conscious of a problem in the Genesis text.

As can be seen, the text of Gen. 18.1-15 is stripped of all its frills. The only thing that seems to have interested the author of *Jubilees* is the announcement of the birth of a son to Abraham and Sarah, and Sarah's disbelieving reaction. *Jubilees* excludes numerous elements in the story, i.e., Abraham's meeting with YHWH, the scene of hospitality where Abraham prepares food and drink for the angels, and the fact of Abraham's and Sarah's old age.

As far as that latter point is concerned, the omission of the couple's old age, not an insignificant element in the Genesis story, is in keeping with what has been already stated earlier in this paper. The *Jubilees* author did not want to put too much stress on this fact because it was not the real issue in his mind, and not central to his plot.

As the passage closes, there is a clear insertion (16.3-4: 'We told her the name of her son as it is ordained and written on the heavenly tablets – Isaac – and [that] when we returned to her at a specific time she would have become pregnant with a son'). The second part is a variation and interpretation of Gen. 18.14, 'At the appointed time I will return to you, in the spring, and Sarah shall have a son'. Curiously, in *Jubilees* this, along with the name of the son, is recorded on the heavenly tablets. In Genesis, the name of the son has already been announced to Abraham earlier in the text: 'Sarah your wife shall bear you a son, and you shall call his name Isaac' (Gen. 17.19). In *Jubilees*, it is announced to Sarah and engraved on the heavenly tablets. Possibly, the 'heavenly tablets' does not mean anything more than the Torah and the reference to these tablets is intended as nothing more than a reference to the biblical text. Nevertheless, it does raise Sarah's status. She is not placed listening behind the tent door but is addressed personally by the angels.

f. *Jubilees* 16.11-31

Jubilees 16.11-31 is the last text to attract our attention in the context of the miraculous birth of Isaac. It contains the rewriting of the birth itself. As can be seen in the synoptic overview, *Jub.* 16.11-14 is a fairly literal rendition of Gen. 21.1-4. There are only some minor omissions, additions and variations. What stands out is the omission of Gen. 21.5-7 and the addition of *Jub.* 16.15-19.

Genesis 21.1-7	*Jubilees 16.11-14*
	11a IN THE MIDDLE OF THE FIFTH MONTH HE MIGRATED FROM THERE b AND SETTLED AT THE WELL OF THE OATH.
[ ] 1a YHWH visited Sarah AS HE HAD SPOKEN,	12a IN THE MIDDLE OF THE SIXTH MONTH the Lord visited Sarah [ ]
b and *YHWH* did for *Sarah* as he had said.	b and *he* did for *her* as he had said.
2a And *Sarah* conceived, b and she gave birth to a son FOR ABRAHAM IN HIS OLD AGE	13a And *she* conceived, b and she gave birth to a son [ ] IN THE THIRD MONTH; c IN THE MIDDLE OF THE MONTH,
at the time of which God had spoken to him.	*on the day that the Lord had told Abraham* – ON THE FESTIVAL OF THE FIRSTFRUITS OF THE HARVEST – [ ] Isaac *was born.*
3a ABRAHAM CALLED THE NAME OF HIS SON WHO *was born* TO HIM, WHOM SARAH GAVE BIRTH FOR HIM, Isaac.	
4a And Abraham circumcised *his son Isaac*	14a And Abraham circumcised *him*
b when he was eight days old, [ ] *as God had commanded him* [ ].	b when he was eight days old.
	c HE WAS THE FIRST TO BE CIRCUMCISED *according to the covenant* WHICH WAS ORDAINED FOREVER.
5a ABRAHAM WAS A HUNDRED YEARS OLD b WHEN HIS SON ISAAC WAS BORN TO HIM.	[ ]
6a AND SARAH SAID: b 'GOD HAS MADE LAUGHTER FOR	

ME;
c EVERY ONE WHO HEARS WILL LAUGH
OVER ME'.

7a AND SHE SAID:
b 'WHO WOULD HAVE SAID TO
ABRAHAM THAT SARAH WOULD
SUCKLE CHILDREN?
c YET I HAVE BORNE HIM A SON IN HIS
OLD AGE'.

Jubilees 16.15-19 (no parallel in Genesis)

15a IN THE SIXTH YEAR OF THE FOURTH WEEK WE CAME TO ABRAHAM AT THE
WELL OF THE OATH.
b WE APPEARED TO HIM
c JUST AS WE HAD SAID TO SARAH THAT WE WOULD RETURN TO HER
d AND SHE WOULD HAVE BECOME PREGNANT WITH A SON.

16a WE RETURNED DURING THE SEVENTH MONTH,
b AND IN FRONT OF US WE FOUND SARAH PREGNANT.
c WE BLESSED HIM
d AND TOLD *HIM* EVERYTHING THAT HAD BEEN COMMANDED FOR HIM:
e THAT HE WOULD NOT YET DIE UNTIL HE BECAME THE FATHER OF SIX SONS
f AND (THAT) HE WOULD SEE (THEM) BEFORE HE DIED;
g BUT (THAT) THROUGH ISAAC HE WOULD HAVE A REPUTATION AND DESCENDANTS.

17a ALL THE DESCENDANTS OF HIS SONS WOULD BECOME NATIONS
b AND BE NUMBERED WITH THE NATIONS.
c BUT ONE OF ISAAC'S SONS WOULD BECOME A HOLY PROGENY
d AND WOULD NOT BE NUMBERED AMONG THE NATIONS,

18a FOR HE WOULD BECOME THE SHARE OF THE MOST HIGH.
b ALL HIS DESCENDANTS HAD FALLEN INTO THAT (SHARE) WHICH GOD OWNS
c SO THAT THEY WOULD BECOME A PEOPLE WHOM THE LORD *POSSESSES* OUT OF ALL THE
NATIONS;
d AND THAT THEY WOULD BECOME A KINGDOM, A PRIESTHOOD, AND A HOLY PEOPLE.

19a THEN WE WENT ON OUR WAY
b AND TOLD SARAH ALL THAT WE HAD REPORTED TO HIM.
c THE TWO OF THEM WERE EXTREMELY HAPPY.

The passage should be disappointing, as far as the theme of the miracles is concerned, as *Jubilees* does not add much to the nature of the miracle, preferring largely to repeat what Genesis has already said: 'In the middle of the sixth month the Lord visited Sarah and he did for her as he had said. And she conceived, and she gave birth to a son in the third month; in the middle of the month, on the day that the Lord had told Abraham – on the festival of the first fruits of the harvest Isaac was born' (*Jub.* 16.12-13). How the Lord visited Sarah, and what he did for her is not related. The interesting element of the rewrite, of course, is the omission of Abraham's age (Gen. 21.2b), which is confirmed by the omission of Gen. 21.5 and 21.7. The age of the parents at the moment of the birth is unimportant, while the author does stress emphatically the date of the occasion: 'In the middle of the sixth month ... she conceived, and she gave birth to a son in the third month; in the middle of the month'. This was, moreover, the time of 'the festival of the first fruits', also called the 'Festival of Weeks' (*Shavu'ot*).[29] Unlike the biblical dating of this festival, according to *Jubilees*, this festival took place in the middle of the third month. This festival is not only a harvest festival, during which offerings had to be brought, but also a festival of the renewal of the covenant. All the festivals of the covenant in the book of *Jubilees* take place on the same day of the year, i.e., the Festival of Weeks: the first covenant with Abraham (*Jub.* 14.1, 10, 18); the second covenant with him (*Jub.* 15.1-5); and the promise to make a covenant with Isaac when God announces his birth (*Jub.* 15.19, 21). Isaac is consequently born during the Festival of Weeks (*Jub.* 16.13); just before Abraham dies, he again celebrates the Festival of Weeks (*Jub.* 22. 1-9), during which he blesses Jacob. The emphasis that *Jubilees* put on the date of the birth is related to the fact that God would establish a covenant only with Isaac and his descendants, as has already been shown. The emphasis on the covenant in the birth scene is confirmed by the addition of *Jub.* 16.14c: 'He was the first to be circumcised according to the covenant which was ordained forever'.

Additions to the birth report will not be examined here in detail. Suffice it to point out the fact that the addition of *Jub.* 16.15-19 is probably related to the omission of the laughter in Gen. 21.6-7. Abraham and Sarah's laughter is interpreted as their joy and happiness. I refer to *Jub.* 16.19: 'The two of them were extremely happy'. The most significant aspect of this addition is the confirmation of the exclusivity of Isaac and especially one of his sons: 'All the descendants of his sons would become nations and be numbered with the nations. But one of Isaac's sons would become a holy progeny and would not be numbered among the nations, for he would become the share of the Most High. All his descendants had fallen into that (share) which God owns so that they would become a people whom the Lord possesses out of all the nations; and that they would become a kingdom, a priesthood, and a holy people' (*Jub.* 16.17-18). The author thus creates a direct lineage from the creation, via Abraham and Sarah to Jacob, and specifically to Levi (the priesthood within Israel).

---

29.   Cf. A. Jaubert, *La notion d'alliance dans le judaïsme aux abords de l'ère chrétienne* (Paris: du Seuil, 1963), 101–4; W. Eiss, 'Das Wochenfest im Jubiläenbuch und im antiken Judentum', in M. Albani, J. Frey, A. Lange (eds), *Studies in the Book of Jubilees* (TSAJ, 65; Tübingen: Mohr Siebeck, 1997), pp. 165–78; J. C. VanderKam, 'Weeks, Festival of', *ABD* VI (1992) pp. 895–97; J.T.A.G.M. Van Ruiten, *Primaeval History*, pp. 247–50.

Conclusions

As has been demonstrated, the story of the birth of Isaac in the book of Genesis is part of the central plot of the story. There is a promise, which continually hangs by a thread, of numerous offspring who will inherit the promised land. In this case, it was threatened by Sarah's infertility and Abraham's and Sarah's old age. However, it is important that the promise be fulfilled by YHWH's intervention. God will keep his promise. He will make the impossible possible. It is the manifestation of divine power, and is based on Israel's understanding of God's continuous sovereignty over the world and its history. It also stresses the exclusive relationship between YHWH and Israel, though the text does not make explicit why the promise of posterity should go through Sarah. Finally, an element of tension between the Abraham story and the story of the forefathers is discernable insomuch as their ages at the conception of their respective first sons are concerned.

The author of *Jubilees* does not add anything to the nature of the God's intervention in the birth of Isaac. It is even doubtful whether he considered the birth of Isaac a specific miracle. However, he was somewhat more explicit about the purpose of the story as such. The differences with Genesis disclose some interesting shifts. In the book of *Jubilees*, it is not Sarah's infertility that is important, it is the origin of Sarah that carries weight, going straight back to the creation of the first man and woman. With this the author changes the purpose of the story completely. It is no longer the story of a promise of numerous offspring which is continually under threat but ultimately fulfilled by the intervention of God, but it becomes a story of pure lineage. The marriage of Abraham and Sarah is put in the same line as the forefathers. The nature of the miracle, i.e., the conception of children in old age, is no longer important. It resolves the tension between the Abraham story and the stories of the forefathers and makes clear why the chosen line should go through Sarah.

ASCLEPIUS' HEALINGS MADE KNOWN

Jan den Boeft

Responding to a call by the god, around 160 CE a gentleman from Mylasa in Karia travelled to Asclepius' famous sanctuary in Epidaurus, in order to be cured of his various health problems, among which was indigestion. During a stop on Aegina the god had ordered him to curb his tendency to become irritated. In the course of his stay at Epidaurus he had to pass through numerous physical exercises and treatment which was not always pleasant, such as 'anointing himself all over with mustard and salt'. It proved to be a successful stay and Apellas – that was the name of the gentleman – expressed his gratitude in a detailed report of his experiences in the *Kurort*. Of course, this inscription, like his entire visit, had been ordered by the god himself, presumably in a dream: ἐκέλευσεν δὲ καὶ ἀναγράψαι ταῦτα. The full text of this well-wrought and fortunately also well-preserved inscription can be found in one of the volumes of the *Inscriptiones Graecae*, but also, with an English translation, in the still indispensable collection of Emma and Louis Edelstein, and, with a German translation, in Hahn's succinct but helpful monograph.[1] As to the question mark in the title of Hahn's monograph, I would be inclined to answer 'both'. The cure can be styled 'medical', but the god prescribes every part of the treatment, Asclepius 'zeigt ihm den Weg zur Heilung', as Hahn rightly says, and, understandably, he wants this success to be registered and indeed advertised, so that all future visitors can read it.

Perhaps somewhat later, a gentleman from Rhodes travelled to another famous sanctuary of Asclepius, in Pergamum. After a successful cure he too put up an

---

1.   F. Hiller von Gaertringen (ed.), *Inscriptiones Graecae* IV².1 (= *Inscriptiones Epidauri*; Berlin: de Gruyter, 1929) 126; E. J. Edelstein, L. Edelstein, *Asclepius. A Collection and Interpretation of the Testimonies* (Publications of the Institute of the History of Medicine, The Johns Hopkins University, 2nd Series; 2 vols.; Baltimore: Johns Hopkins Press, 1945 [= Baltimore, London: Johns Hopkins University Press, 1998]), T 432; P. T. Hahn, *Die Weihinschrift des Apellas: Kurbericht oder Wundererzählung?* (Diss: Erlangen, 1976). There were, of course, many other inscriptions, most of which quite short, in the sanctuary. In studying these in Hiller von Gaertringen one should always take notice of the numerous corrections in W. Peek, 'Inschriften aus dem Asklepieion von Epidauros', *Abhandlungen der Sächsischen Akademie der Wissenschaften zu Leipzig* (Philologisch-historische Klasse, Band 60, Heft 2; Berlin: Akademie-Verlag, 1969).

inscription, which is much shorter and which deserves to be presented in its entirety, as it has been published by H. Müller.[2] Since it was only found in 1983, it is not in Edelstein's collection.

᾽Ασκληπιῶι> φιλανθρώπωι· θεῶι> Πό(πλιος) Αἴ(λιος)
Θέων Ζηνοδότου καὶ Ζηνοδό[τ]ης ῾Ρόδιος
ἑκατὸν εἴκοσι ἡμερῶν μὴ πιὼν καὶ φά-
γὼν ἕωθεν ἑκάστης ἡμέρας λευκοῦ πι-
πέρεος κόκκους δεκαπέντε καὶ κρομμύου
[ἥ]μισυ κατὰ κέλευσιν τοῦ θεοῦ ἐναργῶς ἐκ
[πολ]λῶν καὶ μεγάλων κινδύνων σωθεὶς
[ἀνέ]θηκα καὶ ὑπὲρ τοῦ ἀδελφιδοῦ Πο(πλίου) Αἰλ(ίου)
[Καλλι]στράτου τοῦ καὶ Πλαγκιανοῦ. vac.
[᾽Αντιπ]άτρου τὸ παιδικὸν > εὐχήν. vac.

It can be rendered as follows: 'To Asclepius, a god who loves men, I, Publius Aelius Theon, the son of Zenodotos and Zenodote, from Rhodes, who for 120 days in early morning did not drink and ate 15 grains of white pepper and half an onion, on the order of the god, and was manifestly (ἐναργῶς) saved from many great dangers, have dedicated, also on behalf of my nephew Publius Aelius Callistratus, who is also named Plancianus, Antipater's παιδικόν, ex voto'.[3] What the god prescribed for the early morning is not exactly everybody's wish to start the day with, but from Aelius Aristides' ἱεροὶ λόγοι, 'sacred tales', we know that he had other ordeals for the patients on his programme. 'We were ordered to do many strange things. Of what I remember, there was a race, which it was necessary to run unshod in winter time', and 'He commanded me again to smear on the mud in the same way and to run in a circle about the Temples three times. And the strength of the northwind was indescribable, and the icy cold had increased'.[4] As Galen noted: 'According to Hippocrates himself, in order to gain ready obedience, prognosis and in general the patient's admiration for his physician are an asset. Thus at any rate even among ourselves in Pergamum we see that those who are being treated by the god obey him when on many occasions he bids them not to drink at all for fifteen days, while they obey none of the physicians who give this prescription'.[5]

2.   H. Müller, 'Ein Heilungsbericht aus dem Asklepieion von Pergamon', *Chiron* 17 (1987), pp. 193–233.

3.   The text and an Italian translation can also be found in M. Girone, ᾽Ιάματα. *Guarigioni miraculose di Asclepio in testi epigrafici* (Bari: Levante editore, 1998), pp. 149–50.

4.   Aelius Aristides, *The Complete Works* vol. II: *Orations XVII-LIII* (transl. C. A. Behr; Leiden: Brill, 1981), pp. 289, 306. *Orations XLVII–LII* are 'The Sacred Tales'.

5.   Galen, *In Hippocratis Epidemiarum Librum VI Commentaria* IV 8 (p. 137): πρὸς τὴν τοιαύτην οὖν εὐπείθειαν αὐτὸς ὁ ῾Ιπποκράτης ἔλεγε καὶ τὰς προρρήσεις ὠφελεῖν ἡμᾶς καὶ ὅλως τὸ θαυμάζεσθαι τὸν ἰατρὸν ὑπὸ τοῦ κάμνοντος. οὕτω γέ τοι καὶ παρ᾽ ἡμῖν ἐν Περγάμῳ τοὺς θεραπευομένους ὑπὸ τοῦ θεοῦ πειθομένους ὁρῶμεν αὐτῷ πεντεκαίδεκα πολλάκις ἡμέραις προστάξαντι μηδ᾽ ὅλως πιεῖν, οἱ τῶν ἰατρῶν μηδενὶ προστάττοντι πείθονται.

For hypotheses concerning what is denoted by παιδικόν, the votive gift, I refer to Müller's discussion. Two other details deserve to be noted: Müller rightly rules out the combination of κατὰ κέλευσιν τοῦ θεοῦ (line 6) and ἀνέθηκα (line 8). Theon does not say that he put up his gift on the god's orders – it was an ex voto: εὐχήν – but that Asclepius prescribed the pepper and onion cure. Müller is also right in not taking ἐναργῶς (line 6) as a reference to the clearness of Asclepius' apparition in a dream, as in the case of Tiberius Claudius Severus (see below), but to the evident salutary results of the cure: the adverb belongs to σωθείς (line 7). So the reports of Apellas from Mylasa and Theon from Rhodes both testify to the same facts: Asclepius provided the medical prescriptions and the success was undeniable, and the sanctuaries of Epidaurus and Pergamum were each enriched by one further clear testimony to the god's skill.

Archeological and epigraphical evidence shows that for Asclepius' sanctuary at Pergamum the second century CE was a period of prosperity.[6] Considerable building activities were going on, the city's mint showed Asclepius' image, and many inscriptions testify to the patients' gratitude. For the details I refer to Christian Habicht, who even suggests that Pergamum at the time was the pick of the *Kurorte* in the Graeco-Roman world.[7] It was, however, not the only place in which Asclepius demonstrated his philanthropy. The more recent studies of Sara Aleshire have amply shown the great importance of the Athenian Asklepieion, which, as she says, 'appealed to a wide variety of people of all economic and social strata'. It had been founded in the fifth century BCE and we know about activities

---

6.   According to Pausanias, Epidauros was the original centre of the cult of Asclepius: τὰ γὰρ Ἀσκληπιεῖα εὑρίσκω τὰ ἐπιφανέστατα γεγονότα ἐξ Ἐπιδαύρου, 'I find that the most famous sanctuaries of Asclepius originated from Epidaurus' (2.26.8). The one at Pergamum was founded by a man who had been healed at Epidaurus after a hunting accident. See for the detailed reports on the excavations of Pergamum's Asklepieion O. Ziegenaus, G. de Luca, *Das Asklepieion* (*Altertümer von Pergamon* XI 1-4; Berlin: Walter de Gruyter, 1968–84). A shorter general description can be found in W. Radt, *Pergamon: Geschichte und Bauten einer antiken Metropole* (Darmstadt: Wissenschaftliche Buchgesellschaft, 1999), pp. 220–42. The sanctuary faded away during the third century CE, perhaps also because of the strong Christian presence in the city. C. Habicht, *Die Inschriften des Asklepieions* (*Altertümer von Pergamon* VIII 3; Berlin: Walter de Gruyter, 1969), p. 129, tentatively suggests that a late inscription could be interpreted as 'Protest gegen das sich ausbreitende, vielleicht bereits übermächtige Christentum': Μέγας Ἀσκληπιός, which reminds one of μεγάλη ἡ Ἄρτεμις Ἐφεσίων (Acts 19.34). The importance of the Asklepieion in earlier times can *inter alia* be illustrated by a passage in a famous inscription in honour of a victory of King Attalus III (138–33): a large statue of the king in his armour and standing on the booty was to be placed ἐν τῷ ναῷ τοῦ Σωτῆρος Ἀσκληπιοῦ, ἵνα ᾖ σύνναος τῷ θεῷ (*IPerg.* 246 = *OGIS* 332, 8-9). For a correct assessment of σύνναος, 'sharing the temple', a more widespread phenomenon, the careful analyses of L. Robert, 'Un décret de Pergame', *Bulletin de Correspondance Hellénique* 108 (1984), pp. 472–89 (475), and L. Robert, 'Le décret de Pergame pour Attale III', *Bulletin de Correspondance Hellénique* 109 (1985), pp. 468–81 (475–77), are indispensable.

7.   C. Habicht, *Inschriften*.

in the fifth century CE. Remarkably, the epigraphical evidence contains the participation of very few foreigners.[8] There were Asklepieia in other towns too, though in a number of cases scant evidence is available. Alessandra Semeria has drawn up a list of the sanctuaries in Greece and the Greek islands,[9] and the god had also settled in Rome, on the island in the Tiber, where the hospital of the *Fatebenefratelli* is nowadays continuing his healing practices within another religious framework.[10]

Nevertheless, Epidaurus held its own, as *inter alia* appears from Apellas' experiences and also in the report of one of the best-known travellers of antiquity, Pausanias, who during the second century CE visited many towns and sanctuaries in Greece. Among these were Epidaurus and its Asklepieion. In ch. 27 of the second book of his 'Description of Greece' he describes what he had seen within the enclosure of the sanctuary, such as the image of the god made of ivory and gold, other works of art, various buildings within the precinct and the following: 'Within the enclosure stood slabs; in my time six remained, but of old there were more. On them are inscribed the names of both the men and the women who have been healed by Asclepius, the disease also from which each suffered, and the means of cure. The dialect is Doric'. The ravages of time have fortunately been not too unkind in this case, for some seventeen centuries later, in the last decades of the 19th century, four of these στῆλαι were unearthed during excavations. The fourth of these, στήλη D, is in fact only a small fragment, and the third had been recycled as the threshold of a Christian chapel with due consequences for the legibility of the inscribed text. The state of the remains of στῆλαι A and B is far better. In all, in their present state the four slabs contain seventy ἰάματα, forty of which are complete or almost so. The text can be found in the *Inscriptiones Graecae*, Herzog (with German translation) and LiDonnici (with English translation). Edelstein, *Asclepius*, Testimonium 423 provides only στῆλαι A and B.[11] By way of introduction I use two cases, as these are translated by LiDonnici, A12: 'Euhippos bore a spear head in his jaw for six years. While he was sleeping here, the god drew the spearhead from him and gave it to him in his hands. When day

8.   S. B. Aleshire, *The Athenian Asklepieion: The People, Their Dedications, and the Inventories* (Amsterdam: Gieben, 1989); S. B. Aleshire, *Asklepios at Athens. Epigraphic and Prosopographic Essays on the Athenian Healing Cults* (Amsterdam: Gieben, 1991).

9.   A. Semeria, 'Per un censimento degli Asklepieia della Grecia e delle isole', *Annali della Scuola Normale Superiore di Pisa*. Classe di Lettere e Filosofia, series III, vol. XVI (1986), pp. 931–58.

10.   A brief survey of the history of healing on the island is provided by M. Guarducci, 'L' Isola Tiberina e la sua tradizione ospitaliera', *Atti della Accademia Nazionale dei Lincei, Rendiconti, Classe di Scienze morali, storiche e filologiche vol.* 26 (1971), pp. 267–83. Excavations have brought to light a large number of votive gifts, but many have since disappeared and only a small number belongs to the collection of the Museo Nazionale Romano.

11.   IV².1 121–24; R. Herzog, *Die Wunderberichte von Epidauros* (= *Philologus*, Supplementband XXII, Heft III Leipzig: Dieterich'sche Verlagsbuchhandlung, 1933; Edelstein, *Asclepius*, 1945: T 423; L. R. LiDonnici, *The Epidaurian Miracle Inscriptions: Text, Translation and Commentary* (Atlanta: Scholars Press, 1995). The last named has incorporated W. Peek's critical remarks about Hiller's text of five healings on the third στήλη.

came, he walked out well, having the spearhead in his hands.' A13: 'A man from Torone, leeches. While he was sleeping, he saw a dream. It seemed to him that the god ripped open his chest with a knife, took out the leeches and gave them to him in his hands, and sewed his breast together. When day came he left having the animals in his hands, and had become well. He had drunk them down, after being tricked by his stepmother who had thrown them into a potion that he drank.'

These testimonies are suffused with a spirit which greatly differs from the cures of Apellas and Theon. Here Asclepius performs examples of surgery which at least at the time were beyond human possibilities. The time of the στῆλαι is the fourth century BCE, but the individual healings of the collection are, of course, older than the collection itself. It is on the composition of the latter that LiDonnici primarily concentrates. The author combats the view that the collection was composed in one go at some time in the late fourth century from a variety of materials, and argues that they 'may reflect *several* episodes of a collection and arrangement of tales' and στήλη A 'seems very clearly to have been made up of three smaller, earlier collections'. Thus LiDonnici. Much of this has a hypothetical character, but the idea is attractive in that it reckons with a continuous and conscious handling of the testimonia by those in charge of the proceedings in the sanctuary. The text itself provides some clues about the origin of the collected tales. The patient of A3 was 'looking at the "pinakes" in the sanctuary'. Such tablets could contain some sort of pictorial representation and an inscription, such as is literally quoted in A1 and explicitly stated about our patient: he reads τὰ ἐπιγράμματα. Another source of the tales may have been the inscriptions on particular votive gifts, such as the silver pig which an Athenian lady dedicated on the order of the god, or the precious cup, which, when broken into pieces, had been repaired by the god and which was then dedicated to him. By the way, this story illustrates that not all the tales are ἰάματα proper, some testify to other aspects of Asclepius' salutary competence.

Most tales, however, concern physical illnesses or defects of a wide variety – baldness, lice, headache, gout, speech problems, wounds, ulcers, stones, as in A8: 'Euphanes, a boy from Epidaurus. This boy suffered from stones and slept in the *abaton*, in his dream the god stood by him and said: "What will you give me, if I restore your health?" The boy answered "ten dice". The god burst out laughing and promised to put an end to the disease. At daybreak Euphanes left healthy.' This charming little scene is also an excellent proof of the god's friendly character. He only became angry when he was clearly cheated or deprived of a gift which had been promised.

There are two domains which together make up well-nigh a third of the legible cases. It is not surprising that these are blindness (ten times) and paralysis of limbs (nine), the same physical defects we are all familiar with from reading the Gospels and Acts. At Epidauros too the blind recovered their sight and the lame walked. These were the defects which human resources were powerless to do anything about, but which made it impossible for those affected to function normally in their society. Small wonder that they sought the god's help. During their ἐγκοίμησις, 'incubation', in the so-called '*abaton*', he provided this help, as in B12:

'Antikrates of Knidos, eyes. This man had been stuck with a spear through both his eyes in a battle, and he became blind and carried around the spearhead with him, inside his face. Sleeping here, he saw a vision. It seemed to him that the god pulled out the the dart and fitted the so-called "girls" (κόρας) back into the eyelids. When day came he left well.' The word κόρη in an ophthalmological sense means 'pupil'.

A case of paralysis will presently follow, but before that I have to deal with the question of what the purpose of these lists of healings may have been. They were obviously meant to be visible to all visitors, for not only Pausanias in the second century CE could see them, but, as I just quoted from A3, even before the time of the στῆλαι patients could walk around and look at the individual tablets with their inscriptions. LiDonnici marshals some evidence for the supposition that the στῆλαι stood against one of the walls on the inside of the *abaton*, the hall where the incubations took place, and thus could 'heighten the suppliants' expectations' before they went to sleep. Such an idea, viz. that the patients would have gained courage and confidence, can be further illustrated by two of the healings. First A3, a case of paralysis, which has already been mentioned above: 'A man who was paralyzed in all his fingers except one came as a suppliant to the god. When he was looking at the plaques in the sanctuary, he didn't believe in the cures and was somewhat disparaging of the inscriptions (ὑποδιέσυρε τὰ ἐπιγράμματα). Sleeping here, he saw a vision. It seemed he was playing the knucklebones below the temple, and as he was about to throw them, the god appeared, sprang on his hand and stretched out the fingers. When the god moved off, the man seemed to bend his hand and to stretch out his fingers one by one. When he had straightened them all, the god asked him if he would still not believe the inscriptions on the plaques around the sanctuary and he answered no. "Therefore, since you doubted them before, though they were not unbelievable, from now on," he said, "your name will be 'Unbeliever' (Ἄπιστος)." When day came, he left well.' The message is clear. Even a person who had travelled to Epidaurus with scepticism, or rather pure disbelief, has to admit to have been in the wrong, when experiencing the salutary power which the god, without any hard feelings, put into action. A nickname is his only punishment. There are two other cases of such disbelief, one of a patient, the other of fellow-visitors in the sanctuary. Future patients could therefore note that even a lack of confidence was no obstacle to success.

Are all Asclepian centres equal? one might ask. One of the ἰάματα implies that at least at Epidaurus they were inclined to answer in the negative. B3:

'Aristagora of Troizen. Since she had a worm in her belly, she slept in the *temenos* of Asclepius at Troizen and she saw a dream. It seemed to her that the sons of the god, while he was not there but was in Epidaurus, cut off her head, but they couldn't put it back again so they sent someone to the Asklepieion, so that he would return. Meanwhile the day overtakes them and the priest clearly sees the head removed from the body. When the night finally came again, Aristagora saw a vision. It seemed to her that the god had returned from Epidaurus and put the head on her neck, and after that cut open her belly, took out the worm and sewed it together again, and from this she became well.'

A longer and somewhat different version of this story, without the name of the woman, can be found in Aelian's *De natura animalium*. It is impossible to go into the question of the interdependence of the two texts. For our purpose here the version just quoted seems to imply a clear warning: beware of the amateurism in nearby Troizen, for Epidaurus is the real thing. It is an understandable part of the advertisement which is the objective of the list of healings. One could also express this in Dillon's words: 'The iamata are didactic in nature, being inscribed by the temple authorities to introduce the sick to the powers of the god'.[12] Apellas' cure in 160 CE may have created the impression that later the god gave medical instructions instead of healing the patients himself. However, an inscription from 224 CE shows that such a chronological dichotomy would be too easy:

ʼΑγαθῇ Τύχῃ
Τιβ(έριος) Κλ(αύδιος) Σευῆρος
Σινωπεὺς ʼΑπόλ-
λωνι Μαλεάτᾳ καὶ
Σώτηρι ʼΑσκληπιῷ
κατ' ὄναρ, ὃν ὁ θεὸς
εἰάσατο ἐν τῷ ἐν-
κοιμητηρίῳ, χοι-
ράδας ἔχοντα ἐπ[ὶ]
τοῦ τραχή[λου] καὶ
καρκίνον [τ]ο[ῦ ὠ]τός,
ἐπιστὰς ἐ[ν]αργῶς,
οἷός ἐστ[ι ἐν τῷ ναῷ.
ʼΕπὶ ἱερέω[ς] Μάρ(κου)
Αὐρ(ηλίου) Πυ(θοδώρ)ου
ἔτους ἑ[κ]α[το]σ-
στοῦ πρώτου.

With prosperous outcome. Tiberius Claudius from Severus Sinope to
Apollo Maleatas and Asclepius the Saviour in accordance
with a dream. The god restored him to health in the
sleeping hall, when he had scrofulous swellings in his neck

12.   M. P. J. Dillon, 'The Didactic Nature of the Epidaurian Iamata', *ZPE* 101 (1994), pp. 239–60 (259). As was noted above, Asclepius also provided help in other cases. The Epidaurian list contains *inter alia* the spectacular repair of a broken goblet, and a nice Pergamene inscription of the second century CE began as follows: σοί μὲγ' ἄριστε θεῶν, [ʼΑσ]κληπιὲ θῆκε Διώνη [ἀργύρεο]ν τὸ κάτοπτρον, 'to you, by far the best of gods, Asclepius, Dione has dedicated her silver mirror'. The rest of the inscription is unfortunately lost, but the quoted words are reminiscent of the first lines of Martial's epigram 9.16 about Earinos, the darling of his master: *Consilium formae speculum dulcisque capillos Pergameo posuit dona sacrata deo*, 'the mirror, which is the adviser of his beauty, and his sweet locks have been put here (by Earinos) as gifts dedicated to the god of Pergamum.'

and an ulcer in his ear, appearing to him clearly, as he is (in the temple). During the priesthood of Marcus Aurelius Pythodorus in the 101st year.[13]

Let us now pass to another Asclepian sanctuary, on the southern coast of Crete, which according to his biographer, was once visited by no less a person than Apollonius of Tyana: 'He also travelled to the sanctuary at Lebena; this is Asclepius' temple, and just as Asia flocks to Pergamum, so Crete flocked to this sanctuary, and many Libyans also cross to it; for it faces the Libyan sea close to Phaistos, where the little rock keeps out a mighty sea.' Excavations have brought to light the remnants of the sanctuary and a number of inscriptions. These can be found in Margherita Guarducci's *Inscriptiones Creticae*, but already before the appearance of this volume she showed in an article that at Lebena too, from the second century BCE, the individual testimonies of healings had been gathered in a list, which was inscribed on the wall of the *abaton*.[14] Some words of a partly preserved inscription testify to this: τῶν ἰαμάτων ἀνέγραφη τὼ θιῶ ὁ κατα[and in the next line ἐς τᾶν σανίδων (I.Cret 1: xvii 8). It seems indeed feasible to complete κατα as κατάλογος and to regard the σανίδες as the equivalent of the πίνακες at Epidaurus. Unfortunately only a few items of the list have been preserved, in a fragmentary state at that. Nevertheless, the evidence contains indications that at Lebena the registered healings were either directly worked by the god or resulted from diets he prescribed. A clear example of the former is Lebena 9 (I.Cret 1: xvii 9):

Δήμανδρον Καλάβιος Γορτύνιον ἰσ[χι]-
[ἀ]λγικὸν γενόμενον προσέταξε ἀπο[μο]-
λὲν ἐς Λεβήναν ὅτι θεραπεύσειν, αἶ[ψα]
δ' εὐθόντα ἔταμε καθ' ὕπνον ὑγιὴς ἐ[γέ]-
νετο.

He (= Asclepius) ordered Demandros, son of Kalabis, from Gortyn, who suffered from sciatica, to come to Lebena in order to cure him. Immediately after his arrival he operated on him in his sleep and his health returned.

13. IG IV².1 127; E. J. Edelstein, L. Edelstein, *Asclepius*, T 424; M. Girone, ὁ Ἰάματα, 71–74. On a mountain near the sanctuary of Asclepius was an earlier small temple of Apollo Maleatas, mentioned by Pausanias 2.27.7. Asclepius cured (ἰάσατο) Severus himself. See for the Greek terminology of healing, L. Wells, *The Greek Language of Healing from Homer to New Testament Times* (Berlin: Walter de Gruyter, 1998), and for the phrase κατ' ὄναρ, F. T. Van Straten, 'Daikrates' Dream: A Votive Relief from Kos, and Some Other kat'onar Dedications', *Bulletin Antieke Beschaving* 51 (1976), pp. 1–38. Unfortunately the end of line 13 is lost; ἐν τῷ ναῷ is no more than an attractive completion, based on the plausible assumption that in his dream the patient recognized Asclepius from the image(s) he had seen in the sanctuary. When the emperor Hadrian visited Epidauros in 124 CE, this was declared the first year of a new era in the local calendar.

14. M. Guarducci, *Inscriptiones Creticae* I (Rome: Libreria dello Stato, 1935); M. Guarducci, 'I miracoli di Asclepio a Lebena', *Historia. Studi Storici per l'Antichità Classica* 8 (1934), pp. 410–28, respectively.

The legible part of Lebena 17, which is a personal inscription, may function as an example of a healing via a diet (I.Cret 1: xvii 17):

> 'Ασκληπιῷ[ι]
> Πόπλιος Γράνιος ['Ροῦφος]
> κατ' ἐπιταγήν.
> ἐκ διετίας βήσσοντά με ἀδ[διαλεί]–
> πτως, ὥστε σάρκας ἐνπνύου[ς καὶ]
> ἡμαγμένας δι' ὅλης ἡμέρας ἀ[πο]–
> βάλλειν, ὁ θεὸς ἐπεδέξατο θερ[α]–
> πεῦσαι.
> ἔδωκεν εὔζωμον νήστη τρώγειν,
> εἶτα πεπερᾶτον 'Ιταλικὸν πείνειν
> πάλιν ἄμυλον διὰ θερμοῦ ὕδατος,
> εἶτα κονίαν ἀπὸ τῆς ἱερᾶς σποδοῦ
> καὶ τοῦ ἱεροῦ ὕδατος, εἶτα ᾠὸν καὶ
> ῥητείνην, πάλιν πίσσαν ὑγράν.

To Asclepius Publius Granius Rufus according to command. (Such expressions are very common, also in the cult of other gods; see the lists drawn up by Van Straten.)[15] When for two years I had coughed incessantly so that I discharged purulent and bloody pieces of flesh all day long, the god took in hand to cure me … He gave me rocket to nibble on an empty stomach, then Italian wine flavored with pepper to drink, then again starch with hot water, the powder from the holy ashes, and some holy water, then an egg and pine-resin, then again moist pitch (translation Edelstein).

As may have become clear from the examples from Epidaurus, Pergamum and Lebena, the god acts from beginning to end: he summons the sick, heals them and then orders them to make this success known to enhance his fame. For Asclepius at Rome, the epigraphic evidence is quite small, but we have at least a well-preserved inscription about four cases. It is the only remaining part of a larger list. The text can be found in several collections, e.g. Edelstein T 438 and IGUR 148. The first and third cases are as follows:

> Αὐταῖς ταῖς ἡμέραις Γαίῳ τινὶ τυφλῷ ἐχρημάτισεν ἐλθεῖν ἐπὶ τὸ ἱερὸν βῆμα
> καὶ προσκυνῆσαι, εἶτα ἀπὸ τοῦ δεξιοῦ ἐλθεῖν ἐπὶ τὸ ἀριστερὸν καὶ θεῖναι
> τοὺς πέντε δακτύλους ἐπάνω τοῦ βήματος καὶ ἆραι τὴν χεῖρα καὶ ἐπιθεῖναι
> ἐπὶ τοὺς ἰδίους ὀφθαλμούς· καὶ ὀρθὸν ἀνέβλεψε τοῦ δήμου παρεστῶτος καὶ
> συνχαιρομένου, ὅτι ζῶσαι ἀρεταὶ ἐγένοντο ἐπὶ τοῦ Σεβαστοῦ ἡμῶν
> 'Αντωνείνου

15.　The appendix (21–27) in Van Straten, 'Votive Relief', contains a list of the relevant expressions.

In those days he [sc., the god] revealed to Gaius, a blind man, that he should go to the holy base [sc., of the statue] and there should prostrate himself; then go from right to the left and place his five fingers on the base and raise his hand and lay it on his own eyes. And he could see again clearly while the people stood by and rejoiced that glorious deeds lived again under our Emperor Antoninus (translation Edelstein).

Αἷμα ἀναφέροντι ᾽Ιουλιανῷ ἀφηλπισμένῳ ὑπὸ παντὸς ἀνθρώπου ἐχρησμάτισεν ὁ θεὸς ἐλθεῖν καὶ ἐκ τοῦ τριβώμου ἆραι κόκκους στροβίλου καὶ φάγειν μετὰ μέλιτος ἐπὶ τρεῖς ἡμέρας· καὶ ἐσώθη καὶ ἐλθὼν δημοσίᾳ ηὐχαρίστησεν ἔμπροσθεν τοῦ δήμου

To Julian who was spitting up blood and had been despaired of by all men the god revealed that he should go and from the threefold altar take the seeds of a pine cone and eat them with honey for three days. And he was saved and went and publicly offered thanks before the people.

Obviously the god's feats were an object of public rejoicing and they also added to the glory of the reigning emperor. Moreover, the reader will have recognized the verb χρηματίζειν denoting a divine revelation, which is so familiar from the NT: in Mt. 2.12 'the magi returned by another route, χρηματισθέντες κατ᾽ ὄναρ'.[16] For a minute comparison of a selection of Asclepian *Heilungsberichte* with one another and with those in the New Testament I refer to the interesting analysis by M. Wolter.[17] I am, however, surprised at one of his conclusions, viz. that the Asclepian reports 'nicht an der Person des Heilers, sondern an der Heilstätte haften' (170). According to Greek belief, a god(dess) resided in his (her) sanctuary and Asclepius is always manifestly present, even if at times this is not explicitly stated.

Concerning the men and women involved, it seems reasonable to deduce from the texts that – to borrow Sara Aleshire's phrase – 'a wide variety of people of all economic and social strata placed their confidence in the healing power of Asclepius'. What about intellectuals and philosophers? Were they inclined to a Lucianic scepticism or disbelief? I shall briefly mention three who did not belong to this category, in chronological order. First Galen, who in one of his autobiographical passages says that Marcus Aurelius refrained from urging him to accompany him on a campaign in Germania, ἀκούσας τἀναντία κελεύειν τὸν πάτριον θεὸν ᾽Ασκληπιόν, οὗ καὶ θεραπευτὴν ἀπέφαινον ἐμαυτόν, ἐξ ὅτου με θανατικὴν διάθεσιν ἀποστήματος ἔχοντα διέσωσε, 'when he heard that the

16. See also P. Roesch, 'Le culte d'Asclepios à Rome', in G. Sabbah (ed.), *Mémoires III: Médecins et Médecine dans l'Antiquité* (Saint-Etienne: Université de Saint-Étienne, 1982), pp. 171–79.

17. M. Wolter, 'Inschriftliche Heilungsberichte und neutestamentliche Wundererzählungen: Überlieferungs- und formgeschichtliche Beobachtungen', in: K. Berger *et al.*, *Studien und Texte zur Formgeschichte* (TANZ, 7; Tübingen: Francke, 1992), pp. 135–75.

opposite was ordered by the god of my fathers Asclepius, whose servant I declared to be since he saved me when I had the deadly condition of an abscess' (*De libris propriis* XIX 18).[18] Next Julian, in a passage of his *Against the Galilaeans*. Having said that Asclepius' sanctuaries can be found everywhere, he adds: ἐμὲ γοῦν ἰάσατο πολλάκις Ἀσκληπιὸς κάμνοντα ὑπαγορεύσας φάρμακα, καὶ τούτων μάρτυς ἐστὶ Ζεύς, 'I in any case was often healed by Asclepius, when I was ill and he suggested medicines; Zeus can testify to this.'[19] Finally, the fifth-century Athenian Neoplatonist Proklos. In ch. 29 of Marinus' fascinating biography we find him praying in the Asklepieion for a severely ill young girl whom her doctors had given up on. The parents appealed to Proklos who went to the god: εὐχομένου δὲ αὐτοῦ τὸν ἀρχαιότερον τρόπον, ἀθρόα μεταβολὴ περὶ τὴν κόρην ἐφαίνετο καὶ ῥαστώνη ἐξαίφνης ἐγίγνετο, 'and when he was praying according to the ancient custom, immediately a change in the girl's condition was manifest and suddenly she felt better'. So even in the fully Christian era the god had survived and he was with Proklos in his last illness: μεταξὺ γὰρ ὢν ὕπνου καὶ ἐγρηγόρσεως, εἶδε δράκοντα περὶ τὴν κεφαλὴν αὐτοῦ ἕρποντα, ἀφ' ἧς αὐτῷ τὴν ἀρχὴν ἐπέθετο τὸ τῆς παρέσεως νόσημα, καὶ οὕτως ἐκ τῆς ἐπιφανείας ἀνακωχῆς τινος τοῦ νοσήματος ᾔσθετο, 'between waking and sleeping he saw a serpent creeping round his head, where the affliction of his paralysis had begun. And thus from the epiphany he noticed a subsidence of his illness'.[20] Galen, Julian and Proklos surely were all well versed in philosophy, but like all pagans in antiquity they were also religious. It is therefore only normal that they relied on Asclepius' healing powers, as had been the practice of many thousands of men and women before them.

A brief inscription on an altar, dating from the first century CE, may summarize what Asclepius could offer and how those whom he had healed advertised his power:

> Ἀσκληπιῷ
> καὶ Ὑγείᾳ θεοῖς
> ἐπιφανεστάτοις
> [ὑ]πὲρ κεφαλῆς
> θεραπείας καὶ
> ὀμμάτων βλέψ[ε-]
> ως Ζώσιμος Φλ.
> Μοδέστης πραγμα-
> τευτὴς χρηματισ-
> θεὶς ὑπὸ τοῦ θεοῦ

18. *Claudii Galeni Opera omnia* (ed. cur. C.G. Kühn; Lipsiae: Cnoblochii, 1821–33), pp. 18–19; Edelstein, *Asclepius*, T 458; P. Moraux, *Galien de Pergame. Souvenirs d'un médecin* (Paris: Les Belles Lettres, 1985), p. 106.

19. Giuliano Imperatore, *Contra Galilaeos*. Introduzione, testo critico e traduzione a cura di E. Masaracchia (Testi e commenti, 9; Roma: Edizioni dell' Ateneo, 1990), Fr. 57.

20. Marinus, *Proclus ou sur le bonheur* (Texte établi, traduit et annoté par H. D. Saffrey et A.-P. Segonds; Paris: Les Belles Lettres, 2001) 29 and 30 respectively.

To Asclepius and Hygieia, the gods who clearly manifest themselves, for the cure of his head and his eyesight, Zosimus, the agent of Flavia Modesta, having received an order from the god.[21]

21. M. Büjükkolanci, H. Engelmann, 'Inschriften aus Ephesos', *ZPE* 86 (1991), pp. 137–44 (143–44).

MIRACLE STORIES AND THEIR NARRATIVE INTENT IN THE CONTEXT OF THE RULER CULT OF CLASSICAL ANTIQUITY

Ulrike Riemer

The contest between the priests of the Pharaoh and the leaders of the Israelites, Aaron and Moses, is well known. Although God forecast the obduracy of the Pharaoh with the words, 'And the Egyptians shall know that I am the LORD, when I stretch forth mine hand upon Egypt' (Exod. 7.5), he nevertheless instructed Moses and Aaron to comply with the Pharaoh's demand to prove themselves by performing a miracle (Exod. 7.9). The ensuing contest with the Egyptian prophets was won by the Hebrews. While the Egyptians were generally able to match the feats performed by Aaron and Moses, such as transforming a staff into a snake, turning the waters of the Nile into blood, and summoning a plague of frogs (though the snake from the Hebrew staff swallowed the Egyptian staves), they failed when it came to producing gnats from dust (Exod. 8.18). The priests conceded defeat and said to the Pharaoh, 'This is the finger of God' (Exod. 8.19). However, the Pharaoh's heart remained hard, thus provoking further plagues.

In contrast to Jesus, who refused to give a miraculous sign to demonstrate his power (Mk 8.11; cf. Mt. 12.38-39; Lk. 11.29), Moses and Aaron, acting on God's instruction, obeyed the Pharaoh's command. It is taken for granted in the Old Testament that supernatural, i.e. magical, forces are proof of God's power or demonstrate that the worker of the miracle is acting with God's full consent.

Numerous studies have been made examining the roots of the New Testament miracle stories in Judaism and Hellenistic-religious culture, and a recent contribution to this field is the *Habilitationsschrift* of Bernd Kollmann.[1] Although, when discussing the current status of research in the field, Kollmann addresses 'die Ableitung der ntl. Wundererzählungen aus der hellenistischen Religionsgeschichte' and mentions Emperor Vespasian as one of the miracle-working *theioi andres*, the section that deals with the roots of such stories in classical antiquity does not cover the worship of the Roman emperors as miracle workers, nor does it treat the issue of Jesus as ruler. This omission is all the more surprising given that there are

---

1. B. Kollmann, *Jesus und die Christen als Wundertäter: Studien zu Magie, Medizin und Schamanismus in Antike und Christentum* (FRLANT, 170; Göttingen: Vandenhoeck & Ruprecht, 1996).

conspicuous parallels with accounts of the Roman imperial cult. Whilst these parallels have often been noted by other authors, a consistent interpretation is lacking. Franz Sauter, for example, emphasizes the miracle of the firmament standing still during the birth of Christ, but derogates the equivalent Martial epigram as nothing more than a 'dichterische Spielerei'.[2]

My aim in this paper is to draw parallels between the miracle stories of the New Testament and those texts of classical antiquity that offer accounts of rulers and the miracles they performed, and to set them both in a common context.

I

As one might expect, many of the accounts of imperial miracle working are to be found in the works of the classical poets. Martial in particular praises in his epigrams the divine powers of the Flavian emperors.[3] In his *Book of Spectacles*, Martial describes how an antelope being hunted by a pack of molosser dogs fled to the emperor and stood in front of him like supplicants. The dogs did not touch the antelope (Martial, *Sp.* 30.1-4). The poet comments on this miracle as follows: Caesar (meaning in this case Titus[4]) has divine power (*numen*) that is sacred.[5] By way of explanation, Martial states that wild animals are unable to lie.[6] The reverence shown by the animals was therefore real and not affected. They sensed Caesar's *numen*, through which he protects and punishes.[7] Peace among animals is a common motif in classical texts[8] (cf. Isa. 11.6-9), and is of special significance in this case as the paradisical state is a direct consequence of the emperor's divine influence.

In poems, the divine nature of the emperors is demonstrated predominantly by their powers over the forces of nature. Wild animals and the natural world both respect and honour the superior power of the emperor.

Another of Martial's epigrams, also taken from the *Book of Spectacles*, describes the proskynesis of a wild animal (Martial, *Sp.* 17). An elephant that would

2. F. Sauter, *Der römische Kaiserkult bei Martial und Statius* (TbzA, 21; Stuttgart and Berlin: Kohlhammer, 1934), p. 168.

3. For more information on the following examples see F. Sauter, *Der römische Kaiserkult*, pp. 168–70; M. Clauss, *Kaiser und Gott: Herrscherkult im römischen Reich* (Stuttgart and Leipzig: Teubner, 1999), pp. 347–53. The best reference for dates remains L. Friedländer, *M. Valerii Martialis Epigrammaton Libri* vol. 1 (Leipzig: Teubner, 1886), pp. 50–67.

4. K. Scott, *The Imperial Cult under the Flavians* (Stuttgart: Kohlhammer, 1936), p. 119. O. Weinreich, *Studien zu Martial. Literarhistorische und religionsgeschichtliche Untersuchung* (TbzA, 4; Stuttgart: Kohlhammer, 1928), pp. 21–23, assigns the *Liber spectaculorum* to the year 80, the occasion of celebrations to mark the opening of the Colosseum. Scott concurs, 56.

5. *Numen habet Caesar, sacra est haec, sacra potestas* (Martial, *Sp.* 30.7).

6. *Credite; mentiri non didicere ferae* (Martial, *Sp.* 30.8).

7. O. Weinreich, *Studien*, p. 86.

8. This subject – though without reference to Martial – is addressed in V. Bucheit, 'Tierfriede in der Antike', *WüJb* 12 (1986), pp. 143–67. Cf. A. S. F. Gow, *Theocritus* (ed., with a translation and commentary; Cambridge: Cambridge University Press, 2nd edn., 1952), on Theocritus, *Id.* 24.86–87.

induce fear even in a bull (*tauro metuendus*) approached the emperor in reverence and humility (*pius et supplex*) and worshipped him (*adorat*), i.e. it knelt in front of the emperor and lifted its trunk upward in a manner similar to that in which a person might raise his arms in supplication to the heavens. Elephants are ideally suited for performing in arenas, as they couple immense strength, which enables them to fight with other wild animals, and high intelligence, which allows them to be trained to perform astonishing feats of skill.[9] But Martial emphasizes the impressive spontaneity of the act, which took place without a command being issued (*non iussus*) and without the intervention of a trainer (*nullo docente magistro*). According to Martial, the pious (*pius*) elephant recognized the emperor (Titus) as 'our god' (*nostrum deum*) and honoured him accordingly.[10]

Titus' younger brother and successor Domitian was even shown respect from the stars. So desirous were the night stars to see the emperor in the morning of his triumphal march into Rome to celebrate the end of the Sarmatian wars[11] that they were unwilling to make way for the morning star (Martial, *Epig.* 8.21). The poet recommends that the emperor arrive while it is still night. It shall be permitted that the stars stand still.[12] It is no longer nature, no longer the movement of the heavenly bodies that divides night and day, but the arrival of the emperor. With his appearance, darkness ends and it becomes light.[13]

Elsewhere, an imperial miracle is compared to a miracle worked by the king of the Roman gods (Martial, *Epig.* 1.6). The abduction of Ganymede by an eagle, whose timorous claws (*timidis unguibus*) carried the boy away unharmed, was initiated by Jupiter (1.6.1-2). In the presence of the Emperor Domitian the lions in the circus were so softened by the entreaties of their prey that the hare could play unscathed in the lion's mouth (1.6.3-4). Martial draws a clear comparison between the two occurrences and even asks which of these miracles is the greater. Both were initiated by the supreme being – in the one case, Jupiter, in the other, Caesar Domitianus.[14]

Once again, the miracle concerns the mastering of a wild, untamed creature. Although the attribute 'imperial' (*caesareos leones*) suggests lions in a circus, making it possible to reduce the miracle to a mere act involving trained animals,[15] the more significant factor is that under the influence of the emperor, both predator and prey forgot their original instincts, with the lion carrying the hare

---

9.   O. Weinreich, *Studien*, pp. 74–75.

10.   *Crede nihim, nostrum sentit et ille deum* (Martial, *Sp.* 17). Cf. O. Weinreich, *Studien*, p. 78, and K. Scott, *Imperial Cult*, p. 120. Juvenal speaks of elephants as *Caesaris armentum nulli servire paratum privato* (Juvenal 12.106-7).

11.   F. Sauter, *Der römische Kaiserkult*, pp. 138–39.

12.   *Stent astra licebit* (Martial, *Epig.* 8.21.11).

13.   Cf. K. Scott, *Imperial Cult*, p. 114.

14.   *Quae maiora putas miracula? summus utrisque auctor adest: haec sunt Caesaris, illa Iovis* (Martial, *Epig* 1.6.5).

15.   P. Howell, *A Commentary on Book One of the Epigrams of Martial* (London: Athlone Press, 1980), p. 119.

unharmed in its mouth as a lioness would carry her cubs. Not only did the hare show no fear, it played (*ludit*) in what was a highly precarious situation. The comparison of Domitian to the king of the gods is not unusual.[16] On his triumphal return home from the Pannonian war, Martial dubs him 'Jupiter returned' (*reducem Iovem*; Martial, *Epig.* 8.15.2).[17]

The lion and hare theme is taken up by Martial in other epigrams. For instance, he speaks of the games and jests (*delicias lususque iocosque*, Martial, *Epig.* 1.14) of the imperial lions. The lions even let a hare go free, and the hare ran in complete safety out of and back into their open jaws. The answer to the (rhetorical) question why a greedy lion (*avidus leo*) would let the prey that it had already caught (*captae praedae*) go free again is answered by the poet himself: the lions belonged to the emperor, therefore they were able to do this.[18] As the lion accepted the emperor as its owner and master, it took him as its model and acted accordingly.[19] The lion, the king of the beasts, demonstrated clemency (*clementia*) – an important virtue of Roman leaders since the time of Julius Caesar.

The last of the seven epigrams from the lion–hare cycle begins with a list of astonishing feats of skill. Martial's rhetorical question: 'Who could not but regard this spectacle as the work of gods?'[20] leads in to the actual topic the poet wishes to address. According to Martial, there is nothing greater than these lions hunting hares, for they let their prey go, capture it again and carry it carefully in their jaws between timorous teeth (*timidos dentes*) to avoid damaging the soft bodies. The mildness testified to here is not something that can be attributed to training, but to the lions' knowledge of who their master is.[21] The feats of skill portrayed at the beginning are artistic in origin (*ars*), but are nevertheless admired as divine works. However, Martial regards the lions' *clementia* as something truly divine,[22] as it is achieved not by training, but through knowledge. The lion regards itself as a servant of the emperor. It knows what it owes to the emperor[23] and, like the emperor, the lion demonstrates leniency to an inferior creature. That the lion, itself a king, bows to the will of the emperor, can only be explained by its knowledge of the divine power resting within the emperor.[24]

---

16. See P. Howell, *Commentary*, on this point. Cf. Martial, *Sp.* 16b.3, though this refers to Titus, Domitian's brother and predecessor.

17. K. Scott, *Imperial Cult*, p. 136. Scott's interpretation is based on the important fact that during the triumphal march into the city, the victorious general represents Jupiter Optimus Maximus.

18. *Sed tamen esse tuus dicitur: ergo potest* (Martial, *Epig.* 1.14.6).

19. O. Weinreich, *Studien*, p. 92.

20. *Quis spectacula non putet deorum?* (Martial, *Epig.* 1.104.11)

21. *Haec clementia non paratur arte, sed norunt cui serviant leones* (Martial, *Epig.* 1.104.21–2).

22. Cf. M. Citroni, *Martialis. Epigrammaton Liber Primus. Introduzione, testo, apparato critico e commento* (Biblioteca di studi superiori, 61; Florence: La Nuova Italia, 1975) on this point.

23. O. Weinreich, *Studien*, p. 99.

24. 'Ein Löwe beugt sich einem Gott oder dem Gottkönig', O. Weinreich, *Studien*, p. 101.

In accounts such as these, human patterns of behaviour are attributed to animals. A further example can be found in another epigram in which a gander, acting wholly of its own accord (*ipse*) and with joy (*laetus*), hastened (*properavit*) to the burning altar to sacrifice itself to Mars. By so doing, it fulfilled the vow of the Bithynian proconsul Velius (Martial, *Epig.* 9.31), who promised to make a sacrifice to the god of war to bring luck to his commander Domitian. The gander gave its life freely in sacrifice for the well-being of the emperor. The voluntary nature of the sacrifice was an important element in performing this ritual. An animal that resisted, or even fled, was regarded in Roman eyes as a bad omen. The behaviour of the gander is that of a hero, one who in good spirits and without hesitation sacrifices himself for the common good.[25] A lack of respect for the emperor is immediately punished by nature. A spectator named Horatius made a bad impression at a circus performance, as he was the only one present in a black coat; all others present, including the *princeps*, were dressed in white. A sudden snow shower (in itself something of a miracle in Rome) covers the dark coat with white snow and thus restores unity. The man's crime, his lack of respect in the presence of the divine nature of the emperor (described in the previous line as *sanctus dux*, Martial, *Epig.* 4.2.4), is sanctioned immediately by the forces of nature (Martial, *Epig.* 4.2).[26]

A more severe punishment was meted out to an ungodly (*impius*) Libyan for illegally fishing in a fishpond in Baiae that was owned by Domitian. The Libyan lost his sight and was from that moment on forced to beg for his living at the very site at which he committed his sacrilegious act (Martial, *Epig.* 4.30).[27] According to Otto Weinreich, blinding is 'das allerhäufigste Strafwunder'.[28] While there may indeed be medical reasons why the Libyan lost his sight (in addition to leprosy, certain forms of fish poisoning are known to cause blindness), his blinding is also compatible with talion law. According to ancient belief,[29] fish go blind when they are pulled from the water. It is therefore only just that the person committing such a sacrilegious act should also lose his sight.[30] The fish belong to the emperor for, like the lions, they acknowledge him as their master (*norunt dominum*, Martial, *Epig.* 4.30.4). They even pay tribute to the emperor by licking his hand (*manum lambunt*, 4.30.4), an act that recalls the behaviour of the elephants mentioned earlier. The crime is sacrilegious because Domitian, lord of the fishes, is a god.[31]

25. O. Weinreich, *Studien*, pp. 133–42.

26. See F. Sauter, *Der römische Kaiserkult*, pp. 106–7.

27. See F. Sauter, *Der römische Kaiserkult*, pp. 110–11.

28. O. Weinreich, *Studien*, p. 147, and O. Weinreich, *Antike Heilungswunder: Untersuchungen zum Wunderglauben der Griechen und Römer* (RVV, 8.1; Neudruck, Berlin: de Gruyter, 1969), pp. 189–94.

29. This is supported by St. John Chrysostom (*De mutatione nominum homiliae quattuor*, PG 51.117) who compares the blinding of Saul/Paul on his way to Damascus (Acts 9.8) to the fate of the captured fish.

30. O. Weinreich, *Studien*, p. 150.

31. O. Weinreich, *Studien*, p. 151. A contrasting view is expressed by F. J. Dölger, 'Die Kaiservergötterung bei Martial und "Die heiligen Fische Domitians"', in idem, *Antike und*

It is striking that in all these accounts the emperor is passive; there is no record of his active involvement. He neither rises to tame the lions, nor raises his hand at the circus to summon snow. His presence alone (and in the tale of the sacrilegious fishing, not even that) is sufficient to work the miracle. This is also demonstrated in the following account from Roman prose of an attempt (in this case, a failed attempt) to control the forces of nature. While endeavouring to cross over to Italy and then running into a storm, Julius Caesar had complete confidence in the power of his own person. Caesar calmed the captain, who had become frightened and wanted to turn back, by referring to his own presence (Cassius Dio 41.46.3) and to his proverbial luck (Plutarch, *Caes.* 38.5). However, his proud words proved to be of no use, the ship had to submit to the force of nature and turn back.

In the case of Tiberius, the situation is somewhat different. According to Tacitus, Tiberius's power was transferred even to images of the emperor. A conflagration in Rome in the year 27 CE devastated the entire *caelius* but did not damage a picture (*effigies*) of Tiberius that was in a senator's house (Tacitus, *Annales.* 4.64.3). Even the destructive force of the fire is respectful of the emperor.

In older commentaries, Martial is frequently referred to as the 'Hofdichter' of the Flavian emperors.[32] An early attempt to correct this view of Martial was undertaken by Ludwig Friedlaender.[33] Hanna Szelest[34] and Peter Howell have noted that nowhere does Martial thank Domitian for any gratuity, suggesting that the poet received nothing or, at best, very little from the emperor ('so his flattery should perhaps be seen in the light of an attempt to win greater favour from the ruler').[35] Niklas Holzberg even claims to be able to detect 'getarnte Kritik' in Martial's imperial panegyric,[36] though this is tempered by his observation that, unlike the politically motivated criticism of the republican opposition, Martial's criticism is restricted to 'Fragen der sittlichen Norm und speziell der Sexualmoral'.[37]

Christentum. Kultur- und religionsgeschichtliche Studien 1 (Münster: Aschendorff, repr., 1974), p. 169, who emphasizes that it is not ownership alone that confers sacredness to the fish, but rather the fact 'daß sie die Hand des Kaisers wie die Hand eines gegenwärtigen Gottes lecken und mit der Berührung der göttlichen Hand selbst "Heiligkeit" in sich aufnehmen'.

32. O. Weinreich, *Studien*, p. 159–60, objects to the 'inneren Unwahrheit' of the 'höfischen Epigrammatik'; F. Sauter, *Der römische Kaiserkult*, calls Martial one of the 'Hauptvertreter der [...] höfischen Adulation' (1); H. Bengtson, *Die Flavier Vespasian, Titus, Domitian. Geschichte eines römischen Kaiserhauses* (München: C. H. Beck, 1979).

33. L. Friedlaender, *M. Valerii Martialis Epigrammaton*, p. 15: 'In seinen Schmeicheleien gegen Domitian und dessen Höflingen hat er das Mass des Erforderten kaum überschritten.'

34. H. Szelest, 'Domitian und Martial', *Eos* 62 (1974), pp. 104–14 (114): 'daß sich der Dichter aus Bilbilis weder der Anerkennung noch der Gunst des Herrscher erfreute'.

35. P. Howell, *Commentary*, p. 5.

36. N. Holzberg, *Martial* (Heidelberger Studienhefte zur Altertumswissenschaft; Heidelberg: Winter, 1988), p. 80. Especially, the lion symbolizes 'die Angst des Epigrammatikers vor der Unberechenbarkeit des allmächtigen Zensors', p. 77.

37. N. Holzberg, *Martial*, p. 79.

To conclude, one can say that despite a number of contradictory interpretations, Martial wrote as a child of his time. It would certainly be a mistake to try and portray him as an exception, or to explain the panegyric elements of epigrams as simply reflecting the genre in which he was writing. Reports of imperial miracles are also to be found in the accounts of other authors who wrote in other literary forms.

II

That extraordinary events presage the rule of a major figure is something that is familiar to us from both the Old and New Testaments.

The most famous prodigy in the New Testament is the Star of Bethlehem. To the astrologers of the Orient, it symbolized the birth of a king and led them to the infant Jesus (Mt. 2.2-9). Stars and comets were significant omens in classical antiquity.

The classical idea of stars being assigned to people was passed down by Pliny the Elder, though he himself contradicted the doctrine. According to this belief, a star would appear with the birth of the person associated with it, and would disappear when the person died (Pliny, *Nat.* 2.28). According to Tacitus, comets were popularly believed to be an omen of a *mutatio regis* (Tacitus, *Ann.* 14.22). In his biography of Nero, Suetonius states that a comet was visible for several days, which 'was generally believed to be an omen to the political elite portending ruin' (*quae summis potestatibus exitium portendere vulgo putatur*, Suetonius, *Nero* 36.1). A comet is also said to have appeared at the time of the birth of Mithridates, and another at the time of the birth of Asclepius.[38] The link between a heavenly phenomenon and the birth of a god or, at the least, a ruler is undoubtedly a part of the pre-Christian tradition.

The majority of the commentaries on St Matthew's Gospel draw on examples from Judaism or from the Orient, in which stars announce the birth of a major figure.[39] However, there is also a remarkable similarity with particular events that concerned Augustus, who ruled in Rome at that time. During the games, which Julius Caesar had planned in honour of the mythical first ancestress *Venus Genetrix* and which were held by his grand-nephew, Augustus, a few days after Caesar's death, a comet appeared in the skies. Pliny, quoting from the biography

---

38. Justinus, *Epitome Hist.* 37.2.1–3; Pausanias 2.26.5.

39. For examples of commentaries, see U. Luz, *Das Evangelium nach Matthäus* (EKK, I.1; Düsseldorf and Zürich: Benziger, 5th edn., 2002), pp. 160–61, and W. Grundmann, *Das Evangelium nach Matthäus* (THKNT, 1; Berlin: Evangelische Verlagsanstalt, 6th edn., 1986), p. 81. See also Balaam's prophecy that a star shall come out of Jacob in Num. 24.17. For a discussion of the Hellenistic tradition, see D. Kienast, 'Augustus und Alexander', *Gymnasium* 76 (1969), pp. 431–56, and H. Kyrieleis, 'θεοὶ ὁρανtoί: Zur Sternsymbolik hellenistischer Herrscherbildnisse', in K. Braun, A. Furtwängler (eds.), *Studien zur klassischen Archäologie* (FS F. Hiller; SSAAG, 1; Saarbrücken: Saarbrücker Druck und Verlag, 1986), pp. 55–72.

of Augustus, states that the people took this to be a sign of Caesar's admission to the pantheon. Augustus himself, however, was convinced that the ascending comet symbolized his own rise 'for the salvation of the world' (*salutare id terris fuit*, Pliny, *Nat.* 2.94). The *sidus Julium* soon began to appear on coins, rings, seals, etc. and prepared the ground for the acceptance of the deified *Divus Julius* into the officially sanctioned state religion in 42 BCE. From that point on, his heir could call himself *Divi filius*.[40] Astrological symbolism thus played an important role for Augustus in establishing his own rule. As the Star of Bethlehem is referred to only in the Gospel according to Matthew, the question naturally arises as to whether the account is more theological than historical in nature.[41] For Walter Grundmann the preferred astronomical explanation of the Star of Bethlehem is the conjunction of Jupiter and Saturn in the constellation Pisces, which would have also been visible in Rome. He considers the possibility that 'durch den Hinweis auf den Stern' the story of the Magi has 'eine apologetische Tendenz gegenüber dem Kaiserkult'.[42] Whatever the case may be, it is clear that the star symbolizes a claim to divine rule.

Prodigies play an important role in characterizations of the emperors. In Suetonius's *Life of Augustus*, for example, an entire section is dedicated to an account of the miraculous omens that heralded and accompanied the reign of the first Roman emperor (Suetonius, *Aug.* 94). The following excerpt illustrates what is meant.

> While felling a wood near Munda to clear a site for his camp, Julius Caesar lighted upon a palm tree and ordered it to be spared, as a good omen. The tree then immediately put out a new shoot, which, within a few days, had grown so tall that it overshadowed the parent plant and afforded space for pigeons to build their nests, although pigeons would normally avoid such hard and rough foliage. It is said that it was this prodigy in particular that persuaded Caesar to choose his sister's grandson as his successor (Suetonius, *Aug.* 94.11).

Similar omens are to be found in the lives of the other emperors. In the biography of Vespasian, whose family Suetonius describes as being of 'obscure descent' and of 'boasting no ancestral honours' (*gens Flavia, obscura ... ac sine ullis maiorum imaginibus*, *Ves.* 1.1), and in his *Life of Tiberius*, Suetonius dedicates an entire chapter in each case to detail the prodigies (*Ves.* 5; *Tib.* 14). There are no such accounts in the *Life of Claudius*, whom Suetonius portrays as being 'weak of body and of mind' (*Cl.* 2.1), nor in the biographies of Caligula, Nero, Otho, Titus, or Domitian. Nero's escape from an attempt on his life by the intervention of a snake is dismissed by Suetonius as a 'tale' (*fabula*, *Nero* 6.4) and hence as untrue.

For Galba, the omens are of somewhat dubious character (*Gal.* 4). While it was predicted that imperial rule would come to the grandfather's family, it was the

---

40. P. Zanker, *Augustus und die Macht der Bilder* (München: C. H. Beck, 1987), p. 44.
41. For example, U. Luz, *Evangelium nach Matthäus*, pp. 162–63.
42. W. Grundmann, *Evangelium nach Matthäus*, p. 81.

family and not explicitly his grandson that was mentioned. Galba's grandfather ridicules the prediction saying that it will happen when a mule gives birth to a foal. When, at a later date, this does indeed occur, Galba alone greets the omen as fortuitous while everyone else was shocked at the occurrence (*Gal.* 4.2). The third omen occurs while Galba is asleep. He dreams that the goddess Fortune, who is standing before his door, urges him to admit her saying that she is weary and that unless she is admitted, she shall bestow her favour on another (*Gal.* 4.3). The prodigies are even worse for Vitellius, and Suetonius does not mention them individually, preferring to summarize. Vitellius's horoscope so horrified his parents that they remained opposed to his career throughout his life (*Vit.* 3.2).

It seems that Suetonius uses the omens to explain the careers of particular rulers. As the first Roman emperor, Augustus required divine legitimation for his rule, as did his stepson and successor Tiberius. This is even more true for the 'upstart' Vespasian, who began a new dynasty after the Julian–Claudian line died out. The rulers who came before and after him did not require such 'assistance' as their rule was legitimized by descent. This applies both to the Julian–Claudian emperors Caligula, Claudia, Nero, and to the sons of Vespasian, Titus, and Domitian. It is possible that opinion of their respective reigns also influenced the decision as to which, if any, omens should be included in the biographies. Given the inadequacy (in the case of Claudius) or intolerability of their respective reigns, it may well have appeared inexpedient to portray these rulers as having enjoyed divine protection. Caligula, Nero, and Domitian were murdered, as were Galba, Otho and Vitellius. Claudius died in mysterious circumstances, it being rumoured that he was murdered by his wife Agrippina (Suetonius, *Cl.* 44.2). The three generals (Galba, Otho and Vitellius) who acceded to power in the eighteen months following Nero's death were too insignificant and, like Titus, their reigns were simply too short for any opinion of them to be made.

III

Healing miracles play a special role in Latin prose. Suetonius relates that during the civil war that raged in the year of the four emperors, Vespasian travelled to Egypt. In Alexandria, Vespasian visited the temple of Serapis to consult the auspices about his rule. Immediately after this, news arrived that the Vitellian troops had been routed at Cremona and that Vitellius himself had been slain in Rome (Suetonius, *Ves.* 7.1). Suetonius continues: Vespasian, who had unexpectedly come to power and was a hitherto unknown *princeps* (*inopinato et adhuc novo principi*), lacked authority (*auctoritas*) and, as it were, a certain majesty (*quasi maiestas quaedam*). But these were granted to him when two men, one blind and the other lame,[43] approached him as he was seated on the tribunal and begged him

---

43. Contrary to what B. Kollmann, *Jesus und die Christen*, p. 106, implies, the records are not consistent with respect to the nature of the infirmities. In Suetonius's account, it is unquestionably the leg that is lame (*debili crure*, *Ves.* 7.2).

to heal them, saying that this had been promised to them in a dream by the god Serapis (Asclepius) (*Ves.* 7.2). Vespasian was highly sceptical, but was prevailed upon by his friends. Publicly, in the presence of the assembled multitudes and acting in accordance with the dreams, Vespasian moistened the eyes of the blind man with spittle and touched the lame leg with his heel; and his actions were crowned with success (*Ves.* 7.3).[44]

In Tacitus, the events are reported slightly differently. Besides the blind man there was also a man with an infirm hand who was healed. The latter asked Vespasian to heal his hand by treading on it with the sole of his foot (Tacitus, *Historiae* 4.81.1). According to Tacitus, Vespasian ridiculed this unreasonable request and declined to help as he feared the gossip that could bring him into disrepute were he to fail. However, the flattery of his courtiers caused him to waver and he ordered that physicians should be summoned to give a prognosis as to whether these infirmities were susceptible to human help. The physicians were divided in their opinions, but agreed that the curing of these infirmities – the faculty of sight was not wholly lost and the hand only dislocated – might perhaps be an expression of divine will, and that the request may indicate that he, Vespasian, had been chosen to be the minister of the Gods (*divino ministerio*). Furthermore, as Tacitus does not fail to mention, if Vespasian were to succeed, the glory would be his; whereas the ridicule of failure would be borne by the poor supplicants (Tacitus, *Hist.* 4.81.2). Vespasian acceded to the request and both men were healed. Tacitus concludes by mentioning that both cures were attested in his own day by eye-witnesses.[45] Of the two authors, Tacitus is the more sceptical. He emphasizes the medical possibility of such cures and somewhat weakens their miraculous aura. In Tacitus' account, Vespasian did not merely hesitate, but, after initially thinking that the idea of him working a miracle was absurd, sought assurances by commissioning expert 'scientific' reports before he acted. Furthermore, Tacitus states that Vespasian's visit to the temple was a consequence of the healing, and not, as Suetonius relates, something that preceded it (Tacitus, *Hist.* 4.81.1). But Tacitus too emphasizes the significance of the miracles for Vespasian's rule. Tacitus introduces the miracle narrative by saying that during the months in which Vespasian was in Alexandria many miracles had occurred (*multa miracula*) that were regarded as a sign of the celestial favour (*caelestis favor*) and a certain partiality of the gods towards him (*in Vespasinium inclinatio numinum*, Tacitus, *Hist.* 4.81.1). Whether it was the opinion of the physicians that Vespasian would prove to be administering the divine will, or the prospect of complete 'exemption from punishment' that finally persuaded the emperor is something that Tacitus wisely leaves open.

---

44. Healing, particularly by means of the foot (chthonic forces) and saliva (spiritual forces) is discussed in G. Ziethen, 'Heilung und römischer Kaiserkult', *SudArch* 78.2 (1994), pp. 183–84.

45. As Tacitus emphasizes (*postquam nullam mendacio pretium*, *Ann.* 4.81.3) the witnesses would have gained no personal benefit from lying at this time.

Cassius Dio provides only a brief summary of the events.[46] Vespasian cured two men in Egypt, one blind and the other with a withered hand, by treading on the hand of the one and spitting upon the eyes of the other (Cassius Dio 66.8.1). However – as Cassius Dio then relates – despite such divine honour being bestowed upon Vespasian, the Alexandrians distanced themselves from him, as they had expected to be rewarded for being the first to declare him emperor, but now had even higher taxes levied upon them (66.88.2). Thus even though the gods signalled their goodwill to the emperor, he could find no favour with the people, who took more note of the money in their purse than of heavenly omens.

The crucial point in this narrative is not the implausibility of such spontaneous healing, whose authenticity is attested by citing witnesses. Vespasian's initial refusal should not be attributed to a lack of willingness, but represents an integral part of the way in which figures in classical antiquity were portrayed (modesty topos). The scepticism that is so typical of Vespasian is also to be found in Suetonius' report of the emperor's cynical words on his deathbed: 'Woe is me, I must be turning into a god.'[47] The background to this miracle story is political, and concerns the problems associated with the founding of a new dynasty.[48] With the death of Nero, the Julian–Claudian line of emperors came to an end. Initially just another general who, with his troops, had intervened in the civil war, Vespasian succeeded in asserting himself. He represents the beginning of the Flavian house. Any new dynasty, however, requires its legitimation. Whereas Augustus could at least claim to be distantly related to the gods – his great-uncle and adoptive father Caesar traced his own lineage back to Aeneas, the Trojan hero and son of Venus – no such assertion could be made by Vespasian.[49] He lacked *auctoritas* and *maiestas* (Suetonius), *caelestis favor* and *inclinatio numinum* (Tacitus), characteristics that would have signalled heavenly approval of his rule. All three authors agree that the two miraculous healings demonstrate Vespasian's divine power, revealing him as a god.[50] There is also good reason that these marvels occurred in Alexandria: ascribing healing powers to the emperor reflects traditional Hellenistic practice, as the title *Soter* proves.[51]

46. It should be noted, however, that this episode of Roman history is recorded only in a single epitome written by the monk Xiphilinos.

47. *Vae, inquit, put deus fio*; Suetonius, *Ves.* 23.4. K. Scott, *Imperial Cult*, pp. 18–19, however, sees Vespasian's scepticism as directed against the official deification that awaited Vespasian after his death. The Flavian emperors believed in omens and portents.

48. For a discussion of this point, see K. H. Waters, 'The Second Dynasty of Rome', *Phoenix* 17 (1963), pp. 198–218. Cf. Suetonius, *Gal.* 1: *progenies Caesarum in Nerone defecit*.

49. K. Scott, *Imperial Cult*, pp. 1–2.

50. The authenticity of such miracles does not need to be discussed here. K. Scott, *Imperial Cult*, pp. 10–13, holds that the miracle was deliberately staged by the priests of Serapis 'with or without the knowledge of the emperor himself' (p. 11). Such arguments prove just how important such 'tricks' were to Vespasian and his supporters in safeguarding his rule, and how willing the people were to accept them. S. Morenz, 'Vespasian Heiland der Kranken: Persönliche Frömmigkeit im antiken Herrscherkult?', *WüJb* 4 (1949/50), pp. 370–78 (376), argues that the healing miracles contain 'einen historischen Kern'.

51. H. Kyrieleis, 'θεοὶ ὀραντοί', p. 63. M. Wolter, 'Inschriftliche Heilungsberichte und neutes-

Similar expectations were also held of other emperors. In his panegyric on Trajan, Pliny the Younger provides a very vivid account of how the sick dragged themselves to be present at the arrival of the emperor in the hope of catching a glance of him and thus of being healed (*Paneg.* 22.3).[52]

The very opposite is experienced by a man who has bought the country estate at Velitrae from the grandparents of Augustus. The rooms included a chamber in which, according to the neighbours, Augustus was born. Entering this room without good reason or without the necessary respect would have been regarded as a sacrilegious act. Anyone who recklessly entered would be exposed to terrible sights. Whether by chance or because of high spirits, the new owner chose to sleep in this very room. Together with his bed, he was violently ejected from the room by some mysterious force, and was found half-dead in front of the door (Suetonius, *Aug.* 6).

It is not uncommon to find (divine) punishment and subsequent miraculous healing in close relation to one another. The author of the *Vita Hadriani* in the *Historia Augusta* recounts that the emperor was seriously ill and was entertaining thoughts of suicide (*SHA* 24.8). A woman received an order in a dream to dissuade Hadrian from suicide as he was destined to recover. However, the woman failed to carry out her charge and went blind as a result. She was commanded a second time, again in a dream, to speak to Hadrian and to kiss his knees, and was assured that by so doing she would recover her sight. Immediately after this account, another miracle is reported in which a blind man was able to see again after touching Hadrian who lay ill with fever (*SHA* 25.1–4). One could argue that in the first case the miracle was more attributable to the deity than to the emperor. As it was the deity that punished her, it was in the deity's power to revoke the penalty. However, in the second miracle, which is reported directly after the first, it is clear that the author attributes the miraculous powers solely to the healing touch of the emperor.[53]

It is a conspicuous element in such reports of miraculous healing that the emperor is not usually actively involved. The only exception seems to be the healings performed by Vespasian in Alexandria. Hadrian works miracles despite being ill and weak. In the conflagration in Rome, the image of the emperor is a symbol of his presence. Not even an image is required in the case of Augustus's birthplace, the room itself being sufficient.

Nevertheless, not one of these accounts leaves us in any doubt about who was the cause of the miracle. Unlike in Judaism and Christianity where the ruler is identified as the representative of the divine power responsible for the miracle, in

tamentliche Wundererzählungen: Überlieferungs- und formgeschichtliche Beobachtungen', in K. Berger *et al.* (eds), *Studien und Texte zur Formgeschichte* (TANZ, 7; Tübingen: Francke: 1992), pp. 135–75, describes the character of the healing stories in Roman inscriptions as follows: 'Sie dienen nicht lediglich dazu, eine Wirklichkeit [das Geschehen von Heilungen] abzubilden, sondern ihnen kommt darüberhinaus die Funktion zu, eine andere Wirklichkeit [die Regierung des Kaisers Antoninus] als Heilszeit abzubilden.'

52. *Aegri quoque neglecto medentium imperio ad conspectum tui quasi salutem sanitatemque prorepere*, Pliny the Younger, *Paneg.* 22.3.

53. As M. Clauss, *Kaiser und Gott*, p. 347.

classical antiquity the ruler himself is the god. This is particularly clear in the case
of Vespasian. Although both Suetonius and Tacitus mention Serapis, whose
temple Vespasian visited (before the healings according to Suetonius or afterwards
in Tacitus' account) and whose apparition in the dreams of the two infirm men
gave detailed instructions about their cures, he, the god, does not perform the
healing but sends the sufferers to the emperor to be cured. The emperor proves
his divinity by acting like a god and working a miracle.

The veneration of the Roman emperors is primarily based on 'miraculous' acts
that reveal them as gods on earth. Tales of miracles and, especially, miraculous
healings are an integral part of the topoi of the Roman imperial cult.[54] That divine
faculties, including the ability to perform miracles, were ascribed to the emperors
is ultimately a consequence of the belief in the ruler as a *divus*.[55]

IV

The New Testament teaches us just how difficult the apostolic duty to heal the ill
could sometimes be for the 'miracle workers' (Lk. 9.2). In the Acts of the Apostles,
Paul and Barnabas, fleeing from the Jews and pagans in Iconium, arrive in Lystra
in Lycaonia. Paul healed a man who had been a cripple since birth by imploring
him to stand (Acts 14.9-10). There were dramatic scenes after the miraculous
healing. The crowd began to proclaim that pagan gods had come down to them
in human form. They called Barnabas 'Zeus' and Paul 'Hermes', as he was the
one who spoke. (14.11-12). Paul and Barnabas tore their robes (14.14) and
attempted to convince the crowds that they too were mere mortals, messengers
of the one true God (14.15). The crowds could barely be restrained from offering
sacrifices to them (14.18). But Jews from Antioch and Iconium arrived and
stirred up the crowds against Paul and Barnabas. Paul was stoned, dragged out
of the city and left in front of the city walls (14.19).

Not only does this story prove how dangerous it can be to attempt to try and
stop an excited crowd once it has decided to act, but it is also, above all, an
example of just how strong the belief was at the time of the New Testament, and
within the New Testament itself, that miraculous powers were a demonstration of
godliness.

Some astonishing analogies become immediately apparent when biblical miracle
stories are compared with the accounts of miraculous occurrences of the Roman

54. So much has already been written on the Roman emperor cult that we restrict ourselves
here to selecting just two works from the immense literature on this subject. For information on
Rome and the West, see the recent studies of M. Clauss, *Kaiser und Gott*. For the area covering
Greece and Asia Minor, the definitive work is still S.R.F. Price, *Rituals and Power: The Roman
Imperial Cult in Asia Minor* (Cambridge: Cambridge University Press, 1984). On the concept
of 'Gottmenschen' as the root of the emperor cult, see H.-D. Betz, 'Gottmensch II: Griechisch-
römische Antike und Urchristentum', *RAC* 12 (1983), pp. 234–312.

55. M. Clauss, *Kaiser und Gott*, p. 19. H.-D. Betz, 'Gottmensch', p. 248: 'Der hellenist.-röm.
θεῖος ἀνήρ ... wird tätig als Wundertäter, Krankenheiler, Erwecker von Toten.'

imperial cult. The (successful) mastery of the rough seas is immediately familiar to us from the Gospels.[56] Like Vespasian, Jesus restores sight by placing spittle on blind eyes (Mk 8.23; Jn 9.6). In other instances, the 'healer' is not actively involved, it being sufficient for the sufferer to merely touch his body, as in the case of the Emperor Hadrian, or his robes, and in the story of Jesus and the bleeding woman.[57] Hadrian, we are told, had fever, and Jesus only knew that he had been touched by sensing that 'virtue had gone out of Him' (Mk 5.30; Mt. 9.22). Despite the limited ability of both Hadrian and Jesus to act, a healing effect emanated from them without them becoming actively involved.

There are also clear parallels between the accounts of marvellous natural events, both good and bad, in the apocryphal gospels and those in the texts of classical antiquity. In the *Protoevangelium of James* one reads that heaven stood still during the birth of Christ (*Prot. Jas.* 18): 'All of nature is holding its breath in expectation of the coming great event.'[58] This was also what Martial recounts in his epigram, as the stars are unwilling to move in order not to miss Domitian's triumphal march into Rome. Both accounts underscore the special character of the imminent arrival. The laws of nature are suspended because of the divine nature of the awaited person.[59] The world stands still in anticipation of the godly phenomenon.

In the *Infancy Gospel of Thomas*, the young Jesus commanded that a boy who had run and knocked into his shoulder shall fall down and die (*Inf. Gos. Thom.* 4.1). The parents of the dead boy and other villagers went to Joseph and reproached him (4.2). When Joseph subsequently admonished Jesus, Jesus left Joseph unharmed but the others were smitten with blindness (5.1). As in the story of the fisherman at Baiae, we are dealing here with sanctions meted out after a sacrilegious act has been committed.[60] The villagers and the angler are guilty of disrespect. They must take their punishment and lose their sight.

The direct confrontations of the Old Testament in which adherents of other cults are challenged directly in a contest (Moses and Aaron and the priests of the Pharaoh, Elija and the prophets of Baal) do not occur in the New Testament. This is not the case with the apologists. Origen must face the charges levelled against the Christians by Celsus that the miracles of Jesus are anything but unique, Jesus having learned them, according to Celsus, from the Egyptians (Origen, *Cels.* 1.46). Many old legends and fables include accounts of marvellous happenings (1.67, also 2.55). On the other hand, the church father Augustine simply declares

56. On the tempest: Mt. 8.23-27; Mk 4.35-41; Lk. 8.22-25. On Jesus walking on water: Mt. 14.24-27; Mk 6.45-52; Jn 6.16-21.

57. Mk 5.27-29; Mt. 9.20; Mk 6.56; Lk. 6.19.

58. H. J. Klauck, *Apokryphe Evangelien: Eine Einführung* (Stuttgart: Katholisches Bibelwerk, 2002), p. 95.

59. Or as F. Sauter, *Der römische Kaiserkult*, p. 168, puts it: 'beidemal ist das Numinose der eigentliche Grund des Geschehens'.

60. As H. J. Klauck, *Apokryphe Evangelien*, p. 101, correctly remarks, theologically it is an illustration of just how effective the words of the young Jesus are.

that miracles performed by the pagan gods never occurred or were, at the very least, inferior (Augustus, *C.D.* 10.16). As far as miracles are concerned, Christianity is clearly competing directly with the pagan cults.

Differences are apparent, however, in the roles played by the miracle workers. Neither the Old Testament prophets nor the apostles act because they are the perfect embodiment of power and authority, but because they are God's representatives and what they do is done in his name. In contrast, the Roman emperors are themselves gods, and do not need to appeal to any higher power. The events in Lystra demonstrate clearly these different viewpoints. Whilst the Lystran crowds identify the miracle workers as the pagan gods Zeus and Hermes, the apostles appeal to the authority of their God, regarding themselves as his representatives. Unfortunately, it is difficult to classify Jesus within this framework. He acts not only as his father's emissary ('Your will be done'), but also of his own accord ('I will': Mk 1.41). Adolf M. Ritter justifiably criticizes attempts to classify Jesus as a magician.[61] Ritter argues that although magical practices are described (the laying on of hands, placing of spittle on eyes, etc.), it is the change in awareness ('Your faith has saved you'[62]) that plays the major role here.[63] While it is true that Jesus refers to Old Testament forecasts, not only in the selection (Mt. 11.5 and Isa. 35.5; Lk. 4.18 and Isa. 61.1) but also in the details of a number of his healings (Mk 5.35-43; Jn 4.46-54 and 1 Kgs 17.17-24; 2 Kgs 5.1-14) – making a comparison with Elijah or Elisha certainly valid (cf. Lk. 4.25-27[64]) – Jesus does not, unlike Elijah, act through the medium of prayer, but 'als der an Gott Handelnde ... durch das schöpferische, sofort wirkende und präzis überlieferte Wort.'[65]

Finally, it should also be mentioned that the striking similarity between Christian accounts of miracles and those of classical antiquity may be simply a reflection of the fact that such stories were so widespread. Perhaps the Christian scribes simply recorded and incorporated these ideas without further consideration.

It nevertheless seems reasonable to conjecture that these accounts were included deliberately, that Christians adopted these elements of the pagan ruler cult to demonstrate the greater power of their Lord and Master.

The disputes of the Christian apologists with paganism reflect a very real contest between them. Given the close agreement between the content of the Christian and pagan miracle stories, it became increasingly necessary for the Christians to emphasize their own miracles and thus the supremacy of their God.

---

61. M. Smith, *Jesus the Magician* (New York: Harper & Row, 1978). On Jesus as a miracle worker, see the recent work of M. Hüneburg, *Jesus als Wundertäter in der Logienquelle: Ein Beitrag zur Christologie von Q* (ABG, 4; Leipzig: EVA, 2001).

62. Mt. 9.22-23; 15.28; Mk 10.52.

63. A. M. Ritter, 'Magie im frühen Christentum', in J. Hammerstaedt *et al.* (eds.), *Apuleius. De magia* (Sapere, 5; Darmstadt: WBG, 2002), pp. 316–18.

64. O. Betz, 'Heilung/Heilungen: I. Neues Testament', *TRE* 14 (1985), pp. 764–65.

65. Mk 1.41; 2.11; 3.5; 10.52; Jn 5.8; Lk. 7.7; 13.12; 17.14. O. Betz, 'Heilung/Heilungen', p. 765.

It is significant that the apocryphal gospels play an important part in this contest. Particularly horrific to us today is the tale of the young Jesus meting out punishment, as it appears diametrically opposed to our picture of Christ.[66] We would have no problem, however, assigning this account to the canon of *maiestas* punishments dispensed by the Roman emperors. If we consider when this account was written, it becomes apparent that in view of the increasing confrontation between Christianity and the Roman state in the mid-to-late second century, Christians felt compelled to make greater efforts to demonstrate to the heathens the supremacy of the Christian God by exploiting elements of the pagan miracle tradition. Indeed, this need felt by the early Christians to imitate the traditional pagan miracle stories is analogous to Christianity's adoption of pagan festivals and other traditions such as the celebration of the first day of Christmas on the anniversary of the birth of *Sol invictus*.[67]

66. On Jesus as trickster, see W. Rebell, *Neutestamentliche Apokryphen und Apostolische Väter*, (München: Kaiser, 1992.), p. 135: Jesus appears both to wound (the son of Annas withers and dies, *Inf. Gos. Thom.* 2.1–3.3) and to heal (the man whose foot has been cleaved, *Inf. Gos. Thom.* 10.1-2).

67. Cf. *CIL* I.2 (*Philocal.* 354), p. 278.

MIRACLE TRADITIONS IN EARLY RABBINIC LITERATURE: SOME QUESTIONS ON THEIR PRAGMATICS[1]

Michael Becker

For many years, research on the miracle traditions, especially of the early rabbinic literature, has not been a major topic of scholarly interest. For various reasons, dealing with the early traditions was – and still is – not an easy enterprise. Accordingly, it is not surprising that since the initial controversy between Paul Fiebig[2] and Adolf Schlatter[3] in the early twentieth century only a small number of scholars have contributed to this subject. Nevertheless, several articles and reviews and also a number of books make comments on miracles[4] and related

---

1. Presenting a selection of some of the main results of my Munich dissertation, this article gives an overview, which is necessarily an eclectic task in many points. I would like to thank the audience at the Berlin SBL International Meeting 2002 for the discussion and several comments, especially my Munich colleague Dr. Jutta Leonhardt-Balzer for reading this paper and her remarks on the English version.

2. P. Fiebig, *Jüdische Wundergeschichten des neutestamentlichen Zeitalters unter besonderer Berücksichtigung ihres Verhältnisses zum Neuen Testament bearbeitet. Ein Beitrag zum Streit um die 'Christusmythe'* (Tübingen: Mohr Siebeck, 1911), and the 2nd edition of his: *Rabbinische Wundergeschichten des neutestamentlichen Zeitalters in vokalisiertem Text mit sprachlichen und sachlichen Bemerkungen* (Berlin: de Gruyter, 1933).

3. A. Schlatter, *Das Wunder in der Synagoge* (BFCT, XVI.5; Gütersloh: Bertelsmann, 1912).

4. See e.g. I. Heinemann, 'Die Kontroverse über das Wunder im Judentum der hellenistischen Zeit', in A. Schreiber (ed.), *Jubilee Volume in Honour of Professor Bernhard Heller* (Budapest: Jubileumi Bizottság, 1941), pp. 170–91; A. Guttmann, 'The Significance of Miracles for Talmudic Judaism', *HUCA* 20 (1947), pp. 363–406; M. Kadushin, *The Rabbinic Mind* (New York: Bloch, 3rd edn., 1972), pp. 152–67; L. Sabourin, 'Hellenistic and Rabbinic "Miracles"', *BTB* 2 (1972), 281–307; E. E. Urbach, *The Sages. Their Concepts and Beliefs* (2 vols.; Jerusalem: Magnes Press, 1975 [Hebrew 1969; English reprint in one vol., Cambridge, MA: Harvard University Press, 1987]), chs. 5–7; K. Hruby, 'Perspectives rabbiniques sur le miracle', in: X. Léon-Dufour (ed.), *Les miracles de Jésus selon le Nouveau Testament* (Paris: Éditions du Seuil, 1977), pp. 73–94; K. Schubert, 'Wunderberichte und ihr Kerygma in der rabbinischen Tradition', *Kairos* 24 (1982), pp. 31–37; R. Kasher, 'Miracle, Faith and Merit of the Fathers – Conceptual Development in the Sages' Writings' (Hebrew), in J. Dan (ed.), *Jerusalem Studies in Jewish Thought* V (Jerusalem: 'Daf Noy' Press, 1986), pp. 15–22, VIII–IX; G. J. Blidstein, 'The Halakhic Concept of "Miracle" (NES)' (Hebrew), *Daat* 50–52 (2003), pp. 1–12. Especially on the Babylonian rabbis of the talmudic era and their interest in miracles see J. Neusner, *The Wonder-Working Lawyers of Talmudic Babylonia: The Theory and Practice of Judaism in its Formative*

matters such as the legends of the Jews and magic.[5] Similar to the discussion of Fiebig and Schlatter, most of the current publications on the rabbinic miracle traditions have a secondary interest in this issue because they focus on a comparison with Jesus' miracle-working. Although the interest in Ḥoni the circle-drawer and Ḥanina ben Dosa has increased during the last decades since Geza Vermes published his influential article and books,[6] the problems and questions concerning these traditions are almost comparable to those throughout the controversy of Fiebig and Schlatter.[7] In spite of the relevance of the relationship between the Jesus-tradition and the rabbis, it is not possible to examine this relationship here.[8] Independently of this prominent background, a critical and methodologically reflective investigation into the *early* rabbinic traditions is needed.

Age (Lanham, New York, London: University Press of America, 1987; cf. moreover n. 15). M. Becker, *Wunder und Wundertäter im frührabbinischen Judentum* (WUNT, II.144; Tübingen: Mohr Siebeck, 2002), pp. 15–32. 291–93. 338–42, should be consulted for a more detailed overview of the history of research.

5.   Cf. the most recent monograph of G. Veltri, *Magie und Halakha: Ansätze zu einem empirischen Wissenschaftsbegriff im spätantiken und frühmittelalterlichen Judentum* (TSAJ, 62; Tübingen: Mohr Siebeck, 1997) and the old standard work by L. Blau, *Das altjüdische Zauberwesen* (Nachdruck; Graz: Akademische Druck- und Verlags-Anstalt, 1974). There still exist some more extensive monographs dealing with the legends of the Jews, chiefly of the talmudic era; see, for instance, L. Ginzberg, *The Legends of the Jews* (7 vols; Philadelphia: Jewish Publication Society of America, 1909–38); cf. M. Becker, *Wunder*, 15 n. 28.

6.   Cf. part 3; G. Vermes, 'A Controversial Galilean Saint from the First Century of the Christian Era', *JJS* 23 (1972), pp. 28–50; 24 (1973), pp. 51–64 (reprint in G. Vermes, *Post-Biblical Jewish Studies* [SJLA, 8; Leiden: Brill, 1975]: 178–214); G. Vermes, *Jesus the Jew. A Historian's Reading of the Gospels* (London: William Collins Sons, 2nd edn., 1983); G. Vermes, *Jesus and the World of Judaism* (London: SCM Press, 1983).

7.   The question of dating the traditions – cf. part 1 – is still very controversial, because most publications do not take into account the differences between early rabbinic and talmudic or later traditions.

8.   For different positions concerning the relevance of rabbinic material for the interpretation of the New Testament, cf. e.g. M. Smith, *Tannaitic Parallels to the Gospel* (JBLMS, 6; Philadelphia: Society of Biblical Literature, 1951 [Hebrew 1945]); M. Smith, 'A Comparison of Early Christian and Early Rabbinic Tradition', *JBL* 82 (1963), pp. 169–79; R. Bloch, 'Note méthodologique pour l'étude de la littérature rabbinique', *RSR* 43 (1955), pp. 194–227 [English: 'Methodological Note for the Study of Rabbinic Literature', in W. S. Green (ed.), *Approaches to Ancient Judaism: Theory and Practice* (BJS, 1; Missoula: Scholars Press 1978), pp. 51–75]; G. W. Buchanan, 'The Use of Rabbinic Literature for New Testament Research', *BTB* 7 (1977), pp. 110–22; P. S. Alexander, 'Rabbinic Judaism and the New Testament', *ZNW* 74 (1983), pp. 237–46; M. C. Parsons, 'The Critical Use of the Rabbinic Literature in New Testament Studies', *PRSt* 12 (1985), pp. 85–102; K. Müller, 'Zur Datierung rabbinischer Aussagen', in H. Merklein (ed.), *Neues Testament und Ethik* (FS R. Schnackenburg; Freiburg i.Br.: Herder, 1989), pp. 551–87; J. Neusner, *Rabbinic Literature and the New Testament: What We Cannot Show, We Do Not Know* (Valley Forge: Trinity Press, 1994); J. Neusner, 'Comparing Sources: Mishnah/Tosefta and Gospel', in J. Neusner, *Jewish Law from Moses to the Mishnah: The Hiram College Lectures on Religion for 1999 and Other Papers* (SFSHJ, 187; Atlanta: Scholars Press, 1999), pp. 119–35; C. A. Evans, 'Early Rabbinic Sources and Jesus Research', *SBLSP* 34 (1995), pp. 53–76; D. Instone Brewer, 'The Use of Rabbinic Sources in Gospel Studies', *TynBul* 50 (1999), pp. 281–98.

Against this background of modern Judaistic research, a deepening of our understanding seems only achievable by means of an assessment of the special character of those traditions. For that reason, we have to aim at an overall examination of the various traditions about miracles: to analyse the terminology and the narratives as well as related subjects such as demonology and magic. Beyond this, such an examination requires a close reading of the wider context of these traditions in early Jewish and ancient-pagan frameworks[9] – and in correlation to Christian traditions too, because at that time isolated circles no longer existed in the eastern Mediterranean.

Considering the limitations of space this paper could not attempt a comprehensive enquiry into this background,[10] hence it concentrates on the rabbinic traditions and the opportunity of reconstructing several aspects of the history and the transition of such stories and traditions. The survey is divided into three sections: The first part (1) will discuss some initial and methodological problems defining conditions and boundaries for the understanding of the early rabbinic miracle traditions. In the second part (2), we will look at several miracle traditions in general. The last section of the study (3) will deal with a couple of traditions including human miracle workers.

1. Initial and Methodological Problems

The 'early rabbinic literature' consists of a corpus of individual texts that reached their almost final form by the third and early fourth century CE. *Mishna, Tosefta*, the so-called halakhic midrashim[11] and several additional texts are the basis of this study.[12] This material belongs to the time of the ascent and consolidation of the rabbis as the leading group in Palestinian Judaism after the destruction of the second temple.[13] Although it is difficult to define clear-cut limits between early

9.   Cf. especially for a survey of the Jewish traditions E. Eve, *The Jewish Context of Jesus' Miracles* (JSNTSup, 231; Sheffield: Sheffield Academic Press, 2002); M. Becker, 'Zeichen. Die johanneische Wunderterminologie und die frührabbinische Tradition', in J. Frey, U. Schnelle (eds.), *Kontexte des Johannesevangeliums: Religions- und traditionsgeschichtliche Studien* (WUNT, 175; Tübingen: Mohr Siebeck, 2004), pp. 233–76.

10.   For further discussion, see M. Becker, *Wunder*.

11.   *Mekhilta de Rabbi Yishma'el (MekhY.)*, *Sifra*, *Sifre Bamidbar (SifBam.)*, *Sifre Devarim (SifDev.)* and in addition see the to some extent very fragmentary and reconstructed texts: *Mekhilta de Rabbi Shim'on ben Yoḥai*, *Sifre Zuta*, *Mekhilta to Devarim* and *Midrash Tanna'im*. For a survey of research including the dating of the texts, see G. Stemberger, *Einleitung in Talmud und Midrasch* (München: C.H. Beck, 8th edn., 1992); J. Neusner, *Introduction to Rabbinic Literature* (New York: Doubleday, 1994).

12.   For further details and discussion concerning the selection of texts, see M. Becker, *Wunder*, 9–15. Even if we cannot exclude talmudic and other later rabbinic evidence a priori, the development of the miracle tradition proves a significant change at the end of the Tannaitic period. This makes it highly questionable to include those traditions – even the baraitot of both Talmudim – without a careful inquiry into their tradition-history.

13.   For the evolution of the social structure of the rabbinic movement and their self-understanding in this period, cf. C. Hezser, *The Social Structure of the Rabbinic Movement in Roman Palestine* (TSAJ, 66; Tübingen: Mohr Siebeck, 1997).

rabbinic traditions and those of the talmudic period, there is good reason – especially in the case of the miracle traditions – to regard the period until the rabbis reached political, social and religious acknowledgement as separate. Not only do the rabbinic texts themselves speak in several place of a 'Tannaitic' period, but we also find a substantial change in the self-awareness and understanding of a rabbi at the transition from the Tannaitic to the talmudic era. The increasing number of miraculous traditions and their integration into the image of a rabbi can function as a distinctive mark for this change, as well as the expansion of demono-logical and magical features in the later documents. Additionally it is necessary to take into account some essential differences between Palestinian and Babylonian traditions.[14] In general, we can conclude that for the rabbis of the *talmudic era* charismatic authority did not stem from the miraculous, but from the authority of the Torah. It is not the personal charisma of a rabbi, but the charisma of the Torah as the order of the whole creation that provides a rabbi with charismatic competence in these later traditions.[15]

In contrast to this development, the early rabbinic literature represents a corpus of texts, which in most part is not interested in miracles, demons and magic. With the exception of those texts commenting on biblical miracle-traditions – especially in the *Mekhilta of R. Yismael* and to some extent also in *Sifre Devarim*[16] – the genuine concern of early rabbinic discussions depends on halakhic topics and related exegetical questions. The halakhic constitution of the sedarim and massekhot of the Mishna – which apart from Scripture represents the leading hermeneutical structure for most of the rabbinic texts – holds no special passage asking for a systematic analysis of miracles. Mishna, *Sifra* and both *Sifre* are not interested in such questions in particular, but they are not opposed to an integration of a small amount of material dealing with the miraculous. Only the Tosefta takes an ambiguous stand in this matter, because on the one hand, this textual corpus includes many more miracles than the Mishna, and on the other hand, it contains a very critical prejudice against the incorporation of such material into halakhic discussions. That seems to be caused by the rise of a new problem at the end of the early rabbinic era.

---

14. Cf. M. Becker, *Wunder*, pp. 412–14.

15. On this phenomenon and the special problems of the Babylonian diaspora, see J. Neusner, *A History of the Jews in Babylonia I–V* (SPB, 9, 11, 12, 14, 15; Leiden: Brill I: 1965 [2nd edn, 1969]; II: 1966, 131–33, 147–59; III: 1968, 102–26; IV: 1969, 330–70, 391–402; V: 1970); J. Neusner, 'Rabbi and Magus in Third-Century Sasanian Babylonia,' *HR* 6 (1966), pp. 169–78; J. Neusner, 'The Phenomenon of the Rabbi in Late Antiquity', *Numen* 16 (1969), pp. 1–20; *Numen* 17 (1970), pp. 1–18; W. S. Green, 'Palestinian Holy Men: Charismatic Leadership and Rabbinic Tradition', *ANRW* II.19.2 (Berlin: de Gruyter, 1979), pp. 619–47 (646–47); M. Becker, *Wunder*, pp. 409–14.

16. See esp. §§ 1–54 and 304–357. These haggadic chapters seem to be an additional part of the midrash with a quite different origin than the main corpus of the text; cf. G. Stemberger, *Einleitung*, pp. 268–69.

As a summary of these tendencies, a famous sentence comments on a discussion on several narratives about curious events concerned with the disappearance of a married partner and the permission of remarriage. The last of three items refers to R. Meir: 'Said R. Meir a precedent: "A certain man fell into a large cistern and came up after three days".' The sages who function here as the authority representing perhaps the author(s) of the Tosefta answer him:

> 'They [the sages] do not adduce a miracle-story [מעשה נסים, alternatively: a miraculous event] in evidence' (*tYev*. 14.6).[17]

Despite its negative tenor, this sentence is evidence of a very interesting development among the rabbis. In the first instance, it marks the rejection of such stories; but that is not enough. Because of its fundamental character, this sentence gives some further hint, that near the end of the Tannaitic period a serious debate on the authority of such 'charismatic' proofs of halakhic problems emerges.[18] The tradition in the Tosefta, therefore, is a significant indication of the departure of that discussion. Before this debate, miracles never seem to have been a very problematic issue for the rabbis, because they were aspects of the biblical tradition and for some part also of their daily life. Unfortunately, a conflict about the theological consequences of using miracles and miracle stories as arguments in the debate of halakhic problems arose, escalated,[19] and thus marks a turning point in the rabbinic tradition.[20]

Even though the systematic framework of early rabbinic documents does not confirm a great interest in miracle traditions, the rabbis had some very subtle interest in them. The creation of new terminological applications highlights this in particular.[21] Still using the biblical terminology in citations of the miracles from the past, the rabbis selected several words and gave them new connotations. In accordance with the early Palestinian targumic traditions, the rabbis took a

---

17. Cf. *yYev*. 16.4 (15d) and the baraita *bYev*. 121b; for further discussion of these passages, see M. Becker, *Wunder*, pp. 195–96, 245–49. The sentence is cited elsewhere, cf. *bBer*. 60a; *bHul*. 43a; *ySheq*. 6.4 (50a) and the discussion in A. Guttmann, 'Significance', pp. 391–93.

18. Cf. A. I. Baumgarten, 'Rabbi Judah I and his Opponents', *JSJ* 12 (1981), pp. 135–72; A. I. Baumgarten, 'Miracles and Halakah in Rabbinic Judaism', *JQR* 73 (1983), pp. 238–53.

19. The *locus classicus* for this problem is the discussion about the so-called Oven of 'Akhnai (*yMQ*. 3.1 [81cd]; *bBM*. 59b), where R. Eli'ezer is said to have used miracles in defence of his halakha. This conflict functions as a paradigm because he did not prevail with his opinion. Cf. M. Becker, *Wunder*, pp. 392–95; for further discussion of the text, see A. Guttmann, 'Significance', pp. 374–97; J. Neusner, *Eliezer Ben Hyrcanus: The Tradition and the Man* 2 vols. (SJLA; 3.4; Leiden: Brill, 1973), pp. 422–27; J. Neusner, *In Search of Talmudic Biography: The Problem of the Attributed Saying* (BJS, 70; Chico: Scholars Press, 1984), pp. 37–42; G. Bodenhofer-Langer, '"Sie ist nicht im Himmel!" Rabbinische Hermeneutik und die Auslegung der Tora', *BN* 75 (1994), pp. 35–47.

20. Cf. M. Becker, *Wunder*, pp. 245–49, 388–403.

21. On this process, see M. Becker, *Wunder*, pp. 184–203.

lexeme, not clearly connected with the miraculous in biblical and intertestamental texts,[22] and transformed it into their new keyword. They made נס – best translated as 'miracle' with the connotation '(wondrous) sign'[23] – the main term, when they spoke about the miracles in their own language and of their own days.[24] The use of that terminology[25] testifies a systematic interest in miracle traditions.[26] No discussion of rabbinic miracles can neglect it.

Before turning to particular texts, we still have to address a number of methodological questions – chiefly the problem of reconstructing pre-editorial strata of the early rabbinic texts. The enormous bulk of scholarly publications by Jacob Neusner has uncovered many problems of the literary character of the rabbinic texts. The rabbinic texts are not at all homogeneous; and there are great differences between halakhic and haggadic traditions. In the main part of the halakhic traditions it seems very difficult to extract detailed and reliable information, for instance, about the Pharisees and their opinions in the time before the destruction of the second temple. Therefore, Neusner's method of documentary hermeneutics – so far the latest stage of his methodological journey – seems to be at first glance a realistic procedure to handle these rabbinic traditions.[27] Nonetheless, this is not

22. For the OT connotations of the word נס, see L. Köhler, W. Baumgartner, *Hebräisches und aramäisches Lexikon zum Alten Testament* vol. III (Leiden: Brill, 3rd edn., 1983), pp. 662–63; H.-J. Fabry, Art. נס, in *ThWAT V* (Stuttgart: Kohlhammer, 1986), pp. 468–73.

23. For further discussion of this vocabulary in view of the Johannine Σημεῖα-terminology see M. Becker, 'Zeichen'.

24. For an analysis of the related conception, cf. M. Becker, *Wunder*, pp. 187–96, 204–5; in p. 187 n. 10, the 75 [+11] passages containing the word in early rabbinic literature are listed. Heinemann, 'Kontroverse', pp. 171–72; Kadushin, *Rabbinic Mind*, pp. 152–67 (161–62).

25. In an analogous way, the lexeme גבורות can prove a significant change and restriction of the meaning in the early rabbinic literature. In the case of the גבורות, a miraculous sense of the lexeme already exists in the biblical tradition.

26. The best proof for this development is a discussion of expectations of a miracle in consequence of pious behaviour during a persecution; cf. *Sifra Emor Pereq 9.5*, see M. Becker, *Wunder*, pp. 191–95.

27. J. Neusner's discussion of rabbinic texts can be characterized by two fundamental changes in method: first, he cancelled the biographical and historizing inquiry into rabbinic traditions to look for a more critical and historically controllable method; and in a second step he changed his diachronic reconstruction to a synchronic analysis of the several rabbinic text corpora. This last change depends on three presuppositions: the autonomy of the text corpora, their connection with the structural hermeneutical systems of the Mishna and Scripture, and the continuity of all texts in the canonical framework of rabbinic Judaism. For further information about this method, see J. Neusner, *The Peripatetic Saying* (BJS, 89; Chico: Scholars Press, 1985), nn. 179–90; J. Neusner, 'Documentary Hermeneutics and the Interpretation of Narrative in Classics of Judaism', in J. Neusner, E. S. Frerichs (eds), *Approaches to Ancient Judaism* Vol. VI. *Studies in the Ethnography and Literature of Judaism* (BJS, 192; Atlanta: Scholars Press, 1989), pp. 107–34; J. Neusner, 'The Three Stages in Formation of Rabbinic Writings', in J. Neusner, E. S. Frerichs (eds), *Approaches*, pp. 85–106; J. Neusner, *Making the Classics in Judaism: The Three Stages of Literary Formation* (BJS, 180; Atlanta: Scholars Press, 1989), pp. 1–44. For an overall application of this method, see J. Neusner, *Introduction to Rabbinic Literature*.

the last word in respect of an analysis of rabbinic texts. I mentioned already that miracle traditions offer a specific opportunity for reconstructing several aspects of the history, and in some part the process of the handing down, of such stories and traditions. Not only their narrative character is exceptional in view of the prominent halakhic structure, but a comprehensive analysis of the rabbinic material can also demonstrate divergent theological motivations. This opens access to more than a few points of friction between the traditions and their integration into the frame of the rabbinic text corpora.[28] That means that a number of these traditions do not fit in perfectly with the editorial interests of the rabbis – to be more precise: of a serious rabbinic text – because their interests shift in a certain manner from document to document. If that is true, we can draw further specific conclusions back to the earlier stages of the material in accordance with these points of friction. In some instances, we can even keep on looking for these points of friction in the traditions themselves, and in several accounts the peculiar differences even open up the possibility of separating a specific text from the genuine rabbinic tradition, because it derives from outside the rabbinic movement.[29]

All these factors influence the pragmatics of the miracle traditions in the early rabbinic literature. However, one of the most interesting conclusions in view of the main concern of this study originates from the fact that the rabbis largely used these traditions for their own purposes. Usually they were not interested in miracle stories or miraculous events in themselves. Therefore, only a serious investigation of the frame and the embedding of the traditions into the argumentation of the macro-texts can give evidence of their view. This constitutes the extraordinary character of the miracle tradition in the early rabbinic texts.

2. Miracle Traditions in General

Of course, no discussion is successful without any differentiation. The texts themselves offer two general categories: a temporal factor and a difference in the literary form. In view of the first aspect, we can distinguish between biblical traditions and traditions about current events. The second differentiation runs crosswise to the first and separates predominantly short notes from more detailed narratives. The following diagram demonstrates the relationship between these two categories and gives a survey of the statistical references: traditional vs. current events and detailed vs. abbreviated miracle traditions in the corpus of early rabbinic texts.[30]

---

28. In the case of Ḥoni's famous 'prayer' for rain, the evolution can be demonstrated from a pre-rabbinic kernel throughout several layers of rabbinic reworking with a certain criticism, affirmation and a thorough rabbinization. Cf. W. S. Green, 'Palestinian Holy Men'; M. Becker, *Wunder*, pp. 291–337.

29. Cf. for instance the traditions about the salvage of the coffin of Joseph from the bottom of the River Nile (*MekhY. Beshallah* 1 [Exod. 13.19]; *tSota* 4.7); for a brief discussion of this story, which most probably has its origin in Egypt because of certain parallels to the myth of Isis and Osiris, see below.

30. For further discussion of these categories and a more complete analysis of the various texts and traditions, see M. Becker, *Wunder*, pp. 204–60.

Table 1: Miracle Traditions[31]

	Short notes	Detailed narratives
Biblical traditions	Approximately 115[32]	(5[33])
Current events	12[34]	19[35]

Concerning the biblical traditions, short notes – e.g. small quotations, keywords or abstract generalizations such as 'the miracles at the sea'[36] – dominate the study. It seems that the rabbis identified entire traditions by such short citations. That is not surprising because of the oral culture and rote learning the rabbis practised in their educational system, and because of the many other abbreviations they used in their exegetical effort. In this context, we have to realize that the theoretical categories of the classical *Formgeschichte*[37] and the possibilities of explaining the origins and the development of narratives come to an end here. There seems to exist a difference not only in social status between the rabbis and

31. Each number includes only the passages found in entire (and therefore comparable) rabbinic text corpora.

32. Mishna: 8; Tosefta: 8; *MekhY.*: approximately 50; *Sifra*: 7; *SifBam.*: 16; *SifDev.*: 23. Only in view of this category can we get statistically representative information about the distribution of the passages – even if we have to take into account several problems of separating distinct passages, especially in the case of the *Mekhilta of R. Yismael*. For that reason the relationship between the texts is more important than the absolute number of passages.

33. Mishna: – ; Tosefta: (1); *MekhY.*: (2); *Sifra*: – ; *SifBam.*: (1); *SifDev.*: (1).

34. Mishna: 6; Tosefta: 5; *MekhY.*: – ; *Sifra*: 1; *SifBam.*: – ; *SifDev.*: –.

35. Mishna: 1; Tosefta: 9; *MekhY.*: 2; *Sifra*: 3; *SifBam.*: 1; *SifDev.*: 3.

36. Some of these texts connect different miracle traditions to lists or small collections; cf. *MekhY. Beshallah* 1 (Exod. 13.18); 5 (Exod. 14.16). For further details and on this special part of the oriental *Listenwissenschaft*, see W. S. Towner, *The Rabbinic 'Enumeration of Scriptural Examples': A Study of a Rabbinic Pattern of Discourse with Special Reference to* Mekhilta D'R. Ishmael (SPB, 22; Leiden: Brill, 1973), pp. 145–54.

37. For further discussion of the problems of rabbinic *Formgeschichte* and especially the miracle tradition, cf. G. Stemberger, *Einleitung*, pp. 59–63; W. S. Towner, 'Form-Criticism of Rabbinic Literature', *JJS* 24 (1973), pp. 101–18; A. J. Saldarini, '"Form Criticism" of Rabbinic Literature', *JBL* 96 (1977), pp. 257–74; A. Goldberg, 'Entwurf einer formanalytischen Methode für die Exegese der rabbinischen Traditionsliteratur', *FJB* 5 (1977), pp. 1–41; A. Goldberg, 'Form-Analysis of Midrashic Literature as a Method of Description', *JJS* 36 (1985), pp. 159–74; D. Ben-Amos, *Narrative Forms in the Haggadah, Structural Analysis* (Diss.: Indiana University, 1967); M. Dibelius, *Die Formgeschichte des Evangeliums* (Tübingen: Mohr Siebeck, 6th ed., 1971), pp. 139–49; J. Neusner, *The Rabbinic Traditions About the Pharisees Before 70*, vol. III (Leiden: Brill, 1971; repr. Atlanta: Scholars Press, 1999); J. Neusner, 'Types and Forms in Ancient Jewish Literature', in J. Neusner, *Early Rabbinic Judaism. Historical Studies in Religion, Literature and Art* (SJLA, 13, Leiden: Brill, 1975), pp. 100–136 (107–8, 122–23); D. Noy, 'The Talmudic-Midrashic "Healing Stories" as Narrative Genre', *Koroth* 9 (1988), pp. 124–46. Neusner's turn away from a *formgeschichtliche* analysis in spite of a form-critical description of the texts is a significant mark of the sceptical change in his opus, and has far-reaching consequences for the whole research.

the people handing down New Testament narratives, but also in their strategies for memorizing texts. The rules of the rabbis' hermeneutical discussions and the degree of formalization and ritualised speech-acts are different from the model of orally handed-down stories in the gospel tradition, even if the optimistic view of the classical *Formgeschichte* of reconstructing the oral background was criticised rigorously in the last decades. Nevertheless, the early rabbinic texts also include a number of traditions from outside their movement, which fit the classical theory better; and some of the miracle stories belong to them.[38]

Of the biblical traditions, the exodus and desert stories are most prominent. They serve as the primary subject and reference for the majority of the short notes of the early rabbis. Three major factors function as hermeneutical principles within their exegesis. At first, they understand the biblical stories as traditions, which recall the mighty divine deeds of the past. This seems not to be new, because since the days when those stories were told for the first time, they operate as identity-establishing traditions: not only for the rabbis, but also for Jews of all generations. Recalling the divine deeds gave the rabbis a gleam of hope considering their present situation, which they interpreted after the destruction of the temple in Jerusalem as having fallen into decay.[39]

Of special interest is the distribution of these notes because most of them are in the *Mekhilta of R. Yismael*. The reason for this is that the biblical book of Exodus, as the basic text of this commentary, includes a great amount of miracle traditions. However, a closer look at the *Mekhilta* presents a quite different picture, because central biblical miracle texts do not receive an explanation there, since Exodus 1–11 is not mentioned in this commentary.[40] To cut a long story short, even if the early rabbis did understand the biblical events in a realistic manner and regarded them as the special signature of a divine intervention for the sake of Israel, miracles were not the object of their prominent interest.

A second hermeneutical principle refers to a factor connected with the theology of creation. In some places, we can find short reflections about the specific character of God's miracle-working – including the presupposition that miracles imply a certain intervention into the 'order of creation'[41]. Even if God's omnipotence allows him to overrule this order, the early rabbis did not apply

---

38. It is, therefore, not realistic to use the classical *Formgeschichte* as the primary method of analysing rabbinical texts.

39. See esp. *mSota* 9 and *tSota* 8-15 (with slight, but significant differences).

40. Another example of the selectivity of the rabbinic usage of miracle traditions is the absence of the Elijah and Elisha stories. Apart from the Moses traditions handed down in the Pentateuch, the Elijah/Elisha cycle involves the highest concentration of miracle stories in the biblical tradition. By contrast, it receives only a very limited interest from the early rabbis. Cf. below.

41. Unlike the later haggadic traditions of the midrashim, where the term 'order of creation' (סדרי בראשית) is used more frequently, the early rabbinic texts do not use it (this term is found for the first time in *bShab.* 53b; cf. M. Kadushin, *Rabbinic Mind*, pp. 152–67). But in accordance with *tSota* 10:4 and *MekhY. Wayassa'* 3 (Exod. 16.4) it is said that God changed the eternal order (סדרי עלם) respecting his work of creation (מעשה בראשית) for the generation of the flood and for Israel; cf. *SifDev.* 32 and *SifBam.* 42.

this argument in an expansive and uncritical way. On the contrary, they were sensitive of the miraculous and especially the impossible. Surely, they could expand the story of the creation in view of those things created in the twilight of the first Shabbat evening (e.g. the manna, the rod of Moses or the demons),[42] but they used common sense and the plausible logic of everyday events to differentiate between possible and impossible things.[43] Moreover, in a few places they can discuss philosophical arguments, proving the existence of a wider horizon of this discussion, including the Stoic conception of providence and the Epicurean criticism of miracles.[44]

A third interpretative factor pushes forward the understanding of some of these miracles as the consequence of piety, respectively as a granting of prayer. This way of understanding miracles has two major consequences. Firstly, most miracles were defined in an even stricter sense than in the biblical traditions as proprietary deeds of God himself. No man – not even Moses – could work a miracle by himself.[45] On the other hand, the image of a miracle worker also receives a certain change. If everyone can pray for the help of God, there is no longer a need for a charismatic miracle worker. This seems a bit exaggerated, because the charismatics would not become superfluous, but it is quite clear that their image is subjected to certain changes. This corresponds to a change in the social status of the early rabbis in Palestinian society during the first three centuries CE; and quite a number of those stories about charismatic authorities can give a hint of this change, because there we can observe a conflict between these figures and the rabbinic authorities. During the Tannaitic era a new type of charismatic evolves: he is a very pious man, usually very poor but highly esteemed by the people, and we can study several conflicts with the rabbis even if this is seemingly an inner-rabbinical quarrel. Finally, in the later strata of the early rabbinic literature and in the Talmudim we can observe the integration of the charismatic qualities into the image of a rabbi because of his knowledge of the Torah.[46]

---

42. Cf. *mAvot* 5.6 parr. *MekhY. Wayassa'* 6 (Exod. 16.32) and *SifDev.* 355. Some of these patterns especially serve an anti-dualistic interest. Cf. M. Becker, *Wunder*, p. 133.

43. For example, in every day life the rabbis rejected swearing an oath under impossible, extremely vague and incredible conditions. Cf. *mShevu.* 3.8; *mNed.* 3.2; *tNed.* 2.1; *tGit.* 7.8; M. Becker, *Wunder*, pp. 256–57.

44. Cf. H.-J. Becker, 'Earthquakes, Insects, Miracles, and the Order of Nature', in P. Schäfer (ed.), *The Talmud Yerushalmi and Graeco-Roman Culture* I (TSAJ, 71; Tübingen: Mohr Siebeck, 1998), pp. 387–96 (394–96).

45. Cf. *mRHSh.* 3.8 and *MekhY. 'Amalek* 1 (Exod. 17.11); a central passage in the *Mekhilta* text runs like this: '*And it came to pass when Moses held up his hand,* etc. Now, could Moses' hands make Israel victorious or could his hands break Amalek? It merely means this: When Moses raised his hands towards heaven, the Israelites would look at him and believe in Him who commanded Moses to do so; then God would perform for them miracles and mighty deeds.' For detailed discussion of these and further passages, see M. Becker, *Wunder*, pp. 271–79; cf. pp. 133–35.

46. Apart from the literal tradition, prayer was the most eminent *Sitz im Leben* of the biblical miracle tradition; there it always had been alive.

Finally, the numerical relationship between short notes and stories is very interesting because it gives additional evidence for a lack of interest in any biblical
miracle *story* as such. Without a doubt, the rabbis commemorated the 'facts' of
the biblical past and they made their comments on several details – but they were
not interested in any biblical miracle story in its entirety. Nevertheless, although
they are very rare, there still existed several extended stories – but these passages
did not narrate biblical events. They give various explications subsequent to a
biblical tale, filling and interpreting the gaps of the narratives with legendary
episodes. For that reason the number of these stories is set in brackets in the
diagram.

As an example, I want to refer to an extremely long story.[47] It attempts to explain
the otherwise unknown circumstances of the finding of the coffin of Joseph,
which the Israelites ought to have taken with them when they left Egypt. Although
we have a few intertestamental traditions about the burial of Joseph,[48] this story
is unique, because in the biblical account we hear only about the oath of the sons
of Israel (Gen. 50.25-26.) to take the coffin with them. In Exod. 13.19 it is said
that Moses has done this, and in Josh. 24.32 we are told about the burial of Joseph
at Shechem. However, nothing is said about the manner in which Moses did this
job.

Complementary to these bare facts, the rabbinic tradition fills this gap by telling
us about the legendary finding and recovery of the coffin of Joseph, which was sent
to the bottom of the Nile by the Egyptians. Almost the oldest textual versions of the
story subsist in the Tosefta and – possibly older – in the *Mekhilta of R. Yismael* in
two slightly different versions.[49] In the latter Moses raises the coffin by throwing a
'magic' pebble – or in an alternate textual tradition the Tetragrammaton written on
a golden plate – into the river, whereas in the Tosefta Moses acts only by his word,
calling Joseph's coffin to rise. This account looks like a rationalization and
therefore it is possibly the youngest version. Even if the *Mekhilta of R. Yismael*
also includes some corrective intervention, it delivers a more genuine version with
a distinct 'magical' action. This confirms not only the action of Moses, but also
the manner in which both texts state their קל וחומר conclusion. In the Tosefta
the conclusion *a minore ad maius* merely serves a polemical purpose to subordinate
Elijah and Elisha beneath the authority of Moses,[50] whereas in the *Mekhilta of
R. Yismael* it is motivated by an analogy between the actions of the biblical

---

47.   In the Tosefta and the *Mekhilta* the story is composed of more than 220 and nearly 200
words respectively. One reason for this length consists in the alternative tradition already offered
in the account, but even so this story is atypical for the rabbis.

48.   Cf. *T. Sim.* 8.3–4.

49.   Cf. *tSot.* 4.7 (with certain differences between the texts of the codices Vienna and Erfurt)
and *MekhY. Beshallah* 1 (Exod. 13.19). For an entire interpretation of this story, including a
synopsis of these texts, cf. M. Becker, *Wunder*, pp. 223–37; for further references in the rabbinic
texts, see p. 223 n. 68.

50.   Here it is said: 'Now if Elisha, disciple of Elijah, disciple of Moses, could do things in such
a way, Moses, master of Elijah, all the more so (should be able to do such things)'.

example of Elisha and that of Moses in the story.[51] In any case, we have a tradition reworked by the rabbis integrating some elements of the Osiris-tradition into the plot. For this tradition Plutarch gives a prominent literary account in his book *De Iside et Osiride*, even if there is no proof of literary dependence.[52]

The framework of the Tosefta and the *Mekhilta of R. Yismael* shows that, at the editorial level, the authors are only interested in the fulfilment of the commandment by Moses (cited already in *mSota* 1.9), not in the miraculous aspects. However, the story itself offers a great variety of interesting details on the rabbinic interpretation and integration of an original tradition most probably arranged by Hellenistic Jews of Egypt. Significant are the differences in the discussion of the 'magical' aspects and the rising conflict between Mosaic traditions and those of Elijah or Elisha. The development of both aspects fits very well with the picture of a changing interest of society, including an inner-rabbinic and an inner-Jewish discussion on charismatic authority, as well as an increase of the influence of pagan – and Christian – traditions.

According to the other category – the miraculous events of the present day (indicated in the lower row of table 1) – we see a different picture. Here as well, only a few tales exist, but there are even fewer short notes about such events. To begin with the tales: most prominent, the בת קול (voice of heaven [literally: daughter of a voice])[53] refers to a phenomenon connected with a very interesting discourse about a special approach to revelation[54] and the integration of miracles into the halakhic discussion.[55] Apart from these traditions, only a small number of other stories refer to miracles or their expectation. This critical pre-condition should not be surprising, because miracle stories in other traditions function as material proving the charisma of a person or the reliability of legal and religious matters in a certain discussion. The different interpretations and emphases in

---

51. The *Mekhilta* states: 'If Elisha, the disciple of Elijah, could make the iron come to the surface, how much more could Moses, the master of Elijah, do it!'

52. For further discussion of the religion- and tradition-historical background of this story cf. M. Güdemann, *Religionsgeschichtliche Studien*, (Leipzig: Oskar Leiner, 1876), pp. 26–40; J. Horovitz, *Die Josephserzählung* (Frankfurt am Main: Kauffmann, 1921), pp. 120–46. 154–56; B. Heller, 'Die Sage vom Sarge Josephs und der Bericht Benjamins von Tudela über Daniels schwebenden Sarg', *MGWJ* 2 (1926), pp. 271–76 (273–76); G. Kittel, *Die Probleme des paläs-tinischen Spätjudentums und das Urchristentum* (Stuttgart: Kohlhammer, 1926), pp. 179–93; H. Bietenhard, *Der Tosefta-Traktat Sota: Hebräischer Text mit kritischem Apparat. Übersetzung, Kommentar* (JudChr, 9; Bern: Peter Lang, 1986), p. 79 n. 102.

53. On the traditions of the בת קול, see P. Kuhn, *Offenbarungsstimmen im Antiken Judentum: Untersuchungen zur Bat Qol und verwandten Phänomenen* (TSAJ, 20; Tübingen: Mohr Siebeck, 1989); P. Kuhn, *Bat Qol: Die Offenbarungsstimme in der rabbinischen Literatur. Sammlung, Übersetzung und Kurzkommentierung der Texte* (EichM, 13; Regensburg: Pustet, 1990); A. Guttmann, 'Significance', pp. 366–97; M. Becker, *Wunder*, pp. 240–44; for early rabbinic references see p. 240 n. 112.

54. See *tSota* 13.3-6; cf. P. Kuhn, *Offenbarungsstimmen*, pp. 303–29; M. Becker, *Wunder*, pp. 243–44.

55. See esp. *mYev.* 16.6; *tYev.* 14.7; cf. M. Becker, *Wunder*, pp. 240–43.

relation to the miracle traditions are the cause of our difficulties in deciding whether a story or a note refers to a miracle or to something else. However, when we look at the categories of the rabbis we can see that they also had trouble with that question. Therefore, it is not merely a problem of our modern reception.

A significant example of these problems and the divergent purposes of the rabbis with the miraculous is the story about the fire in the courtyard of Joseph ben Simai (*tShab.* 13.9).[56] It is told in a halakhic discussion of the Mishna that a Gentile coming along at Shabbat and being helpful in putting out a fire should neither be urged to do so nor not to do so – as with Joseph who rejected several soldiers who came to help him. This rejection, as the Tosefta states, is erroneous because it provoked a 'heavenly intervention': a rain-cloud burst and put the fire out. The Tosefta criticises Joseph's rejection as superfluous because of the statement in the Mishna. Even if the Tosefta does not speak directly about the miraculous character of the event,[57] it gives a significant comment on the rabbinic convictions about miracles, although the story does not correspond with the pattern 'miracle story' of the *Formgeschichte*. The coincidence of the contingent – the right thing at the right time, which otherwise could be called a mere accident – plays an important role in the belief of the rabbis. It fits marvellously within the conception of the divine omnipotence and providence. However, the rabbis disagree on the reverse of the argument using this regulative idea as a means of forcing God's help. The expectations of miracles are also the subject of their subtle criticism in other places.[58]

Further stories and notes direct their interest primarily on institutional aspects. The Shabbat, the temple, the Torah and the divine providence[59] can receive confirmation by miracles. Some of the tales function in their context as *Normenwunder*, as Gerd Theißen[60] has classified them; other stories look more like rescue events. In several places, it is not quite certain whether the rabbis understood these stories as miracles at all. For that reason we can see again how important the context in which the rabbis tell a story is. The context operates as one of the main factors of the pragmatics of rabbinic miracle stories.

There are further details about the literary character of such stories and notes. We can list them briefly:

---

56. Very remarkable is the later use of this story in the *Yerushalmi* (cf. *yShab.* 16.7 [15d]; *yYom.* 8.5 [45d] and *yNed.* 4.9 [38d]). These references show how the rabbis can use the same story for different purposes, as the halakhic context requires it.

57. Until the Bavli (*bShab.* 121a) did so, no tradition cared about a miracle.

58. Cf. *Sifra Emor Pereq* 9.5.

59. Cf. *mAvot* 5.5; *tYom.* 2.4; *tSota* 13.7f.; *tSan.* 8.3 par. *MekhY. Kaspa* 3 (Exod. 23.7).

60. On this classification and its functional aspects, see G. Theißen, *Urchristliche Wundergeschichten* (SNT, 8; Gütersloh: Mohn, 6th edn., 1990), pp. 114–20.

61. For further information about the form and function of a מעשה in rabbinic literature, see A. Goldberg, 'Form und Funktion des Ma'ase in der Mischna', *FJB* 2 (1974), pp. 1–38.

• Most stories are introduced as מעשה – as a paradigmatic precedent – in a halakhic discussion.[61]
• Complementary to the first aspect, *Chreia*-like structures outnumber the narratives; but they do not serve personal interests.[62]
• Only a few stories are assigned to a named rabbinic authority; most are handed down anonymously.[63]
• Some narratives and short notes are connected in form of catalogue-like collections and enumerations.[64]

Although we cannot distil a general purpose from those texts and traditions, and though it seems impossible to define their literary function uniquely, we have to recognize that many stories by themselves serve legendary or etiological purposes. But only in a few places are they cited for their genuine purposes. Usually – as stated above – the rabbis have their own strategies for including these texts by means of a catchword or one significant aspect, which is not necessarily the point of the miracle. They use the material for their own purposes, which quite often differ from the genuine purposes of the miracle traditions.

3. Human Miracle Workers

The corpus of early rabbinic texts mentions only a small number of people associated with charismatic authority for performing miracles. These texts are divided into three different groups. *The early rabbinic documents* – contrary to the later texts – provide the smallest amount of information, with regard to their charismatic authority and miracle-working, about genuine rabbis. Only in three cases a study seems to promise success – and even there the most relevant texts are from later sources: these rabbinic authorities – Tannaim of the second, third and fourth generations respectively – are all three closely related with each

---

62. On the use of *Chreia* in rabbinic literature, cf. C. Hezser, 'Die Verwendung der hellenistischen Gattung Chrie im frühen Christentum und Judentum', *JSJ* 27 (1996), pp. 371–439; J. Avery-Peck, 'Classifying Early Rabbinic Pronouncement Stories', *SBLSP* 22 (1983), pp. 223–44.

63. For that reason the otherwise troublesome debate about the dating of rabbinic traditions on account of attributed sayings does not have much relevance in the case of miracle traditions. On this discussion, see W. S. Green, 'What's in a Name? – The Problematic of Rabbinic "Biography"', in W. S. Green (ed.), *Approaches to Ancient Judaism: Theory and Practice* (BJS, 1; Missoula: Scholars Press, 1978), pp. 77–96; W. S. Green, 'Context and Meaning in Rabbinic "Biography"', in W. S. Green (ed.), *Approaches to Ancient Judaism* II (BJS, 9; Ann Arbor: Scholars Press, 1980), pp. 94–111; J. N. Lightstone, 'Names without "Lives": Why no "Lives of the Rabbis" in Early Rabbinic Judaism', *SR* 19 (1990), pp. 43–57; K. Müller, 'Datierung', pp. 559–62; G. Stemberger, *Einleitung*, 70–72; J. Neusner, *Talmudic Biography*; J. Neusner, *Introduction to Rabbinic Literature*; J. Neusner, 'Evaluating the Attributions of Sayings to Named Sages in the Rabbinic Literature', *JSJ* 26 (1995), pp. 93–111.

64. Apart from the already mentioned enumerations (see note 36), see especially *mAvot* 5.4-6. For further information and texts see M. Becker, *Wunder*, pp. 186, 188 with n. 12, 208–9; cf. the compilation about the miraculous events in connection with Shimon the Righteous in *tSot*. 13.7-8; on this text see J. Neusner, *Peripatetic Saying*, pp. 41–47, and G. Stemberger, 'Narrative Baraitot in the Yerushalmi', in P. Schäfer (ed.), *The Talmud Yerushalmi and Graeco-Roman Culture* I (TSAJ, 71; Tübingen: Mohr Siebeck, 1998), pp. 63–81 (77–79).

other:[65] R. Eliʿezer ben Hyrkanos, R. Shimʿon ben Yoḥai, and R. Pinḥas ben Yair.
• R. Eliʿezer[66] in some traditions acts as an expert in the halakhic discussion on 'magic' (*tSan.* 11.5; cf. *ySan.* 7.19 [25d]; *bSan.* 68a). Further on he is involved in the famous discussion about the use of miracles as arguments in a halakhic discourse (*yMQ.* 3.1 [81cd]; *bBM.* 59b) and was involved in a discussion on a charge of מינות (heresy), perhaps because of his contact with Jewish Christians.[67] However, he was not a miracle worker, even if later traditions narrate some miraculous events about him (cf. *yHag.* 2.1 [77b] par. *RutR.* 6.4; *QohR.* 7.8.1.).
• R. Shimʿon[68] is a very prominent candidate for a miracle worker, but, as in the tradition about R. Eliʿezer, only talmudic texts tell us about his ascetic lifestyle and the miraculous purification of Tiberias (cf. e.g. *yShevi.* 9.1 [38d]; *bShab.* 34a; *BerR.* 79.8), various miracles (see esp. *yBer.* 9.3 [13d] and parallels) and even an exorcism (*bMeʾil.* 17b).
• The Rabbinic sources give a small amount of information about a conflict between R. Pinḥas and R Yᵉhuda I (Rabbi). Both seem to argue using miracles to support their opinions in a debate related to the halakha of tithing agricultural products.[69] Moreover, R. Pinḥas was closely related to the pious people called the Ḥasidim, and several miracle stories (see esp. *yDem.* 1.3 [21d-22a]) circulate about him – very similar to those told of Ḥanina ben Dosa in *bTaan.* 24b-25a, demonstrating the devoutness of both.[70]

This result is somewhat amazing because in later documents we can observe a great quantity of traditions even about several Tannaitic sages. However, although we get a lot of information on related rabbinic activities in the later documents, it is difficult to obtain reliable facts about the majority of the rabbis mentioned. Apart from the problems of traditions attributed to named authorities,[71] the amount of texts for the majority of these rabbis is very small; in most cases it is too small for a historical survey. A great number of these traditions seem to have emerged in consequence of the change in the image of a rabbi already mentioned. It is probable that the later talmudic authorities would have liked to adapt their earlier colleagues to their own image, although we cannot exclude the possibility that some of these traditions rest upon older and trustworthy information.[72]

---

65. R. Eliʿezer and R. Pinḥas were teaching at Lydda and R. Shimʿon was the father in law of R. Pinḥas.

66. On R. Eliʿezer, see the publications by J. Neusner mentioned in note 19; Y. D. Gilat, *R. Eliezer Ben Hyrcanus: A Scholar Outcast* (Jerusalem: Bar-Ilan University Press, 1984); M. Becker, *Wunder*, pp. 389–96.

67. Cf. *tHul.* 2.24; M. Becker, *Wunder*, pp. 290–92.

68. Cf. on R. Shimʿon, L. Levine, 'R. Simeon b. Yoḥai and the Purification of Tiberias: History and Tradition', *HUCA* 49 (1978), pp. 143–85; B. Z. Rosenfeld, 'R. Simeon b. Yohai – Wonder Worker and Magician. Scholar, *Saddiq* and *Hasid*', *REJ* 158 (1999), pp. 349–84; M. Becker, *Wunder*, pp. 396–99.

69. Cf. above note 18.

70. Cf. M. Becker, *Wunder*, pp. 399–402.

71. Cf. above note 63.

72. For further discussion of this problem and the rabbinic authorities, see M. Becker, *Wunder*, pp. 382–403. 409–14.

As a second category, we have to look at those texts which give us some suggestions about the already mentioned group of pious people, especially the Ḥasidim.[73]
In some texts, they are associated with the solitaries[74] we will discuss afterwards
or with the so-called 'men of deed'[75], but it seems to be better to characterize them
as a group of their own. Seemingly, this is not a homogeneous party. Only some
of them, for example, make use of the literal impact of miracle stories in halakhic
discussions and even fewer can be characterized as miracle workers. If a movement
of the Ḥasidim ever really existed, R. Pinḥas ben Yair apparently was the archetype
for the connection of piety and miracles, which exercised a heavy influence on the
tradition of Ḥanina ben Dosa.[76] However, the Ḥasidim did not succeed with their
ideas and that is perhaps the reason why only very few texts survive as a basis for
a reconstruction.

Finally, we have to look at those individuals I would like to characterize as
charismatic solitaires. They can be found not really inside, but at the margin of
the rabbinic movement. Even so, we get the most information about them.
Prominent examples of these charismatic solitaires are Ḥoni the circle-drawer and
Ḥanina ben Dosa.[77]

Before turning to the texts, some general remarks on the rabbinic traditions
about miracle workers and the continuity of the heritage of the Hebrew Bible and
early Judaism seem to be necessary. At a first glance, we have already found that
there was very little interest in those questions. Nonetheless, there was a certain
debate about the biblical miracle workers, but it was highly selective and concen-
trated, with a few exceptions,[78] on the Mosaic tradition. Already mentioned are

73. On the Rabbinic Ḥasidim, see D. Berman, 'Hasidim in Rabbinic Traditions', *SBLSP* 2
(1979), pp. 15–33; A. Büchler, *Types of Jewish-Palestine Piety from 70 B.C.E. to 70 C.E.: The
Ancient Pious Men* (London: Jews' College, 1922), pp. 81–87; L. Gulkowitsch, *Die Bildung des
Begriffes Ḥāsîd* (Tartu: K. Mattiesen, 1935); L. Jacobs, 'The Concept of Hasid in the Biblical and
Rabbinic Literatures', *JJS* 8 (1957), pp. 143–54; J. Morgenstern, 'The *HᴬSÎDÎM* – Who were
they?', *HUCA* 38 (1967), pp. 59–73; S. Safrai, 'The Teaching of Pietists in Mishnaic Literature',
JJS 16 (1965), pp. 15–33; S. Safrai, מעשׂה חסידים בתספרות התנאים, in S. Safrai,
ארץ—ישׂראל וחכמיה בתקופה המשׁנה והתלמוד (Jerusalem: Hakibbutz Hameuchad
Publishing House, 1983), pp. 144–60; S. Safrai, 'The Pious (*Hassidim*) and the Man of Deeds'
(Hebrew), *Zion* 50 (1985), pp. 133–54, XII–XIII; G. B. A. Sarfatti, 'Pious Men, Men of Deeds
and the Early Prophets' (Hebrew), *Tarbiz* 26 (1956/57), pp. 126–53, II–IV.

74. Cf. the story replacing the Ḥoni-tradition of the Mishna in *tTaan.* 2.13/3.1; for further
discussion of this text, see below and M. Becker, *Wunder*, pp. 302–5.

75. Cf. *mSota* 9.15 par. (in connection with Ḥanina ben Dosa); for further discussion and
other texts, see M. Becker, *Wunder*, pp. 368–75.

76. Compare the stories in *yDem.* 1.3 (21d-22a) with those in *bTaan.* 24b-25a and esp. the
rescue-story in *yDem.* 1.2 (22a) par. *ySheq.* 5.2 (48d); *DevR.* 3.3 with that in *bYeb.* 121b par.
bBQ. 50a, cf. M. Becker, *Wunder*, pp. 363–64.

77. The story about Yacov from Kfar Sama (*tHul.* 2.22-23) – his healing in the name of Jesus
– seems to be another similar case which cannot be dealt with here; cf. M. Becker, *Wunder*,
pp. 378–82.

78. Apart from the reference to Abraham's astrological knowledge and the tradition about
his ability to cure those who looked at the precious stone he was wearing on a chain around his

the indications of a restrained conflict between Moses- and Elijah-traditions,[79] both
of which are usually associated with different roles in the rabbinic literature: Moses
as law-giver and Elijah as precursor of the *eschaton*. Overall, the rabbis are much
more wary of magical implications and the difficulties of the halakhic discussion.
Considering the very strict attribution of miracle-working to God, they do not
hesitate to criticise some biblical practices in the context of the Mosaic tradition
in a subtle way. Not the raising of the hands of Moses gave Israel the victory over
Amalek (Exod. 17.8-16), but their looking at Moses, believing in the one who
commanded Moses to do so. If Israel believes in such a way, then God performs
for them miracles and mighty deeds.[80]

Apart from this limitation of magical implications, two general observations are
very significant. On the one hand, we have seen that in the rabbinic tradition,
miracle workers do not ordinarily have the authority to perform miracles by
themselves and most rabbis respond in a critical manner to all attempts to
attribute any halakhic demand to personal charisma. A rabbi can only work
miracles in a derived form of authority, for the reason that only God can perform
miracles. Therefore, the rabbis developed a subtle way of discussing this derived
authority in accordance with the conception of a שׁליח.[81] Usually by this term
the rabbinic tradition thinks of an envoy, acting under the order and in the name
of an authoritative sender, and there often exists a connection between this
characterization and juridical acts in daily affairs. However, this stance has much
in common with the biblical and near-eastern conception of a messenger it is
derived from. A religious aspect of a שׁליח ordinarily seems out of the question,
but there are some exceptions where, by analogy with this concept, even a miracle
worker can act as an envoy of God – just like a prophet sent by him.[82] Even if there

---

neck (*tQid.* 5.17), we get some information about Balaam as the negative typos par excellence
(*SifBam.* 157; cf. *mSan.* 10.2; *mAvot* 5.19; *tSota* 4.19; *MekhY. Beshallah* 2f. [esp. Exod. 14.9]
and *SifDev.* 250). As an exception to that rule, see *SifDev.* 357, where Balaam acts next to Moses
(cf. the ambivalent traditions in *MekhY. Baḥodesh* 1 [Exod. 19.2]; 5 [Exod. 20.2] and *SifDev.*
343).

79. Cf. the different versions of the story about the finding and recovery of the coffin of Joseph
mentioned above.

80. *MekhY. ʿAmalek* 1 (Exod. 17.11); *mRHSh.* 3.8; cf. M. Becker, *Wunder*, pp. 271–79.

81. Cf. the surveys of the שׁליח-ʿinstitution' by J. A. Bühner, *Der Gesandte und sein Weg
im 4. Evangelium* (WUNT II.2; Tübingen: Mohr Siebeck, 1977), pp. 181–373; K. H. Rengstorf,
ἀπόστολος κτλ, in *TWNT* 1 (Stuttgart: Kohlhammer, 1933), pp. 406–48 (414–20); for the
discussion of research see M. Lohmeyer, *Der Apostelbegriff im Neuen Testament. Eine
Untersuchung auf dem Hintergrund der synoptischen Aussendungsreden* (SBB, 29; Stuttgart:
Katholisches Bibelwerk, 1995), pp. 18–122; K. Scholtissek, *Vollmacht im Alten Testament und
Judentum: Begriffs- und motivgeschichtliche Studien zu einem bibeltheologischen Thema (mit
einem Ausblick auf das Neue Testament)* (PaThSt, 24; Paderborn: Ferdinand Schöningh, 1993),
pp. 40–42, 129–38.

82. Cf. the discussion in *MekhY. ʿAmalek* 1 (Exod. 17.9), where the rabbis discuss the
opportunity of Elisha to kill and to make alive again. However, the rabbis are not interested in
that act normally reserved for God only. Their interests rest upon the discussion of this act in accordance with the authorization of Gehazi to behave in the same way as his master. The main aspect

are only a few texts – most of them from younger sources – which talk about a שׁלִיחַ in relation to miracle-working,[83] the relevance of this discussion cannot be denied, especially in account of the continuity with the biblical conception.[84]

As a second aspect, we have to take note that the best examples for human miracle workers do not derive from the circles of the early rabbis, even if they went through a thorough rabbinization, which adapted these individuals to the image of a rabbi, changing their perspective in a fundamental manner. This process was first analysed by William Scott Green[85] and some others;[86] and I tried to deepen the argumentation in view of general structures and the diverse conflicts up to the end of the Tannaitic era.

This procedure promises success, because some of the stories themselves offer resistance to the rabbinization, which neglected the charismatic character of the miracle workers. Therefore, we can catch a glimpse of earlier strata of individual miracle traditions. Most fascinating are the stories about Honi the circle-drawer and Hanina ben Dosa. In several of these stories, we are able to reconstruct the process of integration into the rabbinic tradition at various stages. As I cannot go into every detail here,[87] we have to look more closely at the overall structures.

Concerning Honi we are in the lucky position to refer to a parallel tradition from outside the rabbinic movement. Flavius Josephus tells us in his *Antiquities* (14, 22–24)[88] about a certain Onias, whose prayers put an end to a rainless period.

of the rabbinic discussion therefore focuses on the legitimation of such an authorization by a teacher, which transfers his authority to a disciple. However, the basis of the whole argument depends on the proportional analogy of the authorization of Elisha and his miracle-working abilities by God. Cf. M. Becker, *Wunder*, pp. 281–88.

83. Apart from priests, K. H. Rengstorf, ἀπόστολος, pp. 419–20, thinks of Moses, Elijah, Elisha and Ezekiel to fit in this conception of a שׁלִיחַ, but there is no early rabbinic text as a proof of their miracle-working. Most impressive are the traditions of the three keys (of fertility, of resurrection, and of rain) given to a righteous one in *MTeh.* 78.5 and *bBM.* 86b, *bTaan.* 2ab, *bSan.* 113a, *PesR.* 42.7 (*Sim.* 12), *TNeo.* and *TFrag,*[P.V] Gen. 30.22.

84. Noteworthy in the context of miracle-working is the often mentioned *locus classicus* in *mBer.* 5.5, where Hanina ben Dosa is given as an example for a שׁלִיחַ because of his prayer and the consequences of his acting in agency.

85. W. S. Green, 'Palestinian Holy Men', pp. 628–47.

86. Cf. e.g. J. Neusner, 'Story as History in Ancient Judaism. Formulating Fresh Questions', in B. M. Bokser (ed.), *History of Judaism. The Next Ten Years* (BJS, 21; Chico: Scholars Press, 1980), pp. 3–29; J.-M. van Cangh, 'Miracles de rabbins et miracles de Jésus. La tradition sur Honi et Hanina', *RTL* 15 (1984), pp. 28–53.

87. For a detailed analysis of the texts mentioned below, see M. Becker, *Wunder*, pp. 290–337 (on Honi), 337–78 (on Hanina ben Dosa).

88. Cf. G. Vermes, *Jesus the Jew*, pp. 70–71; O. Betz, 'Der Tod des Choni-Onias im Licht der Tempelrolle von Qumran. Bemerkungen zu Josephus *Antiquitates* 14,22-24', in O. Betz, *Jesus, der Messias Israels: Aufsätze zur biblischen Theologie* (WUNT, 42; Tübingen: Mohr Siebeck, 1987), pp. 59–74; W. S. Green, 'Palestinian Holy Men', pp. 638–39; R. Gray, *Prophetic Figures in Late Second Temple Jewish Palestine: The Evidence from Josephus* (New York, Oxford: Oxford University Press, 1993), pp. 145–47; M. Becker, *Wunder*, pp. 294–98.

For that reason, he was asked by the adherents of Hyrcanus II to curse the troops of Aristobulus II at the siege of Jerusalem in the year 65 BCE. This report not only attests the historical relevance of Ḥoni, who was murdered for remaining neutral,[89] but also gives a hint for a closer look at the ambivalence between prayer and curse. The prayer seems to be biased towards the interests of Josephus' presentation of Onias as a reputable person to his Roman and Hellenistic audience.[90]

Facing the rabbinic texts, we find a story that explicitly mentions the rain-miracle of Ḥoni explaining the name-giving act (*mTaan.* 3.8),[91] because he encircles himself and swears not to leave the circle until the right portion of rain has fallen.[92] That this act of forcing God earns a lot of criticism is evident, and after sufficient blessed rain has fallen, Shim'on ben Shetaḥ consequently makes his objection, even if he cannot ban him, because he just acts before God 'like a son who importunes his father, so that he does what he wants.'[93] However, it is very interesting to look at the context, because rabbinic hermeneutics tend to quote this tradition only as an example for a halakhic question, not for the miraculous aspect. This is proved by the Mishna tradition, which interprets the story as an example for the *shofar* not being sounded because of much too much rain.

This picture, painted with a few strokes, confirms that there was a long prehistory of this tradition in the Mishna: building the story, revising, criticising and enlarging it. But not only by reconstructing the highly complex pre-history we can follow the change of the tradition, we can also investigate the ongoing process at the Tosefta (*tTaan.* 2.13/3.1), which does not agree with the compromise represented by the Mishna: quoting the tradition and criticising Ḥoni in form of a paradigm.[94]

---

89. For the background of the death of Onias, cf. O. Betz, 'Tod des Choni-Onias'.

90. The cursing seems remarkable in view of the interpretation of the circle-drawing of Ḥoni in the rabbinic account. Therefore it not only seems to be most likely to think of 'magical' implications in this action – and not only a 'demanding prayer' as Judah Goldin wants to understand his behaviour – cf. J. Goldin, 'On Honi the Circle-Maker: A Demanding Prayer', *HTR* 56 (1963), pp. 233–37 (reprinted in B. L. Eichler, J. H. Tigay [eds.], *Judah Goldin: Studies in Midrash and Related Literature* [Philadelphia, New York, Jerusalem: The Jewish Publication Society, 1988], pp. 331–35). For further discussion, see below and M. Becker, *Wunder*, pp. 309–19.

91. Other stories on Ḥoni (*yTaan.* 3.10 [67a]; *bTaan.* 23a; *MTeh.* 126.1) and his grandchildren (*yTaan.* 3.9 [66d]; *bTaan.* 23ab; *MTeh.* 126.2) cannot be discussed here, although they are fascinating in view of the development of the Ḥoni tradition and the integration of pagan material in rabbinic stories, cf. M. Becker, *Wunder*, pp. 329–37.

92. This act seems to contradict the purpose the story is cited for, because Ḥoni was asked to pray for rain, but this prayer was not successful.

93. It is probable that this objection of Shim'on ben Shetaḥ was an originally independent tradition now connected in the Mishna with the rain-miracle; compare on that account *yMQ.* 3.1 (81d) and *bBer.* 19a.

94. See M. Becker, *Wunder*, pp. 302–5.

This account once more shows the special interests of the Tosefta. Not only does it give a better answer to the question of Mishna-frame, but it also enters into competition with the Mishna account by replacing the Ḥoni-story with a story of the prayer of 'a certain Ḥasid'. Even if the later Talmudim[95] did not follow the Tosefta, because they painted a very harmonistic picture expanding the Mishna up to a happy end, we can observe that there were many conflicts at different stages before and after the account of the Mishna. Nevertheless, one of the major results of this reconstruction consists in the fact that Ḥoni, who is never called a rabbi, neither was a Ḥasid, because this assignment belongs to the argument of the Tosefta, representing the later view of the third century. Just for this reason it seems impossible to reconstruct a Ḥasidic movement up to the first century BCE, including Ḥanina ben Dosa and Jesus as some scholars want to do.[96]

Finally, one other aspect is of interest. In view of the drawing of the circle many problems exist and gave occasion for the conflicting positions,[97] notably for the rabbinization, which at the end has Ḥoni transformed into a rabbinic pious charismatic. Even if there are some 'magical' implications forcing God to do what Ḥoni wants him to do, no tradition – not even the rabbis – placed him outside Jewish self-understanding.

In the case of Ḥanina ben Dosa we are confronted with a much more detailed and expanded tradition. Most of the stories derive from later sources and seem to be younger than the traditions of the early rabbinic sources.[98] These younger traditions show nearly the same picture of a rabbinization to a pious charismatic and Ḥasid – similar to the characterization of Ḥoni.[99] Moreover, looking at the older sources in a critical way also raises many questions about the status of Ḥanina as a rabbi: the description as an agent of the congregation (שליח), as the

95. Cf. *yTaan.* 3.9 (66d-67a); *bTaan.* 23a; for further references, see *TanB.* ואר א 22; *MegTaan. Scholion* 20/22. Adar; (*BerR.* 13.7).

96. Cf. S. Safrai, 'Jesus as Ḥasid' (Hebrew), in *Proceedings of the Tenth World Congress of Jewish Studies, Div. B*, vol. I (Jerusalem: The Magnes Press, 1990), pp. 1–7; S. Safrai, 'Jesus and the Ḥasidim', *Jerusalem Perspective* 42 (1994), pp. 3–22; and Safrai's publications mentioned in note 73; see also K. Wengst, *Jesus zwischen Juden und Christen* (Stuttgart: Kohlhammer, 1999); K. Wengst, 'Der Jesus der Evangelien und die Chassidim in der rabbinischen Literatur', *KuI* 14 (1999), pp. 110–19; G. F. Willems, *Jezus en de Chassidim van zijn Dagen: Een godsdiensthistorische Ontdekking* (Baarn: Ten Have, 1996); for a quite different reconstruction, see Sarfatti, 'Pious Men'.

97. See above note 90.

98. Traditions in the early rabbinic texts are the following stories: Ḥanina's prayer (*mBer.* 5.5 [cf. *tBer.* 3.3 and his healings (from a distance) in *yBer.* 5.5 (9d); *bBer.* 34b and rescuing activities in *bYev.* 121b/*bBQ.* 50a]), his encounter with the reptile (*tBer.* 3.20 [cf. *mBer.* 5.1; *yBer.* 5.1 (9a); *bBer.* 33a; *ShemR.* 3.12; *Tan.* ואר א 4]), three sayings stressing Ḥaninas's wisdom (*mAvot* 3.10f. [cf. *tBer.* 3.3; *ARN.A* 22.1; *ARN.B* 32]), and the end of the 'men of deed' (*mSota* 9.15 [*tSota* 15.5 and parr.]). For an overview of the complete tradition of Ḥanina ben Dosa see M. Becker, *Wunder*, pp. 343–44.

99. See especially the compilation including seven miracle-stories in *bTaan.* 24b-25a and the story about Ḥanina's prevention from using untithed goods in *yDem.* 1.3 (22a).

Mishna-frame interprets Ḥanina and his prayer (*mBer* 5.5), does not fit with the charismatic and individual prayer of the earliest tradition itself.[100] Even if we observe that there are fluid borders between a prayer and some obscure 'magical' acts, the prognostic aspect – Ḥanina knows about the outcome of sick people because of his prayer – makes a difference to the ordinary prayer of a rabbi. Although the integration of Ḥanina into rabbinic society does not seem to be as difficult as that of the Ḥoni-tradition, he was not a rabbi either.

That this integration does not function without any trouble we can see even in the enlargement of the prayer tradition by the stories of both Talmudim (*yBer.* 5.5 [9d]; *bBer.* 34b). There was a controversy about the prognostic aspect and the authority of the charismatic in relation to the rabbis. The authentic character of Ḥanina therefore is not easily described. Perhaps his characterization as the most eminent of the 'men of deed' (*mSot.* 9.15) we can understand best as a popular catchword – even when modern translations, such as 'men of good deed' and 'miracle worker', show the extremes, which in reality belong close together in this characterization.[101]

Very interesting – not only in view of the expansion of the tradition – is the last of the early miracle traditions about the encounter of Ḥanina and the poisonous reptile while he was praying (*tBer.* 3.20).[102] I only want to highlight one point on analogous texts. The nearest parallel for this text we can find is a pagan fragment of Aristotle (*frg.* 191 Rose; *DK* 14,7). There it is said that Pythagoras in Etrury bit the deadly snake that wanted to bite him. The remaining differences should make us cautious of a literal dependence, but this parallel – in the context of many other details in analogous stories – leads directly to the point that the rabbis were not unfamiliar with those pagan traditions and used them for their own purposes.[103]

100. On the 'praying' of Ḥanina, see G. Vermes, 'A Controversial Galilean Saint'; S. Freyne, 'The Charismatic', in J. J. Collins, G. W. E. Nickelsburg (eds.), *Ideal Figures in Ancient Judaism* (SBLSCS, 12, Chico: Scholars Press, 1980), pp. 223–58 (a slightly revised version: S. Freyne, 'Ḥanina ben Dosa. A Galilean Charismatic', in S. Freyne, *Galilee and Gospel. Collected Essays* [WUNT 125], Tübingen: Mohr Siebeck 2000), pp. 132–59 (144–45); B. M. Bokser, 'Wonder-Working and the Rabbinic Tradition: The Case of Ḥanina ben Dosa', *JSJ* 16 (1982), pp. 42–92 (43–46); M. Becker, *Wunder*, pp. 348–55.

101. On the many problems of this characterization, see the discussion in G. Vermes, 'A Controversial Galilean Saint'; S. Freyne, 'Charismatic', pp. 224–27, 244–45; M. Becker, *Wunder*, pp. 368–75; cf. also A. Büchler, *Types*, pp. 81–87; S. Safrai, 'Teaching of Pietists', pp. 15–20.

102. On this story, see G. Vermes, 'A Controversial Galilean Saint'; S. Freyne, 'Charismatic', p. 233; B. M. Bokser, 'Ḥanina ben Dosa'; B. M. Bokser, 'Wonder-Working', pp. 47–51; M. Becker, *Wunder*, pp. 365–68.

103. This seems to be correct even if the immunity against poisonous reptiles is a common topos in ancient literature cf. Mk 16.17-18; Lk. 10.19; Acts 28.3-6; see J. A. Kelhoffer, *Miracle and Mission: The Authentication of Missionaries and Their Message in the Longer Ending of Mark* (WUNT, II.112; Tübingen: Mohr Siebeck, 2000), pp. 340–416.

4. Concluding remarks

Finally, in view of the pragmatics of miracles and miracle stories I want to stress a small number of aspects of the rabbinic traditions. We have seen that the early rabbinic documents have an ambiguous interest in miracle traditions. Directed by the hermeneutical principles of the halakha the rabbis were rather critical – especially in the case of undermining a halakhic argumentation by means of miracle stories. However, that is not the whole truth, because we observed a certain development of their opinions and their texts serve different purposes. Generally, considering the level of the macro-texts, the fact is remarkable that most of the stories we normally characterize as miracle stories are not cited by the rabbis for their original purpose. The stories function as examples for various halakhic aspects, but the rabbis were by no means consistent. This corresponds to several other observations, including the sociological aspect. The rabbis were not a homogeneous group, especially before the end of the Tannaitic period, and therefore we can study conflicts on several levels. They do not seem to be a totally closed group or private party, because we have found a certain integration of pagan material; and there is even an argument for some further Christian influence, which proves a terrain with fluid borders.

Moreover, apart from the deeply-rooted aversions against the proof of the halakha by miracle stories, there exists a genuine interest in miracles, because they are part of the history and object of hope in Jewish self-understanding. Divided into different groups, the extreme supporters of miracles did not overcome the more critical mainstream position among the rabbis, but their opinions had a deep influence on the discussion at various points. At the end of the early rabbinic era there was a certain change in the image of a rabbi. On the one hand a rabbi now fits even better to the conception of a 'charismatic', but on the other hand it is not on account of the miracles that he is a 'charismatic', but the Torah itself bestows all charismatic gifts.

THE FUNCTION OF THE MIRACLE STORIES IN PHILOSTRATUS' *VITA APOLLONII TYANENSIS*

Erkki Koskenniemi

1. Introduction

Most students of the New Testament are familiar with Apollonius of Tyana and perhaps have basic knowledge of the Cappadocian miracle worker, who allegedly lived from the very first years of the first century CE until the reign of Nerva (96–98), but it is certainly useful to repeat the background. We know several Greek writers with the name Philostratus: Some of them[1] belonged to the same family and we have a group of works attributed to them traditionally called the *Corpus Philostrateum*, but it is not easy to attribute an individual work to an individual writer. A long wrestling led to a *communis opinio* in the middle of the 20th century. It is commonly held that the 'second' Philostratus, a man at the court of Severus, wrote almost all the texts and certainly the most important ones, *Vita Apollonii Tyanensis* and *Vitae sophistarum* and the *Letters*, but apparently even *Gymnasticus, Heroicus, Imagines I* and *Nero*.[2] His nephew wrote *Imagines II*. Although there is admittedly reasonable doubt about the authorship of *Gymnasticus, Imagines I, Heroicus* and *Nero* and some smaller works threaten to remain anonymous,[3] the main parts of the *Corpus Philostrateum* were written by Lucius Flavius Philostratus. According to his own words, he belonged to the

---

1.   Philostratus, a historian who wrote an Indian and Phoenician history and is mentioned in Josephus (*Ant.* 10.20-23; 10.220-28, *Apion* 1.144), does not belong among the writers of the *Corpus Philostrateum*.

2.   See W. Schmid, *Der Atticismus in seinen Hauptvertretern 1-5* (Stuttgart: Kohlhammer, 1887–97), pp. 1–11; followed, e.g., by F. Solmsen, 'Philostratos (8-12)', *PRE* 20.1 (1941), pp. 124–77 (124–35); O. Schönberger (ed.), *Philostratos, Die Bilder. Griechisch-deutsch nach Vorarbeiten von Ernst Kalinka* (Tusc; München: Heimeran, 1968), pp. 10–16. On the question, see J.-J. Flinterman, *Power, Paidea and Pythagoreanism: Greek identity, Conceptions of the Relationship between Philosophers and Monarchs and Political Ideas in Philostratus' Life of Apollonius* (Dutch Monographs on Ancient History and Archaeology, 13; Amsterdam: Gieben, 1995), pp. 5–14, and L. de Lannoy's review article 'Le problème de Philostrate: état de la question', *ANRW* II.34.3 (1997), pp. 2362–449 (2412–13).

3.   K. Münscher, a prominent scholar of the *Corpus Philostrateum*, attributed *Heroicus* and *Imagines II* to the 'third' Philostratus; cf. his 'Bericht über die Literatur zur zweiten Sophistik (Rednerische Epideiktik und Belletristik) aus den Jahren 1910-1915', *Bursians Jahresbericht* 1970 (1915), pp. 1–231; and 'Die Philostrate', *PhS* 10 (1907), pp. 467–558. K. Gerth, 'Die Zweite oder Neue Sophistik', *PRES* 8 (1956), pp. 719–82 (764–65), and E. Kalinka, in O. Schönberger,

literary circles of Julia Domna, the wife of the emperor Septimius Severus and the mother of Caracalla and Geta (*Vit. Ap.* 1.3). Two inscriptions attest that he[4] was στρατηγὼν ἐπὶ τὰ ὅπλα in Athens about 200/201–210/211,[5] which means that he was involved with, among other things, cultic matters.[6]

The most famous work of Philostratus is *Vita Apollonii Tyanensis*, Τὰ τοῦ Ἀπολλωνίου τοῦ Τυανέως, which Julia Domna allegedly asked him to write (*Vit. Ap.* 1.3). The work, published apparently between 218 and 222 CE,[7] consists of eight books and describes a philosopher and miracle worker travelling to India and back and meeting personally all Roman emperors from Vespasian to Nerva. Philostratus claims that the work is largely based on a now lost work of Damis, Apollonius' faithful pupil.

Philostratus is never considered a great name in Greek literature, but the golden age of classical studies in Germany dealt extensively with his work, and the new interest in the Second Sophism since Bowersock completes the work of the masters.[8] The interest among theologians has been much stronger since Gillis Wetter and Richard Reitzenstein, when *Vita Apollonii Tyanensis* once again became central to theological discussion, and it has even opened new views on the work. Dietmar Esser tried to define the genre of the work (1969),[9] Gerd Petzke

Philostratos, pp. 10–16, follow his view. Yet according to G. Anderson, it is not possible to say who wrote *Nero, Imagines I, Gymnasticus* and *Heroicus* (*Philostratus. Biography and Belles Lettres in the Third Century A.D.* [London, Sydney and Dover, NH: Croom Helm, 1986], pp. 241–53, 268, 272), but according to A. Beschorner (*Philostratus, Flavius, Helden und Heroen, Homer und Caracalla. Übersetzung, Kommentar und Interpretationen zum Heroikos des Flavios Philostratos* [Bari: Levante, 1999], Pinakes 5:2) the final answer is the 'second' Philostratus.

    4.   On the identification, see L. De Lannoy, 'Le problème', pp. 2385–86.

    5.   See G. Anderson, *Philostratus*, 6; J.-J. Flinterman, *Power, Paidea and Pythagoreanism*, pp. 16–17, and L. De Lannoy, 'Le problème', p. 2383.

    6.   On this office, see G. Anderson, *Philostratus*, p. 6.

    7.   The work is not dedicated to Julia Domna, which indicates that she was already dead (218). Moreover, the work was apparently written before Elagabalus's death – see E. Koskenniemi, *Der philostrateische Apollonios* (CHL 94; Helsinki: Societas Scientiarum Fennica, 1991), p. 43.

    8.   The most important studies after the article of E. Meyer ('Apollonius von Tyana und die Biographie des Philostratos', *Hermes* 52 [1917], pp. 370–424) and the article of F. Solmsen, 'Philostratos (pp. 8–12)', were written by W. Speyer ('Zum Bild des Apollonios von Tyana bei Heiden und Christen', *JAC* 17 [1974], pp. 47–63), E. L. Bowie ('Apollonius of Tyana: Tradition and reality', *ANRW* II.16.2 [Berlin, New York: De Gruyter, 1978], pp. 1652–99), G. Anderson, *Philostratus*, and M. Dzielska (*Apollonios of Tyana in Legend and History* [PRSA, 10; Roma: L'Erma di Bretschneider, 1986]). J.-J. Flinterman's book mentioned above (*Power, Paidea and Pythagoreanism*) is a very learned and important contribution to the research. He represents, on several questions, a view differing from mine, and generally sees more ways to the historical Apollonius than many other scholars. Like many earlier studies, my book mentioned above (E. Koskenniemi, *Der philostrateische Apollonios*) abandons the search for the historical Apollonius and studies the Philostratean tradition, i.e. the ideals and intentions of the writer.

    9.   D. Esser, *Formgeschichtliche Studien zur hellenistischen und zur frühchristlichen Literatur unter besonderer Berücksichtigung der vita Apollonii des Philostrat und der Evangelien*

applied the form-critical method to *Vit. Ap.* (1970),[10] and I tried to examine the way the scholars have used Apollonius in the study of the New Testament (1994).[11]

It is very difficult to define the function of the stories: It was once common to take the stories of the *Vit. Ap.* uncritically and compare them with the stories in the Gospels because scholars thought that Apollonius was the nearest parallel to Jesus with his teaching and miracles. This was not the way of the German scholars of the late 19th and early 20th centuries, who were well aware of the problems involved in such comparison, but it was the method of many eager New Testament scholars who were keen to make the religio-historical method work, but had lost contact with the classical texts.[12] Happily, the critical approach to Philostratus' work has returned, even to New Testament scholarship.[13] In seeking the function of the stories, we must realise that we have to move on three levels, 1) to study Philostratus and his work, 2) to study Apollonius' miracles in the non-Philostratean tradition and 3) to ask what can be said about the reputation of the historical Apollonius.

2. The Function of the Stories
a. Philostratus
The easiest task is to study the function that Philostratus gives to the stories in *Vita Apollonii Tyanensis*. Methodologically it means that the redaction-critical study of the New Testament is *mutatis mutandis* adapted to the study of *Vit. Ap.*, and

---

(Dissertation: Bonn, 1969). Esser was not yet aware of the plausible suggestion that Xenophon's *Cyropaedia* was a model for Philostratus' work (E. L. Bowie, 'Apollonius of Tyana', p. 1665; G. Anderson, *Philostratus*, pp. 231–32).

10. G. Petzke, *Die Traditionen über Apollonius of Tyana und das Neue Testament* (SCHNT, 1; Leiden: Brill, 1970). The work was severely criticised in reviews by Speyer (G. Petzke, 'Die Traditionen von Apollonios von Tyana und das Neue Testament' *JAC* 16 [1973], pp. 133–35) and E. L. Bowie, 'Apollonius of Tyana', p. 1653, and the criticism is justified – see E. Koskenniemi, *Apollonios von Tyana in der neutestamentlichen Exegese: Forschungsbericht und Weiterführung der Diskussion* (WUNT, II.61; Tübingen: Mohr Siebeck, 1994), p. 56.

11. E. Koskenniemi, *Apollonios von Tyana*.

12. Maybe the best example is the role Ludwig Bieler's book played in New Testament scholarship (*ΘΕΙΟΣ ΑΝΗΡ. Das Bild des 'Göttlichen Menschen' in Spätantike und Frühchristentum* [Wien: Höfels, 1935–36]). Bieler's book was a collection of material from various periods and various continents inspired by the contemporary religio-historical study. He collected classical material, but even Christian, Lithaunian and American stories, to illuminate his Platonic view on the life and destiny of divine men. The pattern he constructed mainly from the *Vit. Ap.* and the Gospels was applied to the study of the Gospels by New Testament scholars who did not realise that they used a lot of gospel material to illuminate the background of the Gospels. For a summary of Bieler's study and its impact on the research, see Koskenniemi, 'Apollonius of Tyana – a typical θεῖος ἀνήρ?', *JBL* 117 (1998), pp. 455–67 (455–60).

13. See, e.g., J. P. Meier, *A Marginal Jew* (New York, London, Toronto, Sydney, Auckland: Doubleday, 1991, 1994), vol. 2, pp. 576–81; H.-J. Klauck, *The Religious Context of Early Christianity: A Guide to Graeco-Roman Religions* (SNTW; Edinburgh: T&T Clark, 2000), pp. 168–77.

it is not difficult, although many essential elements of the original methodology do not exist. Although we only have some scarce non-Philostratean sources, if his main source Damis is considered his own invention,[14] we know quite well the world and the circles he lived in, we can study the literary tradition in the works on famous men and conventions known to Philostratus. Above all, we know his wide production and it seems to be easy to define his own point of view on different themes. The non-Philostratean tradition on Apollonius, although scarce, helps to illuminate the intentions of the writer.

A first look at Philostratus' work gives the impression that he plays with form and neglects the content. His Apollonius personally rejects wine, meat and bloody sacrifices, but jovially permits them for his friends (*Vit. Ap.* 2.7; 1.31-32). He understands all human languages and even that of the birds (1.19; 1.20), but needs an interpreter in India (3.28). Many inconsistencies relate to important religious topics: Apollonius flatly denies that gods can have sexual intercourse or children with men (6.40, similarly in *Her.* 25.10), but he is himself a son of Zeus (*Vit. Ap.* 1.6). The entire story about Damis is an obvious fiction, understood as such even by his readers.[15] However, though Philostratus' work is fictive, it does not mean that he did not want to be taken seriously.[16] Although Philostratus seems to play with stories and with the literary form without any deeper purpose, a study of his work defines the areas he never writes lightly upon and the biases occurring always consistently. They are not philosophical or religious topics, but they touch upon his view of the role of Greek culture and the past, and of the role of the philosopher at the ruler's court.[17] Consequently, it can be expected that the miracle stories may have different functions, less or more serious.

Philostratus' work is full of miraculous stories, especially when he describes Apollonius' trip to India. Apollonius sees different παράδοξα, such as men five cubits long, women both black and white, different fabulous animals and even the chains of Prometheus. He follows a common and well-known road in Greek and Latin literature: Herodotus had already inserted good stories among serious history (e.g., 4.2.7-10), and even Caesar wrote on unicorns in Gaul (*Gall.* 6.26-28) between his *res gestae*. The miraculous stories belonged to the tradition and Josephus, for example, tells about the miraculous sand of Lake Beleus (*War* 2.189-191), and about a healing but very dangerous herb (*baaras*) killing the collectors (*War* 7.180-185). These stories were especially popular in the second

---

14. On Damis and other sources Philostratus claims to have used, see below pp. 78–79.

15. See below pp. 78–79.

16. Cf. J. A. Francis ('Truthful Fiction: New Questions to Old Answers on Philostratus' *Life of Apollonius*', *American Journal of Philology* 119 [1998], pp. 419–41), who criticizes the older view that Philostratus' work is either fiction or a serious work. Most of its first readers apparently considered it both a fiction and a serious work.

17. See E. Koskenniemi, *Der philostrateische Apollonios*, pp. 31–57. This is the main theme of Flinterman's book and I agree with him on the main lines concerning Philostratus' view, although not on the analysis of the sources.

century CE. Phlegon, the freedman of Hadrian, wrote exciting stories about ghosts, Aelianus wrote his *Variae historiae* and Favorinus wrote some 24 books on *mirabilia*.[18]

Philostratus was aware of a traditional function of miraculous stories, to simply entertain the reader without any deeper purpose, and it is understandable that a lot of miraculous material is compatible with this tradition. The intention is obvious in the passage dealing with the Indian sages. There was no need to tell them anything because they already knew the names and all about the lives of the visitors (*Vit. Ap.* 3.12). They were rulers over rain and winds as Aeolus once was (3.14), and when they prayed, they were raised two cubits into the air (3.17). They, of course, spoke excellent Greek and were able to solve the traditional problems of the Homeric myths and Greek philosophy (3.17). They were sought as healers and they helped: someone with uneven legs was healed, a blind man got his sight and a lame hand became healthy again (3.39). The sages could also expel a demon who fell in love with a young boy by sending a threatening letter (3.38). Consequently, Apollonius even participates in a dialogue with Achilles' soul and tells afterwards the real history of the Trojan war (4.12, 16). It is easy to see that Apollonius and the Indian philosophers are mostly only Philostratus' tools to tell stories and entertain his readers, and only a few of them took his stories seriously. However, this does not exclude other, more serious functions for the stories.

Philostratus did not write only to entertain. He was himself a philosopher at a ruler's court and he saw, for example, the terrible day on which Caracalla let the soldiers tear his brother and co-regent Geta from his mother's arms to be slain, and started his own rule using terror and informers. Philostratus relates how the teacher of the sons condemned the act (*Vit. Soph.* 607), and though he personally shared the view in a strong letter (*Ep.* 72), he was certainly realistic enough not to give it to the emperor.[19] The climax of *Vit. Ap.* is Apollonius' trip to Rome to meet Domitian, who filled the empire with informers, hated philosophers generally, especially Apollonius,[20] and accused him of, for example, revolutionary aims, sorcery and having an Arcadian boy sacrificed in magical rites. Many of Apollonius' miraculous deeds serve this aim. Domitian puts him in chains, shaving his head (7.34) and stripping him naked to destroy his power and to take away

---

18. On the growing tendency to write miraculous stories, see B. A. van Groningen, 'General literary tendencies in the second century A.D.', *Mnemosyne* 4.18 (1965), pp. 41–56 (51–52).

19. G. Anderson, *Philostratus*, p. 6.

20. It cannot be ruled out that the historical Apollonius had troubles with the rulers as many philosophers had. In any case, Apollonius' letters to Domitian (*Ep. Apoll.* 20-21) attest a clearly more positive view of the emperor than the picture drawn in *Vit. Ap.* The philosopher could send advice to the ruler (see E. Koskenniemi, *Der philostrateische Apollonios*, pp. 35–36). J.-J. Flinterman, *Power, Paidea and Pythagoreanism*, pp. 145–47, attributes some of the material included in *Vit. Ap.* to the pseudonymous work of Damis. However, he does not examine Philostratus' entire work thoroughly enough and overlooks the similarity with the author's other works. Moreover, if the chronology of Maximus is correct, Apollonius was almost a hundred years old when Domitian was murdered (see below p. 80).

his secret amulets (8.3), and orders that he change himself to water, an animal or a tree (7.34). When only Damis is present, Apollonius shows himself able to free his leg from the chain but he puts it back (7.38). He defends himself in court with conventional methods, but after having won the case he miraculously disappears and re-appears in Dicaiarchia (8.5, 12). Far away in Ephesus, he sees that Stephanus murders the emperor in Rome, and accepts it (8.25-26). All these miracles and several others serve Philostratus' goal: to show that a philosopher stands above the tyrants. He followed a strong literary tradition,[21] and was personally acquainted with troubles between rulers and philosophers.

Although many of the miraculous stories are only entertaining or are linked with Philostratus' political view, some of them deserve special attention.

The stories about the young Apollonius in the temples connect the man with miraculous prophecy and knowledge. These traits may be pre-Philostratean and they are treated below. Even Philostratus makes his Apollonius a friend of gods and a reformer of cults. Philostratus deals with his prophecies in an interesting way: on the one hand, they are emphasized and underline Apollonius' special status among men. However, on the other hand, he seems to play down the miraculous, claiming that the ability to prophesy was nothing more than wisdom (4.44). Origen observed Philostratus' inconsistency:[22] Philostratus relates that Apollonius rejected the claims that he was a sorcerer with the fact that he could be bound and did not free himself from the chains (7.34), but later did free his leg from the chains to show that Domitian was not able to bind him (7.38). According to 'Damis', precisely this deed attested his superhuman character (see even 8.13). According to Flinterman, the reason for the tension is that Philostratus is at odds with his sources and tries to play down Apollonius' reputation of being a magician.[23] However, the best way to downplay Apollonius' bad reputation would have

---

21. On this tradition see E. Koskenniemi, *Der philostrateische Apollonios*, pp. 31–44; J.-J. Flinterman, *Power, Paidea and Pythagoreanism*, pp. 165–69.

22. Origen, *Adv. Hieroclem* 35.

23. This is the main reason why Flinterman still supposes that Philostratus indeed used a pseudonymous writing of Damis. According to him, 'a refutation of my argument for the reality of the Damis source requires the following assumption: that Philostratus attributed a report which was too obscurantist for his taste to a source which he had invented himself, as well as commenting on it in order to add credibility to his own fiction. Until ancient parallels can be adduced for a procedure of this kind, it is difficult to contradict the argument of a tension between reports which are attributed to the Damis source, on the one hand, and the attitude of the author of the *Vit. Ap.* to magic/goeteia, on the other' (*Power, Paidea and Pythagoreanism*, p. 232). Philostratus 'rigorously refuses the application of the title *magos* to the sage of Tyana' (*Power, Paidea and Pythagoreanism*, p. 72). It is true that Philostratus avoids the word and is keen to defend Apollonius against the charges of sorcery, but it is easy to see that he is inconsistent in *Vit. Ap.* as well as elsewhere in his production. Flinterman observes that Philostratos even elsewhere defends sophists against the charges of *goeteia* (*Vit. Soph.* 523 and 590; J.-J. Flinterman, *Power, Paidea and Pythagoreanism*, pp. 64–65), but overlooks the fact that Philostratus shows an interest in *mageia* (see below). There is thus a clear tension, but it is not between Philostratus and a 'Damis source', but in Philostratus' thought – typical of his own era.

been to simply drop some stories, but the writer preferred to tell them, drawn either from the sources on Apollonius or other traditions. Philostratus thus defended his hero against the charges that he was a sorcerer, but did not want to eliminate all miraculous skills, and this has led him into inconsistency. His apologetic attitude is obvious from the very beginning of the work (1.2) and following Apollonius' mighty deeds (e.g., 5.12; 7.39; cf. 8.7, 8). However, people in Philostratus' own time were very fond of miracles and found them entertaining, and Philostratus did not want to exclude such stories from his work. On the contrary, Diogenes Laertius, for example, liked to tell about the miracles of the greatest philosophers,[24] and Philostratus tried to beat them all with his Apollonius. He defended Apollonius by comparing him to Anaxagoras and Socrates and other wise men accused of godless teaching or magic, but he is not willing to eliminate the exciting stories supporting the critical voices. His Apollonius seeks the wisdom of magicians in Babylon (1.26), and finds treasures, an activity, which Lucian among others attributes to sorcerers (*Alex.* 5). Elsewhere he accepted astronomy, if it did not lead too far (*Gymn.* 1), but he was apparently not able to define what this meant. Philostratus does not reject μάγοι or μάγων θεολογία (*Vit. Soph.* 490; 494; *Ep.* 8). Philostratus has two intentions difficult to combine: he tried to defend Apollonius against the charges that he was a magician[25] and he tells stories to show his extraordinary ability. As Anderson states, Philostratus tried to sit on two chairs,[26] but he only followed the climate of his time which was fond of miracle stories.

A common ambivalence is thus present here: on the one hand, esoteric wisdom and even magical skills were highly appreciated; on the other hand, a part of magic was hated and even severely punished, and only a few were able to draw the line between the permissible and the forbidden.[27] The apocryphal acts of the apostles show how the method of describing famous men developed in Graeco-Roman culture.

Some rather isolated stories have awakened perhaps the greatest interest among scholars. Apollonius and the Indian philosophers struggle with demons and expel them (*Vit. Ap.* 2.4; 3.38; 4.4, 10, 20, 25). The Indians also act as healers (3.39; 6.42) and Apollonius revives a dead – or seemingly dead – girl (4.45). He eliminates a satyr, which is killing women in a village (6.27), and is even able to help

24. Diogenes Laertius writes on the extraordinary abilities of, e.g., Pythagoras (8.3), Democritus (9.34) and Empedocles (1.114; 6.68-70).
25. This is traditionally considered a central bias in Philostratus' work; see E. L. Bowie, 'Apollonius of Tyana'; D. H. Raynor, 'Moeragenes and Philostratus', *CQ* 34 (1984), pp. 222–26, and M. Dzielska, *Apollonios of Tyana*, pp. 91–92.
26. G. Anderson, *Philostratus*, pp. 138–39.
27. Philo offers a good example on the ambivalence: he accepts the 'true magic' (ἡ ἀληθὴς μαγική) which studies nature scientifically and is practiced by kings in Persia. Another art of magic is κακοτεχνία, which is the way of the charlatans and lower people and it deals with charms and incantations. It is rejected by Philo (*Spec. Leg.* 3.100-03; *Prob.* 74), and he actually considers it a religious duty to kill those who exercise it.

a man to find a treasure (6.39). He left the world in a miraculous way (8.30) and appeared after his departure to a young philosopher (8.31). Although we do not know which stories were connected with Apollonius before Philostratus, the writer apparently has taken a part of this material from the local traditions on Apollonius.[28] The function of these stories varies greatly, from entertainment to support for Philostratus' own political view.

Werner Kahl developed a useful tool for the study of the miracle stories. He tried to separate the different roles in the stories and asked who is the 'Bearer of the Numinous Power' (= BNP), actually performing or causing the miracle; who is the 'Mediator of the Numinous Power' (=MNP), used as the agent of the BNP; and who is the 'Petitioner of the Numinous Power' (=PNP), asking the BNP to perform the miracle.[29] In Philostratus' work Apollonius admittedly sometimes mediates the help of gods to people coming to the temples (esp. 1.9). In any case, the most important role attributed to him (and to the Indian philosophers) is that he is an independent miracle worker, who did not need to ask for the help of the gods. Especially the story about the leg freed from the chain and put back leads Philostratus (using Damis as his masque) to emphasize the art of the deed attesting Apollonius' divine nature: Apollonius did not need a sacrifice or a prayer to make his miracle. In Kahl's terminology, the Philostratean Apollonius is a 'Bearer of the Numinous Power', which clearly separates him from, for example, most of the Hebrew miracle workers in the Old Testament, as well as in the stories of them retold in early Jewish literature. These miracles are specifically related to emphasize Apollonius' special nature. Philostratus states that Apollonius was honoured as a god (1.31) and that a shrine was erected after his earthly life (8.31). That did not mean a lot: the early church fathers mocked deified men by referring to Antinous, the boy Hadrian loved and declared a god after his sudden death.

But did Philostratus use the stories of Apollonius' extraordinary nature to serve missionary purposes? Philostratus certainly had a 'mission', but it hardly had anything to do with Apollonius. His Pythagorean philosopher is inconsistent[30] and Philostratus has little interest in Pythagoreanism in the rest of his works. Philostratus' strongest bias is national and political, not religious,[31] and consequently the miracle stories do not support a religious agenda or reform.

Philostratus thus writes of miracles to entertain his readers and, like many of his contemporaries, he likes exciting stories enough to be inconsistent. He also uses the miracles to support his own view of rulers and philosophers. He certainly has also preserved traditions predating his work.

---

28. See J.-J. Flinterman, *Power, Paidea and Pythagoreanism*, pp. 67–68.

29. W. Kahl, *New Testament Miracle Stories in their Religious-Historical Setting: A Religionsgeschichtlice Comparison from a Structural Perspective* (FRLANT, 163; Göttingen: Vandenhoeck & Ruprecht, 1994), pp. 62–65.

30. Philostratus' 'Pythagorean' philosopher pleads sometimes for good monistic views (see esp. *Vit. Ap.* 3.34). M. Dzielska recognizes middle Platonic views behind Philostratus' traditions (*Apollonios of Tyana*, pp. 129–51).

31. See even A. Billault, *L' Univers de Philostrate* (Collection Latomus, 252; Bruxelles: Latomus, 2000), p. 120.

b. The Pre-Philostratean Tradition

A much more difficult task than studying Philostratus' ideology is tracing the function of the miracle stories in the pre-Philostratean tradition. Philostratus mentions his sources, but very few consider him always reliable. Almost everything comes to us through Philostratus, which increases the difficulty. We do have a collection of Apollonius' letters, but, although some of them may be genuine, many of them are forged, and some of them are obviously written by Philostratus.[32] He also claims to have used Apollonius' work on sacrifices, but says that he had never seen a work on divination mentioned by others (*Vit. Ap.* 3.41). Eusebius quotes a short fragment of Περὶ θυσιῶν (*Praep. ev.* 4.13.1) and there is no compelling reason to doubt the authenticity. At any rate, it seems to be independent of Philostratus. Philostratus claims that he had used ὑπομνημονεύματα of Damis, but very few scholars believe this. Either he used a pseudonym as, e.g., Speyer and Flinterman believe,[33] or more probably invented his own source, and Damis is only a masque of Philostratus.[34] However, the works of Maximus of Aegae and Moeragenes, which Philostratus allegedly used (*Vit. Ap.* 1.3), apparently really existed (see below).

It is thus not easy to distinguish the pre-Philostratean tradition from the Philostratean redaction. Philostratus has invented many of his sources and although he certainly had real sources, we do not know how he used them. However, it seems to be virtually certain that two views on Apollonius existed before Philostratus.

1) Philostratus states that he used as his source a work of Maximus of Aeagae relating everything Apollonius did in Aegae (1.3). Because the work of Damis is considered a fiction, many scholars also doubt the existence of Maximus's book.[35] However, Fritz Graf argued convincingly for the existence of the book and could even reconstruct its main contents.[36] It dealt with the youth of Apollonius when he was living in the temples in intimate contact with gods and able to foresee different events (1.7-12). Apollonius' letters are always a problematic source and especially the ones quoted by Philostratus, but many of them support the view that Apollonius had the reputation of a religious teacher in the pre-Philostratean tradition *(Ep. Apoll.* 26, 65-67). Even the fragment of his work Περὶ θυσιῶν is

---

32. The letters are edited and commented on by R. J. Penella (*The Letters of Apollonius of Tyana* [MnS1 ρ, 56; Leiden: Brill, 1979). He also asks the question of authenticity, but there are no easy answers.

33. See ' /. Speyer, 'Zum Bild des Apollonios', pp. 48–53; J.-J. Flinterman, *Power, Paidea and Pythagoreanism*, pp. 79–88.

34. E. Meyer, 'Apollonius von Tyana'. The survey of the arguments in E. Koskenniemi, *Der philostrateische Apollonios*, pp. 9–15.

35. E. Meyer, 'Apollonius von Tyana', 402; F. Solmsen, 'Philostratos (8-12)', pp. 151–52; V. Mumprecht (ed.), *Philostratos, Das Leben des Apollonios von Tyana*. (Tusc: München and Zürich, 1983), pp. 990–91.

36. F. Graf, 'Maximos von Aigai: Ein Beitrag zur Ueberlieferung über Apollonios von Tyana', *JAC* 27–28 (1984–85), pp. 65–73; see even E. L. Bowie, 'Apollonius of Tyana', pp. 1684–85, and G. Anderson, *Philostratus*, p. 169.

compatible with this view. Philostratus also claims to have used the oral tradition in the temples and there is no reason to doubt him. The picture of a religious reformer is strongly expanded in Philostratus' work, making Apollonius a reformer of cults in various cities, even in Rome. He is rejected from some temples because some people considered him a sorcerer, but Philostratus strongly defends him (*Vit. Ap.* 5.19).

It is not easy to define the role and the function of the miracles in this tradition, but Graf rightly claimed that the reputation of a magician was not present in it.[37] It does, of course, not exclude his abilities to prophesy or to know about the lives of the people visiting the temple, or even give effective advice in Asclepius' temple (1.9–11). Apparently, it belonged to a very late stage of the tradition that Apollonius was honoured as god. The first certain proof of Apollonius having divine status is that Caracalla dedicated a shrine to him (*Vit. Ap.* 8.31; Cass. Dio 77.18.4).

It is difficult to find a parallel to the picture of Apollonius drawn in these parts of the tradition. He was considered to have an intimate relationship to gods, who revealed to him the future and helped him to see what others could not see. According to Josephus, Egyptian priests were excellent at prophecy (*Ant.* 2.205), and although we cannot name them, they certainly were not the only people in temples with such a reputation.

2) Philostratus mentions the work of Moeragenes, which certainly existed and was known to Origen (*Cels.* 6.4). The title of the work (Τὰ ᾽Απολλωνίου τοῦ Τυανέως μάγου καὶ φιλοσόφου ἀπομνημονεύματα) attests the tradition that Apollonius had something to do with magical skills. Philostratus rejects Moeragenes' work, considering it negative, and several scholars have followed the view that it was critical of Apollonius.[38] The view is, however, hardly correct, since the title calls the man 'magician and philosopher'.[39] It means that the magical skills are an essential part of wisdom and that they are not rejected, but proudly presented.

The view of Apollonius having magical skills is also strongly attested elsewhere in the non-Philostratean tradition. Although magic is a theme in only a few of the more than one hundred letters, some of them defend him against the charges. Letters 16 and 17 may be representative: 'Apollonius' rejects only one part of magic and proudly preserves the rest in a debate with Euphrates, a rival philosopher. Lucian offers a very negative picture of Apollonius: he only needed to mention that Apollonius was the teacher of Alexander of Abonuteichus to show Alexander in a very negative light (*Alex.* 5). Cassius Dio knew the story, also related by Philostratus, that Apollonius 'saw' the murder of Domitian although the emperor was killed in Rome and Apollonius was in Ephesus (Cassius Dio 67.18; cf. *Vit.*

37. F. Graf, 'Maximos von Aigai', p. 72.
38. E. Meyer, 'Apollonius von Tyana', p. 393; F. Solmsen, 'Philostratos (8-12)', pp. 141–43; V. Mumprecht *Philostratos*, pp. 990–94; G. Anderson, *Philostratus*, pp. 299–300.
39. E. L. Bowie, 'Apollonius of Tyana', p. 1673; D. H. Raynor, 'Moeragenes and Philostratus'; M. Dzielska, *Apollonios of Tyana*, pp. 85–127.

Ap. 8.26). There is no doubt that these kind of stories also circulated in the oral tradition collected by Philostratus.

What was the function of the miracles in this part of the non-Philostratean tradition? Some ancient writers (Lucian, Origen) unequivocally use his bad reputation to attack Apollonius: he was a magician to be avoided by an honest man. However, the other part of the tradition proudly presents these skills, and Moeragenes is the best example of this view. Esoteric wisdom and the ability to produce all kinds of miracles with all kinds of tricks were not rejected, and the stories were eagerly retold. The paradoxographical literature referred to above shows the strongest interest in entertaining stories. Lucian could laugh at such stories and parody them in his *Philopseudes*, but they were an essential part of the scene in the late second century and became more and more popular. It is easy to find models for Apollonius' reputation. Magical skills were always exercised by professionals, and although we do not know their names, the figures appear already, for example, in Homer, Sophocles and Theocritus.[40] But all professionals did not practice skills forbidden by the laws: Tiberius relied on Thrasyllus (Tacitus, *Ann.* 6.20-21), Otho on Ptolemaeus (*Hist.* 1.22) and Sulla on a Chaldean (Plutarch, *Sulla* 37) as did Sergius Paulus on Bar-Jesus according to Luke in Acts 13.

Philostratus admittedly rejects Moeragenes' work, but it is precisely in this aspect that he is inconsistent and approves what he elsewhere rejects. It is a *communis opinio* that late antiquity was a period of magic,[41] and the Jewish[42] as well as the Christian tradition followed the stream. The pre-Philostratean tradition offered two ways to go and Philostratus took both. This literate man with his Apollonius is a good example of the *Zeitgeist*, but the traditions were not his own invention.

c. The Historical Apollonius?

The most interesting level is almost impossible to deal with: what was the function of the miracles in the life of the historical Apollonius of Tyana? The question must be asked although the prospects for an answer are understandably not very good after everything said above. There is even no consensus on the years Apollonius lived. If he was young in the first decades of the first century CE, he was hardly active when Domitian was murdered in 96, as Philostratus states.[43]

---

40. See E. Koskenniemi, *Apollonios von Tyana*, p. 224.

41. See E. Koskenniemi, *Apollonios von Tyana*, pp. 224–25. We know several Gentile miracle workers from the middle of the second century CE on, but only a few from before that period, see E. Koskenniemi, *Apollonios von Tyana*, pp. 208–17.

42. A good example is how the tradition about the miracles of Ḥanina ben Dosa slowly grows up. Mishna and Tosefta both contain only one miracle story, the Palestinian Talmud 3 and the Babylonian 11 (S. Freyne, 'The Charismatic', in J. J. Collins and G. W. E. Nickelsburg [eds], *Ideal Figures in Ancient Judaism: Profiles and Paradigms* [SBLSCS 12; Chico: Scholars Press, 1980], pp. 223–58 [p. 241–242]). M. Becker lists the miracle stories in the early rabbinic sources (*Wunder und Wundertäter im frührabbinischen Judentum: Studien zum Phänomen und seiner Überlieferung im Horizont von Magie und Dämonismus* [WUNT, II.144]; Tübingen: Mohr Siebeck, 2002.

43. M. Dzielska states her view on Philostratus' work very clearly: 'Moreover, I consider this material useful and historically valuable only when it finds its confirmation in other literary and historical sources' (*Apollonios of Tyana*, p. 15). According to her, Apollonius lived about

The framework into which Philostratus puts most of Apollonius' miracles is, of course, unhistorical. Very few believe that Apollonius ever visited India,[44] and to use Jarchas, the leader of the Indian philosophers, as Theissen and Gnilka do, to illuminate the atmosphere in the first century is simply wrong.[45] The philosopher at the ruler's court, Philostratus, made Apollonius the most important man of the first century, and even used his miracles to achieve this end. Apollonius did not make Vespasian an emperor in Egypt, he was not the patron of Titus, and he was not the main opponent of Domitian and did not disappear from his court, and was not a close friend of Nerva. But the non-Philostratean tradition offers two different reputations for Apollonius. What can be said about the historical Apollonius and the role of his miracles? Was he a reformer of the cult and a religious teacher in the temples, or was he a magician practicing arts suspect in the view of the educated members of society and thrown out of the temples? Or can these views be combined?

Was Apollonius a religious reformer teaching in the temples? Maybe he was, but it is very difficult to say what he really taught and what he did not. The sources are again problematic. Even in some non-Philostratean sources, Apollonius speaks about sacrifices, obviously accepting them (*Ep. Apoll.* 65–67). However, in others he rejects all sacrifices (*Ep. Apoll.* 26), and the work Περὶ θυσιῶν represents precisely this view.[46] Everything in *Vit. Ap.* is apparently merged with the cult of *Sol invictus*, popular before the reform of Elagabalus.[47]

A strong pre-Philostratean tradition says that Apollonius was a master of skills considered problematic. It is very difficult to define which parts of this tradition had something to do with the historical Apollonius and which were connected with him later. According to Dzielska, the letters to Euphrates were an early attempt to exonerate Apollonius from his – historically correct – reputation as a magician.[48]

40–120 CE (*Apollonios of Tyana*, pp. 32–37). Most scholars believe that Maximus has dated the early years of the man correctly (see E. Koskenniemi, *Apollonios von Tyana*, pp. 170–71). This should lead to some scepticism regarding the events during Domitian's rule, especially as only a few letters tell about contacts between Apollonius and Domitian.

44. J.-J. Flinterman sees a nucleus of the travels in the book of Damis (*Power, Paidea and Pythagoreanism*, pp. 101–6). It is obvious that Philostratus' work contains good knowledge on, for example, Taxila, and no one can exclude the possibility that Apollonius travelled to India, but Philostratus had enough material for the story even without the Damis source.

45. See G. Theissen, *Urchristliche Wundergeschichten: Ein Beitrag zur formgeschichtlichen Erforschung der synoptischen Evangelien* (SNT, 8; Gütersloher Verlagshaus, 1974) p. 273, and J. Gnilka, *Jesus von Nazareth: Botschaft und Geschichte* (HTKNTSup, 3. Freiburg, Basel, Wien: Herder, 1990), pp. 120–21.

46. R. J. Penella, *Letters of Apollonius*, p. 105, tries to remove the inconsistency in the tradition by supposing that Apollonius rejected all sacrifices except the bloodless ones to the supreme god. However, the letters mentioned do not criticize the bloody sacrifices and the priests in Olympia in *Ep. Apoll.* 26 did not sacrifice to Apollonius' supreme god.

47. See E. Koskenniemi, *Der philostrateische Apollonios*, pp. 76–79.

48. M. Dzielska, *Apollonios of Tyana*, pp. 90–91.

All the same, we have very scant evidence on his followers, who would have tried to exonerate their master and collected and preserved the tradition.[49] A great part of the tradition is apparently adapted to Apollonius later, although the roots may lie in the first century. But who knows how strong they are?

Many works and articles on Apollonius contain a passage separating fact and fiction. Maybe this article has shown that such a task is very difficult and apparently impossible. We are able to study the function of the miracle stories in Philostratus' work, and can trace some pre-Philostratean traits in the tradition. However, the study of the historical Apollonius seems even here virtually impossible. Apollonius had, very early, two reputations, which can only partly be combined. Graf, for example, takes the first and considers Περὶ θυσιῶν authentic, whereas Dzielska takes the second and considers the reputation as a sorcerer original. Only guesswork is left. A man declaring all sacrifices obsolete (Περὶ θυσιῶν) cannot explain both traditions, because he hardly had much to do with magical rites. An influential religious teacher brought up in Asclepius' temple (as Maximus says), perhaps practising healing outside the temple and later at odds with some temples, maybe could explain both traditions, but it is hard to go beyond speculations.

3. Conclusion

Seeking the function of the miracle stories in Philostratus' *Vita Apollonii Tyanensis* entails: 1) studying Philostratus and his work, 2) studying Apollonius' miracles in the non-Philostratean tradition and 3) asking what can be said about the reputation of the historical Apollonius.

The easiest task is to study the function Philostratus himself gives to the stories, many of which are pre-Philostratean but not necessarily connected with Apollonius before *Vita Apollonii*. They serve to simply entertain the readers who are fond of miraculous stories, and the author gets into difficulties with what is permissible and what is not. However, the stories are also part of a serious message: a philosopher stands above a tyrant, and even an overwhelming power cannot defeat him. Philostratus also relates that Apollonius was deified, but the first certain evidence is the shrine erected by the Severian dynasty, and there are no signs of any missionary functions in the stories in Philostratus' work.

The study of the pre-Philostratean traditions shows that Apollonius already had two contrasting reputations before *Vita Apollonii* and consequently even the function of the miracle stories was different. First, especially the best-known stories about Apollonius and the work of Moeragenes attest that he was considered a magician, and although Philostratus partly attacks this view, he himself strengthens it. But secondly, especially the work of Maximus and the fragments of Περὶ θυσιῶν present Apollonius as a religious teacher in a way which leaves

---

49. Petzke especially suggested a process of tradition comparable to the traditions about Jesus, but there is no evidence of a long chain of tradents between the historical Apollonius and Philostratus (see E. Koskenniemi, *Apollonios von Tyana*, pp. 51–56).

very little room for magical rites, and the only miraculous trait is an intimate contact with gods in the temples.

After all, it is very difficult to define the role of the miracles in the life of the historical Apollonius. Both pre-Philostratean lines described above are equally well based in the sources and it is very difficult to make a choice between them. If we seek a way to explain both traditions, we may tentatively suggest that Apollonius was an influential religious teacher in Asclepius' temple, maybe practising healing outside the temple and later at odds with some temples and accused of sorcery.

PART II

MARKAN MIRACLE STORIES IN HISTORICAL JESUS RESEARCH, REDACTION CRITICISM AND NARRATIVE ANALYSIS

Geert Van Oyen

In this article I would like to present some insights from different methodological approaches to the miracle tradition, some of which at first view cannot easily be brought together: historical Jesus research, redaction criticism and narrative criticism. In fact, historical Jesus research and narrative criticism even seem to exclude each other. Still I think that in the methodology of exegesis it is not a matter of 'either/or' but of 'and', though always with the largest possible respect for the limits and results of each method. I will present my ideas in the form of five complementary theses. The purpose is modest: I present them as a possible stepping stone towards a more coherent 'inter-methodological' approach. When each method is aware of its own chances and limits, a sound dialogue between practitioners of different approaches should be possible. At least for the reader interested in a comprehensive interpretation of miracle stories, the building pieces of the puzzle are made available.

1. In historical Jesus research nothing can be said about the veracity that God truly is the one who is behind the miraculous deeds.
When we start talking about miracles it is useful to agree upon the meaning of the term 'miracle'. I will for convenience use the three elements in the definition of a miracle as proposed by J.P. Meier: '(1) an unusual, startling, or extraordinary event that is in principle perceivable by any interested and fair-minded observer, (2) an event that finds no reasonable explanation in human abilities or in other known forces that operate in our world of time and space, and (3) an event that is the result of a special act of God, doing what no human power can do'.[1] Surely, this definition is not the only one that can be used, but it is in agreement with what many people spontaneously or scientifically are thinking. In the rest of the article I do accept that these three aspects belong to the phenomenon of what is generally called 'miracle'. Now, it is a sound position when historical researchers

---

1. J. P. Meier, *A Marginal Jew: Rethinking the Historical Jesus* vol. II (ABRL; New York: Doubleday, 1994), p. 512.

know the limits of their discipline and do not try to look for what is not the objective of their method. In that sense, in historical criticism it is better not to look for 'an explanation that transcends what we take to be the "natural" laws of cause and effect'.[2] Therefore I think that the third element in Meier's definition cannot be proven nor denied by historical research. Historical research simply leaves the matter open. But historical criticism can ascertain that there are people who ascribe these deeds to God. Whether one considers this belief to be true or false depends on other criteria, like the world-view or belief one is adhering to, but not on historical research. The consequence of this thesis can be formulated in its reversed form as follows, quoting Borg again: 'One cannot solve the historical question by faith or belief'.[3] No exegetical method is capable of detecting if it is really God who is acting in these miracles. Although in some circles this is a very common statement, I think in many other groups misunderstanding about the role of exegesis persists.

I would like to add two remarks. (1) The result of research on the first two elements of Meier's definition may be relevant for those who believe. If the conclusion of historical research on Jesus' miraculous acts is a confirmation that indeed (in general) he did such things, then this conclusion gives believers an idea of who Jesus was and how he brought liberation. This is not without any importance for those who want to study the relation between history and faith.[4] (2) It is, however, a false position when scholars think they are on neutral ground, when they exclude this third element from their research and focus exclusively on points one and two. Neutrality and objectivity are not found by exclusion of the transcendental aspect of miracle stories. Researchers always bring in some ideas of their own pre-understandings about Jesus' identity. This is a very important issue because there is too much arguing between scholars that could be avoided if one would only clarify the presuppositions behind the historical research. This leads me to the second thesis, also in the domain of historical criticism.

2. Historical Jesus research in general agrees on the fact that Jesus has done miraculous deeds (exorcisms and healings) and that they should be compared with similar contemporary traditions in the Jewish and Graeco-Roman world. Scholars disagree on the general interpretation and meaning of this fact.
While in the 'Old Quest' emphasis was laid on the teaching and preaching of Jesus to portray the historical Jesus, most scholars in the 'Third Quest' are defending miracle-working as a major characteristic of Jesus' activity.[5] The main reasons to

2.   M. Borg, *A New Vision: Spirit, Culture, and the Life of Discipleship* (San Francisco: Harper & Row, 1987), p. 57.

3.   M. Borg, *New Vision*, p. 70.

4.   The dichotomy between the historical Jesus and the Christ of faith should be left behind us. These two aspects of one person should be brought together in research. See A. Gesché, 'Pour une identité narrative de Jésus', *RTL* 30 (1999), pp. 153–79 (336–56). See also G. Van Oyen, 'What More Should We Know about Jesus than One Hundred Year Ago?', *LS* (forthcoming).

5.   The division into 'Old', 'New' and 'Third' Quest is too artificial; see G. Van Oyen, 'What More'.

do so are: (1) the massiveness of the traditions in the Gospels is very impressive (six exorcisms, seventeen healing stories, eight nature miracles, according to D. Aune);[6] (2) the socio-religious context and the cultural environment allows without too much problem for a religious person to perform miracles; (3) the world view at Jesus' time was rather positive towards miracles and magic. Thus, 'if the miracle tradition from Jesus' public ministry were to be rejected in toto as unhistorical, so should every other Gospel tradition about him' (Meier),[7] or 'Seine Zeitgenossen hat Jesus vor allem durch Wunder beeindruckt und irritiert' (Theissen–Merz),[8] or 'the mighty deeds of Jesus, exorcisms and miracles alike, are the product of the power which flowed through him as a holy man' (Borg).[9] Briefly, historical research concludes that for the people around Jesus it must have been clear that he did healings and exorcisms. All the above-mentioned prominent authors, as well as E. P. Sanders and J. D. Crossan, further agree that *nature* miracles are later additions and do not belong to the historical Jesus.

It is now also generally accepted that the miracles of Jesus have to be compared with and understood within the context of Mediterranean miracle workers.[10] The sourcebook of W. Cotter, *Miracles in Greco-Roman Antiquity* (with an Appendix on 'Jesus, Torah and Miracles')[11] shows the relevance of these contemporaneous (or earlier or later) stories for the study of the NT miracle stories. Every monograph on the historical Jesus has a chapter on miracle stories in ancient history. Of course, the overall interpretation of Jesus' miracles is influenced by the fact that some scholars put more emphasis on the Jewish (and Old Testament) background, while others search for parallels in the Hellenistic stories. But the general tendency is clear: the miracles Jesus performed cannot be studied as isolated and unique cases. 'Uniqueness' could be used as a category for the miracles of Jesus only because they are to be integrated in the wider context of his message and proclamation of the Reign of God.

What then, after all, makes the difference between the scholars, if it is not the fact that Jesus performed miracles and that these miracles have to be compared with other contemporary stories? The answer is quite simple: it is the interpretation

---

6. J. P. Meier, *Marginal Jew*, p. 618.

7. J. P. Meier, *Marginal Jew*, p. 630.

8. G. Theissen, A. Merz, *Der historische Jesus: Ein Lehrbuch* (Göttingen: Vandenhoeck & Ruprecht, 1996), p. 256.

9. M. Borg, *New Vision*, p. 67.

10. See, e.g., W. Kahl, *New Testament Miracle Stories in their Religious-Historical Setting: A Religionsgeschichtliche Comparison from a Structural Perspective* (FRLANT, 163; Göttingen: Vandenhoeck & Ruprecht, 1994).

11. W. Cotter, *Miracles in Greco-Roman Antiquity: A Sourcebook for the Study of New Testament Miracle Stories* (London, New York: Routledge, 1999). The four parts are: 'Gods and heroes who heal', 'Exorcists and exorcisms', 'Gods and heroes who control nature', 'Magic and miracles'. For special studies, see, for instance, B. Kollmann, *Jesus und die Christen als Wundertäter: Studien zu Magie, Medizin und Schamanismus in Antike und Christentum* (Göttingen: Vandenhoeck & Ruprecht, 1996); G. H. Twelftree, *Jesus the Exorcist: A Contribution to the Study of the Historical Jesus* (WUNT, II.54; Tübingen: Mohr Siebeck, 1992).

or meaning of Jesus as miracle worker within their general interpretation of who Jesus was as a historical figure. To illustrate what I mean I would like to mention the controversy J. D. Crossan has provoked among scholars with his interpretation of miracles, both the historical and non-historical ones, in *The Historical Jesus* (1991).[12] His portrayal of Jesus has had a lot of popular success, but scholarly opposition – apart from the many criticisms in regard to his cross-cultural method and use of non-canonical sources – has to do with the general interpretation of his Jesus. In regard to this general view I first want to mention two difficult points vis-à-vis the orthodox or classic interpretation and then give a three-fold criticism. The first difficulty is that Crossan's exegesis of the miracles fits his overall portrayal of the historical Jesus as a 'revolutionary Jesus': healings and exorcisms perform social integration for the outlaws of society, because the individual sick body is the mirror of the social structure. This interpretation of the historical miracles is based on the connection they have with other important passages in the sources considered by Crossan to be historical, i.e. the complex of 'Mission and Message' and 'Harvest is Great' – about the sending of the disciples – 'where one can see the heart of the Jesus movement most clearly'.[13] According to Crossan it is impossible to know who were the original persons being sent on the mission. It is most probably said for *anyone* who wanted 'to participate more actively in the Jesus movement'.[14] Still Crossan has a very detailed description of them as 'healed healers', sent two by two (Mk 6.7 is historical), of whom one of each couple is a female missionary (cf. Paul in 1 Cor. 9.5). This mission initiated as a consequence of what Jesus had done: healing and exorcising while in exchange he receives a meal and thus establishes a system of 'open commensality', defined as 'a shared egalitarianism of spiritual and material resources'.[15] The problem with this point is of course not the consistency of Crossan's work, but the absolute scholarly uncertainty about the detailed knowledge the author has concerning the heart of the Jesus movement. A socio-cultural interpretation in the light of the wisdom tradition is clearly directing the interpretation of the meaning of the historical miracles Jesus performed.

The second difficulty, maybe even more problematic, is his interpretation of the non-historical nature miracles. Four passages in Mark are considered retrojected apparition stories that originally belonged to the *Cross Gospel* (a hypothetical source within the *Gospel of Peter*). Apart from the Transfiguration story [1/1][16]

---

12. Literature about Crossan's point of view on miracle stories is abundant. For a recent discussion, see P. F. Craffert, 'Crossan's Historical Jesus as Healer, Exorcist and Miracle Worker', *RT* 10 (2003), pp. 243–66; J. D. Crossan, 'Methodology, Healing, Story, and Ideology: Response to the Articles by Pieter F. Craffert and Johan M. Strijdom', *RT* 10 (2003), pp. 296–307.

13. J. D. Crossan, *The Historical Jesus: The Life of a Mediterranean Peasant* (San Francisco and Edinburgh: Harper & Row, 1991), p. 333.

14. J. D. Crossan, *Historical Jesus*, p. 334.

15. J. D. Crossan, *Historical Jesus*, p. 341.

16. The numbers between square brackets refer to the chronological stratum (1 to 4) and to the number of attestations; the number between parentheses refer to Crossan's 'Inventory of the

Crossan mentions (no. 3) Bread and Fish [1/6], (no. 128) Walking on Water [1/2] and (no. 190) Fishing for Humans [2/3]. They are examples of what he calls 'a process creating event'. All four received the code value ± in regard to their historicity and they 'had nothing originally to do with demonstrating the power of Jesus over nature but rather with establishing the power of leadership over the church and especially of some leaders over others'.[17] The background for his argument is the text in 1 Cor. 15.1-11, in which he distinguishes three categories: general community, leadership group and specific leader. These groups are 'crossed' with the three nature miracles (nos. 3, 128, 190) 'in order to suggest a trajectory of revelatory apparition moving the emphasis slowly but steadily from *community* to *group* to *leader*'.[18] As the paschal event itself is a creation of the community (since nobody knew the place where Jesus was buried) the post-paschal nature miracles reflect the conflicts about authority in the church.

This brief sketch of Crossan's interpretation of the miracle tradition is clear enough to mention some of the problems, which I only can enumerate here and not develop. They are meant to help to understand why Crossan's interpretation causes so much reaction in the scholarly world.

(1) A one-sided terminology based on sociological sciences such as in the words 'magic', 'magician', and 'revolutionary, unconventional, undermining, shocking, or surprising' behaviour of Jesus eliminates a number of traditional religious aspects of Jesus' message (like his being a son of God, not even necessarily in the christological sense but as someone whose trust is in God). The kind of language used to talk about Jesus and his miracles is a constitutive part of how scholarly interpretation is received in different milieus. The word 'revolutionary' is used in a double meaning for the position of Jesus within his own context and for the position of Crossan's Jesus within the majority of the scholarly and believing communities today. I do not see why it would not be possible to characterize the Jesus of many 'classic' (for instance, eschatological) interpretations as revolutionary.

(2) The distinction between eschatology and (cynic) wisdom is too exclusive and influences Crossan's view on miracles. In fact, according to him there is only one alternative: whether the miracles were an act of religious banditry by a non-conformist magician or they were symbols of the future eschatological reality of which Jesus was convinced. However, it is very difficult to know what Jesus was really thinking about the miracles he performed. I have the impression that the sources do not allow us to go beyond the unity of present actions that make visible in the present the future Kingdom of God.[19] 'Die Einzigartigkeit der

Jesus tradition by chronological stratification and independent attestation' (nos. 1–522); compare J. D. Crossan, *Historical Jesus*, pp. 427–50. On the use of criteria by Crossan and in modern scholarship, see G. Van Oyen, 'How Do We Know (What there Is to Know)? Criteria in Historical Jesus Research', *LS* 26 (2001), pp. 1–21.

17. G. Van Oyen, 'How Do We Know', p. 397.
18. G. Van Oyen, 'How Do We Know', p. 398.
19. See B. Witherington III, *The Jesus Quest: The Third Search for the Jew of Nazareth* (Downers Grove: InterVarsity Press, 1997), p. 70: 'The question posed by Crossan's interpretation of miracles is whether they should be seen as an act of religious banditry, with Jesus deliberately trying to act outside the normal religious lines to annoy or challenge the religious authorities, or whether his miracles should be seen as not directed against anyone, but rather as acts of

Wunder des historischen Jesus liegt darin, dass gegenwärtig geschehenden Heilungen und Exorzismen eine eschatologische Bedeutung zugesprochen wird'.[20]
(3) There is hardly a reference to the Old Testament. As J. P. Meier and E. P. Sanders and almost every other scholar have argued, one cannot explain Jesus' walking on the water without the OT references. Seen from this background, nature miracles are not stories about the crisis of the disciples' authority, but epiphany stories about the identity of Jesus the Christ. 'I think that the walking on the water is most likely from start to finish a creation of the early Church, a Christological confession in narrative form'.[21]

The second thesis can now be concluded. All scholars recognize the importance of the literary and social *Umwelt* for the explanation of NT miracles. This, however, never leads to a neutral historical approach to the miracles of Jesus. Neutrality simply does not exist: every new parallel story opens the eyes of the researcher for more possible hypotheses about the relationship between Jesus and the world in which he lived. Therefore, in my opinion, the greatest problem in historical Jesus research remains as ever before since the Enlightenment: is there any continuity between the earthly Jesus and the (post-paschal) texts in the Gospels? How smooth and fluent is the transition from the scholarly interpretation of the historical miracles towards their interpretation in the early Church? It is the answer to this question that remains the dividing factor in actual Jesus research, and it will remain decisive in further research. In other words, are the miracles performed by the earthly Jesus integrated by the evangelists into the story of Jesus' life (with parables, passion, resurrection) in such a way that they do not dramatically change their original purpose at the time when Jesus actually did them? Of course, if this continuity exists, there will still always remain the unavoidable problem of interpreting the meaning of these miracles. It is not the purpose to go into this question in detail, but maybe one should start with the very general idea that Jesus and the people around him understood the miracles as signs of the presence of the God of Israel and as symbols of the beginning of a new era. This idea was then taken over by the early Church.

3. No matter what criteria of historicity are used and notwithstanding the different opinions concerning the dates and interrelationship of the canonical and the apocryphal sources, each author's general opinion is 'proven' by the historicity of some individual healing miracles and exorcisms.
A comparison of the opinion of the many recent historical Jesus studies on every miracle story is impossible. Therefore by way of example I would like to compare the views of Crossan and Meier on the basis of Crossan's historical miracles (bold print in the scheme).

compassion performed in conjunction with his eschatological mission. That Jesus' miracles were seen as a threat seems sure, but that does not settle the issue of Jesus' intent'.
   20. G. Theissen, A. Merz, *Der historische Jesus*, p. 279.
   21. J. P. Meier, *Marginal Jew*, p. 921.

J. D. CROSSAN			J. P. MEIER (vol. II)
Stratum I			
3	Bread and Fish	[1/6] ±	
110	**A Leper Cured**	**[1/2] +**	'neither for nor against historicity' (701)
119	Distant Boy Cured	[1/2] ±	
121	**Beelzebul Controversy**	**[1/2] +**	'no countervailing reasons for denying historicity' (657)
127	Sickness and Sin	[1/2] +	'some event in the public ministry' (680)
128	Walking on Water	[1/2] ±	
129	**Blind Man Healed**	**[1/2] +**	'historicity of the core of the story' (694)
130	Dead Man Raised	[1/2] ±	
184	Transfiguration of Jesus	[1/2] ±	
Stratum II			
190	Fishing for Humans	[2/3] ±	
215	In Capernaum's Synagogue	[2/1] ±	
216	Simon's Mother-in-Law	[2/1] ±	
217	Healings and Exorcisms	[2/1] ±	
221	Hand and Sabbath	[2/1] –	
222	Crowds are Cured	[2/1] –	
223	Demons are Silenced	[2/1] –	
228	The Gerasene Demoniac	[2/1] ±	
229	**Two Women Cured**	**[2/1] +**	'non liquet' (710)
231	Herod on Jesus	[2/1] –	
233	Healings at Gennesaret	[2/1] ±	
237	Distant Girl Cured	[2/1] ±	
238	**Deaf Mute Cured**	**[2/1] +**	'some event in the life of Jesus' (714)
245	Possessed Boy Cured	[2/1] ±	
246	**Stranger as Exorcist**	**[2/1] +**	'whether… Jesus or the early days of the church' (415)
256	Healing of Bartimaeus	[2/1] ±	
260	Cursed Fig Tree	[2/1] –	
269	Jesus Arrested	[2/1] ±	
349	Water into Wine	[2/1]	
Stratum III			
429	The Temple Tax	[3/1] –	
442	Widow's Son Raised	[3/1] –	
455	Cripple and Sabbath	[3/1] –	
458	Dropsy and Sabbath	[3/1] –	

According to Crossan a total of seven miracles are historical, four from Stratum I and three from Stratum II:

Stratum I:

110   A Leper Cured: P. Egerton 2b (35-47); Mk 1.40-45 = Mt. 8.1-4 = Lk. 5.12-16; Lk. 17.11-19
121   Beelzebul Controversy: 2Q: Lk. 11.14-15, 17-18 = Mt. 12.22-26; Mt. 9.32-34; Mk 3.22-26
127   Sickness and Sin: Jn 5.1-9a.14; Mk 2.1-12 par Mt 9.1-8 = Lk. 5.17-26
129   Blind Man Healed: Jn 9.1-7; Mk 8.22-26

Stratum II:

229   Two Women Cured: Mk 5.21-43 = Mt. 9.18-26 = Lk. 8.40-56
238   Deaf Mute Cured: Mk 7.31-37 (see Mt. 15.29-31)
246   Stranger as Exorcist: Mk 9.38-39 = Lk. 9.49-50a.

The first interesting thing that has to be said about the method of both authors is that the criteria of judgment for or against historicity differ. Crossan emphasizes the value of multiple independent attestation. But as can be seen from the table where more stories have multiple attestation, this is not the only criterion: nos. 3, 119, 128, 130, 184, 190 do not have a + sign. Meier has a broader range of criteria, especially the combination of dissimilarity and multiple attestation. Notwithstanding this difference, when we compare Meier's conclusion about Crossan's positive examples, it seems that both authors have a similar position, though it must be said that Meier is more nuanced and less certain; he seems to speak more in general terms (see the quotes in the right column). Still the final interpretation of both authors on the *meaning* of the historical miracle stories is completely opposite. The explanation for it is that the criterion which really plays the main role in their reasoning is the argument of coherence with their general view of Jesus. The same historical miracles are integrated within their respective broader interpretation of Jesus. For Crossan, as seen above, the emphasis is on social revolution, for Meier on the coming and the presence of the Kingdom.[22] The latter accepts that Jesus during his lifetime acted as an eschatological prophet in the line of Elijah and Elisha, and thus there is no need to deny that Jesus stands in the line of Old Testament prophets (see also Sanders). According to Crossan, Jesus is a social revolutionary and therefore the miracles that can be explained from this perspective fit in his view on the historical Jesus. It is not easy to say whose interpretation is right and whose is wrong. And there is maybe no 'completely wrong' or 'completely right' in this matter, since any portrayal is a reconstruction and makes use of a specific language within a specific method or approach.

The divergences between both these (and many other) Jesus interpretations reveal that the main question of any historical study of the individual stories is in fact the problem of the religious interpretation of Jesus. Whatever approach people use in their research on Jesus, they eventually will have to deal with the question about the position of Jesus from a religious point of view. In what religious tradition should he be placed? With whom should he be compared in the first (and the second) place? Since the range is very wide, running from Old Testament miracle tradition (Moses, Elijah, Elisha), apocalyptic Judaism (e.g., exorcisms), rabbinical literature (Honi, Ḥanina), Hellenistic cynical magical teachers, wise philosophers (Apollonius), this discussion will always remain a problem. I am rather in favour of a balanced view, where influence from many backgrounds can be detected upon a person and certainly upon the creation of the stories about that person. False opposition should be avoided. In this sense, Crossan's exclusion of the eschatological function of the miracles is most probably a denial of a major part of Jesus' *Umwelt*. But for all interpreters the jump from

---

22. See his preliminary sketch of a synthesis in *Marginal Jew*, pp. 1044–45: '(1) At the very least, in some vague sense Jesus was seen by others and himself as an eschatological prophet. He proclaimed the imminent coming of God's kingly rule and reign. (2) Yet, unlike the Baptist, Jesus proclaimed and celebrated the kingdom of God already present in his ministry.'

literary texts to historically secure ground where we can stand next to Jesus himself remains difficult. And probably interpreting Jesus was no less difficult for the people who originally stood next to him. It is said that historical criticism on Jesus' miracles nowadays is very often a mirror in which the different opinions scholars have on Jesus today are reflected. Whatever they are looking for, they will find it. And because of the complexity of the Mediterranean world in the first century CE they will always find some arguments in the great amount of surrounding miracle traditions of Jesus' time to support their view. It is not impossible that this mirror reflects only the different opinions that were present at the time of Jesus himself.

My third thesis thus leads to a double proposal. The first is that one should take more seriously the limits of the critical methods used in defining what is historical and what is not. I am not saying this because faith would set limits to the use of critical method, but, on the contrary, because critical method itself is confronted with its own restrictions. Maybe we cannot go further than what M. Borg has stated: 'the stories reflect the *kinds* of situations Jesus encountered and the *kinds* of deeds he did, even if we cannot be sure whether a particular story is a stylised "typical" picture or based fairly closely on eyewitness report of a specific event. That is, the verdict that we are dealing with generally historical material does not imply the historical accuracy of all details'.[23] The second proposal is that scholars should clarify their theological standpoints more than they do now when approaching historical problems. Since no historical research on Jesus can be done in splendid isolation, not even outside the theological setting, scholars would help each other a lot if they would try to formulate the relevance of their reconstruction for theology in general.[24]

4. The issue of historicity of miracle workers was not a debated item for the evangelists. The author of the Gospel of Mark, for instance, never doubts the fact that Jesus did miracles, but he interprets them from a christological point of view: Jesus as Son of God cannot be fully explained by his miracles!

Many books since the flowering of redaction criticism in the 1970s have been written about miracle stories in the Gospel of Mark (D.-A. Koch, G. Theissen, K. Kertelge, H. C. Kee, H.-W. Kuhn, etc.).[25] They have focused on many items of the Markan redactional reworking of these *individual* stories, and tried to explain their function in the *whole* of Markan theology, which is after all the ultimate goal of redaction criticism. Points for attention were the grouping of the miracles, the

23. M. Borg, *New Vision*, p. 61.

24. The important role of pre-understanding in interpretation is shown by D. Ingolfsland, 'The Historical Jesus according to John Dominic Crossan's First Strata Sources: A Critical Comment', *JETS* 45 (2002), pp. 405–14. On the basis of the same sources found in Crossan's oldest stratum the author reconstructs a completely opposite 'historical' Jesus, 'as the Jewish Messiah, Savior, and incarnation of God, who performed amazing miracles and rose from the dead' (414).

25. See F. Neirynck *et al.*, *The Gospel of Mark 1950-1990: A Cumulative Bibliography* (BETL, 102; Leuven: Peeters, 1992), pp. 653–54 (Index on Miracle Stories and Exorcisms).

possibility of reconstructing pre-Markan *catena(e)* and Markan additions, Jesus'
transition from Jewish to Gentile soil,[26] the symbolic purposes of some of the
stories (like the healing of the blind men 8.22-26 and 10.46-52; the feeding
narratives 6.34-44 and 8.1-9; the cursing of the fig tree 11.12-15, 16-20, 21-25),
the importance of faith and prayer, and the problem of the hidden identity of Jesus
known as the messianic secret.[27] The last point is the most important one since,
starting with W. Wrede (1901), it is according to many exegetes the overall theme
of the gospel.[28] The least one can say about the function of the miracles in Mark
with regard to the theme of the identity of Jesus in Mark is that they are very
ambiguous. They positively focus on the eschatological liberation Jesus is bringing
and they want to illustrate his epiphanic presence as divine man. But, and this is
the remarkable thing, at the same time they are used to hide his true identity. It
is difficult to generalize and make a statement about all miracle stories, but those
in the section Mark 4–8 are clearly meant to say that Jesus is not, or not correctly,
recognized as the evangelist himself looks at him. One gets the impression that the
miracles are of secondary importance and are subordinated to the main theme of
the gospel, i.e. Jesus' passion. This is clearly a Markan construction which colours
the historical reliability of the tradition: is it possible to find certainty about what
is beyond this theology?

I think the whole discussion cannot be better summarized than in the words of
C. M. Tuckett:

> It may be that Mark is trying to say not so much that the miracles clearly testify to who Jesus
> is, but rather that the miracles *in part* testify to who Jesus is; however, there is more to Jesus
> than (just) being a miracle-worker … Mark is not opposed to the view that Jesus is to be
> seen as (primarily) a miracle-worker. There is simply too much material in Mark supporting
> that kind of a Christology to make such a theory untenable … Nevertheless, the possibility
> that Mark might still be wanting to imply an element of reserve about such a view of Jesus
> should not be ruled out of consideration too quickly … Mark does portray the disciples
> coming to see who Jesus is, and Mark guides his readers through that odyssey. It is a journey
> that takes on board positively the miracle-working activity of Jesus; but, as the gospel as a
> whole indicates, that part of the journey of discovery about who Jesus is, or rather about
> what it means to call Jesus by the various terms and 'titles', is filled in by the second half
> of the gospel, climaxing in the account of Jesus' life and death.[29]

26. See for instance R. Feneberg, *Der Jude Jesus und die Heiden: Biographie und Theologie
Jesu im Markusevangelium* (HBS, 24; Freiburg i.Br.: Herder, 2000).

27. See W. R. Telford, *The Theology of the Gospel of Mark* (Cambridge: Cambridge
University Press, 2001), pp. 89–103 ('The nature and function of the miracles in Mark').

28. Some scholars do not agree and defend the thesis that (some of) the elements composing
the messianic secret are traditional and should be interpreted on their own; cf. H. Räisänen, *Das
'Messiasgeheimnis's im Markusevangelium: Ein redaktionskritischer Versuch* (SFEG, 26; Helsinki,
1976). For a presentation and a discussion of the theme, see the first part of my doctoral thesis
De Studie van de Marcusredactie in de twintigste eeuw [The Study of the Markan Redaction in
the Twentieth Century] (SNTA, 18; Leuven: Peeters, 1993 [with a summary in English]), pp. 36–40
(Wrede), 150–59 (messianic secret in form criticism), 236–59 (redaction criticism).

29. C. M. Tuckett, 'The Disciples and the Messianic Secret in Mark', in I. Dunderberg *et al.*

This quotation summarizes the redaction-critical result of how Mark would have intended the function of miracle stories. The redaction-critical point of view is compatible with what we said above about historical research. The positive choice in historical criticism for a more general description of what Jesus could have done instead of for the impasse of a detailed analysis of each individual miracle story is perfectly in agreement with the fact that the evangelist was not interested in historical exactness but in the *christ*-ological message. The passage from Tuckett's article connects also with the newer narrative approach by mentioning the role of the reader, and thus introduces the fifth thesis.[30]

5. *From a narrative-critical or reader-response-critical point of view, the Markan miracle stories function in the gospel story development as plot events in which Jesus' behaviour is shown as superior to the demons, conflicting with the authorities and mysterious to the disciples. Hence, the readers are constantly challenged about the true identity of Jesus and his relationship to God.*

The renewing aspects of narrative criticism in gospel studies can be summarized in two points: *what* is the plot development ('story') and *how* does the narrator communicate with the readers ('discourse')? The numerous miracles in Mark play an important role in both these aspects. They dominate the narrative line from the beginning of the gospel: after the personal experience of Jesus' struggle with Satan in the desert (1.11-13), the exorcism in 1.21-28 is the first public event and the healing in 1.29-31 is the first private healing. Both stories are followed by a summary about exorcism and healing in general. Mark is orientating the reader's perspective about Jesus' activities from the beginning. Miracles lead to further conflict (3.1–6 as the climax of the conflict section 2.1–3.6), and are the cement of the larger section in Mark 4–8. In that section there is a combination of themes: in doing better than the Old Testament antecedents (Elijah, Elisha) and in being open towards non-Jewish people in an equal way as towards Jews, he is becoming an enigma for his family and for the disciples. He is also becoming an enemy of the authorities. In the light of the whole story, in a certain sense all miracles can be interpreted as examples of one the conflicts present in Mark. Scholars generally distinguish between three levels of conflict with Jesus: one with the non-human forces, another one with the religious and political authorities, and a third one with the disciples.[31] On all of the three levels the miracle stories in the

(eds.), *Fair Play: Diversity and Conflicts in Early Christianity. Essays in Honour of Heikki Räisänen* (NovTSup 103; Leiden: Brill, 2002) pp. 131–50 (149).

30. See also the conclusion of B. D. Ellenburg, *A Review of Selected Narrative-Critical Conventions in Mark's Use of Miracle Material*, *JETS* 38 (1995), pp. 171–80 (180): 'No doubt exists that the author of Mark's Gospel tells a dramatic story and weaves the tale to create powerful effects on the reader. Integral to that story are the miracle pericopae. Narrative criticism is sympathetic to the theory that the miracles function in Mark's world of events in the same way that the parables function in word. Redaction criticism does not dispel such a notion, but a narrative reading allows for a wider appreciation of just such a possibility.'

31. On the three levels of conflict in Mark, see D. Rhoads, *Mark as Story: An Introduction to the Narrative of a Gospel*, (Philadelphia: Fortress Press, 1982).

first half of the gospels are at the heart of the conflict.[32] Exorcisms are the clearest manifestation of Jesus' victory over the evil supra-human forces. But also the terminology in the stilling of the storm (an example of a nature miracle) reminds the reader of the exorcism in 1.23-28, and shows how Jesus is stronger than the demons. The dramatic line in 2.1–3.6 illustrates how Mark intermingles conflict stories about theological or ethical questions (forgiving sins, respect for the Sabbath) with healing stories (healing of the paralysed man, healing in the synagogue). Jesus' miraculous performance is one of the reasons for the conflict with the religious leaders. And a political reading of Mk 5.1-20 ('legion') against the Roman occupation is not impossible. Thus, even if the healings and exorcisms do not seem to explain the full meaning of Jesus' identity, they are an essential part of his portrayal since they inform the reader about critical actions against the power of Satan and the authorities. The third level of conflict is an ambiguous one. The miracles should serve as an instruction for the disciples about Jesus' real identity, but – paradoxically – they seem to understand worse when they are assisting at the miraculous acts of Jesus. The function of the miracles in the larger context of discipleship is that they draw away the attention from the miracle worker Jesus towards the teaching of Jesus about the deeper fundamental ethics of following.[33]

It is through these elements of conflict with the authorities and misunderstanding by the disciples that the communication with the reader about Jesus' identity is created. It is clear from the Markan redactional asides and comments that the evangelist himself mentions these conflict lines as essential for the reader. I give for each of the three lines an example: 3.22-27 (demons), 6.52 and 8.17-21 (disciples), 1.21-28 and 3.5-6 (authorities). This narrative-unifying view of the miracle stories from the perspective of conflict could be of major importance for the interpretation of the whole of the gospel. While, for instance, in redaction-critical interpretations the misunderstanding of the disciples is explained by way of an existing conflict in Mark's community (e.g. about a *theios anèr* Christology), in narrative criticism it is understood as a means of communication with the reader. It brings closer together the two parts of Mark's Gospel; before and after Peter's confession. It does not see the second one (the passion) as a correction of the first one (miracle worker Jesus), but as a consequence and continuation of a former conflict and misunderstanding. The key for understanding the gospel is the fundamental option that is presented to Peter and the disciples and through them to the readers: 'Behind me Satan! For you are setting your mind not on divine things but on human things' (8.33). In other words, is it possible to accept or believe that the same God is present in Jesus' deeds *and* in his death? That is what the

32. The only two miracle stories in the second half of the gospel (9.14–29; 10.46-52) – or three if the cursing of the fig tree is added – can also be seen against the background of the theme of discipleship.

33. D. Rhoads, 'Losing Life for Others in the Face of Death: Mark's Standards of Judgment', in *Int* 7 (1993), pp. 258–69 = D. Rhoads, *Reading Mark: Engaging the Gospel* (Minneapolis, MN: Fortress, 2004), pp. 44–62.

'messianic' secret is about within a narrative-critical reading: the true and deepest divine reality of Jesus is never one hundred percent guaranteed in the miracles, except for those who dare to think further that in Jesus' passion God is still there. The miracles according to Mark, then, reveal that in the human person Jesus, who reacts in his deeds against the power of evil (Satan) and against the non-human aspects of religious and profane institutions, the power of God is present. In this sense it is not the miracles as such that reveal or hide the God of Jesus, but the interpretation of his acts as liberating signs of the Kingdom of God. And according to Mark, this God is the one who was with Jesus in his passion (notwithstanding Jesus' hesitation to openly affirm his own 'divine' status!). One of the new things narrative criticism has introduced into exegesis is the idea of 'perspective'. With regard to the miracle stories, 'perspective' means that the problem in the Gospel of Mark is not whether God is present or not in the miracles Jesus performs. The problem is whether God is present in Jesus' miracles as Mark interpreted them! Since this is a new challenge to believe for every generation, the gap between the Crossan line of a present-day revolution in the miracles of Jesus and the Sanders–Meier line of an eschatological coming of a new era is not as deep as one usually would think.

6. *Summary and conclusion*

There are no historical arguments against the idea that Jesus was a healer and an exorcist. His healings and exorcisms were open to many interpretations, probably already during his lifetime, but certainly after his death. It is very difficult to reconstruct a detailed report of one of Jesus' healing or liberating actions. The earliest gospel interpretation of the miracles sees them as part of the larger idea of the coming of the Kingdom of God. In this sense the miracle interpretation of Mark is critical towards all forms of strangling power and at the same time is a manifestation of God's preference through Jesus for the marginalized people. Moreover, the idea of the Kingdom of God is based upon the paradox that 'if anyone wants to be great, that person is to be least of all and everyone's servant' (9.35) and this finally leads to Jesus' death since he does not abandon this line of thinking. As the first gospel writer wants his readers to understand that this 'wisdom' makes sense only if they believe God is at the side of Jesus at the moment of his death,[34] he covers the miracle tradition with a veil of misunderstanding by the disciples. Thus, he does not only make a distinction between the two halves of the gospel (miracles and passion) but he also unites them, since they are both part of the revelation of the God of Jesus.

---

34. It would lead us too far to explain that this insight is only possible from a post-resurrection perspective.

'Many-Coloured Illnesses' (Mark 1.34):
On the Significance of Illnesses in
New Testament Therapy Narratives

Reinhard von Bendemann

1. The Question of 'Illness' in the New Testament Therapy Narratives

The confession of Christ as a physician is not yet found explicitly within New Testament literature. The earliest reference to Christ as a physician is made by Ignatius of Antioch. In his letter to the Ephesians he writes: 'There is one physician, both fleshly and spiritual ... Jesus Christ, our Lord' (Ign. *Eph.* 7.2; cf. 20.2; *Acts John* 108). Despite its late phrasing, such an interpretation of Christ has not been established without a foundation in New Testament passages. For instance, in Mk 2.17 par. Jesus compares his interaction with sinners with the work of a physician (cf. Lk. 4.23). Moreover, significance has to be deduced from the healing narratives within the Gospels and Acts. The relevant confession, formed later, is based on these, though not only under soteriological presuppositions: here Jesus is a 'physician' not only in the sense of 'saviour'. The above-mentioned passages moreover reflect on Christ as one who actually 'heals'.[1] Such a process of healing itself, however, is described in varying ways. There are indicators provided within the healing narratives which allow for a more clear-cut distinction between the individual illnesses than is often acknowledged in more recent research. As summarized in Mk 1.34 Jesus heals 'many-coloured illnesses'.[2]

In the following discussion, examples of such a differentiation and modification reflected in individual therapy narratives will be analysed. Regarding the history of research on this issue, it becomes clear that the significance of distinguishing illnesses and their appropriate treatment has been widely neglected. In short, it has to be stated that the various illnesses and concrete sufferings, which are reported in the stories as being healed, often receive surprisingly little interest. The research

---

1. For the interpretation of Christ as a medic cf. G. Fichtner, 'Christus als Arzt. Ursprünge und Wirkungen eines Motivs', *Frühmittelalterliche Studien* 16 (1982), pp. 1–18; B. Kollmann, *Jesus und die Christen als Wundertäter: Studien zu Magie, Medizin und Schamanismus in Antike und Christentum* (FRLANT, 170; Göttingen: Vandenhoeck & Ruprecht, 1996), pp. 363–66, and M. Dörnemann, *Krankheit und Heilung in der Theologie der frühen Kirchenväter* (STAC, 20; Tübingen: Mohr Siebeck, 2003).

2. For the formulation in Mk 1.34 cf. Strabo *Geogr.* 5.3.11; Plutarch *Pericles* 15.1; *Quaest. conviv.* 732e; Aretaios 4.9. Cf. further the Anonymus Londinensis Med. (*Iatrika* 7.25).

on miracle stories is often limited to form-historical or narrative-critical approaches; the relevant surveys examine the schemes of the narratives primarily according to form and narrative technique. Consequently, these functional approaches lead to a wide-spread exchangeability of specified diseases and definite sufferings. Therefore, it needs to be questioned whether this approach meets the requirements of the scope of meaning (*Sinnspektrum*) of early Christian narratives dealing with illnesses or whether this widespread lack of interest in the concrete illnesses implies a considerable loss of awareness, even loss of liveliness for the inter-pretation.

Accordingly, some methodological issues need to be clarified at first: The expression 'illness' as such cannot be interpreted as an absolute term. Any mention of an illness, as well as any identification of a particular illness or disease, is based on a certain competence of employing language related to a particular interpre-tation of reality. Any reference to an illness or a disease therefore needs to be under-stood as bound to a reconstruction of reality which is influenced by personal experiences, ethical concepts and imaginations of values. Within certain cultural communities patterns are established by which members must deem themselves 'sick' or 'healthy', and relate themselves to one of these states. In reverse, each individual case of an illness occurring within a community has a potential impact on its framework of perception of 'illness' and 'health'. These mutual and reciprocal attributions and definitions therefore have to be understood as tensions between conformity and deviance, which underlie varying socio-cultural processes of expressing experienced reality (*Erlebnisformierung*). Consequently, whole branches of different sciences are involved with defining and analysing the phenomena of illness and health.[3]

To start with, a history-of-traditions approach regarding early Christian therapy narratives is necessary in order to access relevant data and conditions.[4] One needs to analyse the underlying competence of employing language deliberately and the presupposed conceptions of interpreting particular illnesses within certain narratives, which (indirectly) reflect socio-historical conditions of early Christian writers and the specific living environment of their recipients. Accordingly, the illnesses in the healing narratives can be defined by (A) physical parameters, (B) a framework of social conditions and (C) religious–theological implications and codes, which have to be considered for an interpretation. These three means of

---

3.   For important considerations indebted to a *wissenssoziologischem* approach cf. A. Weissenrieder, *Images of Illness in the Gospel of Luke* (WUNT, II.164; Tübingen: Mohr Siebeck, 2003), pp. 21–42.

4.   'Human sickness as a personal and social reality and its therapy is inextricably bound to language and signification', J. J. Pilch, *Healing in the New Testament: Insights from Medical and Mediterranean Anthropology* (Minneapolis: Fortress Press, 2000), p. 41. Hence, any attempt to distinguish between 'sickness' as a kind of phenomenon per se and 'illness' and 'disease' as means of possible interpretations is bound to fail (cf. pp. 24–25, 59–60, 93, 153, 159 and passim). A. Weissenrieder, *Images of Illness*, p. 36: 'Thus, the body and illness should not be understood as "natural constants" onto which cultural codes are merely appended as epiphenomena.'

identifying an underlying concept of illness can only be distinguished heuristically; within the healing narratives themselves, as well as their social settings, they are inherent and closely related with one another.

A further aspect directly depends on such a tripartite division of interacting factors defining illness: any reference to illness relates to a multidimensional interpretation of reality. This also becomes obvious through the specific form of language which is employed in the healing narratives. Illnesses are part of 'narrated worlds' which are developed from the perspective of the narrators. A three-dimensional character of illnesses in New Testament passages is a part of and is involved in literature. However, although it relates to reality, literature is generically subject to its own laws. For this reason one has to examine what significance may be applied to details of a described illness as part of the overall narrative–theological conception of a particular story.

In the following discussion a *history-of-traditions* approach is related to a 'genre' which has found little interest in the area of New Testament research, although a connection to the possible interpretation of Christ as 'physician' seems to be at hand, namely ancient medical literature. At least a short basic introduction, some more detailed reasons for the selection of texts and the following procedure are necessary. A profile of the competence of employing language which corresponds with analogous ideas and motifs has to be distinguished from genealogical connections. In most cases genealogical connections between early Christian writings and specific medical writings of Hellenistic-Roman origin can hardly be made plausible. At the same time, the temporal proximity of certain writings does not necessarily imply a proximity in world-view as well. As a natural starting point for a comparison, authors which are contemporary with New Testament literature will be taken into consideration; however, older concepts of Hippocratic medicine, for example, might be preserved in texts from the first and second century CE as well.[5] The content and significance of this specific form of medicine were taught and transmitted with the encyclopaedic sciences. For instance, evidence for such knowledge is presupposed and further elaborated in the encyclopaedia of Celsus (1st century CE); writers of later times such as Soran of Ephesus (1st/2nd century CE; his work περὶ ὀξέων καὶ χρονίων παθῶν translated by Caelius Aurelianus), Galen (129–*ca.* 216 CE), Alexander Aphrodisiensis (2nd/3rd century CE), Oribasius (*ca.* 320–400 CE) or Alexander of Tralles (*ca.* 525–605 CE) are also influenced by or dependent on such medical knowledge. Presuppositions about the various medical sources and especially the interdependencies between them are rather complex. Moreover, one can find medical knowledge or allusions to sources with medical contexts in originally non-medical texts as well.[6] Accordingly, refer-

5.   Cf. for Luke, A. Weissenrieder, *Images of Illness*.
6.   For the history of ancient medicine see, for instance, H. Avalos, *Health Care and the Rise of Christianity* (Peabody, MA.: Hendrickson, 1999); M. D. Grmek (ed.), *Die Geschichte des medizinischen Denkens: Antike und Mittelalter* (München: Beck, 1996); R. Jackson, *Doctors and Diseases in the Roman Empire* (London: British Museum Publications, 1988); H. C. Kee, *Medicine, Miracle and Magic in New Testament Times* (SNTSMS, 55; Cambridge, London:

ences to general medical knowledge and related expressions can also be dissem-
inated beyond the borders of the established schools of thought
(*Schulrichtungen*) in the Hellenistic period. Further, along with established
positions one can find medical contents in rather popular (*volkstümliche*)
writings, such as Pliny's *Naturalis Historia* (cf. especially vols. 28–32). However,
the value of a more extensive inclusion of ancient medical sources – as can only
be partially presupposed in the following discussion – can only be justified by
means of examining the relevant New Testament passages themselves.

The following analysis of illnesses and their specific character in New Testament
writings has to be limited to two examples with a selected assessment of data. Some
perspectives for further research and consequences for the understanding of
illness, healing and salvation in early Christianity will eventually be formulated.

2. *Obscurum fascinosum febris*
An approach to the phenomenon of fever in early Christian documents is
confronted with an extensive variety (*Brechungen*) of concepts and interpretations
as documented and reflected in ancient Greek texts as well as in Hellenistic-Roman
writings with medical contexts (and also early Jewish literature). Therefore, it is
impossible to simply base the examination on a general definition of the expression
'fever'.[7]

a. *The Problem of Ancient Pyretology*
A discussion of 'fever' and related phenomena is closely linked with the fundamental problem of a basic or inherent (or later ascribed) definition of 'illness' and

Cambridge University Press, 1986); S. S. Kottek, *Medicine and Hygiene in the Works of Flavius Josephus* (SAM, 91; New York, Leiden: Brill, 1994); A. Krug, *Heilkunst und Heilkult: Medizin in der Antike* (BAB; München: Beck, 1993 [1985]); J. Longrigg, *Greek Medicine from the Heroic to the Hellenistic Age: A Source Book* (London: Duckworth, 1998); T. Newmyer, 'Talmudic Medicine and Greco-Roman Science: Crosscurrents and Resistance', *ANRW* II.37.3 (1996), pp. 2895–911; R. Schmitz, *Geschichte der Pharmazie* vol. 1: *Von den Anfängen bis zum Ausgang des Mittelalters* (Eschborn: Govi-Verlag, 1998), pp. 27–36, 113–204, and H. von Staden, *Herophilos: The Art of Medicine in Early Alexandria* (Gütersloh: Mohn, 1989). See for an overview: R. von Bendemann, J. Neumann, 'Antike Medizin', in K. Erlemann, K. L. Noethlichs, K. Scherberich, J. Zangenberg (eds); *Neues Testament und Antike Kultur* 2: *Familie, Gesellschaft, Wirtschaft* (Neukirchen-Vluyn: Neukirchener Verlag, 2005), pp. 215–22.

7.   Early evidence for concepts of pyretology is provided by Democritus (Diogenes Laertius 9.49). In encyclopaedic literature fever is commonly referred to. For instance, in Celsus' *De medicina* in parts of the third (3.3-17) and the fourth volume (4.14) – basing the arguments on the ancient writings – various kinds of fever are discussed in an aetiological and dietary context. Further, Galen's writing *De differentiis febrium* (in two volumes) is worth mentioning. Reflections on fever also occur in the writing *De curandi ratione per venaesectionem*. The peripatetic Alexander Aphrodisiensis deals with the topic in the writing *De febribus libellus*. More references to fever can be found in passages of Aretaios' writing which deal with severe and chronic diseases (ed. Hude; 59 references to φλεγμονή; 65 references to πυρετός). For more evidence see H.-J. Horn, 'Fieber', *RAC* 7 (1969), pp. 877–909, esp. 878; J. Longrigg, *Greek Medicine*, pp. 114, 120, 139, 158–159.

'health'. Speaking of 'fever' means to distinguish between 'natural' and 'unnatural' heat (cf. Alexander Aphrodisiensis, *De febribus* 1.81-106; Galen, *In Hipp. Epid. 6 comm.* 1.29). Within research literature it is widely assumed that in ancient writings – diverging from modern pyretology – fever is commonly understood as 'illness' rather than as 'symptom'.[8] Such a general assumption, however, can only be sustained with considerable limitations. For Celsus (*De med.* 1.1), for instance, fever is actually part of a third group of illnesses, which has to be defined as neither acute nor chronic, but rather as being alternating. However, in ancient medical texts fever can be described as an indicator and accompanying symptom of various sufferings.[9] Based on the distinction between the Latin expressions *morbus* and *vitium* one can consider fever and related phenomena as appearing and disappearing, and consequently pathological (i.e. part of an 'illness'). However, the distinction of different cyclic forms of fever in Greek and Hellenistic-Roman medical texts indicates that the transition to *vitium* is not clear-cut, but rather fluent. According to Külken conceptional models within the ancient history of curing fever have to be distinguished '*phänotypisch*'.[10] Initially (but not in every group of sources; especially not in the *Corpus Hippocraticum*), one can find an interpretation of fever as a foreign, almost hostile power which takes control of a human body.[11] In contrast, in other sources fever can be regarded as a 'cooking process', a πέψις within the body. Such a pyretological model can be based on the idea of identity and wholeness of the human in a state of balanced harmony of bodily fluids.[12] A modernized form of such a concept (which was fully developed in the Romantic period) is present in models which acknowledge a positive psychological and physical influence of fever on body and soul.[13] In contrast to the ancient conceptions of fever which attempt to integrate fever teleologically in a conceptional scheme of a perceived world, other early models deny a holistic approach to identify diseases and related phenomena (cf. for instance Galen's criticism of the Stoa).

Although the various approaches and perspectives differ considerably, some lines of convergence can be emphasized after all (for the systematic structure cf. Galen,

8. Cf. for instance K. Weiß, 'πυρέσσω, πυρετός', *TWNT* 6 (1959), pp. 956–59 (956); C. Schulze, *Celsus* (Hildesheim: Olms, 2001), p. 45; J. R. Donahue, D. J. Harrington, *The Gospel of Mark* (SPS, 2; Collegeville, MN: Liturgical Press, 2002), p. 82.

9. For deafness and dumbness with feverish accompanying symptoms, see A. Weissenrieder, *Images of Illness*, pp. 114, 116–117, 128. For fever in connection with *flux sanguinis* of women cf. pp. 244, 247 (cf. *Corpus Hippocraticum, Mul.* 2.110). Cf. further Epictetus (*Diss.* 4.9.4) for thirst and an aching stomach in connection with fever; see also Celsus (*De med.* 3.22) for fever as consequence of severe emaciation, and Caelius Aurelianus (*Tard. pass.* 2.15, 28) for a connection between fever and paralysis.

10. Cf. T. Külken, *Fieberkonzepte in der Geschichte der Medizin* (Heidelberg: Verlag für Medizin Ewald Fischer, 1985), *passim* (pp. 12, 98–101).

11. Cf. T. Külken, *Fieberkonzepte*, pp. 15–18.

12. Already in Hippocratic medicine such a disorder can be interpreted as an indicator for supporting the recovery of a human being. For *Eukrasie* and *Dyskrasie* see T. Külken, *Fieberkonzepte, pp.* 21–31. Cf. *Corpus Hippocraticum, Morb.* 2.22.

13. Cf. T. Külken, *Fieberkonzepte*, pp. 87–97.

Diff. febr. 17.273-77). One may gradually distinguish between weak (πυρετοὶ βληχηροί) and mild (πυρετοὶ πρηέες), lukewarm (πυρετοὶ χλιαροί) or burning fevers (πυρετοὶ περικαέες).[14] The ardent fever (labelled as καῦσος, *febris ardens*)[15] and the shivering fit (ἠπίαλος πυρετός or ῥιγοπύρετος; cf. ῥῖγος) offer a separate field for observation and efforts of therapy.

The distinction between 'minor' or 'light' fever on the one hand and 'major' or 'heavy' fever on the other hand is not only established on the basis of external perception of body temperatures (cf. Galen, *Diff. febr.* 17.275; Alexander Aprodisiensis, *De febribus* 18 [1.93]; Lk. 4.38, differing from Mk 1.30). The rate at which a fever spreads is also a means of distinguishing different forms. The understanding of fever as a highly complex anthropological concept receives more support from a further means of classification, namely the location where body heat is developed. The distinct characteristics of the so-called 'ephemeral fever', which in contrast to septic fevers (having their origin in the bodily fluids) and frantic or hectic fevers (depending on the *pneuma*) is situated in the solid parts of the body, are rapid outbreak and dissolution.[16]

A significant role is played by the analysis of the rhythm of alternating fevers which occur periodically. In ancient medicine a fixed system of intermittent fevers is established: 'one-day' or 'quotidian fever' (ἀμφημερινὸς πυρετός, *quotidiana*), 'three-day fever' or 'sandfly fever' (τριταῖος πυρετός; *tertiana*) and 'quartan fever' (τεταρταῖος πυρετός, *quartana*, cf. for instance Hippocr., *Epid.* 1.12)[17] are differentiated. Such distinctions are not limited to the professional knowledge of physicians (cp. Celsus, *De med.* 3.3). For instance, Josephus refers to the quartan fever of Alexander Jannaeus who ignores the disease due to his participation in military campaigns (*War* 1.106), and therefore dies at the age of 51 during the siege of Ragaba (*Ant.* 13.398).[18] A special status in medical literature is provided by the 'three-and-a-half-day fever' (ἡμιτριταῖος πυρετός). Certain days within the course of changing fevers are considered to be especially critical (cf. for the uneven days the opinion of the former physicians: Celsus, *De med.* 3.4).

In the ancient world fever is regularly regarded as a harbinger of death, even if medical or scientific attention is given. In 25 of 42 cases of illnesses dealt with in Hippocrates, *Epid.* 1.3 the disease is lethal.[19] Especially the 'three-and-a-half-day-fever' (ἡμιτριταῖος) is considered dangerous, since the frequent attacks seriously interfere with a prediction concerning the cycle of the fever. According to Celsus,

14. Cf. K. Weiß, 'πυρέσσω, πυρετός', p. 957; *P. Oxy.* 6.924.6.

15. See Celsus, *De med.* 3.7.2; Lucian, *Philops.* 25; Aretaios 2.4.

16. For a distinction of the categories and overlaps cf. H.-J. Horn, 'Fieber', pp. 879–80.

17. Cf. J. Longrigg, *Greek Medicine*, p. 139.

18. Miraculous narratives on the cure of fever of well-known personalities are common: Consul Fabius Maximus is healed from *quartana* at the battle at the Isère (Pliny the Elder, *Hist. Nat.* 7.166). A blind Pannonian cures the fever of Hadrian and becomes healthy himself (*Historia Augusta Vita Hadriani* 25.3-4; 24.9).

19. Cf. P. Potter, 'Epidemien I/III: Form und Absicht der zweiundvierzig Fallbeschreibungen', in G. Baader, R. Winau (eds.), *Die Hippokratischen Epidemien: Theorie – Praxis – Tradition* (SudArch, 27; Stuttgart: Franz Steiner Verlag, 1989), pp. 9–19 (10 n. 15).

the majority of those infected with this fever die due to mistakes made by the physi-cians treating the patient (*De med.* 3.8). The mortality rate of fever is further illus-trated by Ammianus, who lets Julian express the fear that he could lose his life even by a weak fever (Amm. Marc. 24.3.7: *'febricula'*). Similarly, Eusebius describes fever as a lethal disease (*Hist. Eccl.* 1.8.9, following the sequence of Josephus in *Ant.* 17.168-70 and *War* 1.656-60): he narrates not without satis-faction the suffering and death of Herod caused by a fever which is sent by God as punishment for his offence.[20]

b. Microcosm and Macrocosm: Social Implications of Fever
A discussion of fever and related phenomena begs the question of the correlation between 'microcosm' and 'macrocosm'. According to Greek understanding the outbreak of a fever does not only have an impact on the individual body which is damaged, it also affects social life at the same time. Just as fever ruins the body, it disturbs the balance of the community (πόλις). Vice versa, sociological concepts of perception might determine the interpretation of the disease. Fever attacks the body of a human as '*Weltenkraft*', and thus obscures his or her socio-political situation.[21]

The political dimensions of fever are also reflected in the metaphorical use of language. Accordingly, it is possible for Cicero to compare the disorder of the republic caused by the Catilina deception with an organism damaged by fever (*Catilina* 13.1): *ut saepe homines aegri morbo gravi, cum aestu febrique iactantur, si aquam gelidam biberunt, primo relevari videntur, deinde multo gravius vehemen-tiusque adflictantur, sic hic morbus, qui est in re publica, relevatus istius poena vehementius reliquis vivis ingravescet.*[22]

Further examples of fever having an impact on sociological matters can be provided: slaves infected with fever decreased in value (or lost their entire value), and sellers were forced to take them back (cf. Ulpian, *Digesta* 21.1.4). According to Julian (*Digesta* 42.1.60) fever is a plausible explanation for absence from court. Those who were infected with intermittent fevers were regarded as sick by law, even on days when the fever ceased attacking them.[23] Thus, fever corresponds with the understanding of epilepsy as *morbus comitialis*, since it can also result in the cancellation of political meetings (cp. Celsus, *De med.* 3.23.1).[24] Fevers are often mentioned in connection with diseases affecting female organs.[25]

20. Further evidence for the interpretation of fever as lethal disease is provided by H.-J. Horn, 'Fieber', pp. 896–97, 899–900; J. G. Cook, 'In Defence of Ambiguity: Is There a Hidden Demon in Mark 1.29-31?', *NTS* 43 (1997), pp. 184–208 (193–94).

21. See T. Külken, *Fieberkonzepte*, p. 27.

22. Cf. H.-J. Horn, 'Fieber', p. 888, concerning Virgil, *catalept.* 2.3; Plutarch, *Pomp.* 21; *coniug. praec.* 141b; *Pericl.* 6.

23. Cf. H.-J. Horn, 'Fieber', p. 880, with regard to Iavolen (*Digesta* 21.1.53).

24. For evidence cf. M. Wohlers, *Heilige Krankheit: Epilepsie in antiker Medizin, Astrologie und Religion* (MTS, 57; Marburg: Elwert Verlag, 1999), pp. 20, 249–50.

25. For diseases of the uterus, childbed fever, menses and other examples see C. Schubert, U. Huttner, *Frauenmedizin in der Antike* (Tusc; Darmstadt: Wissenschaftliche Buchgesellschaft, 1999).

c. Religious Evaluation and Significance of Fever
Ailments of fever have to be regarded as part of a more complex interpretation of time, world and reality. Next to teleological ideas (which are determined by special concepts of perception) as preserved in medical writings, one is confronted with further-reaching interpretations of diseases in religious–theological contexts. The possibility of regarding fever as God's punishment has already been referred to. Moreover, demonological roots can be identified in one of the pyretological concepts. Where the damage of the disease is apparent and a person sick with fever has obviously lost his balance without a direct trace of an external cause, dark forces and powers were assumed.[26] However, as demonstrated below, one must not take the influence of such demonological patterns of perception as a general basis and the only starting point for the interpretation of the early Christian efforts in curing fevers.[27]

The significance of 'magic' methods for curing fever and the extent of their use cannot be easily determined. Apart from 'scientific' medical approaches and treatments the belief in magical amulets as protective devices against fever was widespread. Major evidence for this assumption is provided by Pliny the Elder (*Hist. Nat.*) who gathered various other sources and listed different (and partially strange) methods, often without avoiding contradictions between those methods or reflecting on their background.[28] According to Alexander of Tralles it was possible to cure fever by writing the Greek letters kappa, rho and alpha on an oil-leaf and placing it on the sick person before sunrise.[29] The belief in statues having the power to influence fever is also attested, for example in the writings of Lucian (cf. *Philops.* 18-20; *Scyth.* 2).

26. For the interpretation of fever as the consequence of curses or divine punishment for those who trespass a sanctuary see *Syll.* 1239–40, similar ideas are reflected in the famous *Fluchtafel* of Rome, where an actor wishes fever for his opponent in order to get him out of the way (cf. R. Egger, *Die Fluchtafel von Rom [Deux Sèvres]: Ihre Entzifferung und ihre Sprache* [ÖAWP, 240; Wien: Kommissionsverlag der österreichischen Akademie der Wissenschaften in Wien, 1962], pp. 17–18). According to H.-J. Horn, 'Fieber', pp. 886–87, the concept of miraculous punishments is rarely found in ancient times. Cf. Diodorus Siculus 36.13.3; Philo, *Exsecr.* 143.

27. For a demonological interpretation of fever as hostile power cf. Philostratus, *Vit. Ap.* 4.10; Pliny the Elder, *Hist. Nat.* 2.16; Lucian, *Philops.* 9; Cyprian, *Confess.* 7; *Cod Paris.* 2316 fo. 433r; PGM 13.15-17; 4Q560 1.4; *T. Sol.* 7.6-7; J. Naveh, S. Shaked, *Amulets and Magic Bowls: Aramaic Incantations of Late Antiquity* (Jerusalem: Magnes, Hebrew University, 1987), no. 2.8–9, 9.1–2 (pp. 44–45, 82–83); cf. J. G. Cook, 'In Defence of Ambiguity', pp. 195 n. 47, 197–98. See also A. Önnerfors (ed.), *Antike Zaubersprüche* (Stuttgart: Reclam, 1991), p. 16. For a critical perspective of a demonological interpretation in Plotin's writing (*Enn.* 2.9.14) see J. G. Cook, 'In Defence of Ambiguity', pp. 203–4. Remarkably, no reference to those infected by fever is made in the *Inscriptions of Epidauros*, since numerous sufferings mentioned in these inscriptions can hardly be explained without assuming them being accompanied by fever. Rufus of Ephesus provides an example for the substitution of a disease: A sick man exchanges epilepsy for *quartana* which can then be cured; cf. Oribasius, *coll. med.* 45.30.1-2, 10-14. For *P. Oxy.* 1381 see H.-J. Horn, 'Fieber', p. 885.

28. See Pliny the Elder, *Hist. Nat.* 8.119; 21.166; 22.38, 60; 28.41, 48, 72, 86, 121; 29.79, 30.30, 95-96, 98-99; 32.113; 37.54; cf. H.-J. Horn, 'Fieber', pp. 881–84.

29. Alexander Tralleis, *De febr.* 1.407. See for similar evidence A. Önnerfors, *Antike*

Besides an understanding of fever as sent by God as a punishment, or even by
demonic forces, another interpretation is possible: in some cases fever and the
accompanying symptoms, such as body heat and shivering fits, can also be
considered as reactions to a positive influence of supernatural powers. Occasionally
one can find descriptions of fever and its accompanying symptoms which lead to
qualified manifestations and actions of the infected persons. In these cases the sick
persons are described as having otherworldly experiences, i.e. contacting other
worlds and plains of existence or even participating in a journey with a
psychopomp. For instance, in Lucian (*Philops.* 25) Cleodemus was firmly locked
in the house suffering from a severe ardent fever. On the seventh day he had a
vision of a man who took him on a tour to Hades. In the underworld he learned
from Pluto that for him the time to die had not yet come – unlike for Demylos
the blacksmith. On his return from Hades Cleodemus is fully recovered (cf. also
Plutarch, *Brut.* 20). Fever can be regarded as a *res ominosa*. According to Aretaios
of Cappadocia, a representative of the so-called 'School of Pneumatics', a person
suffering from fever in a near-death state receives seer-like abilities. Therefore, it
is possible for him to predict the time of his own death as well as the future of
fellow human beings.[30]

An example of the hypothesis that people worshipped what they feared in
ancient time is provided by the existence of the cult of *Dea Febris*: her veneration
aims at protection and avoidance of infection (i.e. it has an apotropaic effect).
According to Valerius Maximus three places of cultic worship were dedicated to
the goddess Febris in the ancient city of Rome, one of them on the Palatine.
Inscriptions underline the age and long history of this cult.[31]

d. Analysis of Pyretology in New Testament Therapy Narratives

New Testament therapy narratives, which give an account of the curing of fever,
reflect no special interest in aetiology, the setting of the disease in the individual's
way of life, the medical prediction (*prognosis*) or dietetic and pharmacological
advice. Therefore, an attempt to introduce and apply modern theories of medicine
is naturally bound to fail. A clear-cut distinction between psychogenic and somato-
genic fever is not to be found within early Christian texts, and specific recogni-
tions, such as the identification of malaria (as frequently proposed in exegetical
analysis as well), are mere speculation. However, an exception to the indifference
towards various forms and symptoms of fever is provided by Luke in Acts 28.8
(as will be discussed below).

Zaubersprüche, pp. 25–26. For possible connections between *Buchstabenmystik* and astrological theories cf. H.-J. Horn, 'Fieber', p. 906; cf. J. G. Cook, 'In Defence of Ambiguity', pp.
190–92, for astrological interpretations of fever cf. *T. Sol.* 18.1-42, and for amulets protecting
from fever in the early church see J. G. Cook, 'In Defence of Ambiguity', pp. 198–203.

    30. See Aretaios 2.4.4. Cf. similarly the effect of *furor* on people within the context of the
treatment of mania in Caelius Aurelianus, *Tard. pass.* 1.150: '… cum quadam vaticinatione …'.

    31. See H.-J. Horn, 'Fieber', pp. 889–91. Cf. Valerius Maximus 2.5.6; Pliny the Elder, *Hist.
Nat.* 2.3.15-16; Cicero, *De Natura Deorum* 3.63-64; Epictetus, *Diss.* 1.19.6.

The Septuagint and the New Testament literature entirely lack the expressions φλεγμονή (which occurs 1726 times in the writings of Galen alone) and φλογισμός (with only three references by Galen). The main term in biblical writings is rather the expression πυρετός.[32]

A. The Healing of Peter's Mother-in-Law (Mark 1.29-31)

The story of the healing of Peter's mother-in-law (cf. 1 Cor. 9.5) in Mk 1.29-31 represents the narrative counterpart to the healing of the 'man with the unclean spirit' in Mk 1.21b-28. The exorcism in the synagogue (concerned with a man) is followed by the miraculous healing in a private household (Mk 1.29, concerned with a female). Mark deliberately dates both examples of appropriate healing narratives on the first day of Jesus' ministry: the healings themselves take place on a Sabbath in order to establish an elaborate model of Jesus' capacity as a healer. The narrative is designed to end in a summary of healing acts set in the evening.[33] In this final summary (Mk 1.32-34) healing miracles and exorcisms are distinguished from each other. More evidence for such a distinction is provided on the narrative level of Mk 1.29-31 itself. Although a demonological interpretation of illness is presupposed in the context (cf. Mk 1.23-28, 32, 34), the illness in Mk 1.29-31 must not a priori be subjugated to such an interpretation.[34]

Compared to possible distinctions between various forms of fever as in Hellenistic-Roman literature, the passage Mk 1.29-31 is rather uninformative. In this expositional passage of the entire narrative (cf. the kerygmatic summary Mk 1.15) phenomenological limitation is carefully avoided; on the contrary, room for further narrative explications is maintained. The assumption that Mark deliberately and carefully placed the only narration concerning the healing of fever at the beginning of his gospel is supported by the following observations:

32. More than three thousand references are made by Galen. In the LXX the expression is exclusively employed in Deut. 28.22. Cf. Philo, *Exsecr.* 143; *Op.* 125 (in a medical context). Cf. similarly Lev. 26.16 and – with some doubts – Num. 11.1-3; Ps. 101.4. For early Jewish ideas and expressions cf. P. Billerbeck, H. L. Strack, *Kommentar zum Neuen Testament aus Talmud und Midrasch* (4 vols.; München: Beck'sche Verlagsbuchhandlung, 9th edn., 1986), pp. 479–80, and J. Preuss, *Biblisch-talmudische Medizin: Beiträge zur Geschichte der Heilkunde und der Kultur überhaupt* (Berlin: Karger, 1911), pp. 182–87.

33. Mk 1.21b-28 and 1.29-31 are probably part of a *Grundbestand* which correlates with the pre-Markan tradition. Mark's own achievements include Mk 1.22, 27, 32a, 34b, 35-38. For the *Überlieferungsgeschichte* of Mk 1.29-31, see B. Kollmann, *Jesus und die Christen*, pp. 222–23; including the relevant literature in nn. 1–2. For the form see D. Lührmann, *Das Markusevangelium* (HNT, 3; Tübingen: Mohr Siebeck, 1987), p. 52, and B. E. Williams, *Miracle – Mission – Competition? Miracle-Working in the Early Christian Mission and its Cultural Environment* (PhD dissertation: Erlangen/Nürnberg, 1988), pp. 266–67.

34. See differently R. Pesch, *Das Markusevangelium* (HTKNT, 2; 2 vols.; Freiburg: Herder-Verlag, 1976, 1977), vol. 1, p. 130; O. Böcher, *Das Neue Testament und die dämonischen Mächte* (SBS, 58; Stuttgart: Katholisches Bibelwerk, 1972), pp. 19–20, and O. Böcher, *Dämonenfurcht und Dämonenabwehr: Ein Beitrag zur Vorgeschichte der christlichen Taufe* (BWANT, V.101; Stuttgart: Kohlhammer, 1970), p. 153. Cf. further J. G. Cook, 'In Defence of Ambiguity', pp. 195–96. An *apopompe* (cf. Mk 1.25) is not present here. The text lacks elements of dispute with an opposition (cf. Mk 1.22; 3.10-12, 22-27; less obvious in 5.1-20; 7.24-30; 9.14-29).

(1) On the borderline between 'illness' and 'symptom', *morbus* and *vitium*, a summarizing potential can be ascribed to fever. Even from a perspective which lacks medical expertise it becomes apparent that fever is a polyvalent phenomenon. For Celsus, for instance, fever is '*vulgare maxime morbi genus*' (i.e. 'exceedingly common', *De med.* 3.3.1).

(2) Suffering from fever includes an ongoing confrontation with a possible lethal outcome. Therefore, already at an early point in his narrative setting Mark is able to portray Jesus' message and work as not limited to the restoration of variable physical defects, but rather deals with the alternative between life and death.

(3) Against the background of religious–theological connotations of suffering a distinction from other reports on fever and cure possibly gains major significance: Peter's mother-in-law who is confined to her bed by fever does not make her choice to 'serve' because she suffers, but rather because she has been cured and raised before by Jesus (Mk 1.31).[35] Therefore, it is implied that fever does not bestow supernatural abilities (see above), but rather hints at agony and suffering which is opposed by 'the Holy One of God' (as before in Mk 1.24; elsewhere in the New Testament in Lk. 4.34; Jn 6.69 and in the Hebrew Bible in Judg. 16.17-12; 2 Kgs 4.9; Ps. 106.16). Accordingly, the act of overcoming the burning fever has to be understood eschatologically, as an example of Jesus' superiority over life-threatening and anti-divine powers. The victory over fever impressively demonstrates a reflection of the idea that the time is fulfilled (Mk 1.15; cf. Isa. 25.8; *1 En.* 5.8-9; 25.6-7; 91.15-17; 96.3; *2 Bar.* 73.1-3, 7; *4 Ezra* 7.7, 21-34, 8.52-54; *Sib. Or.* III 367-80; *LAB* 3.10; 1 Cor. 15.55; Rev. 21.4 etc.).

(4) At the end of Mk 1.29-31 the narrator states that Peter's mother-in-law 'served them' (Mk 1.31; cf. in context 1.13). Employing the form of past tense here indicates the duration of the described action. For ancient readers this continuity of service implied by the verbal aspect excludes the possibility that the illness is only temporarily healed or the symptoms of an intermittent fever are only delayed momentarily: thus, the permanent nature of the cure is emphasized.

Despite the abbreviated character, which corresponds with the introduction of the overall framework, the illness in Mk 1.29-31 has a specific and unique profile and function. The symptoms of fever do not simply provide an exchangeable framework.[36] On the contrary, the physical pain and the consequent socio-religious implications are distinctly opposed by Jesus at the beginning of his service.

---

35.   For the verb ἐγείρειν ('lift up', 'wake up') as a typical element of Mark's healing narratives cf. Mk 2.9-11; 3.3; 5.41; 9.27; 10.49. For the taking of the hand cf. Mk 5.41; 9.27. The question whether or not a transfer of powers is implied needs not to be discussed further here – cf. O. Böcher, *Christus Exorcista: Dämonismus und Taufe im Neuen Testament* (BWANT, V.16; Stuttgart: Kohlhammer, 1972), p. 81; R. Pesch, *Markusevangelium*, vol. 1, p. 130; B. Kollmann, *Jesus und die Christen*, p. 223 n. 4. For the touching of the patient by the doctor's hand see, for example, Celsus (*De med.* 3.6.6). For the cure of fever by prayer cf. *bBer.* 34b. Healing by prayer occurs only rarely in the early Jesus-tradition; cf. Mk 7.34 (where Jesus' gesture of looking up possibly hints at a prayer); Mk 9.29 (directed towards the disciples); cf. Jn 11.41-42; Acts 9.40 (by Peter); 28.8 (by Paul); Jas 5.14-18; Acts 16.25.

36.   See for instance R. Hengel, M. Hengel, 'Die Heilungen Jesu und medizinisches Denken', in A. Suhl (ed.), *Der Wunderbegriff im Neuen Testament* (WdF, 295; Darmstadt: Wissenschaftliche

B. Re-interpreting the Fever in Luke-Acts

According to the progress of the story of the healing of Peter's mother-in-law from its Galilean beginnings in the Lukan version (Lk. 4.38-39), Jesus acts as a 'charismatic' miracle worker rather than as a 'physician'. Thus, his victory over the fever appears to be rather the work of an exorcist than in Mark.[37] From the beginning of the gospel onward Luke demonstrates that evil powers which cause pain and disease are inferior to Jesus who appears in ἐξουσία and δύναμις (Lk. 4.36, differing from Mk 1.27, cf. in essence Lk. 10.18). Jesus' central role in the Lukan version of this miracle is not only reflected by the focus on him in the introductory part (Lk. 4.38, different from Mk 1.29), but also in the section concerned with the woman: the information of her condition from Mk 1.30 is altered into a question directed to Jesus as an expert (Lk. 4.38).

Within the New Testament it is only Luke who adds a further narrative of healing from fever. Thus, the *auctor ad Theophilum* arranges an inclusion between the programmatic healing of a fever following the first public speech of Jesus in Nazareth (Lk. 4.16-30) and the last therapy narrated in Acts: as the protagonist of the second half of Acts it is Paul who – following the shipwreck incident – cures the father of Publius, the chief official of Malta who acts hospitably towards the shipwrecked people.[38] Within the context of Acts 28.1-10, v. 8 represents a therapy narrative in a nutshell. This narrative is deliberately placed within the progress of the story connecting the description of the events in Palestine and Rome (Acts 19.21). For the interpretation of Acts 28.8 the special position within the proceeding plot becomes significant, since the dominant socio-cultural background gradually alters. The closer Paul and his fellow travellers approach their destination Rome, the more prominently a sensual world gains influence on the narrative which readers might associate with the capital of the Roman empire. Accordingly, instead of a wandering Jesus (and wandering messengers and witnesses) as described in the gospel, Acts 27–28 consequently provides a description of Paul's journey by ship as appropriate for a Roman citizen. (Such means of locomotion are also obviously compared to other missionary journeys which Luke has narrated before.) The ship is specified in size as being capable of carrying no less than 276 passengers (Acts 27.37). In addition, a fellow traveller is described in more detail, namely a Roman centurion, whose 'philanthropy' marks him as a model (Acts 27.43). Moreover, Luke

Buchgesellschaft 1980), pp. 338–73 (352), concerning Jn 4. For Theißen the perception of these diseases is entirely limited to the question whether or not elements of exorcisms can possibly be isolated; cf. G. Theißen, *Urchristliche Wundergeschichten: Ein Beitrag zur formgeschichtlichen Erforschung der synoptischen Evangelien* (SNT, 8; Gütersloh: Mohn, 1974), pp. 94–97, 186.

37. Cf. for instance F. Bovon, *Das Evangelium nach Lukas (Lk 1,1-9,50)* (EKKNT 3.1; Zürich: Benziger Verlag, Neukirchen-Vluyn: Neukirchener Verlag, 1989), p. 224. Already in Mark the use of the verb ἐπιτιμᾶν might hint at a connection with exorcisms (though the expression is not exclusively employed in exorcisms); cf. Mk 3.12; 9.25 and 4.39. The meaning has to be derived from the context, cf. Mk 8.30, 32-33; 9.25; 10.13, 48.

38. For a tradition-historical and redaction-historical analysis see S. Schreiber, *Paulus als Wundertäter: Redaktionsgeschichtliche Untersuchungen zur Apostelgeschichte und den authentischen Paulusbriefen* (BZNW, 79; Berlin and New York: de Gruyter, 1996), pp. 122–36.

employs a narrative structure in the given passage which follows a scheme of (1) shipwreck, (2) rescue and (3) a new threat to the people involved; in the final part of the scheme the snakebite is of special relevance.[39] Thus, the frame in which Luke places Acts 28.8 is determined.

(1) Luke exactly identifies the illness he refers to as dysentery (δυσεντέριον) by employing medical terminology.[40] Accordingly, Acts 28.8 constitutes the only example in New Testament therapy narratives concerned with fever where the aetiological background bears significance.

(2) The preposition of the fever preceding the medical specification of the disease is not tautological. Luke rather deliberately identifies the illness in a pyretological way. The plural form possibly hints at an understanding of this fever as a cyclic inter-mittent kind of fever. In other words, one should not assume that a form of fever is in view which could potentially cease on its own.[41] The emphasis on the vehemence of the illness is also displayed by the combination of two therapeutic treatments which Luke normally separates in Luke-Acts. The cure does not succeed due to diet or pharmacology, as often used in the ancient world.[42] Instead, Paul employs two curing acts otherwise always separated by Luke, namely prayer and laying on of hands (simultaneously).[43]

39. For evidence see Homer, *Iliad* 2.718-25; Sophocles, *Phil.* 254-74 etc.; for the scheme cf. *Anthologia Graeca* 7.290 (Statilius Flaccus); 9.269 (Antipatros of Thessalonike); see H.-J. Klauck, *Magie und Heidentum in der Apostelgeschichte des Lukas* (SBS, 167; Stuttgart: Katholisches Bibelwerk, 1996), pp. 129–30. See also J. Wehnert, 'Gestrandet: Zu einer neuen These über den Schiffbruch des Apostels Paulus auf dem Wege nach Rom (Apg 27–28)', *ZTK* 87 (1990), pp. 67–99 (93–94, n. 52, for the ancient Egyptian shipwreck narrative). See A. von Harnack, *Lukas der Arzt: Der Verfasser des dritten Evangeliums und der Apostelgeschichte* (BENT, 1; Leipzig: Hinrich'sche Buchhandlung, 1906), pp. 123–25, for possible medical conno-tations of the snakebite in Acts 28.3-6 (e.g. πίμπρασθαι as a *terminus technicus* for the swelling of the wound, see *SIG3* 1169, 123; Josephus, *Ant.* 3.271, cf. Num. 5.21, 27 [LXX], concerning the κοιλία, see W. Bauer, K. and B. Aland (eds.), *Griechisch-deutsches Wörterbuch zu den Schriften des Neuen Testaments und der frühchristlichen Literatur* (Berlin, New York: Walter de Gruyter, 6th edn., 1988), p. 1325.

40. The expression δυσεντέριον corresponds with the Hellenistic form δυσεντερία (e.g. Josephus, *Ant.* 6.3). W. K. Hobart, *The Medical Language of St. Luke* (Grand Rapids: Baker, 1954 [= Dublin: Hodges, Figgis & Co.; London: Longmans, Green & Co. 1882]), pp. 52–53, identifies this disease as dysentery. See similarly A. von Harnack, *Lukas der Arzt*, p. 123. For the symptoms in the writings of the *Corpus Hippocraticum* see A. Weissenrieder, *Images of Illness*, pp. 341–46. For the chronology of the disease see Aretaios 3.13.16; 4.9. Cf. J. Longrigg, *Greek Medicine*, pp. 22, 108, 111, 120, 191, 199.

41. For harmless forms of fever which possibly cease on their own see Celsus, *De med.* 2.3 (cf. also Caelius Aurelianus, *Tard. pass.* Praef. 2: '… sicut saepe febres acutae solvuntur …'). For the association of dysentery with fever cf. *Corpus Hippocraticum*, *Prorr.* 2.22; *Aphor.* 6.3.

42. Cf. Dioscorides, *Mat. Med.* 1.22.1; 42.1; 64.4; 70.1; 73.3; 74.1; 82.1; 97.1-2; 100.3; 106.1; 107.2 and many other passages. (According to *TLG* the same root occurs 74 times.) For the application of vinegar see Epictetus, *Diss.* 2.21.22.

43. For such an unusual combination cf. the healing of the Pharaoh by Abraham in 1QGenAp 20.29; see also W. Kahl, *New Testament Miracle Stories in their Religious-Historical Setting: A religionsgeschichtliche Comparison from a Structural Perspective* (FRLANT, 163; Göttingen: Vandenhoeck & Ruprecht, 1994), p. 224. For the healing by laying on of hands see in summary

(3) Further social dimensions are implied in the narrative context of Acts 28.8, since the sick person is politically relevant: he is the father of the chief official, the first of the island. (This element corresponds with Peter being the first of the disciples in Lk. 4.38-39; moreover, in both narratives the sick persons are defined by the degree of relationship.) Regarding this fever, one can conclude that the social status of the household is affected: the balance of the community is threatened when the family of the πρῶτος suffers from fever.

(4) Finally, the narrative context of Acts 28.8 (see above) suggests that Luke pays special attention to the connotations of the disease according to Hellenistic-Roman interpretations, namely – approaching the city of Rome – the *cultus febris*.[44] On the basis of considering possible religious–theological connotations of the illness, a further problem, which has intensively occupied the discussion of Acts 28, is to be solved: in Acts 28.6, immediately before the healing narrative, Paul is addressed as 'God'. The question is: why does the *auctor ad Theophilum* 'permit' a deification without obvious critique here, while he makes considerable efforts in Acts 14 to avoid giving divine status to the apostles (Acts 14.11-13, 15-17, 18)?[45]

Various answers to this question have been offered in literature concerned with Acts 28. For instance, it has been proposed that for the reader, after having read Acts 14, it is obvious how Acts 28.6 should be judged. Thus any further critical statement would be unnecessary; it is rather Luke's narrative strategy to involve his readers. They are encouraged to actively reject such an attempt of ascribing divine status to Paul.[46] Further, it has been argued that Luke was not primarily concerned with the witness himself, but with the barbarians who are portrayed positively insofar as they are open-minded for divine acts due to their philanthropy.[47]

Lk. 4.40, cf. W. Kirchschläger, 'Fieberheilung in Apg 28 und Lk 4', in J. Kremer (ed.), *Les Actes des Apôtres* (BETL, 48; Leuven: Leuven University Press, 1979), pp. 509–21 (514–15). For the history of reception cf. H.-J. Horn, 'Fieber', pp. 897–98. For the laying on of hands as an element of healing fever see also *Act. Barn.* 15. Further, 4Q560 1.4; *bShab.* 66b, 67a; HDM A 3.23 reflect on magical elements of healing fever.

44. After meeting the 'barbarians' (Acts 28.2) Paul manages to be introduced to the island's higher-ranking representatives: thus, he gains access to the convention of hospitality (Acts 28.7: φιλοφρόνως ἐξένισεν). A connection with Dike, the Goddess of Fate, is given here (Acts 28.4); see for this H. Conzelmann, *Die Apostelgeschichte* (HNT, 7; Tübingen: Mohr, 2nd edn., 1972), p. 157; J. Roloff, *Die Apostelgeschichte* (NTD, 5; Göttingen: Vandenhoeck & Ruprecht, 2nd edn., 1988), p. 367; A. Weiser, *Die Apostelgeschichte* (ÖTK, 5; 2 vols.; Gütersloh and Würzburg: Mohn and Echter, 2nd edn., 1989), p. 669. Further, the ship which finally allows Paul to leave in Acts 28.11 is ornamented with the Διόσκουροι; cf. F. J. Dölger, '"Dioskuroi": Das Reiseschiff des Apostels Paulus und seine Schutzgötter. Kult- und Kulturgeschichtliches zu Apg 28,11', *AC* 6 (1950), pp. 276–85. However, in the description of the arrival in Rome Luke avoids any critique of the city and its religious connotations diverging from the scenario concerning the events in Athens (cf. Acts 17.16-31).

45. For the tradition-historical background and the local colour of the narrative see C. Breytenbach, 'Zeus und der lebendige Gott: Anmerkungen zu Apostelgeschichte 14.11-17', *NTS* 39 (1993), pp. 396–413.

46. See for instance A. Weiser, *Apostelgeschichte*, p. 669; S. Schreiber, *Paulus*, p. 133 n. 533.

47. See H.-J. Klauck, *Magie und Heidentum*, p. 131.

However, it has to be argued that the reference to Paul as God is not simply accepted or implicitly devalued by Luke; it rather fits into the narrative context and matches the narrative intention. By generating an inclusive correspondence with the first story of a miraculous healing of fever by Jesus in the beginning of Luke-Acts (Lk. 4.38-39), Luke aims at a brief summary of Paul's therapeutic competence at the end in Acts 28. In this final position the emphasis is on the power of Paul, who is portrayed as even victorious over fever. Accordingly, readers can conclude here that the power of the βασιλεία – its proclamation and its active ministry (cf. Lk. 9.1-6 and 10.1-16) – has been preserved without being compromised on the way to the presence of the readers. Accordingly, the island's inhabitants in Acts 28.6 perceive something true and essential according to the narrative progress: Despite Paul's action not being without the support of the power of Israel's God (cf. the prayer expressed by προσευξάμενος in v. 8), Luke's portrayal of Paul as an almost divine physician, who is able to cope with fever and who finally becomes the benefactor of the entire island (Acts 28.9),[48] does not create a deliberate misunderstanding,[49] but has to be interpreted considering the aspect of ἀσφάλεια for the readers (cf. Lk. 1.4).

3. Phenomena Related to 'Paralysis' in the Healing-Stories of the New Testament
a. Implications of Paralysis
The phenomena of paralysis are – next to blindness – ranked high by percentage in the texts of the New Testament.[50] Implications of paralysis can be divided heuristically with regard to the three parameters (see introduction above):

---

48. Cf. the thorough analysis of A. Weissenrieder, *Images of Illness*, pp. 344–46; A. Weissenrieder, '"He is a God!" Acts 28:1-9 in the light of Iconographical and Textual Sources Related to Medicine', in A. Weissenrieder, F. Wendt, P. von Gemünden (eds), *Picturing the New Testament* (WUNT, II 193; Tübingen: Mohr Siebeck, 2005), pp. 127–56. The motif of the snake combined with the healing and the application of divinity might possibly allude to special illustrations of Asclepius as a divine physician (not identified with the snake, but victorious over the animal). A connection of the snake with religious–mythological ideas in a wider sense can be assumed; cf. M. Whittaker, '"Signs and Wonders". The Pagan Background', *SE* 5 (1968), pp. 155–58 (157). However, in Acts 28 the snake is neither part of the healing act nor is it directly linked to the one performing the healing. For Luke the 'miracle' consists in surviving the bite itself (cf. Acts 28.6). The first reaction of the island's inhabitants who fear Paul's death has to be taken seriously (Acts 28.4). For the concept of having power over animals see L. Bieler, *ΘΕΙΟΣ ΑΝΗΡ: Das Bild des 'göttlichen Menschen' in Spätantike und Frühchristentum* (2 vols.; Darmstadt: Wissenschaftliche Buchgesellschaft, 1976), pp. 104–8; S. H. Kanda, *The Form and Function of the Petrine and Pauline Miracle Stories in the Acts of the Apostles* (PhD dissertation: Claremont Graduate School, 1974), pp. 293–94; H. Conzelmann, *Apostelgeschichte*, p. 157; A. A. Barb, 'Der Heilige und die Schlangen', *MAG* 82 (1953), pp. 1–21 (13–18). For the hypothesis of the snake being an embodiment of Dike, which is subordinate to Paul, see J. Wehnert, 'Gestrandet', p. 94; for the critical review of this position, see S. Schreiber, *Paulus*, p. 127 n. 509. The summary of Acts 28.9 is reminiscent of Lk. 4.38-39. The narrative as such recalls the service and salvific efforts of Jesus (cf. the summaries in Lk. 5.15: 6.18; Acts 5.15-16; 10.38; 19.11-12).

49. Cf. for instance S. Schreiber, *Paulus*, p. 136.

50. Statistically a similarity with the Inscriptions of Epidauros is striking despite differences of terminology or concept. Cf. A 3 (stiffness of fingers); 15; 16; B 15 (35)-17; (37); 18 (38) (paralysis of the knee); C 14 (57); 17 (60); 21 (64); D 4 (70).

(1) According to the distinction made by Celsus (*De med.* 3.1), phenomena related to paralysis are generally part of the class of chronic diseases. In Lk. 13.10-17 the duration of the paralysis is specified as eighteen years (Lk. 13.11–16). In Acts 9.33 Aeneas is confined to his bed for eight years. Further, Peter (and John, in Jerusalem: Acts 3.2) and Paul (and Barnabas, in Lystra: Acts 14.8) are confronted with cases of paralysis since birth.[51] The forms of paralysis which affect the whole body (cf. Mk 2.1-12 par. Acts 3.2; 9.33, cf. Mk 2.4 and possibly Lk. 13.11) can be distinguished from other forms which only affect certain organs or regions of the body (cf. Mk 3.1; Acts 14.8 and maybe Lk. 13.11).[52] However, a system which differentiates systematically between 'malfunction of the body' and 'illness' cannot be deduced from the given passages. The perception of the disability to move within the texts is also rather '*leitsymptomatisch*'. Modern medical classifications often only reflect the world-view of the interpreters.[53] An example for an anachronistic interpretation can, for instance, be seen in Mk 2.1-12 where the illness of the paralytic is labelled as 'gout' (the healing of the so-called 'Gichtbrüchiger').[54]

An explanation for the different paralytic phenomena as resulting from the mixture of bodily fluids (as provided in ancient medical writings) is absent in New Testament literature. Various relations of paralysis with other illnesses are not compatible with a systematic classification; those relations are rather defined by a loss of quality of life (cf. Lk. 7.22 par; 14.13, 21; Mt. 15.30; Acts 8.7; Jn 5.3

51. For other data on the duration of the illness see Mk 9.21; Acts 4.22; Jn 5.5; 9.1 and Philostratus, *Vit. Ap.* 3.38-39 (where Apollonius heals a paralysed hand [ἀδρανής]). For the duration in Lk. 13.10-17 cf. Celsus, *De med.* 3.22.8 (cf. *Corpus Hippocraticum, Aphor.* 5.9; *Coa praesagia* 431).

52. For the above-mentioned distinctions see Celsus, *De med.* 3.1.27; Aretaios 3.7; Caelius Aurelianus, *Tard. pass.* 2.2.

53. An understanding of certain symptoms related to an inability to move as rheumatism (e.g. Lk. 13.11-17) bears many difficulties. No evidence for rheumatism based on the so-called *Viersäftelehre* (i.e. rheumatism is related to a cold slime produced by the brain; cf. *Corpus Hippocraticum, De glandulis* 11; *De locis in homine* 10; for the general pattern see J. Benedum, *Die Therapie rheumatischer Erkrankungen im Wandel der Zeit* [*SBWGJWG*, 31.3; Stuttgart: Franz Steiner Verlag, 1994], p. 84) is preserved in the appropriate passages. Cf. the explanation for a hump due to the body's overproduction of slime in *Corpus Hippocraticum, Morb. Sacr.* 6. An assumption that bodily fluids might indeed play a role in some illnesses may possibly be derived from Mk 3.1-6 (cf. Jn 5.3).

54. Such a problematic interpretation is still displayed in the revised edition of Luther's translation from 1984. Cf. also P. Billerbeck, H. L. Strack, *Kommentar*, p. 475; A. von Harnack, *Lukas der Arzt*, p. 131, on Lk. 13.11-17; G. Traub, 'Die Wunder im Neuen Testament', in A. Suhl (ed.), *Wunderbegriff*, pp. 120–76 (149); R. Hengel, M. Hengel, 'Wunderbegriff', p. 365; A. Suhl, *Wunderbegriff*, p. 485. Such a classification projects the *arthritis divitum* into the New Testament text. Cf. Pliny the Elder, *Hist. Nat.* 36.64, 100: '*Podagrae morbus rarior solebat esse non modo patrum avorumque memoria, verum etiam nostra, peregrinus et ipse, nam si Italiae fuisse antiquitus, Latinum nomen invenisset.*' Similarly Galen, *In Hippocratis aphorismi et Galeni in eos commentarii* 28; see J. Benedum, *Therapie*, p. 92.

etc.). The expressions παραλυτικός[55] and χολός[56] can potentially be related to all narrated symptoms (cf. Acts 8.7). Different manifestations of paralysis and diseases of the joints were partly considered to be painful (cf. the severe case in Mt. 8.6).[57] The therapy was painful as well in many cases. For instance, Themison is in favour of drilling holes in the patients' skulls and gives the advice to treat the illness of certain body parts by beating them with a stick (cf. Caelius Aurelianus *Tard. pass.* 2.59). Celsus maintains: 'Those who are gravely paralysed in all their limbs are as a rule quickly carried off, but if not so carried off, some may live a long while, yet rarely however regain health. Mostly they drag out a miserable existence, their memory lost also' (*De med.* 3.27).[58]

(2) The major social feature of the disorders is the dependence on others (cf. Mk 2.31; Acts 3.2-6; Jn 5.7). An example for such dependence is provided by the Inscription of Epidauros W 16 where a paralytic is deprived of his stick by a child. The *Gospel of the Nazarenes* presupposes that the man in Mk 3.1-6 is not capable of working due to his 'withered' hand. Therefore, his only alternative is – as in Acts 3.2 – to become a beggar (cf. Jerome, *Comm. in Mt.* 12.13). It is hardly a coincidence that the paupers are followed by the lame in the list of substitute-guests in Lk. 14.13, 21.

(3) A religious–theological classification of symptoms related to paralysis cannot be standardized. For an analysis of the early Christian perspective of paralysis and its treatment, dependencies on and influences from the Hebrew Bible and early

55.   The expression occurs ten times in the New Testament (Mt. 4.24 in the summary; 8.6; Mk 2.3-4, 5, 9-10 par. Mt. 9.2 [*bis*], 6). In the fourth gospel the term is absent. In writings dated before the New Testament the expression is apparently lacking. According to *TLG* the expression is used since the first century by Dioscorides Pedanius (*Mat. med.* 1.16.2; 3.78.2, 81.1; 4.176.2, 183.2; 5.18.3; *Euporista* 1.226.1); Cyranides 1.1.110; 3.9.12; Galen, *De compositione medicamentorum* 13.1045 and others. Luke prefers the use of the past participle (in the passive) which does not necessarily demonstrate his exclusive medical competence (cf. A. von Harnack, *Lukas der Arzt*, p. 129), but rather reflects the use of a terminology which was more common in antiquity (cf. *Corpus Hippocraticum, Morb. Pop.* 7.1.8; *Coa praesagia* 193.2; Aristotle, *Eth. Nic.* 1102b; Polybius, *Hist.* 8.4.2; 11.14.6; 20.10.9; 32.8.1; Philo, *Spec. Leg.* 2.193; Diodorus Siculus, *Bibliotheca Historica* 8.12.14; 18.31.4; 20.72.2 etc.).

56.   This expression occurs 14 times within the New Testament: Lk. 7.22 par Mt. 11.5; Mk 9.45 par Mt. 18.8; 15.30-31; 21.14; Lk. 14.13, 21; Acts 3.2; 8.7 (without a clear-cut distinction); 14.8; Jn 5.3; Heb. 12.13. From Homer onwards the expression is frequently used and occurs more than 100 times before the first century CE.

57.   An overview is provided by Celsus, *De med.* 4.29-31 (cf. 7.32 for the deformity and distortion of fingers; 8.4-10 for broken bones *a capite ad calcem* – for the sources within the *Corpus Hippocraticum* see C. Schulze, *Celsus*, pp. 73-75). Against these observations cf. Aretaios 3.7.9.

58.   Cf. *Corpus Hippocraticum, Coa praesagia* 307; *Prorr.* 1.118. See for the paralysis also Caelius Aurelianus, *Tard. pass.* 2.15: *Est autem passio generaliter gravis atque difficilis; sed gravior curatione fiet, quoties toto sensu caruerint partes atque motu, et in corporibus iamdudum debilibus vel senibus aut ex alio morbo praevitatis, ut epilepsia, febre, item si plurirmas tenuerit corporis partes vel vit[iat]ae neccarias.* For the dangerous character of paralysis see also 2.20.

Jewish writings have to be considered. A special problem is provided in Mk 2.5.[59] The connection between 'illness' and 'sin' is certainly presupposed here (cf. Lev. 26.14-16; Deut. 29.15, 21-22; Isa. 38.17; Ps. 90.8-9; 107.17-20; Jn 5.14; 1 Cor. 11.29-30; Jas 5.15-16; cf. *bNed*. 41a etc.). Within the context of the Gospel of Mark the link primarily aims at emphasizing the authority of Jesus (i.e. of the 'Son of Man' in Mk 2.10) and at repulsing the accusation of blasphemy (cf. Plato, *Polit.* 2.381e; Mk 3.28-29; 7.22; 14.64; 15.29; Acts 6.11; Rev. 13.6; 16.11, 21).

In Lk. 7.22 paralytics are not only mentioned along with the blind and the deaf (and dumb), but also along with lepers. Therefore, paralysis can be found in combination with an illness which is primarily defined by religious implications in early Christian writings (cf. Lev. 13–14). However, the narrative Lk. 13.10-17 is exceptional among early Christian narratives concerned with healings of the lame: this passage provides the only interpretation of paralysis which presupposes for certain a demonological cause for the illness (Lk. 13.11, 16).

The early Christian narratives dealing with the healings of the lame are in principle based on pre-texts from the Hebrew Bible; especially distinct passages of Isaiah (similar for blindness and deafness) are reflected in the relevant texts. For instance, the sequence of paralysis (Mk 2.1-12) and a 'withered' hand (Mk 3.1-6) – framing the *controversy scenes* in Mk 2.1–3.6 – can be read as being preformed in Isa. 35.3 (in reversed order; cf. further Isa. 33.23; 35.6; Mt. 11.5; 21.14).[60]

---

59. For the problem of the *überlieferungsgeschichtliche* connection between vv. (5b)6-10 and the rest of the narrative see, e.g., D. Lührmann, *Markusevangelium*, pp. 56–57; B. Kollmann, *Jesus und die Christen*, p. 226, including n. 16. For the problem of the so-called *Tun-Ergehen-Zusammenhang* see the summary in M. Rösel, 'Tun-Ergehen-Zusammenhang', *NBL* fasc. 14/15 (2001), pp. 931–34.

60. In comparison the *Wanderlegende* of the healing of Titus Latinius (preserved in different traditions) is influenced by Roman ideas. Cicero refers to this legend in *De Divinatione* 1.55 in the context of his treatise on dreams (1.39-64). A nameless Roman farmer disobeys the orders of an apparition three times. Such disobedience is punished (*illum debilem factum ...*), but he is finally healed after transmitting the content of his dream to the senate (*... cumque senatui somnium enarravisset, pedibus suis salvum domum revertisse ...*). For Cicero's sources (Q. Fabius Pictor; Cn. Gellius; Coelius Antipater) see C. Schäublin (ed.), *Marcus Tullius Cicero: De Divinatione* (Tusc, München and Zürich: Artemis & Winkler, 1991), p. 315. The context of this legend is provided by the so-called *ludi votivi*. For problems concerning identification and dating cf. C. Schäublin, *Marcus Tullius Cicero*, pp. 315–16. The healing of paralysis is regarded as a divine indication for the necessity of an *instauratio* by the Roman senate; cf. W. Eisenhut, 'Instauratio', *PRES* 14 (1974), pp. 197–205 (199–200). Only Cicero refers to the need of a second *instauratio* (*iterum instauratos ...*). Evidence for the legend is also provided by Livy (in connection with Coriolan's stay at the Volscians). He partially modifies and extends the plot: Jupiter himself replaces the anonymous apparition. Further, the Roman farmer is explicitly identified as Titus Latinius. Jupiter appears only twice (and not three times). An *admiratio omnium* is stated at the end (Livy 2.36.1-8). Cf. further Plutarch, *Coriolanus* 24.1-3. For the parallels to Mk 2.1-12 (especially the astonishment of those present) see I. Maisch, *Die Heilung des Gelähmten. Eine exegetisch-traditionsgeschichtliche Untersuchung zu Mk 2,1-12* (SBS, 52; Stuttgart: Katholisches Bibelwerk, 1971), pp. 63–64. Cf. also the healing of a paralysed man through touching the gravestone of a virgin in Lucian, *Philops*. 11-12 (cf. the stretcher in Mk 2.1-12).

b. *The Ambiguity of 'Rest'*

In the Gospels, therapies of paralytics are continually placed within the context of disputes and controversies with Jewish opponents. A special affinity with disputes regarding the Sabbath can be observed. This affinity in Mk 3.1-6 and Lk. 13.10-17 is probably not original with regard to the tradition history. The case is even more complicated in Jn 5.2-9b, the Johannine version of Mk 2.1-12 (cf. the Inscription of Epidauros W 37), which has probably been secondarily expanded as a conflict regarding the Sabbath (Jn 5.10-18). The connection, however, results in a specific meaning and provides a specific sense, which is closely related to the sufferings of immobility (paralysis).

In Mk 3.5 the healing of the human with the 'withered' hand[61] is set against the silence of the opponents in view of the question whether or not it is lawful to perform good deeds or save lives on the Sabbath (Mk 3.4). Formally, the scenario represents a controversy story. Notably, though, an 'illness' is also ascribed to the opponents: they suffer from a 'constriction of the heart' (i.e. from 'stubborn hearts', cf. the phrase πώρωσις τῆς καρδίας in Mk 3.5; cf. also *Corpus Hippocraticum, De fracturis* 23.10; *De articulis* 15.6; 37.37; *Vectiarius* 36.8; *Mul.* 217.7, *De superfetatione* 19.7; Galen, *Ars medica* 1.387.18; *De locis affectis* 8.322.17; *De methodo medendi* 10.161, 438-40, 442; Theophilus *Ad Autolycum* 2.35 etc.). This illness is supposed to be interpreted metaphorically. Mark arranges this illness to culminate in the Pharisees' and Herodians' decision to kill Jesus in v. 6 (cf. Mk 12.13 par. Mt. 22.16; cf. Mk 8.15 *varia lectio*). Thus, the first main part in the presentation of Jesus' ministry in the second gospel is concluded: It begins on a Sabbath in a synagogue (Mk 1.21-28), and consistently ends there on a Sabbath.

---

61. The verb ξηραίνειν in the passive (as usually in the New Testament except for Jas 1.11, where the active form is related to the sun; cf. Thucydides 1.109) refers to the drying-up of liquids (cf. Rev. 16.12; Mk 5.29) or of plants (Mk 4.6 par.; 11.20-21 par.; 1 Pet. 1.24; Rev. 14.15; Jn 15.6). For the adjective in Mk 3.6 par. see Lk. 23.31; Heb. 11.29; Mt. 23.15; Herodotus 5.45. The idea of bodily fluids seems to be related, see *Corpus Hippocraticum, Progn.* 3.25; *Morb. pop.* 7.1.11, cf. A. Krug, *Heilkunst*, pp. 46–49. In Mk 9.18 the verb refers to the stiffness of the epileptic. For a rigid body cf. *Corpus Hippocraticum, Aphor.* 2.20. See also the body of Electra consumed by grief (Euripides, *Electra* 239). For the Inscription of Epidauros A 3 cf. R. Herzog, *Die Wunderheilungen von Epidauros: Ein Beitrag zur Geschichte der Medizin und der Religion* (PS 22.3; Leipzig: Dieterich'sche Verlagsbuchhandlung, 1931), pp. 32, 138; see further the Inscription C 17 (60) (on a dry leg). For ξηραίνειν cf. also Lucian, *Toxaris* 24; Galen, *De marcore liber* 7.666.1; cf. *T. Sim.* 2.12 (a hand is ἡμίξηρος for seven days). Cf. Celsus for the treatment of various consuming illnesses (*De med.* 3.22). In Mt. 15.30-31 (cf. 12.9-14) the human with the 'withered' hand is designated as a κυλλός; cf. U. Luz, *Das Evangelium nach Matthäus* (EKKNT I; 4 vols.; Zürich: Benziger Verlag; Neukirchen-Vluyn: Neukirchener Verlag, 2002, 1990, 1997, 2002), vol. 2, p. 440 including n. 11, with regard to the phrase οὐ μόνον πόδα, ἀλλὰ τὴν χεῖρα; *Suidas* 3.210 [Adler]; cf. also Mk 9.43 par. Mt. 18.8. For the healing in Mk 3.5 cf. the orders in the Inscription of Epidauros A 15; B 15 (35); cf. C 14 (57); C 21 (64) (cf. Mk 2.11; Lk. 13.12; Acts 14.10). In cases of paralytic disorder, exercise is explicitly encouraged in medical texts (cf. Caelius Aurelianus, *Tard. pass.* 2.40, 43, 47). For the depiction of a leg with varicose veins in the Asklepieion of Athens as well as for further votive offerings of people having a leg condition see E. Künzl, *Medizin in der Antike. Aus einer Welt ohne Narkose und Aspirin* (Stuttgart: Theiss, 2002), p. 34.

The healing of the woman who is 'bent over and unable to straighten up in any way' in Lk. 13.11-17 is also integrated into a conflict concerning the Sabbath. This narrative focuses on the reaction of the opponents as well. At the end a twofold reaction of the audience is narrated (Lk. 13.17), which encourages the readers to come to their own decision.[62]

The Sabbath itself is not criticized in these narratives. It is rather presumed that the Sabbath is Israel's day of rest set by God's grace. In early Jewish interpretation the day is moreover qualified eschatologically.[63] Given the character of the Sabbath as a day of rest, a casuistry, which consequently implies paralysing immobility, seems to be absurd and represents a contradiction in itself. In addition to the harmful physical aspects of immobility, a specific and unmistakable potential of socio-religious meaning can be attributed to the illness. Healing of the particular disease can represent the eschatological re-creation, which overcomes misguided rest and pathological immobilization. Thus, in the curing of paralysis the pragmatic dimensions of salvation can be reflected symbolically.[64] On a second level of the narrative the readers are simultaneously involved in these dimensions; implied readers are encouraged to avoid a behaviour corresponding with a 'constricted

---

62. For συγκύπτειν in Lk. 13.11 cf. Aristotle, *Historia Animalium* 572a (concerning the behaviour of animals); Xenophon, *Anabasis* 3.4.19, 21 (concerning military formations); Athenaeus Mech., *De machinis* 18.10; 22.6.8. Cf. also Job 9.27; Sir. 12.11; 19.26 (LXX). Otherwise Lk. 13.11 is interpreted as a depiction of gout by A. von Harnack, *Lukas der Arzt*, p. 131: For him ἀναρθοῦν is a technical term (cf. W. K. Hobart, *Medical Language*, p. 22). Against the assumption of a twofold suffering in Lk. 13.11 see W. Radl, 'Ein "doppeltes Leiden" in Lk 13,11? Zu einer Notiz von Günther Schwarz', *BN* 31 (1986), pp. 35–36. Following A. Weissenrieder, *Images of Illness*, p. 254 etc., one may consider whether or not a readership of the first century CE was able to make a connection to the so-called *hystera-phenomena*. For the narrative structure cf. R. von Bendemann, *Zwischen ΔΟΧΑ und ΣΤΑΥΡΟΣ: Eine exegetische Untersuchung der Texte des sogenannten Reiseberichts im Lukasevangelium* (BZNW, 101; Berlin: de Gruyter, 2001), pp. 279–99. For ἀνακύπτειν in Lk. 13.13 cf. 21.28.

63. Cf. B. Schaller, *Jesus und der Sabbat* (FDV, 3, Münster: Institutum Delitzschianum, 1994), pp. 26–27; C. Dietzfelbinger, 'Vom Sinn der Sabbatheilungen Jesu', *EvT* 38 (1978), pp. 281–98 (296–97). For conditions permitting acts of healing on a Sabbath (e.g. *mYom.* 8.6) cf. the references in P. Billerbeck, H. L. Strack, *Kommentar*, pp. 623–29. For interpretations of the Sabbath as either the day of election or the day in memory of creation and subsequent rest or the day of expected completion, cf. Gen. 2.2-3; Exod. 31.13-16; 35.2; Lev. 23; Deut. 5.12-15; Neh. 13.15-22; 1 Macc. 1.41-44; 2.29-38; 2 Macc. 6.6; *Jub.* 2.16-20, 30; CD 11.4.13-14; 12.3-6; Philo, *Vit. Mos.* 2.22; *Jos. Asen.* 8.9; 22.13; *mShab.*; *MekhY. Shabbeta* (Exod. 31.13). Cf. further Tacitus, *Hist.* 5.4-5; Juvenal, *Sat.* 14.96-106. For a summary see J. Becker, *Jesus von Nazaret* (Berlin: de Gruyter, 1996), pp. 371–78.

64. In a similar way the diseases related to blindness can be accentuated pragmatically (cf. Mk 8.22-26 in its narrative context). Therefore, the arrangement of the blind and the paralytics in pairs (typical for ancient texts) can also be explained based on a metaphorical interpretation of diseases. Cf. for this (in changing order) Lk. 7.22 par.; 14.13, 21 (in reversed order); Mt. 15.30; 21.14; Jn 5.3; 2 Kgs 5.8; Lev. 21.18; Deut. 15.21 (all three in LXX); *Corpus Hippocraticum, sem. part.* 5.2; Aristotle, *Historia Animalium* 585b; Antigonos Paradox., *Historiarum mirabilium collectio* 112a, 1-2; Plutarch, *Pel.* 3.8.4; *Quomodo adolescens poetas audire debeat* 35c; Josephus, *Apion* 2.23; Epictetus, *Diss.* 1.28.9; 4.8.28-29; Ps.-Clem., *Hom.* 6.11 etc.

heart' and narrow-mindedness (cf. Mk 3.5), and respectively to participate in rejoicing over the messianic deeds of glory (Lk. 13.17).[65]

Finally, at least a short comment with regard to the healings of paralysis in Acts is necessary. For the overall narrative perspective of Acts the conflicts concerned with the Sabbath belong (as implicitly also in the Gospel of Mark before) to the past. Accordingly, episodes of healing the lame become part of the history of early Christianity as a structured period. They demarcate certain stages and crucial points within the process of salvation being universalized (cf. Lk. 2.32a; 3.6; Acts 13.47 etc.). Accordingly, Luke has deliberately restricted the healings of the lame to the first half of Acts, previous to the 'Council of the Apostles' (Acts 15). Luke has prepared this thoroughly calculated proceeding in a key passage in his gospel, namely in his version of the parable of the 'great banquet' in Lk. 14.15-24. Here, the 'paralytics' are mentioned along with other substitute-guests (Lk. 14.21; cf. 14.13), who – after the designated guests refuse to appear – are invited in a first re-invitation to participate in the banquet of the βασιλεία. The individual narratives concerned with the healing of paralytics in Acts do not simply resemble Lukan redaction. They are rather shaped according to various traditions, partially influenced by local colour and adjusted to the appropriate narrative context – their setting in Acts corresponds with the unfolding of the plot. At crucial points within the plot, the episodes concerned with healings of lame people reflect the link between missionary words and practice. Luke has his readership in view here as well. Thus, on a secondary level of the narrative, the stories have a special pragmatic impact; the readers of Acts – being in danger of becoming 'paralysed' themselves in hands, legs or the entire body – are implicitly exhorted not to remain passive, but encouraged to move and become active participants in the process of universal salvation.[66]

---

65. The verb πωροῦν is applied to the reception ascribed to the *disciples* in the second gospel (Mk 6.52; 8.17). Already in the LXX versions of Job 17.7 and Prov. 10.20 (A) the verb is used figuratively and alludes to numbness. With the comparable expression σκληρύνειν ('to harden') a warning is addressed to those suffering of a 'constricted heart' in Heb. 3.8 (cf. also 3.13, 15; 4.7). For σκληροκαρδία cf. K. Berger, 'Hartherzigkeit und Gottes Gesetz: Die Vorgeschichte des antijüdischen Vorwurfs in Mc 10,5', *ZNW* 61 (1970), pp. 1–47.

66. The first healing after Pentecost (cp. the summary in Acts 2.43) occurs in Acts 3.1-10, namely the healing of the paralytic beggar at the temple gate called 'beautiful'. From the healing process 'in the name of Jesus Christ [the Nazarene]' (cf. Mk 9.38; Lk. 9.49; 10.17; Acts 4.7, 10; 9.27-28; 16.18; 1 Cor. 5.4; 6.11; Phil. 2.10; Col. 3.17; Eph. 5.20; 2 Thess. 3.6 etc.) by an order and the taking of the right hand (Acts 3.6-7) it can be derived that feet and ankles are affected. For the process of healing in Acts 3.6-7 cf. A. von Harnack, *Lukas der Arzt*, p. 133; I. Maisch, *Heilung*, p. 68. The healing of Aeneas who has suffered from paralysis for eight years (cf. W. Bauer, K. and B. Aland, *Wörterbuch*, p. 475, for the duration; cf. Acts 4.22) in Acts 9.33-35 is integrated into the context of Peter's travels in the communities (cf. 9.31-32). The passage is deliberately set before the plot concerned with Cornelius in Acts 10–11 (cf. B. E. Williams, *Miracle*, p. 300: '... provides a preface ...'). This healing is especially remarkable because it is directly related to the (raised) Jesus Christ by the effectiveness of the word – without involvement of therapeutic practice. Acts 9.34 provides the most obvious anticipation (through the word of the witness) of the later confession of Christ as a physician (cf. the difference of a theological concept in Acts

4. Conclusions and Perspectives

The main perspective implied in the New Testament therapy stories concerning the different illnesses can be qualified as *'leitsymptomatisch'*. Certain symptoms and concrete infirmities are not evaluated diagnostically or prognostically. Rather, a certain symptom, derived by an external awareness of function, becomes the foundation and framework for the awareness and perception itself. This basic symptom, however, is regarded and elucidated from the angle of a 'saluto-genetic perspective'. In other words, the interest is reflected in the concept of salvation within the healing narratives, not 'patho-genetically' in aetiological questions concerned with the mere disease.[67]

A precise analysis of the three parameters of illness (see the introduction above) is significant for the reconstruction of the sensual world of the varying healing narratives. Such an analysis helps to identify specific profiles which cannot be mutually substituted and which remain related to the background and context of their setting in experienced reality. Early Christian narrators demonstrate their ability to distinguish between these conceptional differences, since they do not simply equivocate different therapies, but rather deploy the diverse concrete symptoms of illness deliberately at crucial points within their narratives. The results of the analysis of exemplary passages, only presented in short here, cannot simply be generalized. However, the parameters which have been presented above may prove to be valid for other illnesses and may in some other cases even be defined more precisely (cf. for instance epilepsy in Mk 9.14-29 or dropsy in Lk. 14.1-6). On the whole a field comes into view in which further research is worthwhile. This is especially of importance as far as a more precise reappraisal of ancient medical writings in their relation to early Christian texts and concepts is concerned. New insights and impulses from such a reappraisal are also to be expected for the anthropology of the New Testament. With regard to a socio-historical point of view our knowledge of the early Christians' life-conditions often proves to lack precision and to be in need of amplification. For instance, an examination of the history of hygiene in ancient Christianity has not yet been undertaken. The dimension of death, as linked closely to the conditions in real life, would have to be reappraised against the background of seasonal conditions of mortality, average life-expectancy and socio-religious conditioning of diverse ailments and disorders.

2.22; 4.30; 13.11; 14.15-18; cf. also the prayer in Acts 28.8). The narrative in Acts 14.8-10 (concerned with Paul) corresponds with the narrative in Acts 3.1-10 (concerned with Peter); in both narratives the paralytic diseases are determined as existing from birth; cp. for the distinction of tradition and redaction and appropriate literature, S. Schreiber, *Paulus*, pp. 63–74. As in Mk 2.1-4 the paralytic in Acts 14.8 is introduced step by step. For the command causing the recovery cf. Ezek. 2.1-2 (LXX). The paralytic represents a soteriological example, since he 'hears' (Acts 14.9). The setting of this last healing of a paralytic within Luke-Acts is also carefully planned. Placed within the context of the first so-called missionary journey, the healing occurs in Lystra, where pagan territory is entered before the Council of the Apostles in Acts 15.

67. For a perception of diseases which is *leitsymptomatisch* within *Corpus Hippocraticum*, *Epid.*, cf. P. Potter, 'Epidemien', pp. 11, 16.

Moreover, against this background a further clarification of the complex idea of the so-called '*Tun-Ergehen-Zusammenhang*' is necessary. Early Christianity mainly adhered to the idea of a theological interpretation of illness, which is due to concepts rooted in the Hebrew Bible and in different facets of early Jewish thinking. Due to this background a concept of reality is influential in early Christian texts, according to which both – healing as well as illness – have to be regarded as a result of the activity of the God of Israel. Human medical or pharmacological skill, however, is potentially associated with foreign religious connotations. A strong line of tradition exists (though not completely undisputed and without critique; cf. for instance the book of Job) in which the phenomenon of illness is defined as closely linked to human sin. Some passages, as for example Mk 2.1-12; 9.28-29 (cf. Jas 5.13-15), reflect this point of view. Accordingly, prayer and faith (in patience) can reflect the prevailing ways to deal with illness in early Christianity of the first century, even if 'faith' is developed in a new way as faith in the exalted Christ, who – as a result of a christologizing of an originally theological metaphor – can be confessed as a physician in later texts (cf. Acts 9.34; see above). However, the question of a connection between illness and guilt has not been simply abandoned by the early Christians. Accordingly, the demonological interpretation of illness did not simply come to an end.[68]

A reappraisal of the early Christian healing traditions on the basis of ancient medical knowledge might also be of consequence for the problematic quest for the 'historical Jesus'. It is impossible to discuss implications in detail here. In short, with regard to the general outline of several proposed reconstructions of the message and activity of the 'historical Jesus', one might ask: do traditions as preserved in the story of the curing of the deaf (and dumb) by manual therapy and 'saliva' in Mk 7.31-37, or in the healing of the blind with spittle in two steps in Mk 8.22-26* provide – expressed in a category of textual criticism – '*lectiones difficiliores*' within the synoptic tradition, and should such traditions, which have an affinity to the later confession of Christ as physician (cf. also Mk 9.14-27*), be more emphasized in appropriate reconstructions – consequently from a historical point of view?[69] Moreover, for a description of parameters on this level further clarifications of categories of interpretation are necessary (e.g., the label of 'folk medicine', cf. '*Überwältigungsmedizin*').

68. Despite all efforts in the area of *diakonia* and sensibility with regard to the sick in the early Church, one also has to face the problematic processes of reception. Cf., for instance, Origen's argument in favour of a demonological interpretation of epilepsy, which is directed against a medical explanation and cure of this disease (cp. Origen, *Comm. in Mt.* 13.6). The hypothesis that early Christianity from its beginning diverged categorically from early Judaism in its interpretation of illnesses and appropriate treatment of sick people is certainly too simple and would deserve further critical discussion.

69. A negative answer to this question cannot be given by simply arguing on the basis of Hellenistic-Roman conventions alone. In some cases it is hardly possible to deduce combined motives and concrete practices in early Christian healing stories from the background of history of religion. For instance, the therapy-process in Mk 7.32-36 (cp. also 8.23-35) provides a *mixtum compositum* of practical and verbal actions without any exact analogy in comparable Hellenistic texts. A particular problem in need of further discussion is given with the hypothesis

Finally, as the examples of illness analysed above can demonstrate, a more intensive investigation of illnesses can be expected to provide not only differentiation and amplification of our knowledge about the conditions of life of early Christians and the concepts of interpretation of life and reality they had at their disposal, but some theological and hermeneutical impulses as well. At least some suggestions with regard to the hermeneutical problem will be given for further discussion. With a *magnus consensus* within the history of research and interpretation it can be stressed that the healing narratives are elaborated on the basis of a primarily christological interest, i.e. they emphasize the authority of Jesus and reflect the belief in the acts of the exalted *Kyrios* in differing ways (e.g. in the thought of Mark, that the exalted Christ is to be comprehended paradoxically in connection with his suffering and cross). They can be interpreted within an eschatological framework (cf. Mk 1.15). They may give a preview of humans as a new creation (cf. Mk 7.37; Gen. 1.31). Accordingly, acts of healing narrated in the New Testament literature are granted free of charge, independent of special (holy) locations, and do in principle not aim at the sick human's restoration with regard to his ability to work (cf. the difference between Mk 3.1-6 par. and Jerome, *Comm. in Mt.* 12.13). At the same time, it has to be stressed nevertheless that early Christian healing narratives deal with specific cases of physical harm and a concrete minimizing of life as far as the proximity of death. By way of a narrow correlation with experiences of death in the context of life, the stories do not only just appeal to the level of understanding; they rather reflect experiences, for instance the fear of fever attacks, the failure of exorcism, or touching impure and dying people. Within demonological concepts of interpreting illness, experiences of a personal raggedness may be reflected, as well as the question of illness beyond the individual, such as the effect of a disease on a community or a whole society (cf. e.g. Isa. 1.5). The healing narratives are moreover open towards action, for instance prayer. If, however, the illnesses within the healing stories are often examined exclusively with regard to christological and theological issues, even as far as exegetical research is concerned, the danger of trivializing concrete suffering emerges.

---

of a rivalry between Asclepius and Jesus set as early as the times of the origins of the literature of the New Testament. Cf. for the Gospel of John, K. H. Rengstorf, *Die Anfänge der Auseinandersetzung zwischen Christusglaube und Asclepiusfrömmigkeit* (SGFWL, 30; Münster: Aschendorf, 1953); see for the history of research, E. Koskenniemi, *Apollonios von Tyana in der neutestamentlichen Exegese: Forschungsbericht und Weiterführung der Diskussion* (WUNT II.61; Tübingen: Mohr Siebeck, 1994). Moreover, the idea of a common use of miracle narratives within the Roman imperial cult is problematic. For instance, the famous tradition concerning Vespasian's healings in Alexandria (preserved in different versions) does not indicate a widespread use of such traditions in general (cf. Tacitus, *Hist.* 4.81: … *alius manum aeger eodem deo auctore, ut pede ac vestigio Caesaris calcaretur orabat … igitur Vespasianus … iussa exsequitur. statim conversa ad usum manus …*; cf. Suetonius, *Ves.* 7; Dio Cassius 66.8). On the contrary, this tradition is obviously closely linked to the special circumstances connected with the cult of Sarapis in Alexandria and the problems of the initiation of a new line of Roman regency, namely the Flavian line. See M. Clauss, *Kaiser und Gott: Herrscherkult im römischen Reich* (München and Leipzig: KG. Saur, 2001 [1999]), pp. 114–15.

Contrary to a simple but widespread dualistic concept of 'illness' and 'health' in common modern understanding and interpretation, the healing narratives in early Christian literature may provide hints that illness is more than just the absence of health, because healing is more than simple restoration of physical well-being. Attempts of actualizing the texts, however, are confronted with the challenge of expressing the quality of this 'more' not only with regards to religious knowledge, but also in its physical and social dimensions of real life.[70]

70. This article was finished in March 2004.

FISHING FOR MEANING:
THE MIRACULOUS CATCH OF FISH IN JOHN 21

Michael Labahn

1. Hermeneutical and Methological Introduction

Modern thinking in the western world after the Enlightenment is normally puzzled by miracles or by the report or narration of miracle stories.[1] It is puzzled by miracles and their narration because there seems to be no reasonable place for miracles within the construction of the world of modern minds, which is created according to the rules of natural law. However, we cannot overlook that ancient minds, too, were sometimes puzzled by the narration of miracles and even by their performance; knowing about technical aids for such an achievement.[2]

---

1. Cf., e.g., the overviews given by S. Alkier, 'Wen wundert was? Einblicke in das Wunderverständnis von der Aufklärung bis zur Gegenwart', *ZNT* 4 n. 7 (2001), pp. 2–15; S. Alkier, *Wunder und Wirklichkeit: Ein Beitrag zu einem Wunderverständnis jenseits von Entmythologisierung und Rehistorisierung* (WUNT, I.134; Tübingen: Mohr Siebeck, 2001), pp. 23–54; H. Bee-Schroedter, *Neutestamentliche Wundergeschichten im Spiegel vergangener und gegenwärtiger Rezeptionen: Historisch-exegetische und empirisch-entwicklungspsychologische Studien* (SBB, 39; Stuttgart: Katholisches Bibelwerk, 1988), pp. 63–110; B. Bron, *Das Wunder. Das theologische Wunderverständnis im Horizont des neuzeitlichen Natur- und Geschichtsbegriffs* (GTA, 2; Göttingen: Vandenhoeck & Ruprecht, 2nd edn, 1979), pp. 28ff; E. and M.-L. Keller, *Der Streit um die Wunder: Kritik und Auslegung des Übernatürlichen in der Neuzeit* (Gütersloh: Gütersloher Verlagshaus, 1968); see also the short summary provided by B. Kollmann, 'Images of Hope: Towards an Understanding of New Testament Miracle Stories' (in this volume).

2. Cf., e.g., Lucian of Samosata's (125–190 CE) treatise in the form of a letter called *Alexandros or the pseudo-prophet* addressed to Kelsos his friend who may have been the one who wrote his polemic against Jewish and Christian piety called *Alethes logos* answered by Origin (cf. on Lucian's tractate: O. Weinreich, 'Alexandros der Lügenprophet und seine Stellung in der Religiosität des 2. Jahrhunderts n. Chr.', idem, *Ausgewählte Schriften I. 1907–1921* [unt. Mitarb. v. U. Klein hg.v. G. Wille; Amsterdam: B.R. Grüner, 1969], pp. 520–51). See already the rationalistic critique of ancient myths and miracles by Palaiphatos (4th century BCE); on Palaiphatos cf. S. Fornaro, 'Palaiphatos', *Der Neue Pauly* 9 (2000), pp. 163–64.

On the scepticism of magic (and miracles) in ancient thinking cf. F. G. Downing, 'Magic and Scepticism in and around the First Christian Century', in T. Klutz (ed.), *Magic in the Biblical World: From the Rod of Aaron to the Ring of Salomon* (JSNTSup, 245; London and New York: T&T Clark, 2003), pp. 86–99. See H. C. Kee, *Miracle in the Early Christian World: A Study in Sociohistorical Method* (New Haven and London: Yale University Press, 1983), pp. 265–73, pointing to the 2nd to 4th cent. CE critics (cf. especially his treatment of Lucian: 265–67).

Nevertheless, many people and narrators of ancient times took miracles for granted and narrated them for various purposes. Ancient miracle stories do not simply celebrate a human being or a deity for performing some supernatural deeds which the narrator may admit as an historical fact. It is not, or perhaps not only, the fascination of the 'obscure'[3] which produces miracle stories all over ancient narrative traditions.[4] It should not be overlooked that narrating miracles seems to be a matter of developing 'meaning' or 'ethos' for an intended audience or a group of readers.[5] Furthermore, miracle stories may express personal or group beliefs and, again, establish their ethos or group boundaries – not only within the Christian community.[6] Narrating miracles expresses one's own trust, world-view and construction of reality and, not to forget, one's own existential hopes, which may all be analysed by interpreting ancient textual worlds.[7]

The Gospel of John is an important example of narrating miracles in ancient times. The fourth gospel contains seven miracle stories in John 2–11, which are sometimes called by historic-critical scholarship only a concession to human condition.[8] Compared with the assumed high Christology they were taken as a strange body within Johannine theology,[9] although a closer look at them clearly indicates that the miracle stories are an integral part of the Johannine narrative and its christological portrait of Jesus as well.[10] The miracle stories have an important function for the soteriological characterization of the gospel's main hero Jesus, and his relationship to God, his father, and to the people within the narrative world. The miracle stories even develop the narrative plot in leading the antagonistic character of Jesus' opponents further to their final decision to kill him (cf. Jn 5.16-18; 11.47-53).[11]

---

3.   An exception may be found in ancient novels where miracle stories play an important role in the plot in order to entertain the readers by solving the problems of endangered heroes.

4.   Cf., e.g., H.C. Kee, *Miracle*.

5.   Cf., e.g., the case of the miracles of Dionysos which may be called, with P. McGuinty, 'Dionysos' Revenge and the Validation of the Hellenic World', *HTR* 71 (1978), pp. 77–94 (80), a 'powerful bulwark of Hellenic ethos'.

6.   On the ethic role of miracle stories told in relation to Pythagoras cf. C. Riedweg, *Pythagoras: Leben – Lehre – Nachwirkung* (München: Beck, 2002), pp. 14–15, 52, 'Hauptquelle für die Verhaltensregeln der Pythagoreer aber ist selbstverständlich der Meister selbst, dessen Wundertaten ihn nach ihrer Auffassung als Lehrer eindeutig legitimierten'.

7.   Cf. H. C. Kee, *Miracle*, p. 3.

8.   R. Bultmann, *Theologie des Neuen Testaments* (UTB, 630; Tübingen: Mohr Siebeck, 9th edn, ed. O. Merk, 1984), p. 409.

9.   J. Becker, 'Wunder und Christologie', *NTS* 16 (1969–70), pp. 130–48 (144).

10.   Cf., e.g., M. Labahn, *Jesus als Lebensspender: Untersuchungen zu einer Geschichte der johanneischen Tradition anhand ihrer Wundergeschichten* (BZNW, 98; Berlin and New York: De Gruyter, 1999); D. A. Lee, *The Symbolic Narratives of the Fourth Gospel: The Interplay of Form and Meaning* (JSNTSup, 95; Sheffield: JSOT Press, 1994); U. Schnelle, *Antidocetic Christology in the Gospel of John: An Investigation of the Place of the Fourth Gospel in the Johannine School* (Minneapolis, MN: Fortress Press, 1992); C. Welck, *Erzählte Zeichen: Die Wundergeschichten des Johannesevangeliums literarisch untersucht. Mit einem Ausblick auf Joh 21* (WUNT, II.69; Tübingen: Mohr Siebeck, 1994).

11.   Cf., e.g., M. Labahn, 'Between Tradition and Literary Art: The Miracle Tradition in the Fourth Gospel', *Bib* 80 (1999), pp. 178–203 (180–81).

Taking up rhetorical topics of ancient literature, John indicates at the end of his narrative that he could present more material about Jesus and his exceptional activities (Jn 20.30: 'Jesus did many other signs in the presence of his disciples, which are not written in this book'[12]).[13] This remark is probably more than just a rhetorical game with his readers, for there might have been more narratives and, of course, also more miracle stories of Jesus accessible in his community or school from which the evangelist selected those stories which served best his narrative aim in order to portray Jesus as the God-sent 'giver of life'.[14] John 21.1-14 is a fascinating example of such a miracle story which may stem from the Johannine tradition[15] and which propagates Johannine ethos and/or theology.

The first question concerns the literary–historical problem of John 21. Some scholars have shown that there are close links of John 21.1-14 to the entire context of John 1–20, and especially to John 6.[16] I want to take up these observations for my interpretation because they shed new light on the function of John 21 as a *postludium* to John 1–20. It has been demonstrated that the addition of the miracle story does not happen by chance, but as a clear compositional act which adds new or previously missed matters to the entire narrative already established up to the first compositional unity, which ends in John 20.30-31, without denying the meaning of the preceding narrative.[17]

Let me summarize the evidence again for the literary-critical secondary character of John 21 which seems to me still convincing. John 20.30-31 forms the end of the book, and its literary intention is finally explained. Jesus' appearance in front of his disciples (20.19-29), and especially in front of Thomas (20.26-29), seems to be the final meeting where Jesus spends the spirit and the power to forgive sins (20.21-23). The passage reflects the situation of those later Christians who have not seen the risen Lord personally (20.29). After such a reflection another visual revelation is somehow redundant.[18] Why do the disciples not recognize the risen

12. All biblical quotations are taken from the NRSV.

13. Cf. e.g., U. Schnelle, *Das Evangelium nach Johannes* (THKNT, 4; Leipzig: Evangelische Verlagsanstalt, 3rd ed., 2004), p. 336.

14. Cf. M. Labahn, *Jesus als Lebensspender*, pp. 487ff.

15. The fact that tradition is used can be assumed by tensions between the narrative setting of John 21, the narrative of the miraculous catch of fish itself, and by word statistics; cf. below.

16. Cf., e.g., M. Hasitschka, 'Die beiden "Zeichen" am See von Tiberias: Interpretation von Joh 6 in Verbindung mit Joh 21,1-14', *SNTU* 24 (1999), pp. 85–102; see also B. J. Malina, R. L. Rohrbaugh, *Social-Science Commentary on the Gospel of John* (Minneapolis, MN: Fortress Press, 1998), p. 288; F. Neirynck, 'John 21', in F. Neirynck, *Evangelica II 1982–1991: Collected Essays* (BETL, 99; Leuven: Peeters, 1991), pp. 601–16 (604–05); J. Zumstein, 'Die Endredaktion des Johannesevangeliums (am Beispiel von Kapitel 21)', in J. Zumstein, *Kreative Erinnerung: Relecture und Auslegung im Johannesevangelium* (Pano: Zürich, 1999), pp. 192–216 (205–6).

17. Cf. also J. Zumstein, 'Narratologische Lektüre der johanneischen Ostergeschichte', in J. Zumstein, *Kreative Erinnerung*, 178–91 (188), however, with a different interpretation of the new meaning developed by John 21.

18. Cf., e.g., J. Zumstein, 'Endredaktion', p. 201.

Jesus in Jn 21.4, although they have seen him twice? In John 21 a couple of new motifs are introduced, and there are many words never used in John 1–20.[19] The disciples become fishermen, and the sons of Zebedee are introduced into the narrative, although they did not play any role in the gospel previously. Nathaniel is suddenly connected with Cana, a fact which is not mentioned in John 1–2. Peter now plays a more important role than in any other place in chs. 1–20, and in John 21 the beloved disciple becomes the author of the gospel narrative.[20] Nevertheless, John 21 still represents traits of the Johannine 'sociolect' which indicates that the last chapter of John has to be read as part of the history of the Johannine community.[21]

The miraculous catch of fish is narrated in different settings in Lk. 5.1-11 and in Jn 21.1-14. There are many significant parallels in structure, motifs and partly in wording shared by Jn 21.1-14 and Lk. 5.1-11[22] which make it highly probable that there is an inter-textual relationship between the two texts which will be explored further below. It should be beyond doubt that both versions are variants of the same narrative core (or idea).[23] Therefore, it is highly debated if Lk. 5.1-11, or a tradition like Lk. 5.1-11, was the source of Jn 21.1-14. And it is also debated if either the Lukan setting (an incident during Jesus' life) or John's setting (a resurrection appearance) was more original.[24] However, to take up the main

---

19. Cf. the overview presented by R. E. Brown, *The Gospel According to John XIII–XXI* (AB, 29A; New York: Doubleday, 1970), pp. 1079–80.

20. Cf., e.g., F. J. Moloney, *The Gospel of John* (SPS, 4; Collegeville: Liturgical Press, 1998), pp. 545–46; U. Schnelle, *The History and Theology of the New Testament Writings* (London: SCM, 1998), pp. 490–91; U. Schnelle, *Antidocetic Christology*, pp. 13–15; J. Zumstein, 'Endredaktion', pp. 199–206.

21. On the difference between Johannine 'sociolect' and Johannine 'ideolect' cf. M. Labahn, *Jesus als Lebensspender*, pp. 107–9. R. E. Brown, *The Gospel According to John XIII–XXI*, pp. 1067–77, points to a lot of Johannine words and phrases in Jn 21.1-14.

22. Cf., e.g., G. Blaskovic, *Johannes und Lukas: Eine Untersuchung zu den literarischen Beziehungen des Johannesevangeliums zum Lukasevangelium* (Diss.T, 84; St. Ottilien: EOS Verlag, 2000), p. 43.

23. The list of parallels and differences between the Johannine and the Lucan story does not allow us to understand both stories as going back to different events or being independent narratives which only by chance contain some parallels (two different events are still assumed in the treatment of H. van der Loos, *The Miracles of Jesus* [NovTSup, 9; Leiden: Brill, 1965], pp. 670, 678, and now by B. Witherington III, *John's Wisdom: A Commentary on the Fourth Gospel* [Louisville, KY: WJK Press, 1995], p. 405, n. 8, referring to G. R. Osborne, 'John 21: Test Case for History and Redaction in the Resurrection Narratives', in R. T. France, D. Wenham (eds), *Gospel Perspectives* II: *Studies of the History and Tradition in the Four Gospels* [Sheffield: JSOT Press, 1981], pp. 293–328 [294–95]) as is convincingly shown by, e.g., J. P. Meier, *A Marginal Jew. Rethinking the Historical Jesus* II: *Mentor, Message, and Miracles* (ABRL; New York: Doubleday, 1994), pp. 897–99, and others. There is a relationship which is much disputed but needs to be explained in traditional historical or literary terms.

24. The answer to the question of the original setting heavily depends on the judgement about the relation between John and the Synoptics (cf. on this subject F. Neirynck, 'John and the Synoptics: 1975–1990', in A. Denaux (ed.), *John and the Synoptics* [BETL, 101; Leuven: Peeters

arguments, post-Easter elements[25] do not per se tell anything about a pre- or post-Easter setting of any story. Apart from the age and the originality of either story, both accounts are told and re-told by post-Easter Christians which means that the stories are applied (although – in my view – not completely changed) to their situations and beliefs. Further, a changed setting does not free us from judging any other text in its own way. Moreover, form-critical rules help us to understand individual forms of a genre, but do not neglect the individual creativity behind every form of the genre and setting.

1992], pp. 3–62; D. M. Smith, *John Among the Gospels: The Relationship in Twentieth Century Research* [Columbia, SC: University of South Carolina Press, 2nd edn, 2001]; J. Frey, 'Das vierte Evangelium auf dem Hintergrund der älteren Evangelientradition: Zum Problem Johannes und die Synoptiker' in T. Söding (ed.), *Mitte oder Rand des Kanons: Neue Standortbestimmungen* (QD, 203; Freiburg i.Br.: Herder, 2003], pp. 60–118 [61–76], and M. Labahn, M. Lang, 'Johannes und die Synoptiker: Positionen und Impulse seit 1990', in J. Frey, U. Schnelle in cooperation with J. Schlegel (eds), *Kontexte des Johannesevangeliums: Das vierte Evangelium in religions- und traditionsgeschichtlicher Perspektive* [WUNT, 175; Tübingen: Mohr Siebeck, 2004], pp. 443–515), a problem which has its own clue with regard to John 21 as part of the Johannine redaction (for I. Dunderberg, *Johannes und die Synoptiker: Studien zu Joh 1–9*, [AASFDHL, 69; Helsinki: Suomalainen Tiedeakatemia, 1994] the parallels between John and the Synoptics are due to a literary relationship of the redaction of John to the Synoptics). If there is an oral or a literary relationship between John (or Jn 21) and the Synoptics/Luke, the question of the original setting has to face the problem of inter-textual relationship first and it is quite natural to assume a Johannine re-telling of the Lukan story.

The situation changes by assuming literary and oral independence. In that case both stories may have reached their narrators by different tradents who may have altered or saved the original setting. It is interesting to see that there is no consensus ahead. Insofar as the Lukan account seems not to be narrated in accordance with the rules of New Testament miracle stories, scholars assume that Luke changed an original post-Easter appearance story of Jesus into his pre-Easter setting; cf., e.g., R. E. Brown, *The Gospel According to John XIII–XXI*, pp. 1085–92; J. A. Fitzmyer, *The Gospel According to Luke I–IX* (AB, 28; New York: Doubleday, 1981), pp. 561–62; G. Klein, 'Die Berufung des Petrus', in idem, *Rekonstruktion und Interpretation: Gesammelte Aufsätze zum Neuen Testament* (BEvT, 50; München: Kaiser, 1969), pp. 11–48 (45–46); B. Kollmann, *Jesus und die Christen als Wundertäter: Studien zu Magie, Medizin und Schamanismus in Antike und Christentum* (FRLANT, 170; Göttingen: Vandenhoeck & Ruprecht, 1996), p. 279; J. P. Meier, *A Marginal Jew* II, pp. 899–904; further arguments are that some post-Easter stories are set back into Jesus' lifetime by their narrators; other scholars are not convinced and plead for the Lukan setting as original: e.g., F. Bovon, *Das Evangelium nach Lukas* 1. Teilband: *Lk 1,1–9,50* (EKKNT, III.1; Zürich: Benzinger and Neukirchen-Vluyn: Neukirchener, 1989), p. 234; H. Schürmann, *Das Lukasevangelium. Erster Teil: Kommentar zu Kap. 1,1–9,50* (HTKNT, III.1; Freiburg: Herder, 1969), pp. 273–74; (for further literature cf. the titles mentioned before). According to R. T. Fortna, *The Fourth Gospel and its Predecessor: From Narrative Source to Present Gospel* (SNTW; Edinburgh: T&T Clark, 1989), pp. 65–83, Jn 21.1-14 belonged to the Gospel of Signs, which he reconstructed as source of the fourth gospel. The miracle is placed as the third sign as part of the earthly ministry of Jesus and does not show any reference to his resurrection (68).

25.   E.g. Peter falling on his knees and confessing his sins in Lk. 5.8 is taken as an argument for the post-Easter setting of Lk. 5.1-11; cf. J. P. Meier, *A Marginal Jew* II, p. 901.

The recent article takes Jn 21.1-14 as a Johannine reshaping of an earlier tradition. The post-Easter elements within the miracle narrative are related to the narrator who adds the story to its actual setting so that this frame does not point to a tradition with a post-Easter setting.

If both texts, Lk. 5.1-11 and Jn 21.1-14, serve a missionary aim, as was admitted recently by Thomas Söding,[26] they still have a different narrative setting in their literary context. In the present article, the meaning of Jn 21.1-14 and its narrative role will be explored in more detail by analysing its *intra*-textual relationship (as far as John 21 is a *Fortschreibung* to John 1–20) as well as its *extra*-textual relationship (to Lk. 5.1-11, or a tradition like Lk. 5.1-11).

2. A Story in its Own Right[27]

Analysing the linguistic and structural character of the story in Jn 21.1-14 and its content, one may find a lot of interaction or interrelation with other texts in John 1–20 and, according to my view, in Luke as well. However, it is the story itself that circumscribes its own focus, that forces the reader to read it in its own right.

Framed by a clear heading and by a concluding remark referring back to the heading (see below), the story forms a literary entity within the overall context of John 21.[28] Referring to other disciples besides Peter and the beloved disciple, who also stems from the Johannine narrative world, shows that Jn 21.1-14 is not exclusively focused on the relationship of Peter and the beloved disciple,[29] although the episode enhances a glimpse of the relationship of these two characters within its actual literary context (however the latter is not the focus of this article). Moreover, the meaning of the story of the catch of fish and its contribution to the under-

26. T. Söding, 'Erscheinung, Vergebung und Sendung: Joh 21 als Zeugnis entwickelten Osterglaubens', in R. Bieringer, V. Koperski, B. Lataire (eds.), *Resurrection in the New Testament. FS J. Lambrecht* (BETL, 165; Leuven: Peeters, 2002), pp. 207–32 (209ff.).

27. The character of John 21 as a story in its own right is strongly emphasized by W. S. Vorster, 'The Growth and the Making of John 21', in F. van Segbroeck, C. M. Tuckett, G. van Belle, J. Verheyden (eds), *The Four Gospels 1992* (FS F. Neirynck; BETL, 100; Leuven: Peeters, 1992), pp. 2207–21 (2216–17), who argues in contrast to my study for John 21 as an integral part of the Gospel of John (see also H. Thyen, 'Noch einmal: Johannes 21 und "der Jünger, den Jesus liebte"', in T. Fornberg and D. Hellholm assisted by C. D. Hellholm (eds), *Texts and Contexts: Biblical Texts in their Textual and Situational Contexts* (Essays in Honor of L. Hartmann; Oslo: Scandinavian University Press, 1995), pp. 147–89.

28. Cf., e.g., B. J. Malina, R. L. Rohrbaugh, *Social-Science Commentary*, p. 287. Differently, e.g., C. Welck, *Erzählte Zeichen*, pp. 315–17, who puts more emphasis on the interpretation of John 21 as a literary unit that underscores the credibility and sufficiency of the Gospel of John (p. 323); G. Blaskovic, *Johannes und Lukas*, p. 71; E. Ruckstuhl, 'Zur Aussage und Botschaft von Johannes 21', in E. Ruckstuhl, *Jesus im Horizont der Evangelien* (SBAB, 3; Stuttgart: Katholisches Bibelwerk, 1988), pp. 327–53 (328–29); see also T. Wiarda, 'John 21:1-23: Narrative Unity and ist Implications', *JSNT* 46 (1992), pp. 53–71; J. Zumstein, 'Narratologische Lektüre', p. 188; J. Zumstein, 'Endredaktion', pp. 206–14.

29. C. Welck, *Erzählte Zeichen*, p. 323, calls Jn 21.1-23 a typical beloved-disciple text ('ein typischer Lieblingsjüngertext').

standing of John 21, as well as to John 1–21 as a whole, is to be gained by analysing the miracle story as a literary unit within a larger world of different texts and contexts.

An introduction or heading by the omniscient narrator in Jn 21.1 explains what will happen during the following narrative: Jesus reveals himself to his disciples at the Sea of Tiberias. The end of the revelation narrative is indicated in v. 14 by some kind of inclusion: 'This was now the third time that Jesus appeared to the disciples after he was raised from the dead'. The narrator again uses the verb φανερόω which he has also applied twice in v. 1. All events reported between these two lines function *to reveal Jesus to his disciples as the risen Lord*.

The group of disciples to which the self-revelation will be addressed is mentioned in v. 2: Simon Peter, Thomas, Nathanael, the sons of Zebedee and two further disciples. Simon Peter appears to be the spokesman of this group,[30] addressing the others with his intention to go fishing. The remaining disciples agree and the story starts as a fisherman's tale about the desperate fate of ordinary men: working the whole night long without any success.

In the morning – an important time for resurrection appearances of Jesus (Lk. 24.1, 22; Jn 20.1; cf. Mk 16.9) and a highly symbolic time in John's Gospel as well[31] – Jesus stands at the shore and not one of his disciples acknowledges his true identity (Jn 21.4). This remark prepares for the identification of Jesus in v. 7, and is therefore a link within the narrative to the overall theme of the revelation of Jesus[32] introduced by the narrator in vv. 1, 14. A second feature was added to the story (v. 5): the still unidentified Jesus asks for something to eat (παιδία, μή τι προσφάγιον ἔχετε – 'Children, you have no fish, have you?'). Now it becomes obvious why Peter wanted to go fishing; there was nothing to eat at all – a struggle without success (v. 3: 'they went out and got into the boat, but that night they caught nothing'). Jesus' question points to a shortage which was not changed by working the whole night long. Therefore, Jesus asks them to cast the net on the right side of the fishing boat and a miracle of gift happens – the fishing net is full of fish and no one is able to haul it in.[33] The addressees are called παιδία (children). This is a title used for the members of the community in 1 John (2.14, 18; see also the reference to τεκνία in 1 Jn 2.1, 12, 28). Does Jesus already

---

30. On the role of Peter cf. E. Ruckstuhl, 'Aussage und Botschaft', p. 330.

31. Cf. the remarks by O. Schwankl, *Licht und Finsternis: Ein metaphorisches Paradigma in den johanneischen Schriften* (HBS, 5; Freiburg: Herder, 1995), pp. 110, 352.

32. Cf. O. Schwankl, *Licht und Finsternis*, p. 190, who points to the parallel between Jn 20.14 and 21.4.

33. Taking the empty net in v. 3 as a mere symbolic feature in the narrative preparing only for the self-revelation of Jesus (C. Welck, *Erzählte Zeichen*, p. 334; see also p. 336) takes all the meaning away from the miraculous catch of fish which is reflected within the narrative. Both features have to be taken in account. The self-revelation of Jesus and the catch of fish, which indeed has a symbolic meaning, have to be read as two parts of the story.

On the fishing net, probably a drag net, cf. G. Dalman, *Arbeit und Sitte VI: Zeltleben, Vieh- und Milchwirtschaft, Jagd, Fischfang* (SDPI, 9 = BFCT, 2.41; Gütersloh: Bertelsmann, 1939), pp. 346–51.

address the disciples as 'children of God'[34] or perhaps – more specifically – as those who are called to go out by the symbolic act of the miraculous catch of fish with a missionary aim?

In accordance with Jn 2.1-11, the miracle reveals the passer-by's identity:[35] it is the master (ὁ κύριός ἐστιν, 21.7), as the beloved disciple acknowledges.[36] Again his counterpart from the gospel comes into view. Peter, who becomes aware of his nakedness, jumps into the sea. Peter's nakedness is due to his work as a fisherman at that time, which is, for example, illustrated by different ancient literature and mosaics.[37] However, the notion that Peter puts on his clothes before jumping into the sea is strange and some exegetes propose, as an interpretation, that he straightens his clothes for swimming.[38] It seems easier to understand the remark in accordance with shame which overcomes the narrative character in the presence of the risen Jesus. Furthermore, it may be asked if the notion of Peter's nakedness has – in its recent literary context – something to do with the denial at the high priest's court, which seems to be reflected by the coal-fire in v. 9 and the threefold order to feed Jesus' lambs later on in Jn 21.15-19.

The boat with the disciples and the net full of fishes arrives at the shore. The miracle confirms and identifies Jesus. Surprisingly, at land there is no more need for the former miracle because there was a fire with fish and bread on it (v. 9).[39] Again the focus switches back to the fishes in the net: Jesus asks the disciples to 'bring some of the fish that you have just caught' (v. 10). The net was hauled in by Peter and contained 153 fishes – a large number,[40] which is not explained, but

34. As supposed by B. J. Malina, R. L. Rohrbaugh, *Social-Science Commentary*, p. 288.

35. Cf. Jn 2.11: καὶ ἐφανέρωσεν τὴν δόξαν αὐτοῦ, καὶ ἐπίστευσαν εἰς αὐτὸν οἱ μαθηταὶ αὐτοῦ – 'Jesus did this, the first of his signs, in Cana of Galilee, and revealed his glory; and his disciples believed in him'.

36. Cf. already Jn 20.5-8. The beloved disciple arrives first at the grave (v. 5) but does not enter. Peter enters first and thereafter the beloved disciple (vv. 6, 8a). It is the beloved disciple of whom it is stated that 'he saw and believed' (v. 8b).

37. Some examples are to be found in Bella S. Galil's article 'A Sea of Stone – Biodiversity and History' (http://www.biomareweb.org/3.2.html); another nice example is a 3rd cent. CE mosaic (Sousse Museum) from Hadrumete in Tunisia (http://www.tunisiaonline.com/mosaics/mosaic46b.html).

38. Cf., e.g. F. J. Moloney, *Gospel of John*, p. 553: 'Peter is not entirely naked, but very lightly clad in one garment ... To remove it would have left him entirely naked, so he tucks it up so that he might move freely in the water'. C. K. Barrett, *Das Evangelium nach Johannes* (Meyer-K Sonderband; Göttingen: Vandenhoeck & Ruprecht, 1990), pp. 555–56, refers to the prohibition in Jewish tradition of greeting nakedly.

39. Clearly pointed out by B. Witherington III, *John's Wisdom*, p. 354; however, he still proposes that 'v.10 may suggest that Jesus needed a few more'; see also B. Kollmann, *Jesus und die Christen als Wundertäter*, p. 278 n. 22.

40. A nice mosaic from the middle of the 3rd cent. CE from Tunesia (Sousse Museum) showing fish and shellfish poured from a rush basket may illustrate the richness of the catch by ancient imagery, but does not explain the use of such a concrete number (http://www.tunisiaonline.com/mosaics/mosaic48.html).

which seems to be of some sense[41] – however, the exact meaning seems somehow undetectable now.[42]

The focus switches again to the meal, and it is not said that the fishes already caught were used for it. The change of focus leaves a 'gap', which gives room to speculate how many fishes were needed to be consumed; it clearly highlights that there is a deeper meaning in the whole account which does not need a narrative harmonization. Here, the reader may suppose that there is a deeper meaning behind the miraculous catch of fish and he or she is really forced to develop a symbolic reading of the whole narrative account.

Again, Jesus invites the spectators in the narrative to eat and again the author takes up the theme of recognizing Jesus in a strange manner, which may best be called a retarding element. The narrator states that the disciples do not dare to ask Jesus for his identity. He gives a reason: the disciples know that he is the *Lord*; however, in that case there was no need to ask any more who he is.

The next scene presents Jesus as a house-father who takes the bread, blesses it, and offers it to his guests (v. 13). He acts similarly with the fish. The whole scene closes with a further comment of the narrator: 'This was now the third time that Jesus appeared to the disciples after he was raised from the dead' (v. 14).[43] With that cataleptic element the narrator points back to John 1–20 and clearly signals to the reader that he presupposes the Johannine narrative; a fact which is indicated

---

41. An interesting parallel to the miraculous catch of fish in which the number of fishes plays an important role is told of Pythagoras (Porphyrius, *Vit. Pyth.* 25; Iamblichus, *Vit. Pyth.* 36). He said that he was able to predict the exact number of fishes which their weighty net contained although it was in the sea. The fishermen promised to do everything he ordered if he was right. Of course, he predicted the right number, and his order to let the fishes live and to put them back into the water was fulfilled. No fish died during counting. The whole story may provide propaganda for Pythagorean 'vegetarianism' (cf. C. Riedweg, *Pythagoras*, pp. 93ff.). The miraculous catch of fish in John 21 and the story about Pythagoras do not have much in common (cf. W. Fauth, 'Pythagoras, Jesus von Nazareth und der Helios-Apollon des Julianus Apostata. Zu einigen Eigentümlichkeiten der spätantiken Pythagoras-Aretalogie im Vergleich mit der thaumasiologischen Tradition der Evangelien', *ZNW* 78 [1987], pp. 26–48 [38–39]); however, they both do not intend merely to characterize their different heroes, but also to develop the group's own ethos.

42. For the search of meaning, cf., e.g., C. R. Koester, *Symbolism in the Fourth Gospel: Meaning, Mystery, Community* (Minneapolis, MN: Fortress Press, 2nd edn, 2003), pp. 311–16. J. Zumstein, 'Endredaktion', p. 211: 'Das mit 153 Fischen gefüllte Netz, das er (sc. Petrus), ohne dass es zerreisst, ans Ufer zieht, präfiguriert die pastorale Funktion des Apostels, die zahlreichen Gemeinden in der Einheit zu sammeln'. For further recent attempts to explain the number cf., e.g., T. Niklas, '"153 große Fische" (Joh 21,11): Erzählerische Ökonomie und "johanneischer Überstieg"', *Bib* 84 (2003), pp. 366–87; M. Oberweis, 'Die Bedeutung der neutestamentlichen "Rätselzahlen" 666 (Apk 13.18) und 153 (Joh 21.11)', *ZNW* 77 (1986), pp. 226–41 (236–41); J. Werlitz, 'Warum gerade 153 Fische? Überlegungen zu Joh 21,11' in S. Schreiber, A. Stimpfle (eds.), *Johannes aenigmaticus* (FS H. Leroy; BU, 29; Regensburg: Verlag Friedrich Pustet, 2000), pp. 121–37 (135–37).

43. The first two scenes are Jn 20.19-23, 24-29.

indirectly by mentioning the actors (Simon Peter: 1.42; 6.68; 13.9, 24, 36; 18.10, 15, 25; 20.6;[44] Thomas called Didymus [Θωμᾶς ὁ λεγόμενος Δίδυμος]:[45] 11.16; 20.24; Nathanael: 1.45-49;[46] for the other two disciples cf. 1.35: ἐκ τῶν μαθητῶν αὐτοῦ δύο; for the μαθητὴς ὃν ἠγάπα ὁ Ἰησοῦς cf. Jn 13.23-26; 19.26-27; 20.2-10), as well as the narrative world (Sea of Tiberias; cf. Jn 6.1) and by taking up language from the preceding text.[47]

A close look at the story so far indicates that the narrator combines different subjects under the overall heading of the third post-revelation appearance of Jesus. A miracle is due to a revelatory story as well as the recognition of the revealed one. Also, it is no surprise in such a story that the revealed one shares community with his addressees. But what is the true meaning of the miracle, which is connected with the narrative frame without really being necessary (there is food on the fire) and which is combined with a puzzling number (153 fishes)? Why did the narrator in v. 12 mention that the disciples did not dare to ask for the identity of Jesus although he immediately states that they know Jesus (v. 12)?

Craig R. Koester has correctly called Jn 21.1-14 a 'symbolic action'.[48] The miraculous catch of fish has something to do with people recognizing Jesus' identity and being brought to Jesus. The story has a christological focus, which is underlined by the narrator in the twofold question of Jesus' identity (vv. 4, 12), in Peter's servile behaviour (v. 7), and in Jesus' order to cast the net (v. 6) with the miraculous good catch (vv. 6, 11). The miracle as well as the action itself is motivated by the quest for food, although it is never stated that the catch has any relevance for food supply. Therefore the miracle is best explained as a symbolic action which stands for something else, which is brought to Jesus on his demand. One may wonder – and many exegetes have considered this solution – if the catch represents a symbol of the missionary activity of the Johannine group itself,[49] which is ordered by the risen Jesus (cf. Mt. 28.16-20). In the light of other texts to which the narrator points, this conclusion may be assured (section 3), so that the inconsistencies of the story may best be explained by reading the story in the light of other

44. Cf. R. E. Brown, *The Gospel According to John XIII–XXI*, p. 1067.

45. For Thomas as an important narrative figure in John cf., e.g., P. Dschulnigg, *Jesus begegnen: Personen und ihre Bedeutung im Johannesevangelium* (Theologie 30; Münster: LIT, 2000), pp. 220–36.

46. For Κανὰ τῆς Γαλιλαίας cf. Jn 2.1, 11; 4.42.

47. For the use of μετὰ ταῦτα cf. Jn 3.22; 5.1, 14; 6.1; 7.1; 11.11; 13.7; 19.38; on ἐφανέρωσεν ἑαυτὸν πάλιν cf 1.31; 2.11; 3.21; 7.4; 9.3; 17.6; for ὑπάγω, which is mostly christologically used, cf. 7.33; 8.14, 21-22; 13.33, 36; 14.4, 28; 16.5, 10, 17 – the question of Jesus' true identity is often raised in the fourth gospel. A linguistic parallel can be found in Jn 1.19; 8.25; see also 4:10. For Jn 21.13 cf. 6.11.

48. C. R. Koester, *Symbolism*, pp. 134ff.

49. Cf., e.g., B. Witherington III, *John's Wisdom*, p. 355, although slightly reluctant concerning the symbolic character of the narrative. By calling the event a 'narrative action' there is no judgement implied concerning the historical value of the event for the narrator.

stories. Furthermore, we can detect aspects of the prehistory of the Johannine narrative (section 4) and we have to reflect the changes of the narrative setting of a miraculous account of Jesus (section 5).

3. A Story in the Light of Other Stories
a. Johannine Stories
John 21.1-14 has to be read as a resumption of the Johannine meal scenes in Jn 6.1-15 and Jn 13.1-20. It also points back to another public scene at the fire in Jn 18.18: 'Now the slaves and the police had made a charcoal fire (ἀνθρακίαν) because it was cold, and they were standing around it and warming themselves. Peter also was standing with them and warming himself.' That remark prepares the scene in Jn 21.15-19. Furthermore, the story submits a collection of names of Jesus' disciples in John pointing to Jn 1.35-51,[50] to 11.16; 14.5; 20.24-28 (Thomas) and to 13.23-26 (see also 19.26; 20.2) where the beloved disciple is mentioned for the first time.

A well-known influence on Jn 21.1-14 is the feeding of the five thousand. The relationship is obvious from the same location at the sea of Tiberias (6.1; 21.1). Also, both scenes share the same food: fish and bread. Both texts also refer to fish in a comparable manner.[51] Nevertheless, fish play their own role in John 21 for they are caught miraculously in the morning. The fish should be brought to Jesus, but Jesus is already near the fire where the reader will find bread and fish, which will be distributed in a way comparable to Jn 6.11.[52] Although Jn 21.13 reads bread in the plural, a reference to John 6 is not unlikely.

Therefore, the reader is reminded of features of the feeding of the crowd in John 6. Jesus, who proved to be the true bread of life by being killed on the cross for his friends (Jn 15.13; cf. 11.50) or for his own people (Jn 10.11) and who is risen and again alive, provides bread and fish as a symbol of giving his life for the benefit of the multitude. If we read the catch of 153 fishes not as fishing for food, but as a symbolic act of 'catching people' then John 21 may be read as a powerful authorisation of the disciples by Jesus to catch men and women from all over the world in order to make them participate in Jesus based on his death and resurrection.

---

50. Cf. e.g. G. Blaskovic, *Johannes und Lukas*, pp. 76–77.
51. Jn 21.13: Καὶ τὸ ὀψάριον ὁμοίως.
   Jn 6.11: ὁμοίως καὶ ἐκ τῶν ὀψαρίων.
52. Jn 21.13: ἔρξεται Ἰησοῦς καὶ λαμβάνει τὸν ἄρτον καὶ δίδωσιν αὐτοῖς.
   Jn 6.11: ἔλαβεν οὖν τοὺς ἄρτους ὁ Ἰησοῦς καὶ εὐχαριστήσας διέδωκεν τοῖς ἀνακειμένοις.
   For sure, Jn 6.11 has verbal agreements with the eucharistic tradition of the New Testament and an influence from there is frequently assumed (cf. the discussion in M. Labahn, *Offenbarung in Zeichen und Wort: Untersuchungen zur Vorgeschichte von Joh 6,1-25a und seiner Rezeption in der Brotrede* [WUNT, II.117; Tübingen: Mohr Siebeck, 2000], pp. 95ff). However, there is no need to think of an extra-textual reference to eucharistic traditions if Jn 21.13 could be fully explained within the Johannine context. The only possible extra-textual reference may stem from Lk. 24.30. However, this influence could not be proved seriously.

One may find some links to the entire context of the feeding of the five thousand. After the feeding of the five thousand, the disciples of Jesus at the evening ('Ὡς δὲ ὀψία ἐγένετο) went to the sea (κατέβησαν οἱ μαθηταὶ αὐτοῦ ἐπὶ τὴν θάλασσαν; 6.16) and into a boat (καὶ ἐμβάντες εἰς πλοῖον).[53] Without Jesus, who was on top of a mountain (6.15: ἀνεχώρησεν πάλιν εἰς τὸ ὄρος), they went into a dangerous storm at night. Separated from Jesus, they experienced their helplessness, which is surpassed by Jesus' miraculous appearance on the sea and the miraculous landing of the ship on the shore. When re-establishing community with Jesus the danger was removed.[54] In John 21, it is night-time and the disciples are in the boat without Jesus and without success (21.3). Jesus' revelation again re-establishes community (21.13).

Craig Koester points to another important intra-textual link between John 21 and 6: In John 21, it is mentioned twice that the net is hauled in: vv. 6, 11. John 6.44 states that nobody can come to Jesus as life-giving bread unless he or she was drawn by God himself: 'No one can come to me unless drawn by the Father who sent me' (οὐδεὶς δύναται ἐλθεῖν πρὸς με ἐὰν μὴ ὁ πατὴρ ὁ πέμψας με ἑλκύσῃ αὐτόν).[55] Furthermore, Jesus reveals himself as the one who draws people into his community after he will be lifted up to the cross (12.32: 'And I, when I am lifted up from the earth, will draw all people to myself' [πάντας ἑλκύσω πρὸς ἐμαυτόν]).[56] It is Jesus' example his disciples are invited to follow.

a. Lukan Stories

The post-Easter account at the Sea of Tiberias resembles two Lukan stories: (1) the miraculous catch of fish in Lk. 5.1-11, which belongs to the special material of Luke and replaces the call to discipleship of four fishermen in Mk 1.16-20 par Matt 4.18-22,[57] and (2) the disciples on their way to Emmaus, Lk. 24.13-35, which is also part of the Lucan special material unparalleled in the other Synoptic Gospels.

1. Luke. 5.1-11[58]

John 21.1 locates the account at the θαλάσσῃ τῆς Τιβεριάδος, which obviously refers back to Jn 6.1 as mentioned above. However, Luke informs his readers that Jesus 'was standing beside the lake of Gennesaret' (ἦν ἑστὼς παρὰ τὴν λίμνην

---

53. The disciples try to get Jesus on board without success: 6.21.

54. For that interpretation cf. M. Labahn, *Offenbarung*, pp. 28ff.

55. Cf. M. Theobald, 'Gezogen von Gottes Liebe (Joh 6,44f): Beobachtungen zur Überlieferung eines johanneischen "Herrenworts"', in K. Backhaus, F. G. Untergassmair (eds), *Schrift und Tradition* (FS J. Ernst; Wien: Schöningh, 1996), pp. 315–41 (335–36).

56. Cf. C. R. Koester, *Symbolism*, pp. 134–35.

57. There are some parallel features between both kinds of call stories (cf., e.g. R. C. Tannehill, *Luke* [ANTC; Nashville: Abingdon, 1996], p. 99), so that both lines of tradition, which do not depend upon one another, may go back to the memory of a call of fishermen to be disciples of Jesus.

58. Cf. the references made by F. Neirynck, 'John 21', pp. 605–9.

Γεννησαρέτ), thus using another more common expression for the Sea of Galilee in the New Testament.[59] Later on, the Johannine narrator mentions that Jesus 'stood on the beach' (21.4: ἔστη ... εἰς τὸν αἰγιαλόν). The expression, which may be understood as a sudden revelatory appearance resembling Jn 20.19, 26 (ἔστη εἰς τὸ μέσον) and may hint at Lk. 5.1, which also refers to Jesus standing at the shore of lake Gennesaret.

At first sight, the list of disciples seems to be a Johannine one (see above section 2). However, Simon Peter as the spokesman of the disciples is a rather unusual element in John[60] and better known from the Synoptic Gospels. The role of Peter in Jn 21.1-14 is in accordance with Lk. 5.8.

The proposed inter-textual relationship is more clearly indicated if the reaction to the miracle by the witnesses itself is compared. In Lk. 5.8 Peter kneels down in front of Jesus and confesses his sin. In Jn 21.7 Simon Peter, after having acknowledged that the *Kyrios* had appeared, recognizes his nakedness, dresses and jumps into the sea. Jn 21.2, 7 may have Lk. 5.8, or some information comparable to it, as its background. The miraculous catch of fish refers to the appearance of something extraordinary, or, more specifically, divine in one's life which leads to fear and surprise.[61] With special regard to Old Testament texts this fear of the divine appearance may be understood as the confrontation between God and sinful mankind.[62] In front of the overall Johannine literary context, it may well be a hint at a special sin, which is later on referred to in Jn 21.15-17 when Peter's threefold denial from 18.15-18, 25-27 is answered by Jesus threefold missionary order: 'Feed my lambs'.

The sons of Zebedee are surprisingly never mentioned in John 1–20 at all. On the other hand, they are closely connected with Simon (Peter) in Lk. 5.10: 'James and John, sons of Zebedee, who were partners with Simon.' The mention of the sons of Zebedee is carried forward by Jesus' famous words on Peter's missionary order: 'from now on you will be catching people'. The impact of the miraculous catch of fish is the call to discipleship characterized by missionary activity. Moreover, the sequence of the text indicates that the outcome, the extraordinary catch of fish, stands for the success of the missionary activity Peter and his partners are called to.[63] Therefore, the narrator takes the miracle as a 'symbolic

59. Cf. M. Labahn, *Offenbarung*, pp. 82–83.

60. Cf. U. Schnelle, *Evangelium nach Johannes*, p. 315. However, Peter takes this position also in Jn 6.68, the Johannine version of Peter's confession; on the important role of Peter's confession in John 6 which shows that Peter may represent the disciples merely at one point of the Johannine narrative cf. M. Labahn, 'Controversial Revelation in Deed and Word: The Feeding of the Five Thousand and Jesus' Crossing of the Sea as a "Prelude" to the Johannine Bread of Life Discourse', *IBS* 22 (2000), pp. 146–81 (175–77).

61. Cf. F. Bovon, *Evangelium nach Lukas 1*, p. 234; R. C. Tannehill, *Luke*, p. 101.

62. Cf. Isa. 6.5-7; see also Exod. 33.18-20; Judg. 6.22-23; 13.22-23; cf. H. Hübner, A. Labahn, M. Labahn (eds), *Vetus Testamentum in Novo* vol. I.2: *Evangelium Secundum Iohannem* (Göttingen: Vandenhoeck & Ruprecht, 2003) on Jn 1.18.

63. See also, R. C. Tannehill, *Luke*, p. 100: 'This shift to metaphorical language [Jesus' word on catching people] invites the audience to understand the great catch of fish on a second level:

action' foreshadowing and guaranteeing[64] the success of mission. The catch of fish in John 21 may well be explained as a symbolic action which depicts the missionary activity ordered by Jesus so that it may well be assumed that the Johannine account is inspired by a Lukan, or Lukan-like story.

In the Gospel of John, Jesus' disciples are never connected with fishing. Such a duty may be presupposed, but it is never mentioned directly or referred to at all. For sure, Lk. 5.2 ('the fishermen [οἱ δὲ ἁλιεῖς] had gone out of them [their boats] and were washing their net') is not the only possible source for the information, but it fits with other references to Luke 5 in John 21.

Although the fact that someone goes on board a ship is part of the narrative plot of any fishing scene, it cannot be overlooked that there is some agreement between the entering of the fishing boat by Simon Peter in Jn 21.3 (εἰς τὸ πλοῖον) and that of Jesus in Lk. 5.3 (Jesus ἐμβὰς δὲ εἰς ἓν τῶν πλοίων; cf. as well Jn 6.21, see above section 2).

Most significant is the hint at the fishermen's failure at night which is alluded to in Jn 21.3 (καὶ ἐν ἐκείνῃ τῇ νυκτὶ ἐπίασαν οὐδέν) and in Lk. 5.5 (δι' ὅλης νυκτὸς κοπιάσαντες οὐδὲν ἐλάβομεν). The situation is cleared in Jn 21.6. The appearance of Jesus interrupts the scene. Due to the narrative setting as post-resurrection narrative, Jesus is not involved in the scene from its beginning (vv. 4-5).[65] Also, the disciples' failure to identify Jesus indicates a changes in the scene (v. 4). The misfortune of fishing at night, a time when fishing was usually successful, is countered by the order to cast the net anew on the right side of the boat, succeeded by a successful catch of fish. Here are the closest parallels in the motifs and activities of the actors of both narratives – however, there are only a few verbal agreements.[66] In both texts, Jesus is recognised as *kyrios* (Lord)[67] and

as a symbolic narrative of the amazingly successful mission that Jesus is starting and that Simon and others will continue.' See also C. H. Talbert, *Reading Luke: A Literary and Theological Commentary on the Third Gospel* (New York: Crossroads, 1982), p. 61.

64. The narrator takes the story for granted and that is the reason that it can be taken also as a symbolic narrative.

65. However, Jesus suddenly standing at the shore has parallels in Jesus' appearance in front of his disciples in John 20 as well as in the narrative setting of Lk. 5.1 (see above).

66. Jn 21.6b: βάλετε εἰς τὰ δεξιὰ μέρη τοῦ πλοίου τὸ δίκτυον.
Lk. 5.4: ἐπανάγαγε εἰς τὸ βάθος καὶ χαλάσατε τὰ δίκτυα ὑμῶν εἰς ἄγραν
Jn 21.6d: ἔβαλον οὖν.
Lk. 5.5b: ἐπὶ δὲ τῷ ῥήματί σου χαλάσω τὰ δίκτυα
Jn 21.6e: καὶ οὐκέτι αὐτὸ ἑλκύσαι ἴσχυον.
Lk. 5.7: καὶ κατένευσαν τοῖς μετόχοις ἐν τῷ ἑτέρῳ πλοίῳ τοῦ ἐλθόντας συλλαβέσθαι αὐτοῖς
Jn 21.6f: ἀπὸ τοῦ πλήθους τῶν ἰχθύων.
Lk. 5.6a: καὶ τοῦτο ποιήσαντες συνέκλεισαν πλῆθος ἰχθύων πολύ, διερρήσσετο δὲ τὰ δίκτυα αὐτῶν

67. Jn 21.7d: ὁ κύριός ἐστιν.
Lk. 5.8: ἰδὼν δὲ Σίμων Πέτρος προσέπεσεν τοῖς γόνασιν Ἰησοῦ λέγων· ἔξελθε ἀπ' ἐμοῦ, ὅτι ἀνὴρ ἁμαρτωλός εἰμι, κύριε; cf. Jn 21.7e-i.

there is a shameful reaction by Peter. In Jn 21.8 it is because of his nakedness, in Luke it is because of his sinfulness.[68] Again, there are parallels in structure and motif but apart from *kyrios* nearly no verbal agreements can be found.

Finally, the success of the miraculous catch is stated as Simon Peter pulls the net ashore: Jn 21.11 (cf. v. 6), again showing parallels to Lk. 5.11, 6b.[69] The rest of the Johannine story does not show literary influence from Lk. 5.

The conclusion taken from these discussions will be drawn in section 4 by trying to understand the compositional act behind the story.

2. Luke 24.13-35
During the narrated incident, the question of the identity of the resurrected Jesus was raised (Jn 21.4, 12). Standing on the shore, his disciples do not know who he is. There is a close Johannine parallel in Jn 20.14 (Mary Magdalene 'turned around and saw Jesus standing there, but she did not know that it was Jesus'). However, a connection with Lk. 24.16, 31 seems to be plausible as well,[70] for in the Lukan Emmaus story the recognition of Jesus is connected with the breaking of bread (Lk. 24.30: 'When he was at the table with them, he took bread, blessed and broke it, and gave it to them'). The linguistically and theologically Johannine question σὺ τίς εἶ (You, who are you?)[71] in Jn 21.12 is followed by a meal scene with Jesus taking, blessing and distributing bread and fish. Both accounts of non-recognition of Jesus are part of Jesus' post-Easter appearances.

It is difficult to prove that the Emmaus account is influential on the *productive side* of the author. There are some indications which point to a coincidence of the two narratives but there is no strong indication for it – however, any early Christian reader who was familiar with the four Gospels would not ignore these links.

---

68. Jn 21.7e-i: Σίμων οὖν Πέτρος ἀκούσας
    ὅτι ὁ κύριός ἐστιν
    τὸν ἐπενδύτην διεζώσατο
    ἦν γὰρ γυμνός
    καὶ ἔβαλεν ἑαυτόν εἰς τὴν θάλασσαν.
    Lk. 5.8: ἰδὼν δὲ Σίμων Πέτρος
    προσέπεσεν τοῖς γόνασιν Ἰησοῦ λέγων
    ἔξελθε ἀπ' ἐμοῦ
    ὅτι ἀνὴρ ἁμαρτωλός εἰμι
    κύριε
69. Jn 21.11b: καὶ εἵλκυσεν τὸ δίκτυον εἰς τὴν γῆν; cf. v. 8.
    Lk. 5.11: καὶ καταγαγόντες τὰ πλοῖα ἐπὶ τὴν γῆν ἀφέντες πάντα
    ἠκολούθησαν αὐτῷ
    Jn 21.11e: καὶ τοσούτων ὄντων οὐκ ἐσχίσθη τὸ δίκτυον
    Lk. 5.6b: διερρήσσετο δὲ τὰ δίκτυα αὐτῶν
70. Cf., e.g., U. Schnelle, *Johannes*, 317.
71. Cf. Jn 1.19: ὅτε ἀπέστειλαν πρὸς αὐτὸν οἱ Ἰουδαῖοι ἐξ Ἱεροσολύμων
    ἱερεῖς καὶ Λευίτας ἵνα ἐρωτήσωσιν αὐτόν· σὺ τίς εἶ
    Jn 8.25: ἔλεγον οὖν αὐτῷ· σὺ τίς εἶ
    Cf. Jn 4.10: εἰ ᾔδεις τὴν δωρεὰν τοῦ θεοῦ καὶ τίς ἐστιν ὁ λέγων σοι· δός μοι πεῖν, σὺ ἂν
    ᾔτησας αὐτὸν καὶ ἔδωκεν ἄν σοι ὕδωρ ζῶν

4. A Story in the Making

Frans Neirynck has strongly recommended reading John 21 as a rewriting of synoptic sources.[72] Using the inter-textual paradigm, this methodological approach was reworked by Manfred Lang in his Halle dissertation on John 18–20.[73] Lang concludes that the Johannine passion story is an inter-textual play with synoptic pre-texts. In a slightly different way both exegetes recommend reading John as a rewriting of a synoptic pre-text.

According to my narrative analysis, the Johannine fishing story is *a story in its own right* but it is *not a story without narrative seams*. The fishing story plays an important role while it is embedded in a frame which connects the fishing narrative with the context of John 1–20. These observations refer to the tradition used by the narrator of John 21. Traits of redactional narrating can be found especially in the narrative frame in Jn 21.1-2[74] and vv. 12-14. But there seems to be also a redactional reworking in the body of the narrative itself: 4b,[75] 5,[76] 7, 9 although

F. Neirynck, 'John 21', p. 604, stresses that the disciples already knew the identity of Jesus as stated at the end of v. 12. However, there is still the puzzling comment that the disciples do not dare to ask 'Who are you?', so that the recognition of Jesus remains vague; that is why the community of the Lord has to be provided with the common meal; cf. R. E. Brown, *The Gospel According to John XIII–XXI*, p. 1070: 'there is still hesitation in v. 12'.

72. F. Neirynck, 'John 21', pp. 605–9; see also G. Blaskovic, *Johannes und Lukas.* pp. 83–87; G. Blaskovic, 'Die Erzählung vom reichen Fischfang (Lk 5,1-11; Joh 21,1-14): Wie Johannes eine Erzählung aus dem Lukasevangelium für seine Zwecke umschreibt' in S. Schreiber, A. Stimpfle (eds), *Johannes aenigmaticus*, pp. 103–20 (116–19).

73. M. Lang, *Johannes und die Synoptiker: Eine redaktionsgeschichtliche Analyse von Joh 18–20 vor dem markinischen und lukanischen Hintergrund* (FRLANT, 182; Göttingen: Vandenhoeck & Ruprecht, 1999).

74. The names of the disciples clearly link Jn 21.1-14 with John 1–20, as shown above. Nevertheless, some of them may have been mentioned in the tradition as well; cf. the remark of J. Becker, *Das Evangelium des Johannes: Kapitel 11–21* (ÖTbK, 4.1; Gütersloh: Gütersloher Verlagshaus; Würzburg: Echter Verlag, 3rd edn, 1991), p. 761, that the list of disciples in v. 2 does not mention the beloved disciple of v. 7. The belated introduction of the beloved disciple may be due to dramaturgic effects but could also hint at a list of disciples from any tradition lacking the beloved disciple.

75. The reference that the disciples did not recognize Jesus contradicts the appearance stories of Jesus in front of his disciples in John 20. That is the reason why R. Pesch, *Der reiche Fischfang: Lk 5,1-11, Jo 21,1-14: Wundergeschichte, Berufungserzählung, Erscheinungsbericht* (KBANT; Düsseldorf: Patmos, 1969), pp. 94–95, and R. Schnackenburg, *Das Johannesevangelium 3. Teil: Kommentar zu Kap. 13–21* (HTKNT IV.3; Freiburg: Herder, 6th edn, 1992), p. 421, attribute v. 4b to a traditional '*Erscheinungsbericht*' which is called by F. Neirynck, 'John 21', p. 603, 'the weakest side of the theory'. A remark like v. 4b is necessary to narrate the catch of fish as a revelation story; that is intended by the author of John 21. Verse 4b indicates that the disciples do not have the knowledge they may have after John 20, and that they are characters who do not have the knowledge the omniscient narrator provides to the readers by identifying Jesus as the person standing on the shore.

76. The content of v. 5 may be traditional but the wording shows Johannine traits; cf. the Johannine λέγει οὖν and παιδία (cf. p. 131); cf., e.g., F. Neirynck, 'John 21', p. 604.

the exact extent is difficult to estimate (material from the following verses probably belongs to the tradition: 21.2-4, 6, 8, 10-11).[77]

Rudolf Pesch has proposed to split the tradition into two stories: a catch-of-fish miracle and an ecclesiological appearance story.[78] However, there is no need to draw a line between the missionary ideas and the miracle in the tradition, it is sufficient to distinguish a miracle tradition reflecting the foundation of the disciples' missionary activity from a frame placing it within a post-Easter appearance story. That story serves now also a literary aim in characterizing Peter and the beloved disciple.

Although there is a high degree of parallel in structure and motifs in the Johannine fishing scene to Lk. 5 (cf. Jn 21.3-4, 6, 8, 11), there is also a remarkably low degree of verbal agreements between both stories. Admittedly, gospel narrators do not necessarily imitate their source, which is evident within the mostly undisputed literary relationship of the Synoptic Gospels in nearly all the theories used for explaining the relationship. That may also be true for the narrator of Jn 21. 1-14. However, he clearly indicates the relationship to John 6 by verbal agreements, which have no counterpart within the proposed inter-textual relationship with Luke 5. The main observation speaking against a direct literary relationship of Jn 21.1-14 and Lk. 5.1-11 is that the agreements do not belong to those parts of the fishing scene which can convincingly be ascribed to the narrator's activity. Most of the parallels belong to the traditional layer of the scenes.

Hence, some scholars assume that John 21 may go back to an early version of the miraculous catch-of-fish story independent of Luke 5, but sharing a more or less limited common core. One may ask if this independent version was a post-resurrection narrative, the setting of which was better preserved in John 21, or if Luke had preserved the setting of the core better than John.[79]

Another more plausible explanation has to be taken into account, which is the phenomenon of 'secondary orality', otherwise called 're-oralization',[80] which I have

77. Other scholars provide different kinds of reconstruction which are connected with divergent sorts of source-critical hypotheses which cannot be discussed here in detail; cf., e.g., R. T. Fortna, *The Gospel of Signs: A Reconstruction of the Narrative Source Underlying the Fourth Gospel* (SNTSMS, 11; Cambridge: Cambridge University Press, 1970), pp. 87–97 (part of the 'Gospel of Signs'; cf. R. T. Fortna, *The Fourth Gospel and its Predecessor*, pp. 68–70; R. T. Fortna, 'Diachronic/Synchronic Reading John 21 and Luke 5', in A. Denaux [ed.], *John and the Synoptics*, pp. 387–99); H.-P. Heekerens, *Die Zeichen-Quelle der johanneischen Redaktion: Ein Beitrag zur Entstehungsgeschichte des vierten Evangeliums* (SBS, 113; Stuttgart: Katholisches Bibelwerk, 1984), pp. 78–91 (part of a signs source with only three miracles).

78. Cf. R. Pesch, *Der reiche Fischfang*, pp. 86–107. See also J. Becker, *Das Evangelium des Johannes: Kapitel 11–21*, pp. 761–63; R. Schnackenburg, *Das Johannesevangelium 3*, pp. 411–12.

79. See above p. 128.

80. S. Byrskog, *Story as History – History as Story: The Gospel Traditions in the Context of Ancient Oral History* (WUNT, 123; Tübingen: Mohr Siebeck, 2000), pp. 138–44. Cf. the remarks on the relationship of the *Gospel of Thomas* to the Synoptic Gospels made by R. Uro, 'Secondary Orality' in the Gospel of Thomas?, *Forum* 9 (1993), pp. 305–29 (306, 313).

adapted to the relationship of John and the Synoptics in my dissertation *Jesus als Lebensspender*.[81] The term 'secondary orality' describes the possibility that a written text is retold orally, and that the text goes anew through a process of oral transmission. The theory of secondary orality takes the instability of vocabulary during oral transmission seriously.[82] However, a story does not get rid of all its wording during the oral transmission. Catchwords and central motifs especially are still preserved. The process of oral transmission does also maintain the basic structure of words and narratives at hand. Such a theory may, hence, explain:

(a) Jn 21.1-14 is using a miracle story taken from tradition,
(b) the high degree of structural coherence between Jn 21.1-14 and Lk. 5.1-11 (with differences as well), and
(c) the remarkable but not very high degree of verbal agreement.

The fundamental reason (d) for assuming a relationship of Jn 21.1-14 to Luke 5 itself and not only to a Lukan-like tradition can be given by the composition history of Lk. 5.1-11. It is an interesting and intriguing fact that the Lukan story has a missionary aim (Lk. 5.10) which is connected with the call to discipleship. The call to discipleship of missionary activity is not originally connected with the miraculous catch of fish and may best be explained as due to the Lukan narrative activity; regardless of whether Luke uses an independent logion[83] or depends on Mk 1.17.[84] Such a link is also to be found in Jn 21.1-14 with structural and verbal parallels ([b] and [c]). If this is true, than it follows, that the tradition of Jn 21.1-14 (a) *depends on the account of the miraculous catch of fish combined with a missionary point as it is presented in Luke 5*. In the transmission process the Lukan account was retold and transmitted with its own interpretation of the missionary order. The Johannine account develops its own version of the relation of miracle and missionary success.

5. Making Sense by Narrating a Miracle Story

It is an interesting fact that one and the same miracle story of Jesus is told in different narrative settings which are, on the narrative level, separated by the events

---

81. M. Labahn, *Jesus als Lebensspender*, pp. 195ff.; M. Labahn, *Offenbarung*, pp. 272–75; cf. the description with critical sympathy by D. M. Smith, *John Among the Gospels*, pp. 195–98.

82. C. Breytenbach, 'MNHMONEUEIN. Das "Sich-erinnern" in der urchristlichen Überlieferung – Die Bethanienepisode (Mk 14,3-9/Jn 12,1-8) als Beispiel, in A. Denaux (ed.), *John and the Syoptics*, pp. 548–57 (554–55), has given some remarks on the process of the re-organization of stories in the human mind which are helpful for understanding the work of an author using sources but also for the meaning of memory in oral transmission: 'Wenn der Hörer nun aber zum Erzähler wird, greift er nicht auf die von ihm damals gehörte Phonemkette zurück. Diese hat er nicht mehr im Ohr. Er hat sie aber beim Hören in eine semantische Textbasis, die situationell organisiert ist, umgesetzt. Er greift auf diese kognitive Repräsentation in seinem eigenen Gedächtnis zurück und formuliert mit Hilfe seiner gedanklichen Vorstellung der Situation, von der die Erzählung handelte, eine neue Erzählung, die seinem neuen kommunikativen Kontext entspricht.'

83. F. Bovon, *Evangelium nach Lukas 1*, p. 234.

84. J. A. Fitzmyer, *The Gospel According to Luke I–IX*, p. 562; B. Kollmann, *Jesus und die Christen als Wundertäter*, p. 278; R. Pesch, *Der reiche Fischfang*, pp. 72–76.

of the cross and the resurrection. It seems that one miracle story was brought into different literary contexts serving different aims. That transformation of the story shows that the ancient narrators did not read the miracle as a mere historical fact with just one particular sense presenting a specific historical circumstance. A miracle story is, first of all, a narrative and serves a narrative's basic function, i.e. to generate a meaning in a world in which people have to live and organize their daily life.

Miracle stories, therefore, partake of the basic function of narrative stories. Elaborating past events by using miraculous motifs and ideas is a way of reconstructing history by narrative means. A miracle story was told in order to generate sense for an actual situation and purpose. If a miracle story refers to a person and/or an event of the past then it does not attempt to preserve the past event per se – or what is assumed to have happened once upon a time in the past. It refers to the past event in order to interpret the present time in a way that enables people to manage their future.[85]

Such a comprehension of the miracles does not necessarily mean that early Christian narrators did not believe that Jesus performed miracles which they subsequently altered into various narrative topics. However, the narrators' belief in Jesus encourages them to realize that Jesus' miracles do not merely present past events, but reflect events with a strong impact for their current situation and orientation in life. Hence, the narrators use, or better re-use, what they believe that Jesus once did, in order to narrate something new which helps their communities to believe in Jesus and manage their present life.

A miracle story with its utopian elements or claims transcends the reality of recent human power and strength. The narrated events surpass human abilities when presenting – to mention only a few motifs – an unexpected military conquest, good health after severe illnesses or even an unexpected catch of fish after a hard night's work, as is reported in the miracle story of John 21. Thereby, miracle stories establish hope and confidence in order to manage future tasks, especially if they are connected with a religious figure venerated by a community like the early Christian movement. Narrating of a powerful religious hero, the story also authorizes ethical demands as well as theological or philosophical claims.

---

85. Cf. J. Rüsen, *Historische Vernunft: Grundzüge einer Historik I: Die Grundlagen der Geschichtswissenschaft* (KVR, 1489; Göttingen: Vandenhoeck & Ruprecht, 1983), p. 56, on the function of the historical mind and its narrative potential: 'Das historische Erzählen mobilisiert die Erinnerung an den zeitlichen Wandel des Menschen und seiner Welt in der Vergangenheit so, daß in ihrem Lichte die in der Gegenwart erfahrenen zeitlichen Veränderungen einen Sinn bekommen, d. h. in die Absichten und Erwartungen des zukunftgerichteten Handelns eingehen können. Diesen Brückenschlag von der Vergangenheit über die Gegenwart in die Zukunft leistet das historische Erzählen mit Kontinuitätsvorstellungen, die die drei Zeitdimensionen übergreifen und zur Einheit eines Zeitverlaufs zusammenschließen … Das historische Erzählen vergegenwärtigt die Vergangenheit immer in einem Zeitbewußtsein, in dem Vergangenheit, Gegenwart und Zukunft einen inneren, schlüssigen Zusammenhang bilden, und eben dadurch konstituiert es Geschichtsbewußtsein'.

Further, there is not a great difference between re-narrating a past event and re-using a narrative topic. Both were narrated for current time, and what is important for the present understanding is taken up. I do not dispute that there is a conservative or preserving element in the Christian narrative activity, for the historical Jesus was understood by his disciples as a messenger of God's kingdom with great authority. Moreover, believing in the resurrection of its hero, the early Christian movement preserves the memory and tradition of its Messiah. However, he is understood to be present in the spirit, so that Christian narrators are encouraged to transmit their tradition in the presence of their *kyrios*.[86] Basically, remembering the past is always an interpretative act which forms history: history and memory are made by the present mind to make sense of past events in order to understand the present time.

John 21.1-14 is in many ways linked with the gospel as a whole, and is to be read in light of the preceding narrative which the final chapter intends to resume and at last to bring to an end (cf. 21.24-25). Therefore, John 21 does not introduce itself as a mere addendum, moreover it wants to be read as an 'epilogue' which opens the reader's view to a situation that extents the end of the entire story.[87]

Despite the gift of the spirit to the disciples, the author of John 21 misses an explicit and christologically-centred order of the risen Lord to perform his mission. However, missionary activity is not a subject strange to the Gospel of John (cf., e.g., Jn 4.35-38). By re-narrating the orally transmitted story of the miraculous catch of fish from the Gospel of Luke, which goes along with its missionary impact, the author of John 21 adds an order for missionary activity into the post-Easter self-revelation of Jesus. The revelatory language in the frame and the motive of community by using the meal scene strongly binds the missionary theme to the presence of the Lord.

For the narrator's mind the risen Jesus continues the activity of the earthly Jesus, sent by his father from heaven, which he clearly marks by taking up motifs from the narrative setting of John 6. For this kind of continuity, he can change the narrative setting of his tradition from a former pre-Easter appearance to a yet post-Easter shape.

By retelling the story he highlights the christological orientation. The order is based on a word of the risen Lord encouraging people to 'haul in' from the world and to become part of his community by knowing his identity. For the ones who are hauled in by Jesus' order through his disciples the question σὺ τίς εἶ (20.12) is answered, for they are hauled in by God/Jesus (6.44/12.32), because they know Jesus' identity (εἰδότες ὅτι ὁ κύριός ἐστιν). That means, they believe in his life-giving activity as the Son of God (20.31).

---

86. The conception of the paraclete teaches and reminds the Johannine community of past events (Jn 14.26) and gives evidence for an awareness and reflection of such productive activity in the Johannine school.

87. Cf. J. Zumstein, 'Der Prozess der Relecture in der johanneischen Literatur', in J. Zumstein, *Kreative Erinnerung*, pp. 15–30 (23).

The rearrangement of an older story points to the community's present time. Their missionary activity is authorized by a symbolic action of the risen Lord. Their work has a particular meaning, for it is founded in Jesus' activity itself. The miracle transmitted in John 21 serves to establish or strengthen the community's ethos as far as their activity has its roots in the order of the Lord. Narrated as a miracle, the order is a powerful act which gives trust in the power of God standing behind the group's activity.[88] Therefore, the miracle also serves as an encouragement in a situation when the missionary activity of the community is disputed or otherwise needs theological foundation.

With the retelling of a past event the author intends to establish orientation and sense in life so that his community will be able to manage the needs with which it is presently confronted. Thus, the miracle is not an obscure act, but generates meaning for the present life of the community.

---

88.   By changing the setting of the miracle, the author does not necessarily doubt the historicity of the event he retells – such an assumption would revoke his own argumentation. Rather, he is convinced that the story itself is open to more than one setting.

BEING THERE:
THE FUNCTION OF THE SUPERNATURAL
IN ACTS 1–12

Matti Myllykoski

Right from the beginning of the critical study of Acts, the role of miracles in Luke's work has been an essential question. In spite of all the labour done for a deeper understanding of Luke's historiography and theology, this issue has often been neglected. In his survey of research on Acts written back in 1977, Erich Grässer summarizes well the situation of scholarship that is prevalent even today. He characterizes the resurrection of Jesus as *the* miracle for Luke, emphasizes his practical and apologetical, but not quite successful, effort to separate the Christian miracles from Jewish and Gentile magic, and notes the large amount of space given to the miracles in his narrative. In the light of all this, Grässer finds it astonishing that 'there is almost nothing' in scholarship on this theme.[1] An extensive presentation of miracles in Acts, their literary function and theological message, was lacking then and is still lacking today, in spite of the quantity of ink spilled on Acts in past decades.[2] The theme is often neglected in comprehensive and otherwise useful books and collections of articles.[3]

---

1.   E. Grässer, 'Acta-Forschung seit 1960 (Fortsetzung)', *TRu* 42 (1977), pp. 1–68 (15–16). See also the history research written by Francois Bovon on the Lukan theology: *Luc le théologien: Vingt-cinq ans de recherches (1950-1975)* (Geneva: Labor et Fides, 2nd edn, 1988) – studies on miracles are absent from both the table of contents and the index.

2.   As far as I can see, the most comprehensive treatise dedicated to miracles in Acts is M. McCord Adams, 'The Role of Miracles in the Structure of Luke-Acts', in E. Stump, T. P. Flint (eds), *Hermes and Athena: Biblical Exegesis and Philosophical Theology* (Notre Dame: University of Notre Dame Press, 1993), pp. 235–65. M. McCord Adams extends the thesis of P. J. Achtemeier, 'The Lukan Perspective on the Miracles of Jesus: A Preliminary Sketch', *JBL* 94 (1975), pp. 547–62. Achtemeier mostly discusses miracles in the Gospel of Luke. An excellent history of research is offered by F. Neirynck, 'The Miracle Stories in the Acts of the Apostles', in J. Kremer (ed.) *Les Actes des Apôtres: Traditions, redaction, théologie* (BETL, 48; Leuven: Leuven University Press, 1979), pp. 169–213.

3.   The great collection of articles in the five volumes of *The Book of Acts in Its First Century Setting* (1993–96) has only one article that partly treats the question of miracles ('Peter and Ben Stada in Lydda' by J. Schwartz, vol. 4, pp. 391–414). The 39 articles published in the Leuven volume *The Unity of Luke-Acts* (1999) have nothing on miracles, even though there are some

There are several possible reasons for this somewhat perplexing situation. Some major themes have dominated the discussion: salvation history, church and Israel, different theological issues (Christology, pneumatology, eschatology, use of Scripture etc.), the difficulty of assessing the relationship between historiography and theology in Luke's work as well as the corresponding lack of consensus on the literary genre of Acts – and in all this the problem of unity and diversity in Luke-Acts. The question of miracles has been set aside partly because it produces difficulties for constructive theological approaches to Acts – a problem that becomes visible in the history of research. The literary problems of the Lukan miracle stories gnawed at the historical reliability of Acts and they were displaced to the margin of scholarly discussion, particularly among those who defended Luke's reliability as a historian. In the first part of this article I want to point out the distance that scholarship has created between Luke's theology and the miracle traditions that he used. I think that this distance is partly due to the fact that scholars have limited the focus of their studies either to miracles or to other related phenomena in Acts. Instead, in the second part of this article, I propose that the miracles belong to a wider category of supernatural events and influences that Luke uses for particular purposes in his narrative. In the third part, I try to rough out how the supernatural works in the plot of Acts 1–12 in order to – fourthly – make some conclusions and suggestions concerning Acts 1–12 as a whole.

1. Miracles and Method: The Case of Acts 1–12

Protestant critical study of early Christianity can be traced back to *Verfallstheorie*, the idea that the Church fell away from the glorious and exemplary life of its earliest days as portrayed in Acts. For Johann Lorenz Mosheim (1693–1755), the first Christians were purer and less sinful than the later ones, even though the quarrels in Corinth prove that there were some who did not live up to the high standards of the Christian faith. Most importantly for miracles in Acts, Mosheim assumed that the power of the Holy Spirit enabled the apostles to perform miracles, which indeed were much more common in the golden age of early Christianity than in later times. Johann Salomo Semler (1725–91) turned this model upside down by portraying the early period of Christianity as the childhood of the new faith, a childhood that was characterized by materialistic particularism of Jewish Christianity, including a special fondness for miracles.[4]

The rationalist criticism of the New Testament documents was particularly focused on miracles. However, as Ward Gasque states, 'the essential trustworthiness of Acts as a historical document was first challenged by Wilhelm Martin Leberecht de Wette (1780–1849)'.[5] Dividing Acts into two parts, chs. 1–12 and 13–28, de Wette

---

articles on related themes (the role of the Spirit, divine visits, and divine communication).

4.   On Mosheim and Semler, see S. Alkier, *Das Urchristentum: Zur Geschichte und Theologie einer exegetischen Disziplin* (BHTh, 83; Tübingen: Mohr Siebeck, 1993), pp. 14–46; on miracles: pp. 14, 18, 20, 31 (n. 144).

5.   W. Gasque, *A History of the Criticism of the Acts of the Apostles* (BGBE, 17; Tübingen: Mohr Siebeck, 1976), p. 24.

considered the first part more defective than the latter,[6] which was closer to Luke in time and partly based on information received from an eye-witness (the so-called 'we'-source). This overall view was a natural starting point for most subsequent scholarship.[7]

As Frans Neirynck states in his research history on miracles in Acts, 'with the *Tendenzkritik* of the 19th century, the miracles were central in the discussion of the apologetic purpose of Acts'.[8] In his work on the purpose of Acts (*Über den Zweck der Apostelgeschichte*), Matthias Schneckenburger paid attention to the pervading similarities between miracle stories told about Peter and Paul. His findings may be summarized with the following table:[9]

PETER		PAUL
3.2, 9-10	Healing of a lame man	14.8-10
	Strafwunder	
5.1-11	Ananias and Sapphira / Elymas	13.6-12
	Actio in distans	
5.15	Shadow / Handkerchiefs	19.2
5.16	Driving out unclean spirits	19.15
(8.7)	(<Philip)	16.16-18
8.14-24	Overcoming magicians	13.6-12
		16.16-18
		19.13-19
9.33	Paralytic / Fever patient	28.8
9.36-40	Raising the dead	20.9
(2.43)	Fear and respect	(28.9-10)
(5.13)	(all apostles)	
10.25-26	Rejection of worship	14.15
5.16; 8.6-7	General references	28.9; 19.11

6.   W. M. L. de Wette, *Kurze Erklärung der Apostelgeschichte* (Leipzig: Weidmann, 3rd edn, 1848), pp. 173–74: 'Ueberhaupt erweckt es Zweifel, dass der Verfasser manchmal einer schwankenden Ueberlieferung zu folgen scheint (I.4ff.; vgl. Luc. XXIV,44ff.; I,8; vgl. Matth. XXVII,5ff.), welche die Thatsachen theils in einem sonderbaren Wunderlichte (VIII,26-40, besonders Vs. 39), theils nach einem offenbaren Missverständnisse (II,5-11; vgl. X,46; XIX,6; I Cor. XIV,2ff.) darstellt'.

7.   See, for example, E. Renan, *Les évangiles et la seconde generation chrétienne* (Paris: Calmann Lévy, 1877), p. 440, who holds Luke, the companion of Paul, to be the author of Acts and formulates the consequences of this view on the interpretation of Acts 1–12 as follows: 'Ces premières années étaient comme un mirage lointain, plein d'illusions. Luc était aussi mal placé que possible pour comprendre ce monde disparu. Ce qui s'était passé dans les années qui suivirent la mort de Jésus était envisagé comme symbolique et mystérieux. Au travers de cette vapeur décevante, tout devenait sacramentel.'

8.   F. Neirynck, 'Miracle Stories', p. 172.

9.   M. Schneckenburger, *Über den Zweck der Apostelgeschichte: Zugleich eine Ergänzung der neueren Commentare* (Bern: Fischer, 1841). See also F. Neirynck, 'Miracle Stories', pp. 173–75.

These findings were taken up by the Tübingen school which started the critical study of miracles in Acts. The parallels that Schneckenburger regarded as a harmless use of similar traditions now turned into a weapon against the reliability of Luke's historiography. In his extensive work on Acts, which first appeared as articles in *Theologische Jahrbücher* (1848–51), Eduard Zeller aptly summarized the Baurian view. For the Tübingen school, the parallels demonstrated that, with the miracles of Peter and Paul, we find ourselves on a thoroughly unhistorical foundation because it is unlikely that such parallels developed in the tradition used by Luke. These parallels – which often go into details of the narrative – presuppose a unified plan by the author and the selection of suitable material from his specific point of view.[10] These findings were enriched with parallels between Jesus' miracles in the Synoptic Gospels and the miracles of Peter and Paul in Acts. The following summary of the Jesus–Peter correspondences in Acts 1–12 can be collected from the evidence presented by Bruno Bauer and Eduard Zeller:[11]

Acts		Mark and Luke
3.6; 9.33-34	Healing of the Lame Man	Mk 2.11; Lk. 5.23-25
3.10		Mk 2.12; Lk. 4.38
5.15-16	Many Healings	Mk 6.55-56; 3.10; Lk. 6.19; 8.46
9.36, 40	Raising a Dead Woman/Girl	Mk 5.40-41
9.40-41		Lk. 7.15

The notion of parallels between miracles performed by Peter and Paul, and Jesus and Peter/Paul was just part of the criticism that the Tübingen school directed against the Lukan narrative. Baur's own treatment of Acts 3–5 is a case in point. In his work on Paul, Baur wanted to demonstrate that, in the hands of Luke, the apostles turn into superhuman beings who impress their audiences with their miraculous powers. Luke's narration is not based on the natural historical development of events but on an idealizing tendency that purports to present the

---

10. E. Zeller, *Die Apostelgeschichte nach ihrem Inhalt und Ursprung kritisch untersucht* (Stuttgart: Mäcken, 1854), pp. 321–22; similarly, but more briefly A. Schwegler, *Das nachapostolische Zeitalter in den Hauptmomenten seiner Entwicklung* I-II (Tübingen: Fues, 1846), pp. 76–77. For the positive reception of this basic view in later scholarship, see W. M. L. de Wette, F. Overbeck (1870: 195 n. 1); H. J. Holtzmann, *Die Apostelgeschichte* (HNT, 1.2; Tübingen, Leipzig: Mohr, 3rd edn, 1901), pp. 18–19. On the development of the discussion on Peter–Paul parallels, see F. Neirynck, 'Miracle Stories', pp. 178–82. Some among the Catholic scholars accepted the idea that Luke deliberately introduced a parallel between the miracles of Peter and Paul, without embracing the Tübingen theory of reconciliation between the Petrine and Pauline Christianity in Acts; on this discussion, see the remarks of J. A. Hardon, 'The Miracle Narratives in the Acts of the Apostles', *CBQ* 16 (1954), pp. 303–18 (308–10).

11. B. Bauer, *Die Apostelgeschichte: Eine Ausgleichung des Paulinismus und des Judentums innerhalb der christlichen Kirche* (Berlin: Hempel, 1850), p. 12, with Jesus–Paul parallels. The Lukan parallels in the first three instances stem from E. Zeller, *Apostelgeschichte*, pp. 428–29, 430. On the predecessors and followers of Bauer, see F. Neirynck, 'Miracle Stories', 182–88, who also offers useful lists of parallels and strengthens the significance of parallels with his own observations. M. McCord Adams, 'Role of Miracles', pp. 260–61.

apostles as great and glorious and to shame and humiliate their opponents. Baur ridicules Luke's aim to make the healing of the lame man by Peter (3.1-10) a matter of ultimate importance. Five thousand men convert, and the very next day all groups of Jewish leaders stop their daily routines and rush to Jerusalem (4.5). In spite of all this urgency, they completely underestimate the respect of the crowds for the apostles (4.13). Their incomprehensible thoughtlessness is underlined by the presence of the healed lame man in the trial against the apostles. If the members of the Sanhedrin were indeed so much afraid of the people, they would not have dared to arrest the apostles and cast them into prison when they were surrounded by the crowds (4.1-3). According to Baur, the second encounter between the apostles and the Sanhedrin merely repeats the first, but puts it on a greater scale (5.12-16). After the miraculous deliverance of the apostles, the Jewish leaders can only give them a meaningless order not to teach in the name of Jesus (5.28).[12] Baur emphasized that the tendentious and miraculous story is a whole; it is unconvincing to set its miraculous aspects aside and take the rest as historical. He rejected all interpretations that mix the natural with the miraculous in theological or psychological terms.[13] Through this criticism, Baur reaches, I think, his key statement: the healing of the lame man is the starting point for awakening the interest of the crowds in the preaching of the apostles – particularly because he could appear at suitable occasions and bear physical witness to their message.[14]

The defence of Luke as a trustworthy historian against the claims of the Tübingen school mostly concerned the historical background of Paul's journeys and the reconciliation of Luke's chronology with the information provided in the Pauline letters, particularly in the case of the so-called apostolic council (Gal. 2 and Acts 15).[15] The criticism directed against the Tübingen school concerning miracles in Acts was more or less based on undermining or simply neglecting the significance of the Peter–Paul and Jesus–Peter/Paul parallels.[16] On the other hand, the studies of both Zeller and Lekebusch demonstrated that Acts as a whole – including the 'we'-passages – must stem from one single author. Lekebusch argued

---

12. F. C. Baur, *Paulus. Der Apostel Jesu Christi: sein Leben und Wirken, seine Briefe und seine Lehre* I-II (Leipzig: Fues, 2nd edn, 1866–67), pp. 20–24.

13. F. C. Baur, *Paulus*, pp. 25–33, particularly against Neander and Olshausen.

14. F. C. Baur, *Paulus*, p. 34: 'Aber die Predigt der Apostel für sich hätte eine so grosse Wirkung nicht hervorgebracht, sie musste selbst einen Anknüpfungspunkt haben, das Interesse des Volkes musste erst durch ein in die Augen fallendes, Aufsehen erregendes Ereignis geweckt werden. Wie konnte diess anders geschehen, als durch ein von den Aposteln verrichtetes Wunder? Aber nicht jedes Wunder würde sich für diesen Zweck gleich gut geeignet haben. Es konnte nur ein solches sein, das nicht blos momentane Bedeutung hatte, sondern seiner Natur nach so beschaffen war, dass es die öffentliche Aufmerksamkeit auf sich fixirte und den Wunderact auch, nachdem er schon geschehen war, der Anschauung gegenwärtig erhielt.'

15. On the history of the defence, see W. Gasque, *History*, pp. 107–63.

16. See, for example, B. Weiss, *Lehrbuch der Einleitung in das Neue Testament* (Berlin: Hertz, 1886), p. 564.

that this was Luke, the personal acquaintance of Paul,[17] while Zeller suggested that it was written by an unknown Paulinist in Rome between 110 and 130.[18] However, defending Luke's historiography in the first half of his work in most cases lead to theories about early written and oral sources, which must have guided Luke's work more than the advocates of the Tübingen school were willing to realize.[19]

Adolf Harnack was also among the source critics who rejected the *Tendenzkritik* of the Tübingen school. Between 1906 and 1911, he wrote three major contributions to the study of Luke-Acts. For him, it was impossible to imagine the historiographical achievement of Luke without recognizing a direct contact to the past that he described.[20] His characterization of the basic idea realized by Luke in Acts further emphasized the unity of the faith put forward by Jesus: 'The power of Jesus' Spirit in the Apostles, historically presented'.[21] He regarded Luke as a rather reliable witness of the events and held that his description of all main events in Acts bears the stamp of historical authenticity; in the so-called 'we'-passages, he speaks as an eyewitness.[22] According to Harnack, the real weakness of Luke as a historian must be found in his credulity concerning 'miraculous healings and pneumatical successes' in the ministry of the apostles, a bias which can be explained by his literary style.[23] Harnack sought to prove the reliability of Luke's historiography with the chronological, geographical and local information stored in Acts; all this does not reveal any bias at all.[24]

However, Harnack saw the miracles and works of the Spirit so prominently present in Acts that he called Luke a 'pneumatical' doctor whose Christianity is thoroughly determined by such elements.[25] He considered the language of Acts

17. E. Lekebusch, *Composition und Entstehung der Apostelgeschichte*. (Gotha: Perthes, 1854), pp. 79–81; see W. Gasque, *History*, pp. 67–70.

18. E. Zeller, *Apostelgeschichte*, pp. 466–88.

19. B. Weiss, *Lehrbuch*, p. 565, assumed that Luke certainly had here and there a special interest in editing his sources, but it is not possible to point out what kind of procedure that was. He emphasized that Luke wanted to understand and portray the deepest motifs of the history of the earliest Christianity. He thought that Luke had a quite extensive source of Peter's works and speeches at his disposal (pp. 571–74). On miracles and source criticism of Acts, see F. Neirynck, 'Miracle Stories', pp. 188–95.

20. A. Harnack, *Die Apostelgeschichte* (BENT, 3; Leipzig: Hinrichs, 1908), p. 2: 'Nur eine direkte Fühlung konnte eine solche Geschichtsschreibung ermöglichen, wie sie in der Apostelgeschichte vorliegt.'

21. A. Harnack, *Apostelgeschichte*, p. 4.

22. A. Harnack, *Apostelgeschichte*, pp. 10–11. He considers most discrepancies in his work as minor lapses, including the chapter on the apostolic council.

23. A. Harnack, *Apostelgeschichte*, p. 18.

24. A. Harnack, *Apostelgeschichte*, pp. 21–100. Note the comment of G. Lüdemann, *Early Christianity according to the Traditions in Acts: A Commentary* (trans. J. Bowden; Minneapolis: Fortress, 1989), p. 3: 'we may describe the Tübingen school's and Harnack's analyses of Acts as the two great extremes in German Protestant research at the turn of the century; there were numerous intermediate positions between them.'

25. A. Harnack, *Apostelgeschichte*, p. 111: 'er selbst ist ein "pneumatischer" Arzt, und sein Christentum erscheint von hier aus sehr durchgreifend bestimmt'. Harnack pays attention to the

1–15 to be thoroughly Lukan, but thought that sources can be identified on the basis of orientation to places and persons. Thus Harnack distinguishes two major sources in the first half of Acts. The tradition that was related to Antioch came to Luke partly as a written source, partly orally from Silas. It was concerned with Stephen, Barnabas and Saul/Paul, presenting the foundation of the Gentile mission. It consisted of the following passages:

6.1-8.4   11.19-30   chs. 13–15

In addition to this reliable tradition, Harnack thought that Luke learned the story behind 9.1-28 directly from Paul.

The rest of Acts 1–15 is oriented towards Jerusalem, including the traditions of Samaria (Philip) and Caesarea (Peter), but Harnack assumed that these texts did not form a unity. On the basis of doublets, he found it possible to separate the historical and coherent source A from the legendary and illogical source B.

A   3.1-5.16   8.5-40   9.29–11.18   12.1-24
B   2.1-47   5.17-42

Source A stemmed, both in written and oral form, mostly from Philip and his daughters, while source B was late and oral.

Correspondingly, Harnack did not exclude a psychosomatically plausible background for the miracles in source A. He thought that they were based on real events: suggestive healings (3.1-10; 9.32-43), ecstasy (4.31), death of a cursed or suspicious couple (5.1-11), vision (8.26, 39), beliefs and exaggerations of friends (12.1-11). Source B was not as reliable since it was based on the highly developed Pentecost miracle. In source A this event was described in a much more comprehensible manner, like an earthquake that can be interpreted as an originally ecstatic phenomenon (4.31). For Harnack, the ascension story was an even later legend.

Unlike Harnack, some defenders of Luke's historiography sometimes tended to read his miracle stories psychologically, e. g., the Spirit of the Lord snatching Philip away after he had baptized the Ethiopian eunuch (8.39).[26] However, the main

major role of miracles in Acts 1–15 and in the so-called 'we'-passages; he counts about 77 'pneumatical' pieces in the former and 14 in the latter. In the rest of the book he finds only 10 such pieces (pp. 111–19). This survey leads him to conclude that in Acts 1–15 Luke drew upon sources that corresponded to his spiritual art that is so predominant in the 'we'-passages. In the 'sober' parts of his work he relied on other kind of sources that were more distant from his character.

26.   According to E. Meyer, *Ursprung und Anfänge des Christentums* III (Stuttgart, Berlin: J. G. Cotta'sche Buchhandlung, 1923), p. 276, it is natural that Philip was an ecstatic person, since he had four prophetic daughters: 'Die Grenzen zwischen Wahrheit und Phantasie werden sich bei ihm noch stärker vermischt haben als beim nüchternen Menschen.' O. Bauernfeind, *Die Apostelgeschichte* (THKNT, 5; Leipzig, 1980 [1939]), p. 129, is inclined to suppose something similar: 'Die Entrückung darf nicht als Beweis für einen weiten Abstand zwischen dem

point to be made here is that the anti-Baurian source criticism was inclined to disassociate Luke from his miracle stories. For these scholars, Luke was a serious historian who acknowledged the miracle stories of his sources as essential elements in the history of the earliest Christian communities. Because he relied on sources, it is not meaningful to assume that he had a particular bias towards the miraculous in the first half of Acts. In spite of the decline of source criticism concerning the first half of Acts, some scholars still claim that Luke drew upon written sources of the earliest communities.

The form-critical studies on the synoptic tradition shed a side-light on the miracles in Acts – a side-light that was to diminish the role of sources in Acts. In his seminal article of 1923 on the style criticism of Acts, Martin Dibelius focused on the *pericopae*, originally independent small units in oral tradition, that can be separated from their context and be classified according to their characteristic features.[27] Dibelius claimed that Luke had no guiding 'thread' for his presentation of the life of the earliest Christian community. He had too small a grasp of the course of its inner developments and he had to confine himself to 'general summaries which, interposed between various scenes and narratives, provide links and elaborations'.[28] As Neirynck has observed, this theory of isolated pieces of tradition toned down the parallels with the miracle stories. Dibelius explained it as a difference of genre (3.1-10 is a *Novelle* while 14.8-18 is a *Legende*) and similarity of topic (the Jairus story in Mk 5.35-43 and the Tabitha legend in Acts 9.36-43), and he was followed by his influential student Ernst Haenchen.[29]

Haenchen developed the seminal ideas of Dibelius in his influential commentary on Acts. For him, miracle stories and brief traditions on some other events formed the main bulk of the tradition used by Luke in the first half of Acts.[30] The commentary of Haenchen reinforced the trend that became current in German scholarship for four decades: Luke was a theologian rather than a historian, and, even as a historian, he was a theologian of salvation history. For many prominent German scholars, he was a pious theologian of *Frühkatholizismus* who described the events of the wonderful times of early Christianity from a notable distance.[31] The redaction-critical interpretation of Haenchen was influential, mostly in Germany, but in recent decades the trustworthiness of Luke's historiography has found new defenders. Even though the language and style of Acts are thoroughly

---

geschichtlichen Vorgang und unserer Legende angesehen werden; gerade dieser Schluss kann sehr wohl von Philippus selbst erzählt worden sein.'

27. M. Dibelius, *Studies in the Acts of the Apostles* (trans. M. Ling; London: SCM Press, 1956; German original, 1951), pp. 11–25.

28. M. Dibelius, *Studies*, p. 9.

29. F. Neirynck, 'Miracle Stories', pp. 198–99, referring to M. Dibelius, *Studies*, p. 21 n. 43; p. 12 n. 24, and E. Haenchen, *The Acts of the Apostles: A Commentary* (trans. B. Noble *et al.*; Oxford: Blackwell, 1971), p. 425 n. 4, 7, pp. 426, 586.

30. E. Haenchen, *Acts*, pp. 81–82, 83–84.

31. This view is often taken as an accusation against Luke; see E. Grässer, *Forschungen zur Apostelgeschichte* (WUNT, 137; Tübingen: Mohr Siebeck, 2001), pp. 15–19.

Lukan, it is possible to assume that he had access to numerous traditions that described the life of the earliest Christian community.[32] These two alternatives have limited the evaluation of the miracle stories in Acts to take place in the framework of Luke's theology or historiography. Miracle traditions are seen as independent units that Luke articulated in his salvation-historical scheme or elements of his historiography. This easily implies a clear distinction between 'tradition,' which is virginal collective data, and Luke's 'redaction', which follows a carefully designed literary plan. The too easily forgotten parallels in the Lukan miracle stories are a symptom of this problem. A further difficulty concerns the dividing line that has generally been drawn between miracles and other supernatural events and influences in Acts. Since the supernatural as a whole plays a major role in the plot of Acts 1–12, it is necessary to see the problem in a wider scope.[33]

2. Supernatural in Acts 1–12: A Survey
In Acts 1–12, very few significant events are portrayed as something that a modern reader would call 'natural'. Luke would not disagree with the viewpoint of his modern readers. He clearly separates divine action and influence from the things that human beings are able to do. The very first thing Peter says to the 'Israelites' after the healing at the Beautiful Gate is that they should not stare at the apostles 'as though by their own power or piety' they had made the lame man walk (3.12). Luke has the crowd stare at them, in the same way as he has the

32. For the trustworthiness of Luke's historiography, see particularly M. Hengel, *Zur urchristlichen Geschichtsschreibung* (Stuttgart: Calwer, 1979). Another pioneer of this view is J. Jervell, *Luke and the People of God: A New Look at Luke-Acts* (Minneapolis: Fortress, 1972), pp. 19–40, J. Jervell, *Die Apostelgeschichte* (KEK, 3; Göttingen: Vandenhoeck & Ruprecht, 17th edn, 1998), pp. 61–72 (64). He discards the pessimistic view of Haenchen and others about the sources on the earliest times, because there certainly were living pieces of tradition about apostles and other leaders of the communities; furthermore, the letters of Paul refer to contents of early traditions and exchange of news between Christian communities, including information about the community of Jerusalem. Concerning Acts 1–12, A. Weiser, *Die Apostelgeschichte: Kapitel 1-12* (ÖTK, 5.1; Gütersloh: Mohn, 1981), p. 37, offers a good example of conservative exegesis. According to him, there were various written traditions: lists of names (1.13; 6.5), miracle stories about Peter (3.1-10; 5.1-11; 9.32-43; 12), separate pieces of information about community life in Jerusalem and Antioch (e.g. 4.36-37; 6.1-6; 11.26), stories on persecution (chs. 4–5, 6–7 and 12), as well as other traditions (1.15-26; 8.26-40; 10–11).

33. In his extensive work on Acts and Hellenistic historiography, C. J. Hemer, *The Book of Acts in the Setting of Hellenistic History* (ed. C. H. Gempf; WUNT, 49; Tübingen: Mohr Siebeck, 1989), devotes a brief chapter to the question of miracles (pp. 433–43). While defending the historical reliability of Luke's work, Hemer thinks that the miracles in Acts must be seen in broad terms. He distinguishes ten categories of miracles: 1) divine events of fundamental significance, 2) references to great salvation events, 3) acts of power, 4) acts that might be natural, 5) summarized references to 'signs and wonders', 6) God's providence, 7) divine intervention, 8) ecstatic phenomena, 9) fulfilment of scripture, 10) overcoming magic powers opposed to God. According to Hemer, modern scholars cannot arrogantly play our world-view against a different world-view of the past; the presence of miracles in a story is no argument per se against its historicity.

apostles themselves gaze towards heaven as Jesus departs from them (1.10). Luke attributes a natural, misguided explanation of the divine miracle to some who observe the Pentecost event: those who speak in tongues are drunk (2.13-15). He stresses that the apostles and all other believers are merely recipients of supernatural gifts and powers. As bold and numinous as Peter and John are in their words and actions, in front of all the Jewish leaders these companions of Jesus amazingly turn out to be 'uneducated and ordinary men' (5.13). As the story of the release of Peter from prison by an angel reveals, Luke's understanding of natural events is somewhat different from ours. He indicates that individual guardian angels are visible beings (12.12-15). On the other hand, in the same story he allows the just-released Peter to assume that he was seeing a vision, i.e., something unreal in contrast to real events (12.9). Luke indicates that visions *can* be delusive, but all the visions he actually relates are true because they include a message from God. In the narrative of Acts, he draws a clear line between mighty acts of God and things imagined or done by human beings (cf. 26.19).

In his article that appeared in 1954, John A. Hardon offered a list of 'all the phenomena in the Acts which occurred after the Ascension and which are traditionally regarded as miraculous events'. He divides the material into descriptive categories that, concerning Acts 1–12, cover the following texts:[34]

I. Individual miraculous phenomena
    A. Resuscitations from the dead   9.36-42
    B. Miraculous cures and exorcisms   3.1-16; 9.17-18; 9.33-35
    C. Miraculous penalties and afflictions   5.1-11; 9.8-9; 12.23
    D. Nature or cosmic miracles   2.2-6; 4.31; 5.17-25; 8.39; 12.5-11
II. Collective miraculous phenomena   2.43; 5.12, 15, 16; 6.8; 8.6-8, 13

Hardon stresses that he has listed 'only physical miracles ... which transcend the sensible forces of nature'. He has left out all instances where human beings are filled with the Holy Spirit, excluding 2.2-6 and 4.31 which include a 'nature miracle'. However, in 8.14-25, Simon Magus recognizes the transmission of the Spirit as a visible, powerful phenomenon that he also would like to master. Hardon also excludes visions from his list, even though they influence the physical reality as powerfully as cures, penalties and the like.

Frans Neirynck has limited his list of miracle stories in Acts to include healings (H), raisings of the dead (R), punishments (P), liberations from prison (L), and summary reports (S).[35] His categories help to sort out different kind of miracles performed through the apostles, but he also includes miracles done to them by angels (L). However, in this case it is problematic to exclude other miracles performed by angels – and other supernatural beings. Partly due to this exclusion,

---

34. J. A. Hardon, 'Miracle Narratives', pp. 304–5.

35. F. Neirynck, 'Miracle Stories', pp. 170–71. See also M. McCord Adams, 'Role of Miracles', p. 259.

there are two interrelated miracles in Acts 1–12 that are missing from his list: the
risen Jesus blinding Saul (9.8-9) and Ananias, commissioned by Jesus, returning
him his sight (9.10-19). Furthermore, Neirynck also includes the encounter
between Peter and Simon Magus (8.18-24), even though Peter only threatens
Simon. If the Simon Magus episode and instances of L (5.17-21; 12.3-17) are
excluded and the missing miracles in 9.8-9, 10-19 are added, I accept Neirynck's
proposal as far as it concerns *miracles performed through apostles and their
followers*:

S	2.43	Many signs and wonders performed by the Apostles
H	3.1-10	Peter heals the lame man at the temple gate
P	5.1-11	The death of Ananias and Sapphira
S	5.12	Many signs and wonders by the Apostles
S	5.15	Peter's shadow
S	5.16	Healing of the multitudes
S	6.8	Signs and wonders by Stephen
S	8.6-7, 13	Signs and wonders by Philip in Samaria
P?	9.8-9	The risen Jesus blinds Saul
H	9.10-19	Saul regains his sight [and receives the Spirit] through Ananias
H	9.32-35	Peter heals the paralytic Aeneas
R	9.36-42	Peter raises the disciple Tabitha

The dominant role of Peter is striking, but the summaries let the reader understand
that his miracles are only part of what was done by all the apostles (2.43; 5.12
['many signs and wonders']; 8.6-7, 13) as well as by Stephen the deacon (6.8). As
the parallels of Schneckenburger presented above demonstrate, Luke writes
mainly about Peter because he represents the mission to the Jews as much as Paul
represents the mission to the Gentiles. In Acts 1–12, Luke reports conveniently
through his summaries that miracles happened in all places that the apostles
entered.

The list of Neirynck can – and must, I think – be supplemented with a list of
specific activities of supernatural beings. God must be excluded here, even though
he responds to the prayer of the apostles and shows by lot who should replace
Judas (1.24-26).[36] The horrible death of Judas (1.18-19) can also be considered
a divine *Strafwunder*, even though there is no agent mentioned. The risen Jesus
(RJ) – several times called 'the Lord' – appears on some important occasions, not
only as an observer, but also as an active participant in the events of the narrative.
He appears and speaks in visions, as Luke thought was prophesied in Joel 2.28
(LXX; Acts 2.17), and he guides the mission of his church (Acts 2.22, 47; 11.21).
He is the actual miracle worker since all miracles of the apostles are performed
in his name, i.e., by his power. Similarly, it is difficult to imagine the risen Jesus

---

36.   Luke reserves the term καρδιογνώστης for God alone (Acts 15.8; cf. Hermas *Man.*
4.3.4; *Ap. Const.* 2.24.6; Ps.-Clem. *Hom.* 10.13.2). Against this common opinion, R. F. O'Toole,
'Activity of the Risen Jesus in Luke-Acts', *Bib* 62 (1981), pp. 471–98, finds it probable that 'Jesus
picks Judas's replacement' (p. 476), because he is the one who has chosen the twelve.

inactive in contexts where people are 'added to' the Lord (5.14; 11.24), turn to him (9.35; 11.21) and believe in him (5.14; 9.42; 11.17). However, references to the 'Lord' often remain obscure, since we do not always know whether Luke is talking about God or Jesus.[37] In Luke-Acts, the Holy Spirit (HS) or the Spirit of the Lord is not just a mechanical vehicle of God's action in the created world or a theological principle since Luke often specifies the Spirit as a personified supernatural being. He speaks to believers (Acts 8.29; 10.19; 11.12) and through the prophets (1.16) and can even 'snatch' Philip (8.39). It is wrong to deceive, test or resist him (5.5, 9; 7.51). Luke portrays the Spirit as the inaugurator of the Church and its mission, and, after the Pentecost, the Spirit is active among the apostles and other believers. Peter, Stephen, Saul and even all the appointed deacons are filled with the Holy Spirit as they bear witness to Jesus and serve the community (4.8; 6.3, 5, 10; 7.55; 9.17). The Spirit also 'comforts' the communities and increases them in number (9.31). In the Cornelius story, Peter first receives a vision (10.9-16) that is interpreted by a heavenly voice (V), and immediately thereupon, the Holy Spirit speaks to him and guides him to take the next action (10.17-23). The Spirit does not 'appear', but talks to and falls upon human beings and works through natural phenomena. Furthermore, Luke keeps angels coming and going (A). Releasing the apostles (5.17-21) and later Peter (12.3-17) from prison is not all that they do in Acts 1–12. They also appear as interpreters of events (*angelus interpres*) and as guides or helpers. Angels are close to the characters of the story even when they are not really there: Stephen can look like an angel (6.15) and Peter can be assumed to be one (12.15). If we leave aside more general references to the influence of the supernatural on the life of the apostles and believers, the following list of the specific activities of the supernatural beings in Acts 1–12 may be compiled:[38]

RJ	1.1-9	The appearances and ascension of Jesus
A	1.10-11	Two men interpret Jesus' ascension to the apostles
HS	2.1-12	The Pentecost: Spirit and glossolalia (cf. 1.1-8; 2.14-42)
HS	4.31	Filling with the Spirit
HS	5.1-11	Spirit punishes Ananias and Sapphira with death
A	5.17-21	Angel delivers the apostles from the prison
RJ	7.54-60	Risen Jesus receives the spirit of his martyr Stephen
HS	8.14-17	The Samaritan believers receive the Spirit
A	8.26	Angel guides Philip

37. R. F. O'Toole, 'Activity', pp. 473–96, presents evidence for all the activities of the risen Jesus in Luke-Acts under six headings: Lord, witness, the Eucharist, the Spirit, name, and salvation. He states that (p. 478) 'Luke's frequent lack of concern to distinguish carefully between κύριος as applied to the Father and to Jesus tells us something about his view of the activity of the risen Christ'. Even though O'Toole concedes that 'God the Father achieves everything which happens in Christ' (p. 473), there is a danger of stretching the christological idea too far. Precisely because Luke uses the title κύριος ambiguously, he also seems to deprive it from its specifically christological content. God and Christ belong functionally together.

HS	8.29	Spirit guides Philip
HS	8.39-40	Spirit snatches Philip away and takes him to Azotus
RJ	9.1-9	Risen Jesus appears to Saul and blinds him
RJ	9.10-16	Risen Jesus appears to Ananias
HS	9.17-19	Saul [regains his sight and] receives the Spirit through Ananias
A	10.1-8	Angel appears to Cornelius (cf. 10.30-33; 11.13-14)
V	10.9-16	Peter sees a vision interpreted a heavenly voice (cf. 11.4-10)
HS	10.17-23	Spirit guides Peter to receive the men sent by Cornelius (cf. 11.11-12)
HS	10.44-48	Gentiles are filled with the Spirit and speak in tongues (cf. 11.15-17)
HS	11.27-30	Spirit predicts through Agabus that a severe famine will come
A	12.3-17	Angel delivers Peter from the prison
A	12.19-23	Angel strikes Herod dead

It is safe to conclude that the risen Jesus, the Holy Spirit and angels played significant roles in the stories told among the Christians. Luke is not in the least bothered by their continuous and often overlapping presence in his narrative, and he quite obviously did not intend to make distinctions concerning their respective functions. On the contrary, he wants to assure his readers that God constantly and in various ways took care of his own people in the times of the apostles. Luke makes clear that the course of their history was also guided by *divine providence*. Divine care becomes apparent in long-term developments that cannot be traced back to exclusively supernatural factors, as the advice of Gamaliel demonstrates (5.38-39).[39] The idea of divine necessity is emphatically present when Luke reports the first act of the new community, i.e., choosing a replacement for Judas (1.16-26). The next ones are related to God's plan and salvation history (3.21; 4.12), the proper human response to them (5.29), and the election of Saul (9.6, 16).

Against those who think that Luke drastically limits the human dimension of events when referring to necessity (δεῖ), Cosgrove has rightly pointed out that Luke-Acts includes 40 instances of δεῖ, but at least 13 of them are 'ordinary', i.e. they do not refer to divine necessity.[40] It is striking, however, that only one of the

38. Cf. the survey of B. J. Koet, 'Divine Communication in Luke-Acts', in J. Verheyden (ed.), *The Unity of Luke-Acts* (BETL, 142; Leuven: Peeters, 1999), pp. 745–58, (746–50, esp. 747) who treats the appearances of the risen Jesus and the angel in chs. 9–10 under the heading of 'dreams and visions'. He seems to separate Paul's vision of Jesus from that of Ananias because the former has physical impact on its receiver. However, can we assume that Luke made such a distinction?

39. On the theme of providence and characterization in popular religious writings, see R. Pervo, *Profit with Delight: The Literary Genre of the Acts of the Apostles* (Philadelphia: Fortress, 1987), p. 74.

40. C. H. Cosgrove, 'The Divine ΔΕΙ in Luke-Acts: Investigation into the Lukan Understanding of God's Providence', *NovT* 26 (1984), pp. 168–90 (172–73), pointing his critique especially at S. Schulz, 'Gottes Vorsehung bei Lukas', *ZNW* 54 (1963), pp. 104–16.

six instances in Acts 1–12 is 'ordinary' (5.29). Cosgrove is surely right in claiming that the Lukan δεῖ is not a *terminus technicus* expressing divine predestination, but rather carries a wide range of meaning: it expresses the rootedness of the keryg-matic history, summons to obedience and points to the surprise reversal effected by the miracle, the guarantee of God's providence. When writing about God's providence, Luke uses a large vocabulary and an unreflective conception of the whole matter and therefore cannot be blamed for making his characters act like human puppets.[41] However, the Lukan δεῖ is reflective in its retrospection: Luke exhorts his audience to look back at the history of the early church and take it as a completely providential period, including God's work and human action. Those who heard the story of Luke were called to cast a yearning and respectful look at the first Christians and so make their nostalgic enthusiasm about them become part of that history.

For Luke, the *forces that oppose the divine action* are mostly human. In spite of the overarching presence of the supernatural in Acts 1–12, he does not demonize the Jewish ruling class. Unlike in his gospel, Luke does not write about 'demons', but about 'unclean spirits' that the apostles drive out of the possessed (5.16; 8.7). The parallel to the events in chs. 10–11 is striking: the apostles were able to remove real impurity while God soon guided Peter and others to understand that the Gentiles, as such, were not impure and could receive the faith and the gift of the Spirit (10.28). Furthermore, Luke once refers to the activity of Satan, by making Ananias (5.3) a counterpart to Judas (Luke 22.3) who betrayed Jesus for money. The devil appears once, as Peter reminds his audience how Jesus 'went about doing good and healing all who were oppressed by the devil' (Acts 10.38; cf. 13.10).

If we strip away the constant presence and continual intervention of the super-natural powers from Acts 1–12, no story is left. Luke clearly needs all of that and nothing less to convey the whole story to his audience. This is hardly irrelevant for our attempts to understand what he wanted to say to his readers.

3. How Does the Supernatural Work?

As miracles and other supernatural events are not a special theme in treatments of the Lukan theology, so are they seldom discussed as important elements in the plot of Acts. Salvation history and everything that relates to it is essential: Luke the historian and Luke the theologian; Israel and the church; Christology, pneuma-tology, eschatology and the like. Since Luke intended to write a story, 'an orderly account of the events that have been fulfilled among us' (Lk. 1.1), proceeding to the period of the Christian mission up to the last years of Paul, his theology must be reconstructed from this overall story, taking into consideration the dynamic historical development he portrays, the suggestiveness of his presentation, and the interweaving of various theological themes into the plot of his narrative. Miracles and other supernatural events and influences cannot be separated either from the plot of Acts or from the theological issues presented in it.[42] The supernatural

41. C. H. Cosgrove, 'Divine ΔΕΙ', pp. 183–87.
42. An interesting example of this is offered by J. J. Pilch, *Healing in the New Testament.*

elements in the Lukan story cannot be silently bypassed as 'tradition' which is less significant than 'redaction', or as 'mythology' which is not as important as 'theology' or 'history'. The very same Luke who can be compared to historians like Thucydides can equally well and in the same breath be compared to the myth-makers despised by Lucian. Miracles and interventions of supernatural beings are vitally important to Luke.

Throughout Luke's narrative, miracles and supernatural events have a generative function; they cause a chain reaction in the story by leading to events that must follow from the powerful act of God. In the following list, I have marked the exceptions to this rule in *italics*:

The risen Lord and his promise of the Spirit; his ascension (1.1-12)
  Foundation of the community in Jerusalem (1.13-14)
  Supplementing the twelve by casting lots (1.15-26)
The Pentecost (2.1-13)
  Speech of Peter and mass conversion (2.14-41)
  Miracles and the ideal life of the community (2.42-47)
The healing of a lame man (3.1-10)
  Speech of Peter (3.11-26)
  Arrest of Peter and John (4.1-22)
  Prayer of the community; God's response (4.25-31)
Community of goods (4.32-37)
  Ananias and Sapphira: *Strafwunder* (5.1-10)
  Fear seizes everybody (5.11)
Signs and wonders by the apostles (5.12-16)
  Apostles before the council and the advice of Gamaliel (5.17-42)
The election of the seven (6.1-7)
  Power and proclamation of Stephen (6.8-10)
  Arrest of Stephen (6.10–7.1)
  Speech of Stephen (7.2-53)
  Martyrdom of Stephen (7.54-60)
  Persecution of the community and the scattering of the apostles (8.1-3)
  The power and proclamation of Philip in Samaria (8.4-8)
  Simon is amazed (8.9-13)
  Peter and John bring the Spirit (8.14-17)
  Simon wants to buy the power (8.18-24)
  Mass conversion; Peter and John return to Jerusalem (8.25)

Insights from Medical and Mediterranean Anthropology (Minneapolis: Fortress, 2000), pp. 110–11, who claims that the body zones affected by illness in Acts are related to the theological agenda of Luke. There are no healing miracles that concern the mouth–ears zone (proclamation); all the more the apostles and other believers heal illnesses of heart–eyes zone (thought/understanding) and hands–feet zone (acting, following on the Way). Unlike Luke with Jesus' mouth–ears zone miracles, Acts is a book of open proclamation; on this difference, see also below the discussion on resurrection and ascension of Jesus.

An angel tells Philip to go towards Gaza (8.26)
>   Philip meets the Ethiopian eunuch (8.27-28)
>   Guided by the Spirit, Philip converts and baptizes the Eunuch (8.29-38)
>   Spirit takes Philip away (8.39-40)

Jesus appears to the persecutor Paul (9.1-5)
>   Jesus tells Paul to go to Damascus (9.6-9)
>   Jesus tells Ananias to go to Paul (9.10-16)
>   Paul regains his sight and is filled with the Spirit (9.17-19a)
>   Paul in Damascus and Jerusalem (9.19b-30)
>   The community lives in peace (9.31)

Peter visits the believers and heals Aeneas in Lydda (9.32-33)
>   Local residents turn to the Lord (9.34)
>   Peter raises Tabitha in Joppa (9.35-41)
>   Many believe in the Lord (9.42)
>   Peter stays in Joppa (9.43)

The vision of Cornelius (10.1-4)
>   Angel tells him to send men for Peter (10.5-8)

The vision of Peter (10.9-16)
>   The men of Cornelius arrive (10.17-23a)
>   Peter goes to Caesarea and hears what Cornelius has to say (10.23b-33)
>   Peter understands his vision: the Gentiles are accepted into the people of God (10.34-43)
>   Spirit falls on the Gentiles present; they are baptized (10.44-48)
>   Peter tells everything to the other apostles in Jerusalem and the recognize it (11.1-18)
>   First Gentile Christian community in Antioch (11.19-26)
>   Collection in Antioch for the poor of Jerusalem (11.27-30)

Herod persecutes the Christians; James is killed and Peter is arrested for trial (12.1-4)
>   The community prays to God and an angel releases Peter (12.5-11)
>   Peter goes to the believers and then to 'another place' (12.12-17)
>   Herod is killed by an angel (12.18-23)
>   Growth of the community (12.24)
>   Barnabas and Saul (12.25)

Not surprisingly, the most obvious, straightforward and programmatic cases come up in the first chapters of Acts.[43] The risen Jesus instructs the apostles about

---

43. This kind of emphatic start is supported by specific references to the fulfilment of Scripture. Although in speeches Luke constantly allows the apostles and other believers to quote the Scriptures in order to demonstrate that they are fulfilled in Jesus and his church, specific references concentrate in the beginning of the book (1.16-20; 3.18; cf. 2.1 and the 'pesher interpretation of Scripture' in 2.22-36). For a survey, see D. Peterson, 'The Motif of Fulfilment and the Purpose of Luke-Acts', in B. W. Winter, A. D. Clarke (eds) *The Book of Acts in Its First Century Setting*, Vol. 1: *Ancient Literary Setting* (Grand Rapids: Eerdmans, 1993), pp. 83–104 (94–100).

the coming of the Spirit, and they act accordingly. The coming of the Spirit leads to their powerful witness for the resurrection of Jesus. Next, one specific public miracle leads to a new chain reaction, calling forth faith in the crowds and the hostile action of the powerful men of the temple. The ensuing events are based on the same supernatural foundation: faith of those who see, hostility of those who see but do not want to believe, and the excitement of the crowds. God is doing his mighty works, miraculously guiding his believers to embrace the right things at the right moment and blessing them in wonderful ways.

In this basic framework, the supernatural events and influences that appear in the plot of Acts repeatedly serve particular purposes which I think can be presented in terms of four overlapping categories:

1) The resurrection and ascension of Jesus is the foundation miracle for the whole narrative of Acts. All subsequent supernatural events and influences bear witness to the truth of this miracle. When they follow the proclamation of the apostles, they serve as successful validation of the divine status and power of Jesus. Supernatural events and influences are *conditio sine qua non* for the astonishing success of the mission of the apostles among the Jews in Judaea.[44]

2) Supernatural events and influences are vital parts of the apostles' activity that leads to accelerating conflicts with the unbelieving, desperate and vicious temple authorities.

3) Supernatural events and influences are manifestations of God's acts, which take place in proper order and as foretold in the Scriptures and which guide the believers, provide theological insights and legitimize the salvation history, particularly the inclusion of the Gentiles in the realm of the new faith.[45]

4) Supernatural events and influences are related to God's providence that guides apostles and other believers and strengthens them in faith, unity and exemplary lifestyle (devotion, purity of heart, care for each other, and community of goods).

Luke has developed these themes in close interrelations to each other. In the following survey, I try to flesh out how these themes come up and develop in the Lukan narrative.

a. *The Resurrection and Ascension of Jesus (Lk. 24; Acts 1.1-11)*
These must be seen as the foundation miracles for the whole narrative of Acts. The end of Luke and the beginning of Acts are very much devoted to demonstrating

---

44. J. A. Hardon, 'Miracle Narratives', p. 310, points out correctly: 'at every point where the Gospel was first established among a certain people, the foundation was made in a miraculous context, with manifest showing of signs and powers worked by the hands of the Apostles.' Cf. also P. J. Achtemeier, 'Lukan Perspective', p. 553: 'It is rather clear in Acts that miracles were an effective device for turning people to faith'. On some occasions Luke makes this happen without mentioning that the word was proclaimed (9.35, 42), but he is clearly conscious of the problem of miracles and magic; see below the discussion on 8.4-25. Achtemeier, 'Lukan Perspective', pp. 556–58, concludes his survey on the Gospel of Luke: 'In sum, there is as much evidence that Luke has toned down the magical aspects of Jesus' miracles, as there is that he presents such stories under the particular influence of the Hellenistic understanding of magic.'

45. Cf. M. McCord Adams, 'Role of Miracles', p. 238.

the truth of Jesus' resurrection, the cessation of his physical presence among the apostles and his new, exalted status after his ascension to heaven (cf. Acts 3.21). In his epoch-making work on the messianic secret in the Gospels, William Wrede also wrote a minor chapter on the theme of secrecy and the ignorance of the disciples in Luke that included an important observation. In the lifetime of Jesus, no one could have understood his suffering and resurrection because God had concealed these coming events from everyone – even though Jesus had clearly announced them to his disciples.[46] With the progressive development of the recognition theme throughout Luke 24, Luke wants to make it perfectly clear that the evidence for Jesus' bodily resurrection is as incontestable as it can be and that all that had happened to him was predicted long ago in the law and by the prophets. Then the disciples can perceive the promise of 'power from on high' (vv. 44-49). I think that these perceptions of Wrede have lasting significance for understanding the resurrection stories of Luke and their culmination in the ascension of Jesus.

In the beginning of Acts, Luke concludes his description of manifold and progressive witnesses to the resurrection and ascension of Jesus loudly and clearly (1.3). Jesus' last appearance to his disciples (vv. 4-11)[47] during forty days includes thorough instructions, particularly the repeated command to stay in Jerusalem for the outpouring of the Spirit.[48] The Lukan Jesus also turns down the disciples' inquiries concerning whether this is the time when he will 'restore the kingdom to Israel'[49] in order to direct their full attention to the missionary task that follows after they have received the power of the Spirit from above.

With the opening scene of Acts, Luke communicates to his readers the idea that nobody will see Jesus on earth before the final days (cf. 3.21). The end is postponed to much later times. But in the time of the apostles, by divine guidance, everything had to take place in a proper order. The apostles and their companions remain in Jerusalem and organize their community in a proper manner by choosing a

46. W. Wrede, *Das Messiasgeheimnis in den Evangelien: Zugleich ein Beitrag zum Verständnis des Markusevangeliums* (Göttingen: Vandenhoeck & Ruprecht, 1901), pp. 163–79. He noticed that Luke repeated the Markan pattern of Jesus' commands to silence, but no longer understood their negative meaning (pp. 173–74). However, Luke put particular emphasis on the ignorance of the disciples in his versions of Markan passion proclamations (Luke 9.45; 18.34). Wrede pointed out that this motif had both historical and dogmatic significance for Luke. This was not so, because there was a danger of taking Jesus to be a national liberator and political Messiah. For Luke, the disciples were ignorant because their ignorance had to be removed by the revelation of the risen Lord and his exegesis of the scripture (p. 171).

47. It is virtually impossible to separate redactional elements and reconstruct a primitive tradition behind 1.1-11. M. Parsons, *The Departure of Jesus in Luke-Acts: The Ascension Narratives in Context* (JSNTSup, 21; Sheffield: JSOT Press, 1987), p. 143, finds it possible 'to argue for faint traces of a pre-Lukan ascension tradition, preserved particularly in v. 9'.

48. Cf. R. C. Tannehill, *The Narrative Unity of Luke-Acts: A Literary Interpretation* vol. 2, *The Acts of the Apostles* (Minneapolis: Fortress, 1990), p. 10.

49. The presentation of Luke implies that, during all those forty days that Jesus kept on appearing and teaching his disciples about the kingdom of God, he did not make it clear whether the kingdom would come immediately or much later.

replacement for Judas Iscariot. The particular person chosen is unimportant for the Lukan narrative; what is of importance is only that the replacement took place and that the leading group of the believers is whole again and prepared to receive the Spirit. In their mission, they will represent the twelve tribes of all Israel; using the same symbolism, Luke states that the believers numbered about one hundred and twenty persons.[50]

b. The Pentecost Miracle (2.1-13)

The appearances and departure of Jesus happened only among his followers; there were no outsider witnesses (cf. 10.40-41).[51] The Pentecost miracle (2.1-13),[52] in turn, must be a large public event that compels all those present to respond to God's mighty acts among those who believe in Jesus. The audible and visible coming of the Spirit is witnessed by the believers alone, but the following speaking in 'other tongues' is heard by 'devout Jews from every nation under heaven living in Jerusalem' (2.5), and they all are 'amazed and astonished' to hear the Galilean believers speak in their native languages (v. 7-8). It is essential to note that the crowd consists of 'devout men' (ἄνδρες εὐλαβεῖς), men of the same spiritual quality as those who buried Stephen (8.2). With this reference, Luke creates a plausible framework for the mass conversion that takes place after the speech of Peter (2.41). These devout men are receptive to the perplexing phenomenon: they *all* ask each other what it means, while *some* mockingly say that these people are merely drunk (vv. 12-13). Luke focuses on the latter group in order to give a starting point for Peter's powerful speech (vv. 14-15).

Luke has Peter introduce the quotation from Joel 3.1-5 as a prophecy fulfilled in the Pentecost miracle. Some notable changes in the text reveal his intentions. Instead of μετὰ ταῦτα in Joel 3.1 (LXX) Luke reads ἐν ταῖς ἐσχάταις ἡμέραις (Acts 2.17), emphasizing that the time of call to repentance and faith in Jesus that starts at the Pentecost will cover the last days as a whole (cf. v. 21).[53] In the light of 1.7-8, there will be a notable interval between the Pentecost and the very last days. The idea that the earliest years of the Church were full of miracles and other supernatural events is important for Luke since it corresponds with the cosmic

50. *Communis opinio*; see e. g. J. Roloff, *Die Apostelgeschichte* (NTD, 5; Göttingen: Vandenhoeck & Ruprecht, 1981), p. 31; A. Weiser, *Apostelgeschichte*, pp. 68–69; R. C. Tannehill, *Narrative Unity*, p. 22; J. Jervell, *Apostelgeschichte*, p. 123.

51. Cf. Celsus's argument against Jesus' resurrection: Jesus preached publicly but 'after rising from the dead showed himself secretly only to one woman, and to his own companions' (Origen, *Cels.* 2.70). This argument was later taken up by Hermann Samuel Reimarus.

52. Scholars usually regard the list of the peoples (2.9-11a) and the coming of the Spirit (vv. 1-4) as separate traditions. Luke interpreted them in terms of Christian prophecy and mission; see e.g. G. Lüdemann, *Early Christianity*, pp. 40–42; J. Jervell, *Apostelgeschichte*, pp. 137–39.

53. With A. Weiser, *Apostelgeschichte*, p. 92; J. Jervell, *Apostelgeschichte*, p. 143, and others. E. Haenchen, *Acts*, p. 179, thinks that the last days refer to later times, since God will pour out his Spirit on *all* flesh only during the mission that takes place after the Cornelius event. However, this process has starts with the Pentecost miracle and the phenomenon repeats itself among both Jews and Gentiles.

events of the very last days. His additions to the quotation in vv. 18-19 – 'and they shall prophesy', as well as the emphatic distinction between *wonders* in the heaven *above* and *signs* on the earth *below* – make the Pentecost miracle and all ensuing supernatural events in the life of the first believers something that begins the period of the last days. In their time, the 'signs on the earth below' are to some extent supplemented by 'wonders in the heaven above' (2.2; 7.55-56; 9.3; 10.11), but the actual heavenly wonders described in vv. 19c-20 belong only to the final events. Luke, who lives in a less miraculous period between the wonderful times of the early Church and the last events, is clear about the main thing: 'Then everyone who calls the name of the Lord [i.e., Jesus] shall be saved' (v. 21).

Just as Jesus' 'deeds of power, wonders and signs' were attested and known to all Israelites, the Pentecost miracle now provides proof for his resurrection. Luke has Peter say to the crowd that they 'crucified and killed [Jesus] by the hands of those outside the law'. These devout men for their part fulfilled 'the definite plan and foreknowledge of God' (v. 23): Jesus had to be crucified and raised from the dead, but now the time has come to understand why God planned all this. Luke thus indicates that these devout men acted in ignorance (cf. 3.17). Now, after having heard the language miracle and having it explained, they ask what they should do (v. 37; cf. Lk 3.10). In this very first public supernatural scene of Acts, the miracle itself did not lead the audience to faith.[54] Those present are puzzled, but correctly disposed to the supernatural event, and so they receive an explanation that leads them to repentance, baptism, forgiveness of sins, reception of the Holy Spirit (v. 38), breaking out of 'this corrupt generation' (v. 40) and communion with other believers (v. 42). Unlike the scene prior to Peter's speech, there are no mockers around in the final scene, only a receptive audience that believes that God has raised Jesus from the dead and that God's miracles and great works continue to take place among his followers who now have received the Holy Spirit. Three thousand persons are baptized and added to the community.

Luke reveals that the proper reaction of a believer to the presence of the supernatural power is awe. This protects the unity of the community (2.42-43) and guards it from acting against the Holy Spirit (5.11). The incredible amount of converts, extraordinary faith and joy of the believers, their spiritual unity, community of goods and 'the goodwill of all the people' summarily described by Luke are undoubtedly consequences of the Pentecost miracle. Without the coming of the Spirit, the community would not have been like that.[55] The apostles must

---

54. P. J. Achtemeier, 'Lukan Perspective', p. 550, emphasizes Luke's 'attempts to balance Jesus' miraculous activity and his teaching in such a way to give them equal weight'. M. McCord Adams, 'Role of Miracles', pp. 237–38, agrees with him and extends this idea to Acts.

55. Drawing upon the narrative theory of Uspensky, M. Parsons, *Departure*, pp. 174–75, claims that 2.46 is the first reference that includes an 'inside view' of the disciples. According to him, Acts 'begins from an external point of view' and 'entry into the narrative world from the psychological point of view is slow, but sure'. I think that this is related to the point made by Wrede on the gradual dissipation of the disciples' ignorance and Luke's emphasis on the hard supernatural evidence of Jesus' resurrection and ascension; see above, the discussion on Luke 24 and Acts 1.

also have changed, even though Luke has already portrayed them as miracle
workers during the ministry of Jesus (Lk. 9.2, 6; 10.8). In Acts, their miracles must
first of all create a conflict and a split within Israel.

c. The Healing of the Lame Man (3.1-10)[56]

This is an indisputable and evident miracle, the impact of which Luke has drama-
tized with rich novelistic details.[57] The very first thing Peter says to the astonished
crowd after the miracle is that he and John have not done such a thing by their
'own power or piety' (v. 12). The miracle that has happened 'by faith in his name'
(v. 16) proves that God has raised from the dead the very same Jesus whom the
'Israelites' have killed and whom Pilate wanted to release (vv. 13-15). The idea that
'the faith that is through Jesus has given him this perfect health in the presence
of all of you' has often been characterized as awkward. Even though there is no
indication that the lame man believes, Luke clearly wishes to extend the motif of
faith – faith that Peter wants to evoke in his audience – to the healing episode.[58]
As after the Pentecost miracle, Peter's call to repentance appeals to the people,
resulting in five thousand fresh converts (4.4).

From among many miracles that could open the public activity of the apostles,
Luke has chosen this one that takes place as a challenging intrusion into the
domain of the temple authorities who become the enemies of the believers. They
put Peter and John in prison because they preach 'that in Jesus there is the resurrection of the dead' (4.2) – a belief that Luke held to be genuinely Jewish.[59] Luke
stresses again that the evident miracle accomplished by uneducated and ordinary
men proves that the resurrection of Jesus is an undeniable fact (cf. 3.12 and 4.13):
miracles are done in his name and by his power. Because the crowds acknowledge
the miracle, willingly listen to the apostles and admire the community of the
believers, the temple authorities are not able to act in a straightforward manner
against the apostles (vv. 13-22). In spite of their helplessness, the leaders of the
people will soon show how violent they can be.

56. According to E. Haenchen, *Acts*, p. 201, this was originally a simple healing miracle –
without the alms motif (vv. 3-6a) and therefore similar to 9.32-35 – emphasizing the saving power
of the risen Jesus. For Luke, it prepared for the following arrest of Peter and John, and Peter's
testimony for Jesus as the only saviour of humankind. Similarly G. Lüdemann, *Early Christianity*,
pp. 50–53; J. Jervell, *Apostelgeschichte*, pp. 161–62.

57. D. Hamm, 'Acts 3.1-10: The Healing of the Temple Beggar as Lukan Theology', *Bib* 67
(1986), pp. 305–19 (308–15, 318), thinks that the ninth hour, the Beautiful Gate, the gazing and
leaping motif, the silver and gold and the tension between passivity and activity in the story
parabolically hint at restoration of Israel at the end of time.

58. I find it plausible that Luke has added the idea of Peter telling the lame man to look at
him and John (v. 4b-5a) in order to make such a reference sensible. Hamm, 'Acts 3.1-10', pp.
311–12, thinks that Luke wanted to stress the role of the apostles as *mediators* of the healing
power of the risen Jesus

59. J. Jervell, *Apostelgeschichte*, p. 175.

d. Unity and Community of Goods among the Believers (4.23–5.16)

After the initial conflict of the apostles with the leaders of the temple, Luke devotes four scenes to the theme of the unity and community of goods among the believers. The community responds to the report of Peter and John with a prayer to God the Creator (4.24-30), a prayer that refers to the activity of Herod and Pontius Pilate against his 'holy servant' Jesus as the fulfilment of Ps. 2.1-2. This reference is obviously *malplacé*, but it may stem from a traditional proof from prophecy that Luke, in spite of all difficulties, wanted to use here.[60] However, the prayer of the community makes an insightful difference between the bold proclamation of the 'servants' supported by God, and healings, signs and wonders that are done by God's own hand (4.29-30). God responds to this prayer by a numinous shaking of 'the place in which they were gathered together' (v. 31). 'They were all filled with the Holy Spirit and spoke the word of God with boldness', even though there were no outsiders to listen to their proclamation. However, with this scene Luke wants to stress God's precise and immediate response to the prayer and the continuous impact of the Pentecost miracle in the community (v. 33).[61] The correct mind-set of the believers and the close presence of the supernatural in their midst enable Luke to refer to the community of goods among the believers (v. 32). The spontaneous donation of Joseph (vv. 36-37) does not fit the rule, but Luke seems to indicate that the ideal state of affairs was reached spontaneously.[62]

e. The Fate of Ananias and Sapphira (5.1-11)

In the light of the preceding episodes, the terrible fate of Ananias and Sapphira[63] underlines the exceedingly high standards of the life of the community and the transparency of the behaviour of all its members. This story also demonstrates Luke's particularly strong aversion to the lust for money; it is not just evil, but belongs to the realm of Satan (Lk. 22.3-6; Acts 5.3; 8.18-20). As speedily as God answered the prayer of the community, he here kills two of its members who have lied to him.[64] The story implies that the members had no way of lying to or deceiving their leaders in the early Christian communities. On the one hand, the

---

60. With E. Haenchen, *Acts*, p. 228; G. Lüdemann, *Early Christianity*, p. 59. For a traditional prayer argue J. Roloff, *Apostelgeschichte*, p. 85; J. Jervell, *Apostelgeschichte*, p. 189.

61. A. Harnack, *Apostelgeschichte*, 142–144, thought that v. 31 transmits the tradition of the original Pentecost miracle.

62. It is difficult to avoid the impression that the case of Joseph was rather exceptional (with E. Haenchen, *Acts*, 234) than just a example of Luke's interest in biographical details (thus J. Jervell, *Apostelgeschichte*, 193).

63. According to E. Haenchen, *Acts*, 234, and G. Lüdemann, *Early Christianity*, 63–65, the original story was only about Ananias; it ended with the frightful reaction of everybody (vv. 1-5). However, v. 4 is added by Luke, who extended the story and added it as an impressive counterpart to the tradition about the community of goods (4.32-37). J. Roloff, *Apostelgeschichte*, 92–93, and J. Jervell, *Apostelgeschichte*, 198–99, exclude only v. 4 as Lukan redaction.

64. Luke gives the impression that all members of the community who owned lands or houses spontaneously and without any pressure sold their property in order that the money so gained could be distributed 'to each as any had need' (4.34-35). Thus Peter can remind Ananias of the

presence of the divine power caused fear and awe (2.43; 5.6, 11); on the other hand, joy and sincerity (2.46) among the believers – and fear and respect among many outsiders (5.6, 11, 13).

After the shocking story of Ananias and Sapphira, Luke could not just go on to the next, more aggressive stage of persecution against the believers. He had to reassure his readers of the missionary success of the community, this time emphasizing the 'signs and wonders' that happened through the apostles and went together with mass conversions (5.12a, 14-15).[65] In addition, he wanted to stress the numinous impact of the story about Ananias and Sapphira on the people (v. 13). These two interests collide and lead Luke into somewhat contradictory statements in vv. 12-16.[66] It is possible to hear Luke saying that the great majority of people feared and respected the believers while a mighty minority was 'added to the Lord'. It seems that the only group that is not indicated here are the temple authorities who immediately go on the attack.

f. The Arrest and Trial of the Apostles (5.17-42)
The summary in 5.12-16 tells about fear and respect as the majority response to their miracles and does not refer to the proclamation of the apostles at all. Correspondingly, the arrest and trial of the apostles by the high priest and the Sadducees, the increasing success of the new movement and the accelerating envy of the temple authorities go hand in hand.[67] They arrest the apostles, but their release by an angel makes the vigorous efforts (v. 23: 'the prison doors securely locked and the guards standing at the doors') of these vicious men look ridiculous and foolish.[68] Now they have to arrest the apostles 'without violence' (v. 26), even though they want to kill them (v. 33). They are calmed down by the pragmatic

voluntary character of his offer and that, even after the piece of property was sold, he could keep the proceeds at his disposal. Unlike J. Jervell (*Apostelgeschichte*, pp. 196-97), I do not find it likely that Luke meant to say that Ananias either had to sell his property or leave the community. Luke rather emphasizes the spontaneous side of selling possessions.

65. Cf. E. Haenchen, *Acts*, pp. 243–44; J. Roloff, *Apostelgeschichte*, p. 96.

66. In the days of source criticism it was typical to separate vv. 12, 14-15 and 12b-13 from each other as independent traditions; see the summary of E. Haenchen, *Acts*, pp. 243–44. Haenchen himself thinks that Luke articulated the traditional material between the *Strafwunder* and the new wave of persecution in order to keep up the success factor in the activity of the apostles. The tension between the statements 'none of the rest dared to join them' (v. 13a) and 'yet more than ever believers were added to the Lord' (v. 14a) was already in the traditional material used by Luke. J. Roloff, *Apostelgeschichte*, p. 97, assumes that Luke has composed the summary by using traditional motives. The pious fearfulness in v. 13a hints at fear reported in v. 11, while the note on the high esteem and success of the believers (v. 13b-14) prepares the reader for the trial in 5.17-42. J. Jervell, *Apostelgeschichte*, pp. 202–3, thinks that v. 12 is added by Luke who uses the tension between v. 13a and 14 a to demonstrate that Israel was now divided. G. Lüdemann, *Early Christianity*, p. 67, notes that there is no intrinsic connection between vv. 12a and 12b, and also between vv. 13a and 13b, but traces the whole back to Lukan redaction.

67. R. Pervo, *Profit*, pp. 27–28, sees in the malicious envy of the temple authorities a theme familiar in romantic novels.

68. R. Pervo, *Profit*, 61–62, chraracterizes the scene as 'burlesque and rowdy'.

advice of Gamaliel who actually recognizes the truth of the new faith (vv. 34-39). The miracles that have happened through the apostles are something completely different from the attempt of Theudas to repeat the miracle of Joshua (v. 36). This time the apostles are flogged and released with the same unrealistic and hopeless order as at the first arrest (vv. 40-42).

The passage as a whole prepares the reader for the first story of Christian martyrdom, showing how the wise words of Gamaliel have fallen on deaf ears – and how the authorities are suddenly no longer afraid of the people. Correspondingly, Luke's references to the immensely great popularity of the believers among the Jewish people start to wane after these events. The supernatural elements of the narrative that served the purpose of demonstrating successfully the truth of the faith are, from ch. 6 on, tacitly turned to support the unity of the believers and their unanimous opening to the Gentile mission.

Luke treats the strife between the Hebrews and Hellenists about a practical issue as a problem that was solved in a proper and completely satisfying manner (6.1-6). The number of disciples increases again greatly and even 'a great number of priests became obedient to the faith' (v. 7). As a representative of the new group of Hellenists, Stephen stands out of the crowd, not as a waiter on tables (v. 2), but as a man of grace and power, signs and wonders (v. 8). In spite of this, Luke does not stress that his mission was a success. On the contrary, it is easy for his theologically weak opponents to cause some men to 'stir up the people as well as the elders and the scribes' against Stephen. In Luke's scheme, Stephen cannot convert thousands or become respected by the people since he has to catalyze the process that leads to the rejection of the new faith among the Judean people and its salvation-historical turn to the Gentiles. His message seems to break with the strongest pillars of Judaism, the law and the temple (vv. 13-14), and he is arrested. In his long speech in front of the Sanhedrin, Luke indeed has Stephen state that 'the Most High does not dwell in houses made with human hands' (7.48, supported by quotation of Isa. 66.1 in vv. 49-50) and that the Jews 'received the law as ordained by angels' and did not keep it (7.53; cf. 15.10). Since Luke presents the accusers of Stephen as false witnesses (6.13-14), he seems to indicate that Stephen – from the Christian point of view – did not break with the relative, salvation-historical functions which God originally ascribed to the law and the temple. That was, of course, something completely different from what the temple authorities had heard him saying.

The speech of Stephen has no missionary intention; it does not even call the temple authorities to repentance, but blatantly condemns them. He portrays the history of Israel as supernatural guidance that the Israelites themselves have always rejected. As they once rejected Moses, they have now rejected the prophet whose coming was foretold by him (7.35-44). Stephen directs his words to the members of the Sanhedrin, but with his scriptural examples, he more or less attacks the people as a whole. The dying Stephen's vision of Jesus as the Son of Man legitimates his pessimistic view of the Jewish people and leads the Lukan narrative towards the Gentile mission. In 8.1-3, Luke no longer tells about the missionary success of the apostles, but about a great persecution. With his historically unreal-

istic statement that 'all except the apostles were scattered throughout the
countryside of Judaea and Samaria' (8.1), he prepares his readers for the mission
of the Hellenist table-servant Philip in Samaria, but simultaneously emphasizes
that, even in the midst of persecution, the community of Jerusalem was kept up
by its leaders. This, of course, implies that they were protected by divine powers,
even though the great period of their mission is over; in 9.31, Luke confines himself
to saying that 'the church throughout Judea, Galilee, and Samaria had peace and
was built up'.

g. The Mission of Philip in 'the City of Samaria' (8.4-25)[69]
This repeats the pattern of 'signs and wonders', proclamation of the gospel and
successful mass conversions related about the apostles' activity in Jerusalem.
Luke dramatizes Philip's success by introducing Simon the Magician and
mentioning that 'all of them [i.e., the Samaritans], from the least to the greatest,
listened to him eagerly, saying, "This man is the power of God that is called great".'
(v. 10). Simon has amazed the crowds with his magic, but Philip converts them
with his proclamation of the 'good news of the kingdom of God' and baptizes
them in the name of Jesus (v. 12). It is interesting to see that precisely here Luke
separates the miracles from the proclamation that leads to conversion; the activity
of Philip must be something completely different from the magical skills of
Simon.[70] Furthermore, a striking moral difference follows. As Simon is converted
and baptized with the others and Peter and John are sent from Jerusalem to lay
their hands on the baptized so that they receive the Holy Spirit,[71] Simon starts to
crave that miraculous power, and he senselessly offers money for it. The severe
words and threats of Peter strike him with awe and submission. The miraculous
power of the apostles is not only something that truly comes from God, but it also
includes the right understanding of God's will and the correct lifestyle that goes
with it.[72] Luke leaves the transmission of the Holy Spirit and further proclamation

69. According to E. Haenchen, *Acts*, pp. 307–8, the early form of the story was about Philip
working as a victorious Christian missionary in Samaria. His greatest triumph was over his
successful adversary Simon the Magician who wanted to buy the secret of his power. A similar
conclusion is drawn by J. Roloff, *Apostelgeschichte*, 132–133, and G. Lüdemann, *Early Christianity*,
pp. 98–99, who further assumes that the tradition – stemming most likely from a cycle of stories
about Philip – portrayed a clash between the supporters of Simon and the Christian religion. J. Jervell,
Apostelgeschichte, p. 267, thinks that the story is a combination of separate traditions (mission of
Philip; Philip vs. Simon; apostles come from Jerusalem and transmit the Holy Spirit; Peter vs. Simon).
He remains indecisive whether it was only Luke himself who combined the traditions.

70. H.J. Klauck, *Magic and Paganism in Early Christianity* (trans. B. McNeil; Edinburgh: T&T
Clark, 2000), p. 14; cf. J. Jervell, *Apostelgeschichte*, p. 262.

71. C. K. Barrett, 'Light on the Holy Spirit from Simon Magus (Acts 8,4-25)', in J. Kremer (ed.)
Les Actes des Apôtres: Traditions, redaction, théologie (BETL, 48; Leuven: Leuven University Press,
1979), pp. 281–95 (293), assumes that Luke here combined two traditions 'to coordinate the Seven
and the Twelve, apportioning baptism to the one and confirmation to the other'.

72. C. K. Barrett, 'Light', pp. 288–91, points out that, in Acts, those who receive the Spirit are
ready to give away money while those who desire to make money are in league with evil powers.

in 'many villages of the Samaritans' (v. 25) to the apostles, smoothing the way for the spontaneous coming of the Spirit in the beginning of the Gentile mission (10.44-48).

h. The Conversion of the Ethiopian Eunuch (8.26-40)

As the second Philip story, the conversion of the Ethiopian eunuch[73] – whom Luke introduces as a court official of the Candace, the queen of the Ethiopians – is a salvation-historical step between the conversion of the Samaritans and that of the Gentiles. Luke does not – and cannot – openly say that this man was a God-fearing Gentile.[74] He is not interested in the mission that could take place in Ethiopia, but he may hint that precisely here the mission of the apostles reached the 'ends of the earth'.[75] Luke stresses the supernatural guidance that Philip receives: an angel tells him to go to the road 'that goes down between Jerusalem and Gaza' (v. 26), and the Spirit guides him to go to the chariot of the eunuch and join him (v. 29). The eunuch does not receive the Spirit, but goes on his way rejoicing, which foreshadows the full acceptance of Gentiles in the Cornelius story. The Spirit snatches Philip away and brings him to Azotus (vv. 39-40), from whence he proclaims the gospel on his way to Caesarea. Thus Peter can find newly established Christian communities when he enters Lydda and Joppa (9.32-43).

i. The Conversion of Saul (9.1-19)

The conversion and call of Saul the persecutor into Paul the missionary (9.1-19) is one of the key scenes in Acts. Luke relates the Damascus event three times (9.3-19; 22.3-16; 26.9-18).[76] Though it reads like a biographical conversion story,[77] its significance in Acts is salvation-historical and apologetical. Consistent with the statement of the risen Jesus in 9.15, the Lukan Paul uses his miraculous conversion as argument for the gospel before 'the people of Israel' (ch. 22) and 'Gentiles and kings' (ch. 26).[78] Accordingly, the conversion of Saul the persecutor

---

73. E. Haenchen, *Acts*, pp. 315–16, assumes that Luke used a Hellenist-Christian tradition that originally told about the first Gentile conversion and that Luke revised it in order to subordinate it to the conversion of Cornelius by Peter. He finds it possible that Luke has made the conversion of the eunuch a miracle story by introducing the angel. J. Roloff, *Apostelgeschichte*, 139, regards the whole story as traditional and traces only the quotation of Isa. 53.7 in Acts 8.32-33 back to Luke. Similarly argues J. Jervell, *Apostelgeschichte*, pp. 272, 275, who thinks that possibly even the quotation was taken from the tradition. A. Weiser, *Apostelgeschichte*, p. 208, and with him G. Lüdemann, *Early Christianity*, pp. 104–5, assume that the tradition was much simpler, consisting merely of the baptism of the Ethiopian eunuch by Philip (vv. 27b, 36a, 38-40a*).

74. E. Haenchen, *Acts*, p. 314.

75. Thus R. Pervo, *Profit*, p. 70; R. C. Tannehill, *Narrative Unity*, pp. 108–9.

76. The synoptic comparison of G. Lüdemann, *Early Christianity*, pp. 107–10, leads to the result that the second account presupposes the first (22.12) and the third version is an abbreviated version of the two previous ones.

77. For criticism of attempts to point out parallels to the story and to define its genre, see J. Jervell, *Apostelgeschichte*, p. 291 n. 60.

78. The wording of v. 15 points to situations of persecution and public accusation. The persecutor becomes the persecuted who will suffer much for the sake of Jesus' name (v. 16).

is as supernatural as a conversion can be. The risen Jesus, who appears as light – something known from the traditional imagery of theophany – and as a voice addressing his words to Saul, almost dictates to the stricken and blinded man what he shall do. There is no place for repentance, but only for an abrupt and complete metamorphosis because the conversion of Saul has a particular role in the divine plan. Luke strengthens this impression by introducing here the mutually verifying visions of Saul and Ananias (9.10-16) and the miraculous healing of Paul's blindness through Ananias (vv. 17-19), followed later by a report to the disciples in Jerusalem who are at first incredulous (v. 26-27).[79] He repeats the pattern of 'double vision' and its verification in the Cornelius story (10.1–11.18) in order to emphasize the completely unmistakeable divine guidance in both events. This strategy further explains the emphatic role of Ananias whom the Lukan Paul, later before the Jewish crowd, characterizes as 'a devout man according to the law and well spoken of by all the Jews living there' (22.12). Paul's conversion becomes both a publicly known miracle in Damascus that immediately triggers a persecution against him (9.19b-25) and a new turn in God's plan that the Jerusalem leaders come to validate (vv. 26-28). As Tannehill puts it, Luke wanted to present the divine initiative in the lives of Philip and Saul pointing towards the Gentile mission before they verify what has already happened.[80]

Ananias is – unlike Philip in Samaria – able to transmit the Holy Spirit to Paul, who is baptized afterwards. After visiting the disciples in Jerusalem, demonstrating his faith and disputing with the Hellenist Jews, he is sent to Tarsus (vv. 29-30), where Luke keeps him waiting for the official recognition of the Gentile mission, which first happens through Peter and then through other apostles in Jerusalem. Only later will he present Paul as a miracle worker; in ch. 9, his proclamation and the persecution directed against him publicly demonstrate the divine power behind his miraculous conversion.

j. The Healing of Aeneas and the Raising of Tabitha (9.32-43)

In 9.31, Luke indicates that, immediately after the conversion of the former persecutor, the communities in Judaea, Galilee and Samaria lived in peace and that Peter now had the opportunity to visit all these Jewish-Christian communities. Their growth, which is no longer dramatic but constant, is brought about by the Holy Spirit. Luke chooses to relate two miracles that Peter performs after his arrival at Lydda, the healing of the paralyzed Aeneas in Lydda and the raising of Tabitha from the dead in Joppa.[81] Both of these miracles partly resemble two miracles of

79. For the strategy of 'double vision', see G. Lohfink, *The Conversion of St. Paul: Narrative and History in Acts* (trans. B. J. Malina; Chicago: Franciscan Herald Press, 1976), pp. 73–77. C. Burchard, *Der dreizehnte Zeuge* (FRLANT, 103; Göttingen: Vandenhoeck & Ruprecht, 1970), pp. 59–86, compares Acts 9 to Apuleius and *Joseph and Aseneth*.

80. R. C. Tannehill, *Narrative Unity*, p. 113. He further suggests that it would have been possible for Luke to place the material in 8.26–9.30 after the Cornelius episode – if he 'wished to make the point that the gentile mission is initiated through Peter'.

81. It is commonly assumed that these stories are separate local legends that Luke has bound together in order to bring Peter closer to Caesarea and to show how Christianity conquered new

Jesus: the healing of the lame man in Mk 2.1-12 and the raising of the daughter of Jairus in Mk 5.21-24, 35-43. The Jesus-like Peter is called, after the first miracle in Lydda, to do a greater one in Joppa. This remains the last miracle performed by him in Acts and perhaps therefore is so highly emotional.[82] These miracles cause mass conversions both in Lydda (9.35: 'all the residents … saw him and turned to the Lord') and Joppa (v. 42: 'many believed in the Lord'); no proclamation of the gospel is needed. The same Peter who faithfully cares about all these Jewish believers is soon to witness the extension of God's plan to concern the Gentiles as well. Luke finds it important to indicate that neither the mission of Philip nor the vision, conversion and groundbreaking commission of Saul has made Peter think about such a dramatic turn. The 'double vision' prepared for the God-fearing centurion Cornelius in Caesarea and for Peter in Joppa must take him completely by surprise.

k. *The conversion of Cornelius (10.1–11.18)*

In the important and repetitious section on the conversion of Cornelius, Luke strongly validates the Gentile mission that was already breaking through in the mission of Philip and the conversion of Saul. This takes place through the 'double vision' of Peter and Cornelius, the guidance of the Holy Spirit and finally through the descent of the Spirit on the whole God-fearing household of Cornelius, his relatives and close friends (cf. 10.24). After all these events, Peter goes to Jerusalem and relates them to the circumcised believers who have accused him of associating and eating with uncircumcised men (11.1-3):

10.1-8	Angel appears to Cornelius	10.30-33;
		11.13-14
10.9-16	Peter sees a vision interpreted a heavenly voice	11.4-10
10.17-23	Spirit guides Peter to receive the men sent by Cornelius	11.11-12
10.44-48	Gentiles are filled with the Spirit and speak in tongues	11.15-17

Starting from the conversion of Saul, visions in Acts are inextricably related to the Gentile mission and its validation.[83] From the point of view of Luke's narrative strategy, the climax is reached in 10.34-35, where the significance of all these supernatural events dawns on Peter. Luke clearly indicates that, without manifold and

---

areas and that the Tabitha story was already traditionally related to 1 Kgs 17.17-24; 2 Kgs 4.19-37 and Mk 5.40-41; see E. Haenchen, *Acts*, pp. 339–40; J. Roloff, *Apostelgeschichte*, pp. 158–59, and J. Jervell, *Apostelgeschichte*, pp. 298–99. G. Lüdemann, *Early Christianity*, p. 122, thinks that the Aeneas story 'has been considerably compressed by Luke' while the Tabitha story 'gives the impression of being a miracle story with a developed style'.

82. M. Dibelius, *Studies*, 12–13, classifies the story as an edifying personal legend; R. Pervo, *Profit*, 67, relates it to corresponding unrealistic scenes in romantic novels ('death is merely apparent, but believed').

83. B. J. Koet, 'Divine Communication', pp. 749–50, emphasizes all visions in Acts – including the scriptural proof in 2.17 (Joel 2.28 [LXX]) but excluding the vision of Stephen in 7.55-56 – reveal the same message: the Gentile mission is a divine command.

mutually-related divine visions, messages and actions, such a turn would not have been possible, even though he portrays Cornelius as a pious God-fearer who gave alms generously and prayed constantly (10.2). As he does not hesitate to relate the conversion of Saul three times, he does not hesitate to repeat the miraculous key events of the Cornelius story. It remains much disputed whether the salvation-historically epoch-making chain of events related in ch. 10 stems from the tradition[84] or whether it is composed by Luke.[85]

Be that as it may, in the very next passage Luke tells how the Gentile mission is, without any divine intervention, set in motion by 'some men of Cyprus and Antioch who, on coming to Antioch, spoke to the Greeks' (11.19-20). Relying on the acceptance of the Gentile converts (11.18), Luke can say that Barnabas is sent from Jerusalem to fetch Paul from Tarsus to Antioch.[86] However, unlike in the case of the mission in Samaria, he does not mention that Barnabas would have transmitted the Holy Spirit to the new converts. Luke characterizes him as 'a good man, full of the Holy Spirit and of faith' (v. 24), i.e., as someone who fully accepts the newly initiated Gentile mission. With Barnabas, Paul tacitly becomes a relatively independent preacher of the gospel. In 11.19-26, Luke has combined and interpreted independent traditions and matched them with his Cornelius story. The prediction of a severe famine 'over all the world' through Agabus and the pre-emptive relief sent by the Antiochian community to the believers in Judaea (11.27-30) underlines the unity and solidarity between the Jewish and Gentile Christian communities. Even though the foretold famine did not come over the whole world and his own piece of information rather indicates a local disaster,[87] Luke wants to stress that Christian prophecy has global dimensions.

l. Peter's Release from Prison and the Death of Herod (12.1-23)
Before moving on to the mission of Paul, Luke describes the exit of Peter from the narrative in miraculous terms. Peter's release from prison and the death of the Herod Agrippa[88] constitute a whole that hints at the outcome of the mission

---

84. J. Roloff, *Apostelgeschichte*, pp. 164–67; J. Jervell, *Apostelgeschichte*, pp. 318–19.

85. M. Dibelius, *Studies*, pp. 120–22; E. Haenchen, *Acts*, pp. 361–63; G. Lüdemann, *Early Christianity*, pp. 130–32. Dibelius and Lüdemann think that Luke drew upon a traditional story of the conversion and baptism of Cornelius and a tradition directed against separation between clean and unclean foods. Haenchen considers the latter was also created by Luke himself.

86. G. Lüdemann, *Early Christianity*, p. 136, assumes that this is 'a Lukan fiction'.

87. At the time of Claudius there was a local famine in Judaea; Josephus, *Ant.* 20.50-53; 20.101.

88. E. Haenchen, *Acts*, p. 391–92, assumes that Luke preserved the traditional release story (vv. 4-17) mostly untouched, with exception of vv. 12 and 17b. The following Lukan vv. 18-19 lead to the originally separate traditional story about the dramatic divine punishment and death of Herod Agrippa (vv. 20-23; cf. Josephus, *Ant.* 19.343-350). Similarly argue J. Roloff, *Apostelgeschichte*, pp. 186–88, and J. Jervell, *Apostelgeschichte*, pp. 337–39. G. Lüdemann, *Early Christianity*, p. 143, considers the traditional account of Peter's release notably simpler and shorter: vv. 3-4, 5b-6a, 9b-c, 11 and 17 are Lukan, as well as some redactional features in vv. 13-16. He assumes that the Lukan version of Agrippa's death is 'an abbreviation of that of Josephus' (p. 144).

among the Jews. Instead of chief priests, now it is Agrippa who persecutes him and other apostles. The execution of James the son of Zebedee (12.2) 'pleased the Jews', which further encouraged Agrippa to arrest Peter during the Festival of Unleavened Bread (v. 3-4). This ominous note echoes, on the one hand, the role of the Jews in the arrest, trial and crucifixion of Jesus (2.23; 3.13-15), and, on the other, the liberation symbolism of Passover and the resurrection of Jesus.[89] After the introduction of the Gentile mission, the miraculous missionary success and the high esteem for the believers among the people of Jerusalem (5.13-14) has – without any explanation – changed into outright hostility. The release story reminds the reader of its parallel in 5.17-21. This time only Peter is arrested and released, but he does not return to the temple or any other public place to teach (cf. 5.25), but instead goes 'to another place' (12.17). Luke uses this entertaining biographical legend[90] to demonstrate the internal unity of the believers, as becomes clear from the fervent prayer of the community for the imprisoned Peter (v. 5). Once again Luke relates the events in a way that emphasizes the undeniable truth of the supernatural event, this time associated with the exodus story. First, when the angel has released Peter and led him through the iron gate of the city – which opens miraculously – he realizes that he is not seeing a vision but that a miracle has happened (vv. 6-11). In the scene that follows, the incredulity of the fervently praying believers is revealed when they turn down the announcement of the maid Rhoda that Peter is at the door. While the escaped Peter is still knocking and waiting, they rather want to assume that the maid has heard the voice of his guardian angel, but finally come to see for themselves. Again, God has taken care of them beyond their own limited expectations (vv. 12-17). Luke wants to point out that God did not reject the community of Jerusalem when the mission was gradually rejected among the Jews and more and more successful among the Gentiles (13.46-47). In all its stages, the mission follows God's plan and foreknowledge.

The tradition of Herod Agrippa being killed by an angel (12.20-23) was formed according to an old scheme: those who despise God must face a horrible death (2 Macc. 9.4-10).[91] Luke uses the story to show how a persecutor of the church was punished for his godless arrogance. Even though Luke plainly states that the majority of the Jews were on the side of Agrippa and against the community of believers in Jerusalem, he injects a positive note between the Agrippa story and the mission of Paul (12.24): 'But the word of God continues to advance and gain adherents'. It is not clear what this means, but a moderate and obscure statement like this is certainly intentional, as it was in 6.7. Luke implies that the community

---

89. Cf. W. Radl, 'Befreiung aus dem Gefängnis: Die Darstellung eines biblischen Grundthemas in Apg 12', *BZ* 27 (1983), pp. 81–96 (87–95), who convincingly argues that the association between the Passover feast and Peter's miraculous release from the prison (emphasized in vv. 11 and 17) stems from Luke.

90. On the entertaining qualities of the story, see R. Pervo, *Profit*, pp. 62–63.

91. On Herod Agrippa I and his death, see H.-J. Klauck, *Magic and Paganism*, pp. 38–44.

in Jerusalem prospered, but more than that, he seems to point forwards to the Gentile mission that is growing in Antioch and already on its way to new conquests.

4. Being There: The Genre of Acts and the Art of Storytelling

It is relatively easy to locate the supernatural events and influences in the framework of the Lukan theology known from numerous scholarly presentations. In the beginning of Acts, divine interventions – the Pentecost miracle and the healing of the lame man – validate the apostles' proclamation of the resurrection of Jesus. The final days have come. In the community of believers, prophecies are fulfilled and the gospel is the only way salvation is offered to the whole of Israel. The miracles performed by the apostles are the backbone of their missionary success, but they also point at solidarity, unity and the high moral standards that are realized in the community. The punitive deaths of Ananias and Sapphira take this impression to the extreme. The temple authorities have, right from the beginning, persecuted the apostles and killed Stephen, but their blind hatred and envy only increase the success of the apostles. However, the glory days of the community in Judaea are over, and the majority of the Judaean Jews seem to reject the gospel, even though Luke hints at this only in 12.3. The community remains a mighty minority in the region. But supernatural events, and with them, every-thing else now starts to take place elsewhere. As Stephen's speech makes clear, God's plan, which he realized through the patriarchs and Moses and which the Jews so often fought against, continues in the Church, among those who believe in Jesus Christ. By miraculously converting Paul in Damascus and Cornelius in Caesarea, God directs his mission more and more towards the Gentiles. In Luke's narrative, God is in charge and his powerful works initiate everything; therefore, the salvation history is generated and guided by supernatural events and announcements.

For whom did Luke write this story? What kind of audience did he have in mind? The content of chs. 1–12 speaks against the idea that he meant Acts to be a defence of Paul addressed to Roman authorities or citizens. The harsh treatment of contemporary Judaism makes it very unlikely to assume that Luke wrote specifically for sympathetic Jewish readers. From the beginning of Acts, Luke more or less presupposes the Christian proclamation and looks at the development of the salvation history from an inside point of view; therefore, it is difficult to see that he aimed to evangelize Gentiles. The survey above supports the conclusion that Luke had Christian readers in mind.[92] He wanted to assert to them that the miracles and other supernatural events that happened in the time of Jesus and the apostles were true, that the Christian faith would overcome its enemies, that the salvation history inherited by his audience was amazingly being guided by God himself, and that the early Christian communities were excellent – even though unattainable – models of faith and life for all of them. The evidence is too weak

---

92. For the intended readers of Luke, see e.g. the survey of J. Jervell, *Apostelgeschichte*, 86–90.

to support the assumption that Luke fought against some specific internal dangers like Gnosticism or docetism.

Why did Luke write as he did? Scholars have often approached Acts as historiography or – more specifically – as a historical monograph that deals with a limited subject and period.[93] The presence of miracles per se is no problem for this view, but Luke's particular inclination towards the fictitious, sensational and miraculous has led some scholars to qualify Acts as tragic-pathetic – or better: mimetic – historiography that aimed at invoking the emotions of the reader by describing tragic and spectacular events.[94] This genre allows more space for the kind of historiography that we find in Acts 1–12, especially considering that Luke did not use the miraculous just for exciting emotions, but for the validation of the Christian faith and the edification of his readers.[95] However, examples for such historiography stem from the sphere of public life or political history, while Acts is a mimetic history of a specific religious movement written for its believing members.[96] Luke does not have the same distance from his materials as the Graeco-Roman historians, and his definite ideological purpose of relating miracle stories does not resemble their various reasons for including such stories in different historical and political contexts.[97] However, there are enough formal

93. D. Palmer, 'Acts and the Ancient Historical Monograph', in B. W. Winter, A. D. Clarke (eds) *The Book of Acts in Its First Century Setting* Vol. 1: *Ancient Literary Setting* (Grand Rapids: Eerdmans, 1993), pp. 1–29, draws upon Polybius' criticism of 'particular' historians, Sallust's 'selective' monographs and Cicero's remarks. He thinks that Hellenistic Jewish historiography, particularly 2 Maccabees, is helpful in classifying Acts as a historical monograph.

94. Thus E. Plümacher, 'ΤΕΡΑΤΕΙΑ: Fiktion und Wunder in der hellenistisch-römischen Geschichtsschreibung und in der Apostelgeschichte', *ZNW* 89 (1998), pp. 66–90, who portrays the mimetic historiography through the lenses of its critics like Polybius and Lucian (69–82). Polybius argued that exaggeration, miracles and emotional effects gained by such means belong to tragedy.

95. E. Plümacher, 'ΤΕΡΑΤΕΙΑ', p. 82, concludes that Luke, in using so much fiction and miracles, simply applied methods that were popular among the historians of his time. Just as Cicero justified his harsh actions against the Catilinians by a divine sign ('a great and bright flame issued forth from the ashes of the burnt wood') that was given him by vestal virgins who offered to *Bona Dea* (Plutarch, *Cic.* 20.1-2), similarly Luke allowed Paul to justify the Gentile mission by pointing at signs and wonders that happened among the Gentiles (Acts 15.12; pp. 80–81, 83–84). Plümacher agrees with E. Haenchen, *Acts*, p. 103, that Luke wrote Acts to edify his Christian readers and therefore introduced miracles, not unlike Plutarch who wanted to educate the masses: he dared to claim that when there are numerous and credible witnesses they can be supported by imagination – like dreams – and some find their faith validated precisely in such manifestations of divine power (Plutarch, *Cor.* 38.4-5).

96. Cf. W. C. Van Unnik, 'Luke's Second Book and the Rules of Hellenistic Historiography', in: J. Kremer (ed.), *Les Actes des Apôtres: Traditions, redaction, théologie* (BETL, 48; Leuven: Leuven University Press, 1979), Plutarch, *Cic.* 37-60: '[Luke] gives his view and reminiscences and impressions of the mission and expansion of Christianity in the first three decades of its existence, in other words, a history of a religious movement. That was something unheard of in Antiquity' (p. 39).

97. Cf. the conclusions of J. S. Lown, 'The Miraculous in the Graeco-Roman Historians', *Forum* 2 (1986), pp. 36–42 (41–42), on the miraculous in the works of Plutarch, Polybius and Livy.

indications that Luke at least wanted to execute his task as a historian:[98] he used sources (such as the disputed 'we'-sections) related to his subject, selected his material carefully and presented it in more or less chronological order, brought vividness into his narrative, composed rhetorically qualified speeches for important occasions and included suitable – both reliable and unreliable – pieces of historical information in his treatise.[99] But this is not all. In Acts, Luke shows a fondness for adventurous themes that bring his work close to ancient novels.[100] The adventurous is often related to the miraculous, and it is difficult to deny the entertaining qualities of Luke's second treatise.

How to explain the repeated novelistic features such as danger, suspense and deliverance in the work of Luke the historian? One thing is sure: Luke tells about the great times of the apostles with special love and affection, and he has a warm and intimate orientation towards his Christian audience. This stems from something other than mere willingness to be a mimetic historian. I assume that the popular and novelistic way of describing events is not originally related to Luke's literary ambitions, but to his career as an excellent storyteller. It is difficult to imagine that such a gift would have been developed by a person who merely taught and preached in the community – like Matthew or John – or collected sources and dictated a historical work in his chamber – like Eusebius. It is easier to imagine Luke as an experienced storyteller who loved to stand in front of a live audience and let his stories edify and charm his hearers. His way of telling about Jesus and the apostles 'combined profit with delight' (Horace, *Ars poetica* 343-44). I assume that he wanted to produce the same reaction among his audience that Jesus so naturally brought about on the road to Emmaus (Lk. 24.32): 'Were our hearts not burning within us while he was talking to us on the road?' Like Paul, Luke himself might have every now and then been 'speaking until midnight' (Acts 20.7), charming his audience with stories about great acts and the guidance of God, the heroic faith of the apostles before their vicious enemies, the wonderful unity of the believers in those times – and among many things, self-ironically relating the story about the boy who could not stay awake (vv. 9-10). All this does not exclude, but rather precedes his interest in historical details and his willingness to become a historian.

---

98. R. Pervo, *Profit*, pp. 3–4, denies this. He rightly emphasizes that Luke and Acts represent different genres, but is unwilling to see Acts – and Luke, for that matter – to be historiography because of the thoroughly non-historical character of its material and presentation.

99. Cf. the characteristics of a Hellenistic historian and his work as discussed by W. C. Van Unnik, 'Luke's Second Book', pp. 45–60.

100. This is the thesis of R. Pervo, *Profit*. See e.g. his analyses on 12.4-17 (pp. 62–63) and 20.7-12 (pp. 65–66). Like popular literature, Acts is 'action-packed'; there is much adventure (miracles, success, danger, deliverance; conspiracies, riots, trials, travels and the like, pp. 12–57), humour and wit, and peeping into the life of the high society (pp. 58–85). There is something undeniably true in all this, even though it is clear that Acts is precisely not popular but a specific kind of religious literature. E. Plümacher, 'ΤΕΡΑΤΕΙΑ', 87 n. 116, does not find any 'sweet blend of pathos and humor' in the story about 'the boy who could not stay awake' (20.7-12). I think that it is precisely the warmth and intimacy of Luke's storytelling that he misses here.

If this scenario works, it is somewhat problematic to separate 'tradition' and 'redaction' in Acts. If Luke was a storyteller, he adapted most of his stories long before writing them down. During the telling of stories, he polished them, developed them in various ways, located them in different contexts, developed suitable speeches and appealing narrative details, and combined them with other stories into meaningful wholes that he later used to compile his book of Acts. This might well explain Luke's interest and ability in developing the Jesus–Peter–Paul parallels as efficient and elegant ways of producing a rich variation of exciting miracle stories for his audiences. I assume that, in Acts, Luke-the-storyteller was the main source of Luke-the-author.[101]

In Luke's days, things were not going so well; Christian communities were threatened by disunity (20.29-30) and the many other difficulties that accompany that. Precisely such lack of orientation produced the great need to tell about the good era of the apostles, particularly about their miracles and God's supernatural guidance in all wonderful things that happened then. It was not just about being informed, exhorted, edified, moved or entertained. It was about all of those: strengthening the insecure Christian identity with stories about an ideal *Urgemeinde* that never existed as such but gave a perfect model of identification.

---

101. I think this might throw some light on the puzzling fact that Luke was a historian whom the later church historians did not want to imitate. The world of such storytelling was irrecoverably lost. Eusebius's approach was formal, even though he also wanted to demonstrate how God works in history; see A. Nobbs, 'Acts and the Subsequent Ecclesiastical Histories', in B. W. Winter, A. D. Clarke (eds), *The Book of Acts in Its First Century Setting* Vol. 1: *Ancient Literary Setting* (Grand Rapids: Eerdmans, 1993), pp. 153–62.

PAUL THE MIRACLE WORKER: DEVELOPMENT AND BACKGROUND OF PAULINE MIRACLE STORIES

Bert Jan Lietaert Peerbolte

In many studies Paul is depicted as a preacher, a theologian or a missionary manager who started and organized new congregations in order to continue his preaching in yet another town.[1] Rarely, however, is Paul treated from the perspective of the performance of miracles.[2] The larger part of this contribution will focus on the narrative traditions of Paul's miracles found in later sources, and on a number of remarks made by authors in the second and third centuries that will help us understand the discourse of miracle stories. Only in the final section will the step be made of looking back to Paul himself. It will be argued that there is ample evidence that Paul's ministry was interpreted by the generations after Paul in a way that considered the performance of miraculous deeds as part of his ministry. On the basis of the evidence from Paul himself, the conclusion will eventually have to be that he did indeed perform such miraculous deeds, but also that he used these 'miracles' as performative presentations of the power of Jesus Christ.

The starting point for this discussion will not be the letters of Paul, as one might expect, but the book of Acts. Section 1 will be dedicated to the narrative depiction of Paul's ministry offered by the *auctor ad Theophilum*. After that, the focus will shift in section 2 to Pauline miracles described by some second-century sources, especially the apocryphal *Acts of Paul*. Section 3 will take a look at a number of

---

1. The emphasis in most books on Paul is on his thoughts, his 'theology'. The fact that this theology should be situated in a very specific religio-historical context, however, demands that we look into other aspects of Paul's ministry like, for instance, his performance of 'miracles'.

2. Notable exceptions to this rule are S. Schreiber, *Paulus als Wundertäter: Redaktionsgeschichtliche Untersuchungen zur Apostelgeschichte und den authentischen Paulusbriefen* (Berlin: De Gruyter, 1996), and S. Alkier, *Wunder und Wirklichkeit in den Briefen des Apostels Paulus: Ein Beitrag zu einem Wunderverständnis jenseits von Entmythologisierung und Rehistorisierung* (WUNT, 134; Tübingen: Mohr Siebeck, 2001). See also G. H. Twelftree, 'Signs, Wonders, Miracles', in: G. F. Hawthorne, R. P. Martin, D. G. Reid (eds.), *Dictionary of Paul and his Letters* (Downers Grove, Leicester: Intervarsity Press, 1993), pp. 875–77, and the literature Twelftree mentions.

second- and third-century Christian authors whose descriptions betray something of the purpose of narrating miracle stories. Finally, section 4 will go back in time to discuss the evidence we find in the letters of Paul himself.

One final preliminary remark is necessary: what is it that we define as a 'miracle story'? The present article uses an expanded version of the definition given by Wendy Cotter in her excellent reader in miracle stories: 'we mean those narratives in which a wonderful rescue or salvation of someone takes place by the overturning of the "canons of the ordinary" through the intervention of a deity or hero'.[3] The expansion of this definition is that not only stories of rescue or salvation, but also exorcisms, can be reckoned as miracle stories.[4]

1. Paul the Miracle Worker in Acts

Let us start with a preliminary remark. The book of Acts may contribute to our understanding of Paul, but its narrative structure is so much defined by its theological agenda that we can nowhere trust its historical descriptions at face value.[5] As we will see, this observation is especially valid when we look into Acts' portrayal of Paul.[6] The miracles that the author incorporates into his work are narrative descriptions he created either on the basis of oral traditions or for literary purposes.[7] For our present goal they are of double interest. Firstly, they reflect an early response to Paul's ministry. Although we should estimate that an entire generation of the Christ-movement lies between Paul and the writing of Acts, this work does reflect the view its author and at least a number of his contemporaries must have held of Paul. Secondly, the book of Acts is a narrative work, which far better enables us to observe the dynamics of miracle stories than Paul's letters do. Of course, these letters should serve as the prime sources on Paul, and that is what they will eventually do in the final section of this article, when we use these letters to step from the world of the literary into the real world.

---

3.   W. Cotter, *Miracles in Greco-Roman Antiquity: A Sourcebook* (London, New York: Routledge, 1999), p. 2.

4.   The evidence in section 3 will point out, that authors in antiquity regarded exorcisms as fully comparable with 'healings' and other miracles.

5.   The discussion of the credibility of Acts was re-opened in the 1970s by Martin Hengel. See especially his *Acts and the History of Earliest Christianity* (London: SCM Press, 1979), and the discussion of the topic by Myllykoski in the present volume. For the present author's position in the debate, cf. L. J. Lietaert Peerbolte, *Paul the Missionary* (CBET, 34; Leuven: Peeters, 2003), pp. 99–105. *In summa*: the author of Acts did use older traditions, but they need to be reconstructed from the narrative and theological framework of the writing as a whole.

6.   L. J. Lietaert Peerbolte, *Paul the Missionary*, p. 105: 'the Book of Acts does at first sight appear to add important information to what is known from Paul himself. At a closer look, however, this information cannot be trusted that easily.'

7.   This approach to Acts has succesfully been pursued by G. Lüdemann in his *Das frühe Christentum nach den Traditionen der Apostelgeschichte: Ein Kommentar* (Göttingen: Vandenhoeck & Ruprecht, 1987).

There are a number of stories in Acts that especially tell us something about the author's view of Paul. In Acts 13.6-12 Paul encounters the sorcerer Bar-Jesus; in 14.8-12 Paul and Barnabas heal a crippled man; in 16.16-24 Paul casts out a demon; in 19.11-20 we find a description of Paul's magical healing powers, as well as an episode on demons who refuse to be cast out by someone other than Paul; and, finally, in 20.7-12 we find a description of Paul's raising of Eutychus.

F. F. Bruce has noted the parallels these stories draw between Paul and Peter:

> Incidents … seem to be selected by Luke in order to show how Paul's apostleship was confirmed by the same signs as was Peter's. Does Peter heal a lamed man (iii.2ff)? So does Paul (xiv.8ff). Has Peter's shadow healing power (v.15)? So have Paul's kerchiefs (xix.12). Does Peter exorcize (v.16)? So does Paul (xvi.18). Has Peter a victorious encounter with a sorcerer (viii.18ff.)? So has Paul (xiii.6ff.). Does Peter raise the dead (ix.36ff.)? So does Paul (xx.9ff.).[8]

It is obvious from Bruce's observations that the way in which Paul is depicted in Acts was influenced to a high degree by the author's urge to put Paul on the same level as Peter, even though he apparently refuses to use the title 'apostle' for Paul (with the exception of 14.4 and 14).[9] According to Bruce, 'the parallel incidents were (not) invented by the author in order to minimize the difference between Peter and Paul; the truth is that the author selected from the records of actual events accessible to him those which best subserved the aim he had in view in composing his work'.[10] In the present author's opinion it would be better to substitute *narrative traditions* for the 'events' Bruce mentions. We don't have direct access to any event underlying the narrative of Acts, but we can assume that the author made use of traditions that were available to him – reliable or not. The author of Acts apparently selected these specific traditions about Paul to enable himself to depict Paul as he did with Peter: as an envoy of Jesus Christ, legitimated by the miracles that God worked through him. In what follows, a short description and analysis are given of the most important miracle-stories about Paul in Acts.

a. Acts 13.6-12
Paul and Barnabas encounter a man who is introduced as a 'Jewish magician', a 'false prophet' named 'Bar-Jesus' (ἄνδρα τινὰ μάγον ψευδοπροφήτην Ἰουδαῖον ᾧ ὄνομα Βαριησοῦ). The designations by which this Bar-Jesus is introduced are remarkable: he is not only a 'false prophet', but also a 'magician'. The word μάγος is used only here, but for the reader it does bring Simon to mind, who tried to use

---

8. F. F. Bruce, *The Acts of the Apostles: The Greek Text with Introduction and Commentary* (Grand Rapids: Eerdmans, 1951), p. 33.

9. E. Haenchen, *Die Apostelgeschichte* (KEK; Göttingen: Vandenhoeck & Ruprecht, 5th edn, 1965), ad loc., states that Acts denies Paul the status of apostle; this view is criticized by S. Porter, *The Paul of Acts: Essays in Literary Criticism, Rhetoric, and Theology* (WUNT, 115; Tübingen: Mohr Siebeck, 1999), pp. 196–97.

10. F. F. Bruce, *Acts*, p. 33.

the power of the 'name of Jesus Christ' for purposes of gain (8.9-13), and was heavily rebuked for that (8.14-25). This Simon is said to practise μαγεία and the author of Acts clearly thinks of that as something detestable.[11] Paul curses the magician for his opposition, and the 'hand of the Lord' indeed does what Paul predicts it will do: Bar-Jesus is blinded.

The interesting thing about this pericope is that it is not a healing narrative, nor an exorcism, but it is a curse of a magician that pictures Paul as a strong and powerful envoy of Christ. The expression he uses is clearly reminiscent of LXX-vocabulary, where 'the hand of the Lord' refers to the power of YHWH.[12] In the literary context of Acts, however, the reference is probably to Jesus. Jesus is identified as the 'Lord' throughout the book, and the clearest expression of this is found in Peter's words in 2.36. There, Peter identifies Jesus as both the Lord and the Anointed One: καὶ κύριον αὐτὸν καὶ Χριστὸν ἐποίησεν ὁ θεός, τοῦτον τὸν Ἰησοῦν ὃν ὑμεῖς ἐσταυρώσατε. If this identification is indeed correct, Paul blinds the magician Bar-Jesus by the power of Jesus, while referring to this power in traditional words as 'the hand of the Lord'. The description therefore points out that the power of Jesus is superior to the powers invoked by magicians.

b. Acts 14.8-12

Paul and Barnabas are described here as the two envoys from Antioch, sent as ἀπόστολοι τῆς ἐκκλησίας. They visit Lystra, to find a man 'crippled from his birth'. The introduction of the crippled man shows a strong parallel with 3.2, which described a similar healing of a crippled man, this time by Peter and John.

The similarity in introduction points to a similarity in function of these two accounts: in 14.8-12 Paul performs a miracle that Peter had also performed earlier. Peter instructs the cripple in Jerusalem in the name of Jesus (3.6), while Paul simply tells 'his' cripple to stand up and walk. In both cases the event is used to introduce a sermon. Peter aims his preaching of Christ at the Jews present in the temple (3.11-26), and Paul takes the Greeks' misinterpretation of his identity as his starting point for a sermon in 14.14-17.

It is difficult to decide whether or not the episode in 14.8-12 reflects an independent tradition of Paul as a miracle worker,[13] but the obvious parallel with 3.2-10 should make us suspicious: it may well be that Luke purposely doubled the narrative about Peter to point out that Paul's task in respect of the Gentiles was fully comparable to Peter's apostolate to the Jews. But also if the author of Acts did use an existing tradition for Paul, it is important to note that within the literary structure of Acts, Paul is presented as equal to Peter by means of the narrative device of a miracle story.

---

11. On the negative depiction of magic in Acts, see H.-J. Klauck, *Magie und Heidentum in der Apostelgeschichte des Lukas* (SBS, 167; Stuttgart: Verlag Katholisches Bibelwerk, 1996).

12. See 1 Sam. 5.3, 6; 7.13; 12.15; 1 Kgs 18.46; Ezra 7.6; Ezek. 3.14.

13. Lüdemann argues in favour of a redactional origin of this passage: G. Lüdemann, *Das frühe Christentum*, p. 166: 'Die Geschichte von der Heilung eines Lahmen an dieser Stelle ist redaktionell ... und auf der Basis der Apg 3 erzählten Geschichte entworfen'.

c. Acts 16.16-24

In the first of the 'we'-passages in Acts, a description is given of a slave-girl who followed Paul and his company.[14] She has a 'spirit of divination' (ἔχουσαν πνεῦμα πύθωνα), that earned the girl's masters a lot of money. This spirit announces the identity of Paul and Silas as that of 'slaves of the Highest God'. Apparently, Paul becomes annoyed by this situation and rebukes the spirit. He exorcises the girl and casts out the demon merely by saying: 'I command you in the name of Jesus to go out from this girl' (v. 18). The story continues with the anger of the girl's masters with regard to Paul's deed. They indict Paul before the magistrates of the town and the opposition against Paul and Silas is further enhanced by the crowd that is gathered. The episode ends with the narration of Paul and Silas being stripped of their clothes, beaten, humiliated and jailed (vv. 23-24). Ultimately, Paul and Silas are of course freed from jail, first by a miraculous intervention resulting in the conversion of the warden, and ultimately by the repentance of the magistrates (vv. 25-39).

This story has a number of elements that continually recur throughout the book of Acts: a local conflict is caused by the fact that Paul preaches the gospel or performs a miraculous deed, he is jailed or thrown out of town, and subsequently Paul is liberated. The important thing in this exorcism story is, however, that Paul casts out the spirit 'in the name of Jesus Christ'. It is remarkable that within New Testament writings this precise formula only occurs in the book of Acts. It is used in 3.6 by Peter, who heals the lame man at the gates of Jerusalem; it is used in 4.10 by the same Peter to proclaim the salvation that has come in Jesus, and it is used here in 16.18 by Paul who casts out the spirit of divination from the girl who is following him. The narrative function of this formula is clear from the episode in 19.11-17 (cf. below), but within the pericope itself, the name of Jesus appears to hold power even over demons and spirits. This was clear already from 3.6 where the healing power of the name became evident, and here the power of exorcism appears related to that of healing.

d. Acts 19.11-20

This passage falls into two minor sections: vv. 11-12 and vv. 13-17. Verses 18-20 conclude the pericope, but can be left out of consideration here.

1. Acts 19.11-12

In these two verses Paul is presented as a miracle worker whose healing powers are so strong that even the handkerchiefs and aprons he has worn on his skin have healing powers.

Although the passage contains a number of *hapax legomena* (χρώς, σουδάρια, σιμικίνθια, ἀπαλλάσσω used for sickness, ἐκπορεύομαι for evil spirits), and is

---

14. On the 'we'-passages, see S. Porter, *Paul of Acts*, pp. 10–46. Porter regards these passages as an incorporated 'we'-source. For a good survey of the discussion about the 'we'-passages, see V. Fusco, *Da Paolo a Luca: Studi su Luca-Atti*, vol. 1 (Brescia: Paideia, 2000), pp. 57–84.

therefore very likely formed out of traditional material, it should in its present form be considered as a redactional transition to the story of vv. 13-17.[15] Very likely the core is formed by a tradition of Paul as a miracle worker. If we consider the *hapax legomena* as proof of this tradition, it spoke of Paul as one who could even heal the sick and expel evil spirits by means of clothes he had been wearing.

2. Acts 19.13-17

In one of the most hilarious passages in the entire Bible an evil spirit refuses to be cast out by the sons of the otherwise unknown Sceva. The narrative starts with the introduction of some Jewish exorcists who try to cast out evil spirits by using 'the name of Jesus, whom Paul is proclaiming' (vv. 13-14). The fact that these exorcists are identified as 'the seven sons of a certain Sceva' suggests that they were unknown to the intended audience, but also that they could be easily traced.[16] The exorcists use the proclamation of Paul in order to perform their task, but they are rebuked by the spirit. By the answer of the spirit ('Jesus I recognise, and Paul I know, but who are you?', v. 15) the connection between Jesus and Paul is confirmed in an unforseen way: the exorcists are apparently rebuked for using Paul's proclamation as a magical formula, and it is they who are driven out (v. 16). They are overwhelmed by the possessed man, their clothes are torn from their bodies, and they have to flee naked. Verse 17 describes the effect of this episode: all Jews and Greeks living in Ephesus hear what has happened, become afraid, and praise 'the name of the Lord Jesus'.

There are a number of important observations to make on the basis of this episode. In the first place, it is clear that in the narrative portrayal in Acts the name of Jesus holds power when proclaimed by one of his envoys, but cannot be used as a magical formula by others. The author of Acts thus clearly takes a stand against the practice of magic, and restricts the power of Jesus to the envoys of Jesus. It is not by magic that they perform their miracles, but by their divine commission. In fact, it is not even Paul who performs the miracles – it is Jesus who uses Paul to do this.

In the second place, the status of Jesus' envoys is pointed out by the authority they hold. If Jesus' name cannot be used as a magical formula, the divine commission of his envoys does place these envoys on a higher level than any competitor.

And thirdly, the narrative uses the same device we find in the Gospels, viz. the recognition of divine authority by demons. In the episode of Mark 1.23-28, the demon that bound the man in the synagogue of Nazareth speaks to Jesus in similar fashion as the spirit in Acts 19.15 does to the sons of Sceva: 'I know who you are – you are the Holy One of God.' The author of Acts uses the same literary device and informs his readers of the authority of the main character of his narrative by mouth of a demon or spirit. This is obviously a strong narrative mechanism,

---

15. *Pace* G. Lüdemann, *Das frühe Christentum*, p. 220.
16. See G. Lüdemann, *Das frühe Christentum*, p. 221.

because within the narrative it implies a legitimation of authority by no less a being than a spirit. The effect the author of Acts wants to evoke in his description of Paul is more or less the same as the effect Jesus' exorcism in Nazareth had on those present in Mark's narrative: 'He even commands unclean spirits!' (Mark 1.27).

e. Acts 20.7-12

Between the lines, the passage on Eutychus shows us how the author depicts Paul as standing in a long tradition of miracle workers in the history of Israel. The literary structure is lucid: verses 7-8 form the introduction to the scene, where the setting is described, Eutychus is introduced, and Paul's digressions are characterized as lengthy, and implicitly as tiresome. Verse 9 informs the reader of the death of Eutychus; verse 10 of Paul's raising of the dead man; verses 11-12 describe the effect on Paul (v. 11), and Eutychus and the by-standers (v. 12). The words of v. 9 (ἤρθη νεκρός) clearly characterize Eutychus as having died. Therefore, Paul's action in v. 10 (ἐπέπεσεν αὐτῷ) is explicitly an attempt to revive Eutychus. Paul's remark, however, seems to imply that the boy had not died, but was still alive: ἡ ... ψυχὴ αὐτοῦ ἐν αὐτῷ ἐστιν (v. 10). Why doesn't the author add the word πάλιν? Given the description in v. 9, it is clear to the reader that Eutychus was really dead. Paul's action in v. 10 is highly reminiscent to the episode of 2 Kgs 4.25-37.[17] In that pericope Elisha raises the dead son of a Shunammite woman by laying upon the child, thus giving him back the power of life. Although the words differ, Acts 20.10 can hardly be read in another way than as a rewriting of 2 Kgs 4.34 (4 Kgdms 4.34). Notwithstanding the differences, the parallels are obvious:

LXX 2 Kgs (4 Kgdms) 4.34	Acts 20.10
ἀνέβη	καταβὰς δὲ ὁ Παῦλος
καὶ ἐκοιμήθη ἐπὶ τὸ παιδάριον	ἐπέπεσεν αὐτῳ
καὶ ἔθηκεν τὸ στόμα αὐτοῦ ἐπὶ τὸ	καὶ συμπεριλαβὼν εἶπεν
στόμα αὐτοῦ καὶ τοὺς ὀφθαλμοὺς	
αὐτοῦ ἐπὶ τοὺς ὀφθαλμοὺς αὐτοῦ	
καὶ τὰς χεῖρας αὐτοῦ ἐπὶ τὰς	
χεῖρας αὐτοῦ	

Furthermore, Elisha raises a child, where Paul raises 'a young man' (νεανίας, v. 9), who is also called 'a boy' (παῖς, v. 12).[18] This narrative background of 20.7-12 makes it highly probable that the Eutychus account is indeed meant as a narrative-theological exposition of Paul's character as a miracle worker. Even the name Eutychus ('Good fortune'!) implies that the story has a deeper significance than the telling of a historical account.[19] Could anyone have more fortune than this boy?

---

17. For more parallels in the vocabulary, see C. K. Barrett, *Acts*, vol. 2 (ICC; London, New York: T&T Clark, 1998), pp. 954–55.

18. Next to the Elisha account, there are also reminiscences of the story of Elijah in 1 Kgs 17.17-24; see C. K. Barrett, *Acts*, vol. 2, pp. 954–55.

19. Barrett's verdict on the relation of the name to the historicity of the account is in itself

If the above observations are correct, Paul is depicted here in terms of Elisha, the 'man of God'.[20] This narrative equation of Paul and Elisha is not typical of the entire picture of Paul in Acts, but it does mean that a narrative on Paul could be modelled after a narrative on one of the greatest miracle workers in the history of Israel. It cannot be without purpose that the author of Acts uses the model of Elisha to depict Paul in this particular story.

f. Paul the Miracle Worker in Acts
The miracle stories about Paul in Acts have a double focus. On the one hand they are narrated in such a way as to point out that Paul holds the same authority as Peter held. Even though Paul is not mentioned as an 'apostle' in Acts, he does share the same divine authorization that Peter was sanctioned by. So one function of these stories is to legitimate Paul's authority within the narrative setting of Acts. On the other hand, Paul's authority and his power are consistently depicted as coming from Jesus Christ. Paul does not act on his own behalf, he is not a miracle worker who has the capacity to perform miracles or exorcisms by himself – he is merely an instrument of the power of Jesus Christ. This probably accounts for the fact that the reworking of the Elisha narrative in 20.7-12 does not explicitly state that Paul raised the boy Eutychus. Thus, we find that the stories in Acts have a double focus: they function as a narrative authorization of Paul as an envoy of Christ, and they depict the power of Jesus Christ as the decisive factor. As will become clear in the next section, it is exactly these two factors that are prominent in later miracle stories of Paul.

2. Paul the Apocryphal Miracle Worker
During the second century, a number of legendary miracle stories featuring Paul were written down. The *Acts of Paul*, for instance, contains an account of Paul's curing and raising of two men in Myra.[21] A man named Hermocrates comes to Paul and asks him to be healed by referring to Jesus as Paul's great example: 'Nothing is impossible with God but especially with him whom you preach, for when he came he healed many, he whose servant you are. Lo, I and my wife and my children cast ourselves at your feet that I also may believe just as you believed in the living God.'[22] Paul's answer is clearly intended as a literary introduction to the miracle story that follows after the dialogue: 'through the name of Jesus Christ you shall become whole in the presence of all these'. Here, the name of Jesus

---

correct: 'there is no need to suspect (the accounts') historicity simply because of the occurrence of this name' (*Acts*, vol. 2, p. 953).

20. See 2 Kgs 4.27. The title 'man of God' is consistently used for Elisha (2 Kgs 4.21-25; 4.40, 42 etc.), but also for Moses (Deut. 33.1; Josh. 14.6) and Elijah (1 Kgs 12.22, 24; 13.1-5 etc.).

21. Translation by J. K. Elliott, *The Apocryphal New Testament: A Collection of Apocryphal Christian Literature in an English Translation* (Oxford: Clarendon, 1993). For critical editions of the *Acts of Paul*, see J. K. Elliott, *Apocryphal New Testament*, pp. 357–59.

22. The quotations are from J. K. Elliott, *Apocryphal New Testament*, pp. 374–75.

Christ is mentioned in a way that is fully comparable to what happens in the canonical book of Acts. What follows is a complicated story. First, the father, Hermocrates, 'fell as if dead', to be healed by Paul immediately afterwards. One of the two sons, Hermippus, is angry with Paul, because 'he wished that his father should not be healed, but die, so that he might quickly be master of his property'. As it appears from the fragmentary text, Hermippus attacks Paul but by accident kills his brother Dion. Hermocrates mourns his son Dion, but 'as he sat at Paul's feet he forgot that Dion was dead'.

Nympha, Hermocrates' wife, enters the scene and brings Dion's death to Paul's attention. Upon hearing this message, Hermocrates is literally blinded by grief, but Paul raises up Dion.[23] Next, he lays his hands on Hermocrates and cures him. The conclusion of the story comes in Hermocrates' words: 'Paul came and laid his hands upon me while I wept. And in that hour I saw all things clearly'.

Fragmentary as it is, this story evidently aims at picturing Paul as a trust-worthy envoy of Jesus Christ in whose name he acts. It is not the preaching of Paul that is central to this account, but his performance of miracles. But the interpre-tation of these miracles in the words of Hermocrates does point out that the events narrated should be interpreted at more than one level at the same time. The story is about Paul curing Hermocrates, raising Dion and then physically opening Hermocrates' eyes, but Hermocrates' words clearly point out that that event has a metaphorical meaning. It is interesting to note that Paul's portrayal in this episode lacks the reluctance that was typical of his picture in Acts, where the miracles Paul performes are evidently pictured as worked by Christ and not Paul.

The miraculous element in the *Acts of Paul* comes to a climax in the events in Ephesus. Paul has been captured and will be executed in the arena by a lion. The story is probably a narrative elaboration of Paul's remark in 1 Cor. 15.32, where he states that he had been forced to fight with wild animals in Ephesus. As the *Acts of Paul* depicts the event, there was little fight. The lion that Paul has to fight happens to be an old acquaintance of his. First the verdict on Paul is summarized in a way that points out how Paul was perceived of:[24] 'Away with the sorcerer! Away with the poisoner!' Then the lion enters, but it 'looked at Paul, and Paul at the lion. Then Paul recognized that this was the lion which had come and been baptized. And borne along by faith Paul said, "Lion, was it you whom I baptized?" And the lion in answer said to Paul, "Yes." Paul spoke to it again and said, "And how were you captured?" The lion said with its own voice, "Just as you were, Paul."' The Roman official Hieronymus now sends many other beasts to kill Paul, as well as archers to kill the lion, but the two miraculously escape. A severe hail-storm hits their enemies and they safely leave Ephesus.

23. Unfortunately, the account of this event is missing. The fact that the resurrection of Dion is ascribed to Paul is clear, though, from the words of Hermippus, who states that Paul 'raised up my brother'. Also the message 'Dion is risen' makes this clear.

24. Translation J. K. Elliott, *Apocryphal New Testament*, pp. 376–79.

The lion episode not only builds upon Paul's remark in 1 Cor. 15.32, but it also elaborates the Demetrius story of Acts 19. It clearly takes up traditional information about Paul to depict him in a more elaborate and legendary way. The same phenomenon occurs, in a somewhat different form, in the *Martyrdom of Paul.*[25] This text opens with an account of the death and raising of Patroclus, a cupbearer of emperor Nero. The episode has clearly been influenced by the account of Acts 20, the raising of Eutychus:

> A certain Patroclus, a cupbearer of the emperor, who had come too late to the barn and could not get near to Paul on account of the throng of the people, sat on a high window, and listened as he taught the word of God. But Satan, being wicked, became jealous of the love of the brethren and Patroclus fell down from the window and died; speedily it was reported to Nero. Paul, however, having learned it by the Spirit, said, 'Brethren, the evil one has obtained a way to tempt you; go forth and you will find a boy who has fallen down and is dying. Lift him up and bring him here.' This they did. When the people saw him they were frightened. Paul said to them, 'Now, brethren, show your faith. Come, let us mourn to our Lord Jesus Christ, that the boy might live and we remain unharmed.' When all began to lament, the boy took breath and, having put him on an animal, they sent him away alive with all those who were of the emperor's house.

Later, the emperor Nero asks the boy how it could be that he was alive again, and who was responsible for that. The boy answers: 'Christ Jesus, the king of the ages.' This answer enrages Nero to such an extent that he subsequently orders all Christians to be killed. After Paul has been executed, he appears to Nero, 'and in the presence of all he said, "Caesar, behold, here is Paul the soldier of God; I am not dead but live in my God. But upon you, unhappy one, many evils and great punishment will come because you have unjustly shed the blood of the righteous not many days ago."'

It appears from the three examples quoted above that Paul is depicted in apocryphal sources from the second century as a miraculous envoy of Jesus Christ. As is the case in the book of Acts, the *Acts of Paul* and the *Martyrdom of Paul* present the miracles he is said to have worked as originating in the power of Jesus Christ. Therefore we may infer that the accounts, too, had a double function: firstly, they attest to the active power of Jesus Christ in whose name even the dead could be raised; and secondly, they prove the divine authorisation of Paul. His activities prove to the reader the immense power of Jesus and God, as well as the fact that Paul has been especially commissioned by Jesus. Quite possibly these stories also had a third function, which cannot be ruled out in the case of the book of Acts either: that of entertainment. The narrating of these miraculous events must have entertained both the narrator and his audience. But unfortunately, there is little evidence to substantiate this suspicion. What we do have is evidence that the combination of the first two characteristics mentioned, the proclamation of the power of Jesus Christ and the legitimation of his envoys, was indeed recog-

---

25. J. K. Elliott, *Apocryphal New Testament*, pp. 385–88.

nized in early Christianity. Let us take a look at some of the evidence we have for the narration of miracle stories in the early Church.

3. Exorcisms and Miracle stories as Religious Propaganda

A number of sources from the second and third centuries tell us something about the perception of miracles and exorcisms. Stories of healings and exorcisms are not always equated, but they are at least strongly connected, and Justin Martyr's treatment of exorcisms does point out that the two categories at least overlapped. For obvious reasons a selection of the evidence has been made. This selection consists of passages from Justin Martyr, Minucius Felix, Irenaeus, Origen, and Eusebius who is quoting Cornelius.[26]

a. Justin Martyr, Dialogus cum Tryphone *and* Apologia

In his *Dialogue with Trypho* Justin Martyr discusses the practice of exorcisms many times. For the present purpose a number of these passages should be looked into. In *Dial.* 30.23, for instance, Justin casually mentions the name of Jesus Christ as having power over demons. But not only that – Justin also refers to the practice of exorcism by expelling demons 'in the name of Jesus Christ who was crucified under Pontius Pilate' (ἐξορκιζόμενα κατὰ τοῦ ὀνόματος Ἰησοῦ Χριστοῦ, τοῦ σταυρωθέντος ἐπὶ Ποντίου Πιλάτου)[27]:

> Furthermore, it is equally clear as the word of the prophecy, speaking in the name of one of his followers, metaphorically affirms that we believers beseech him to safeguard us from strangers, that is, from wicked and deceitful spirits.
>   We constantly ask God through Jesus Christ to keep us safe from those demons who, while they are strangers to the worship of God, were adored by us of old; we pray, too, that after our conversion to God through Christ, we may be without blame. We call him our Helper and Redeemer, by the power at whose name even the demons shudder; even to this day they are overcome by us when we exorcise them in the name of Jesus Christ, who was crucified under Pontius Pilate, the Governer of Judea. Thus, it is clear to all that his Father bestowed upon him such a great power that even the demons are submissive both to his name and to his preordained manner of suffering.[28]

The situation Justin portrays here is also reflected in 49.8 and 76.6. The latter passage especially is clear on the link between exorcism and belief in Jesus: 'And now we, who believe in our Lord Jesus, who was crucified under Pontius Pilate, when we exorcise all demons and evil spirits, have them subjected to us'. The idea is plain and simple: Jesus subjected demons and evil spirits to himself, and because of this his followers hold the same power.

---

26. Other texts that could have been taken into account are e.g. Tertullian's *Apologia* 23, 27, 32, 37; Cyprianus, *Ad Demetrianum,* 15; and Augustine, *C.D.* 22.8.

27. See M. Marcovich (ed.), *Iustini Martyris Dialogus cum Tryphone* (PTS, 47; Berlin: De Gruyter, 1997), p. 118.

28. Translation T. B. Falls, T. P. Halton, M. Slusser, *St. Justin Martyr. Dialogue with Trypho* (Selections from the Fathers of the Church, 3; Washington: Catholic University Press of America, 2003), pp. 45–46.

The most lucid expression of this idea is found in *Dial.* 85.2. There, Justin states that all demons are subdued by the power of Jesus' name. Note, by the way, the confession formula with which Justin refers to Jesus:

> Every demon is vanquished and subdued when exorcised in the name of this true Son of God (κατὰ γὰρ τοῦ ὀνόματος αὐτοῦ τούτου τοῦ υἱοῦ τοῦ θεοῦ)[29] who was the first-born of all creatures, who was born of a virgin, who was crucified by your people under Pontius Pilate, who died and then, after his resurrection from the dead, ascended into heaven.
>
> But, if you attempt to exorcise them in the name of any man born among you, whether kings, just men, prophets, or patriarchs, not one of the demons will be subdued. Whereas, if any man among you should exorcise them in the name of the God of Abraham and the God of Isaac and the God of Jacob, they will, perhaps, be subdued. But some of your exorcists, as I have already noted, adjure the demons by employing the magical art of the Gentiles, using fumigations and amulets.[30]

It is clear that Justin cannot deny that some Jewish exorcists are effective as well, but he immediately adds that most of them use pagan methods. The basis of their authority is, of course, that they call upon the name of the God of Abraham, Isaac and Jacob, who is the same as the God and Father of Jesus Christ. But, Justin hastens to say, the authority of followers of Jesus Christ is much stronger, because they derive it from the Son of God, and do not use pagan methods.

The fact that the mere name 'Jesus' was considered as holding power and authority is clearly explained by Justin in his second *Apology*. In an interesting passage (6.4-6), Justin mentions the fact that the use of this name was instrumental in acts of exorcism:

> But 'Jesus', His name as man and Saviour, has also significance (Ἰησοῦς δὲ καὶ ἀνθρώπου καὶ σωτῆρος ὄνομα καὶ σημασίαν ἔχει).[31] For He was made man also, as we before said, having been conceived according to the will of God the Father, for the sake of believing men, and for the destruction of the demons (ἐπὶ καταλύσει τῶν δαιμόνων). And now you can learn this from what is under your own observation. For numberless demoniacs throughout the whole world, and in your city – many of our Christian men exorcising them in the name of Jesus Christ, who was crucified under Pontius Pilate, have healed and do heal, rendering helpless and driving the possessing devils out of the men, though they could not be cured by all the other exorcists, and those who used incantations and drugs.[32]

Apparently many Christians in Justin's day actively practised exorcism and people came to them in order to have their demons cast out. Justin describes it more or less as though the Christians were travelling doctors who cured others from their demons. What is especially revealing in this respect is the close connection he

---

29. M. Marcovich, *Dialogus*, 216.

30. T. B. Falls, *et al.*, *Dialogue*, 132.

31. M. Marcovich, *Iustini Martyris Apologiae pro Christianis* (PTS, 38; Berlin: De Gruyter, 1994), p. 146.

32. Translation taken from L. W. Barnard, *St. Justin Martyr. The First and Second Apologies* (ACW, 56; New York and Mahawah: Paulist Press, 1997), pp. 77–78.

makes between exorcism and healing ('men exorcising them ... have healed and do heal'). It is clear from this text that the practice of healing in the second century overlapped with the practice of exorcism. To a certain extent the two activities could even be considered equal.

b. Minucius Felix, Octavius 27.5-7
In his defence of the Christians, Minucius Felix discusses the 'unclean spirits, demons' (*impuri spiritus, daemones*, 27.1) that hold people in possession. According to Minucius Felix, these 'demons' are regularly known to 'Magi and philosophers', but the *Christiani* hold power over them. Interestingly enough Minucius Felix includes major deities in this group of demons:

> All this, as most of your people know, the demons themselves admit to be true, when they are driven out of men's bodies by words of exorcism and the fire of prayer. Saturn himself, Serapis, Jupiter, or any other demon you worship (*et quicquid daemonum colitis*), under stress of pain, confess openly what they are; ... when adjured in the name of the one true God, reluctantly, in misery, they quail and quake, and either suddenly leap forth at once, or vanish gradually, according to the faith exercised by the sufferer or the grace imparted by the healer. Challenged at close quarters they run away from Christians (*sic christianos de proximo fugitant*).[33]

The traditional Graeco-Roman deities are obviously characterized here as 'demons', and they are expelled by the name of 'the one true God'. The demons even flee at the sight of Christians! This view of the Graeco-Roman pantheon has doubtless been strongly influenced by Jewish polemics against idolatry, and did form part of the attraction of the Christian alternative.[34] Minucius Felix's remark on the flight of the demons at the sight of the Christians is unmistakably a rhetorical hyperbole, but nonetheless it does say something about the views Christians in the second century held of Graeco-Roman deities: they considered their own God as far superior to those 'demons' and apparently thought they even held power over the pagan gods.

c. Irenaeus, Adversus Haereses 2.32.4
In his defense of Christianity against 'the heresies', Irenaeus, too, mentions the practice of exorcism and the fact that miracles are worked through the name of Jesus Christ (*Against the Heresies* 2.32.4):

> But if they say the Lord has done [his miracles] merely in appearance we shall take them back to the prophetic writings and show from them that all these things had been predicted

---

33. Taken from T. R. Glover, G. H. Rendall, *Tertullian: Apology, De Spectaculis. Minucius Felix* (LCL; Cambridge, MA: Harvard University Press; London: Heinemann, 1984).

34. See D. B. Martin, *Inventing Superstition. From the Hippocratics to the Christians* (Cambridge, London: Harvard University Press, 2004), *passim*, esp. p. 243: 'Christianity may indeed have been as successful as it was because, among other factors, it offered answers to a problem that most people considered a real one: the threat of harm from possibly malicious daimons.'

of him, and that they really happened, and that he alone is the Son of God. Therefore his real disciples have received grace from him and use it in his name for the benefit of other men, as each has received the gift from him. Some really and truly drive out demons, so that often those who have been cleansed of evil spirits believe and are in the church, and some have foreknowledge of the future, and visions and prophetic speech, and others lay their hands on the sick and make them well, and as we said, even the dead have been raised and have remained with us for many years. Why should I say more? It is impossible to tell the number of the gifts which the church throughout the world received from God in the name of Jesus Christ (*in nomine Iesu Christi*[35]), crucified under Pontius Pilate, and uses each day for the benefit of the gentiles, neither deceiving nor making profit. For as it freely received from God, so it freely ministers.[36]

For Irenaeus, the Church is on its way to becoming a carrier of special power, for the followers of Jesus share in his power. Note especially the fact that, like Justin, Irenaeus mentions the 'name' of Jesus Christ, and adds a short confession-like formula 'crucified under Pontius Pilate'. The formula is shorter than in Justin, but it is there all the same.

d. Origen, Contra Celsum 1.6

A few decades after Ireneaus, Origen mentions the topic of exorcism and links the special power the Christians have to the name of Jesus Christ. In paragraph 6 of the first book of his defence of Christianity against Celsus, Origen refutes Celsus' claim that the Christians perform their exorcisms by means of magic, thereby following the example of Jesus who, according to Celsus, was also nothing but a sorcerer:

After this, through the influence of some motive which is unknown to me, Celsus asserts that it is by the names of certain demons, and by the use of incantations, that the Christians appear to be possessed of (miraculous) power; hinting, I suppose, at the practices of those who expel evil spirits by incantations. And here he manifestly appears to malign the gospel. For it is not by incantations that Christians seem to prevail (over evil spirits), but by the name of Jesus (ἀλλὰ τῷ ὀνόματι ᾿Ιησοῦ), accompanied by the announcement of the narratives which relate to Him; for the repetition of these has frequently been the means of driving demons out of men, especially when those who repeated them did so in a sound and genuinely believing spirit. Such power, indeed, does the name of Jesus possess over evil spirits, that there have been instances where it was effectual, when it was pronounced even by bad men, which Jesus Himself taught (would be the case), when He said: 'Many shall say to Me in that day, In Thy name we have cast out devils, and done many wonderful works.' Whether Celsus omitted this from intentional malignity, or from ignorance, I do not know. And he next proceeds to bring a charge against the Saviour Himself, alleging that it was by means of sorcery that He was able to accomplish the wonders which He performed; and that foreseeing that others would attain the same knowledge, and do the same things, making a boast of doing them by help of the power of God, He excludes such from His kingdom. And his accusation is that if they are justly excluded, while He Himself is guilty of the same

35. N. Brox (ed.), *Irenäus von Lyon. Adversus Haereses - Gegen die Häresien II* (FC, 8.2; Freiburg: Herder, 1993), p. 280.

36. R. M. Grant, *Irenaeus of Lyons* (London, New York: Routledge, 1997), pp. 121–22.

practices, He is a wicked man; but if He is not guilty of wickedness in doing such things, neither are they who do the same as He. But even if it be impossible to show by what power Jesus wrought these miracles, it is clear that Christians employ no spells or incantations, but the simple name of Jesus, and certain other words in which they repose faith, according to the holy Scriptures.[37]

It is remarkable to note how Origen states that Jesus' name may even cast out demons when 'pronounced by bad men' (ὑπὸ φαύλων ὀνομαζόμενον). This situation goes certainly a step beyond what Acts described, viz. that the name of Jesus could not be used by those who have not been divinely commissioned to do so (cf. above, Acts 19.11-17). The situation Origen depicts is one in which exorcisms were even practised by many 'in the name of Jesus' while they ought not to be reckoned among the followers of Jesus.

e. Eusebius, Historia Ecclesiastica *6.43.11*
Not only were exorcisms actively performed in early Christianity, but the office of exorcist also became one of the officially recognized functions of the Church. In his *Ecclesiastical History* 6.43.11, Eusebius quotes from a letter of Cornelius, who was the bishop of Rome and wrote his letter around 250 CE to Fabius, bishop of Antioch. Cornelius refutes the heretic Novatus and in doing so describes the situation in his church:

> This assertor of the gospel then did not know that there should be but one bishop in a catholic church, in which, however, he well knew (for how could he be ignorant?) that there were forty-six presbyters, seven deacons, seven sub-deacons, forty-two acoluthi, exorcists, readers, and janitors.[38]

Cornelius mentions the office of exorcist in such an off-hand manner that it is clear that by the time he wrote this letter, the function of 'exorcist' was recognized as one of the offices of the church. The debate Cornelius is involved in is not on the office of exorcist, but on Novatus' leadership of the group of the Cathari (43.1). Therefore, there is no discussion in this letter of the office of exorcist – it is just mentioned as one of the tasks of the church.

f. Narrative and Practice
If we may draw some tentative conclusions from the texts mentioned in this section, they would have to be the following. First of all, the exorcisms mentioned in the texts presented above function as proof of the superiority of the Christian God, or rather Jesus Christ. The fact that certain believers can cast out demons who hold individuals in their power proves to these believers that Jesus, in whose

---

37. Translation by F. Crombie, *The Writings of Origen*, vol. 1 (ANCL, 10; Edinburgh: Clark, 1939), pp. 402–3.
38. Translation by C. F. Cruse, *Eusebius' Ecclesiastical History* (Peabody: Hendrickson, 1998), p. 231.

name the exorcism is performed, holds greater power than the demons that are cast out.[39] The names of God and Jesus are all-important in this respect. Demons are cast out 'in the name of the Lord' or 'in the name of Jesus'.[40] The passages presented further show us that exorcisms were not merely narrated, but also actively performed in the second and third centuries. This happened to such an extent that the office of 'exorcist' was counted among the official tasks in the church by 250 CE. Finally, it should be noted that healing rituals were considered to be closely related to exorcisms. This becomes especially clear in the text mentioned from Justin's second *Apology*.

Since it is highly unlikely that the practice of healings and exorcisms was restricted to the second and third centuries, we may safely infer that followers of Jesus Christ did perform healings and exorcisms in the first century as well. It simply makes no sense to suppose that the narration of miracle stories in the first century resulted in the practice of healings in the second and third centuries. It must have been quite the reverse: the literary device of narrating miracles and exorcisms must have had the actual practice of miraculous deeds like healings and exorcisms as its religious *Sitz im Leben*. This observation enables us to go back from the narrative traditions we discussed in the first two sections to the man who is the prime subject of these traditions, Paul himself.

4. Paul the Miracle Worker

If we take a look at the undisputed letters of Paul,[41] we find that Paul himself describes his ministry as characterized by more than words alone. Paul uses the traditional expression of 'signs and wonders' as a characterization of what he did. He does so in 1 Cor. 2.1-5, in 2 Cor. 12.12, and Rom 15.19.

In 1 Cor. 2.1-5 Paul refers to his preaching of the gospel among the Corinthians. He points out that he did not come to them with great rhetoric or philosophical wisdom, but ἐν ἀποδείξει πνεύματος καὶ δυνάμεως (v. 4). The display of power Paul gave must have been connected to his understanding of the Spirit.[42] Somehow Paul must have done something different from just preaching the gospel. In 1 Cor. 1.17 Paul explicitly states that he sees himself as sent to preach the gospel, but here in Acts he points out that the way in which he did so was not just by talking. He stresses the fact that he did *not* bring the gospel in the manner of a rhetorician or a sophist (cf. 2.1: ἦλθον οὐ καθ᾽ ὑπεροχὴν λόγου ἢ σοφίας). The point is under-

---

39. S. Schreiber, *Wundertäter*, pp. 149–50, points out that it is God who is depicted in Acts as ultimately responsible for the performance of miracles by Paul.

40. The 'name of Jesus' or 'the Lord' is mentioned several times in the early chapters of Acts – see e.g. 2.38; 3.6, 16; 4.7, 10, 12, 17-18, 30. In ch. 9 Saul is called to proclaim the 'name' of Jesus among the Gentiles: cf. 9.15-16, 21, 27 and numerous passages later in Acts.

41. Romans, 1 & 2 Corinthians, Galatians, Philippians, 1 Thessalonians and Philemon.

42. S. Schreiber, *Wundertäter*, 252, concludes that Paul did not speak about the performance of miraculous deeds in 1 Cor. 2.4. Also, in the case of 1 Thess. 1.5, Schreiber argues that Paul does not speak of any miracles performed by Paul: 'Von einer Wundertätigkeit Pauli ist in keiner Weise die Rede'. It would seem to the present author that Schreiber is too cautious here.

lined by Paul's remark on the subject in 4.20: οὐ γὰρ ἐν λόγῳ ἡ βασιλεία τοῦ θεοῦ ἀλλ᾽ ἐν δυνάμει. Romans 1.16 shows us that Paul understood the gospel itself as a δύναμις from God, and thereby proves that in Paul's vision the gospel was not just a collection of words. For Paul, it was a force working through the spirit, and his own task was to present this force. We may safely infer that Paul did so not merely by preaching, for the word δύναμις clearly refers to a more than just verbal activity.[43]

An even stronger indication of this is given in 2 Cor. 12.12. There, Paul speaks of the 'signs of an apostle' he had performed among the Corinthians: τὰ μὲν σημεῖα τοῦ ἀποστόλου κατειργάσθη ἐν ὑμῖν ἐν πάσῃ ὑπομονῇ, σημείοις τε καὶ τέρασιν καὶ δυνάμεσιν. The expression Paul uses, 'signs of the apostle', may have been a known characterization of the appearance of an apostle.[44] But also, if it was not, Paul does indicate that he included the performance of 'signs and wonders and mighty works' in his ministry. Here Paul uses the expression σημεῖα καὶ τέρατα again, this time to explain the σημεῖα τοῦ ἀπόστολου. It is very likely that Paul uses this expression to refer to the miraculous deeds that were expected from an apostle. This specific ability of an apostle to perform miraculous deeds was no doubt related to the gift of 'workings of powers' Paul describes in 1 Cor. 12.7 as one of the *charismata* in the congregation. Therefore, both passages mentioned point out that Paul regarded the performance of 'powers' or 'wonders' as a gift by the spirit, given to believers in general and apostles in particular.

It is remarkable that Paul refers to these 'signs' by the expression σημεῖα καὶ τέρατα. For our understanding of what it is Paul means by this expression, it is important to note that the words used are a stock phrase derived from the Exodus tradition (see e.g. Exod. 7.3, 9; 11.9, 10; Deut. 4.34; 6.22; 7.19; 11.3).[45] According to Deut. 13.2-3, the performance of a sign or a wonder is a typical activity for a prophet.[46] It may therefore not be by accident that we find this expression used

43. See W. Grundmann, s.v. δύναμαι, δύναμις in: *TWNT*, 3, pp. 286–318, 313: 'In der Verkündigung des Paulus ist der Christus als πνεῦμα gegenwärtig und erweist sich als die δύναμις Gottes.' By this description, however, Grundmann seems to limit the 'power' Paul displayed to the *content* of his proclamation. See also C. E. Arnold, 'Power, NT Concept of', in *ABD*, 5, pp. 444–46. Arnold points at the fact that Jesus' 'works of power should produce repentance and incite faith.'

44. See the verdict by G. H. Twelftree in the *Dictionary of Paul and his Letters*, p. 876: 'The phrase may have come from the Corinthians or perhaps from his opponents'. Regardless of whether this is true or not, the phrase links the performance of 'signs' to the authority of an apostle.

45. In combination with δυνάμεις it is also used in Rom. 15.19, and in Acts 2.22; 6.8; 2 Thess. 2.9; Heb. 2.4. The triple combination of σημεῖα καὶ τέρατα is found nowhere in the LXX, but the combination of σημεῖα καὶ τέρατα with the singular δύναμις does occur in Bar. 2.11, again in a description of the salvation God has established in the exodus event (καὶ νῦν κύριε ὁ θεὸς Ισραηλ ὃς ἐξήγαγες τὸν λαόν σου ἐκ γῆς Αἰγύπτου ἐν χειρὶ κραταιᾷ καὶ ἐν σημείοις καὶ ἐν τέρασιν καὶ ἐν δυνάμει μεγάλῃ καὶ ἐν βραχίονι ὑψηλῷ καὶ ἐποίησας σεαυτῷ ὄνομα ὡς ἡ ἡμέρα αὕτη).

46. It is for this reason that the performance of signs and wonders turned into a standard characteristic of a false prophet as well; see W. A. Meeks, *The Prophet King: Moses Traditions*

by Isaiah and Jeremiah as well.[47] In the various descriptions of eschatological adversaries of Israel or Christ found in early Jewish and Christian sources, the performing of 'signs and wonders' is also a standard element. In Paul's day this characteristic is clearly part of the picture of a prophetic figure, either true or false, and all who act with the authority of the spirit show this by performing 'signs and wonders'.

Could it be, though, that Paul used the expression in a metaphorical way? Isaiah 8.18 especially should make us aware that the words 'signs and wonders' do not automatically refer to the performance of miracles. In this text, the prophet Isaiah describes himself and his children as 'signs and wonders' given by God to the house of Israel.

There are two indications against a metaphorical interpretation of the phrase in Paul. The first is that Paul speaks of the 'signs of an apostle' as *actions* that Paul himself had *performed*. Therefore, his use of the expression can hardly have been merely metaphorical. Should this fail to convince, we have some more substantial evidence in Rom. 15.19. There, Paul speaks about his ministry as a whole as characterized by the fact that it was performed 'in word and deed' (λόγῳ καὶ ἔργῳ), ἐν δυνάμει σημείων καὶ τεράτων, ἐν δυνάμει πνεύματος θεοῦ. Here we find a combination of elements which we also encountered in 1 Cor. 2.4 (ἐν ἀποδείξει πνεύματος καὶ δυνάμεως) and 2 Cor. 12.12 (σημείοις τε καὶ τέρασιν καὶ δυνάμεσιν). Especially the expression λόγῳ καὶ ἔργῳ indicates that Paul did do something other than preaching alone. The word ἔργον Paul uses here is not very likely to refer to the communities he has built, but it is explained by the words that follow.[48] This means that we are not allowed to interpret Paul's use of the expression 'signs and wonders' as merely a metaphor. Apparently Paul did perform some miraculous deeds.

From the few passages discussed above, we are allowed to conclude that Paul must have done more than just preach the gospel in words alone. His ministry must also have consisted of some miraculous deeds; ἔργοι that Paul did, 'signs and wonders' he performed. This observation points out that Paul legitimized his ministry by miraculous deeds, thereby pointing out that he was a prophetic envoy of Christ.[49]

As to the character of Paul's miraculous deeds, his 'signs and wonders', we are unfortunately in total darkness. We have no evidence that Paul expelled demons,

and the Johannine Christology (NovTSup, 14; Leiden: Brill, 1967), pp. 47–55; L. J. Lietaert Peerbolte, *The Antecedents of Antichrist: A Traditio-Historical Study of the Earliest Christian Views on Eschatological Opponents* (JSJSup, 49; Leiden: Brill, 1996), p. 80.

47. See Isa. 8.18; 20.3; Jer 39.20-21.

48. In 1 Cor. 9.1 Paul uses the word ἔργον to refer to the community of the Corinthians. There is no indication that this specific use of the word is intended here, too.

49. The performance of miracles is to be seen as an element of the prophetic tradition rather than a characteristic of Paul as a *theios aner*. For a criticism of this category related to the performance of miracles, see C. R. Holladay, *THEIOS ANER in Hellenistic Judaism: A Critique of the Use of This Category in New Testament Christology* (SBLDS, 40; Missoula: Scholars Press, 1977), pp. 236–37.

performed healings or even tried to raise the dead. All we have is the indication
that Paul did not confine his ministry to preaching alone. He apparently did
perform some symbolic actions or indeed miracles to prove the authenticity of his
preaching and the divine power of Jesus Christ. Seen from this angle, the reception
of Paul as a miracle worker in later writings was a narrative elaboration, a
characteristic that was indeed present in Paul's ministry.

But how should the 'miracles' Paul apparently performed be evaluated? First
of all, it is important to see that the performance of divine deeds did belong to the
core of what people expected from an envoy from God. It is clear that that was
the situation in the second and third centuries, and there is enough Jewish and
pagan evidence to surmise that this pattern was no Christian invention.[50] Paul,
therefore, was part of his religious context, and the religious discourse of his day
simply entailed the performance of divine deeds.

Next to this, it is important to take into account what Paul himself states
about the 'signs and wonders' he performed. In 2 Cor. 12.11 he introduces his
mention of the signs he performed by referring to himself as a 'fool' (γέγονα
ἄφρων). Paul's boasting of his signs is part of a rhetorical outburst, commonly
known as the 'Fool's Speech'.[51] In this speech Paul uses the tactics of his opponents
– boasting – to point out that he himself is superior to them, while at the same
time indicating that the elements he could boast of in fact did not matter at all.
The speech presents us with a number of difficulties, but they need not be treated
in this contribution. What is clear about this piece of rhetoric is that Paul inverts
his argument by pointing out that he is superior to his opponents. Thereby, he gives
two signals: first, that his capacities and the effect of what he did mattered more
than those of his opponents; and second, that the boasting on these things was
entirely vain. It is a masterly rhetorical device in which Paul communicates his own
superiority, while at the same time pointing out that that superiority actually means
nothing, since the true power behind his deeds comes from God.

With regard to the 'miracles' Paul must have performed, this means that he does
mention them as part of his ministry, part of the way in which he proclaimed the
gospel. And at the same time he points out that he is 'weak' and that the purpose
of his weakness is that he may receive the 'power of Christ' (12.10). Therefore,
Paul implicitly refers to the δύναμις τοῦ Χριστοῦ as the ultimate force in his
ministry. This means that Paul himself makes a double statement here: on the one
hand, miracles matter; on the other hand, it is not Paul who works them, but the
power of Jesus Christ or the Gospel.

In Paul's presentation of the signs and wonders he performed, we find therefore
the same double message that appeared to be present in later narrative traditions
about Paul: the deeds he performed were to be regarded as a confirmation of his

---

50. For pagan as well as Jewish stories on 'heroes who heal', see W. Cotter, *Miracles in Greco-Roman Antiquity*, pp. 35–53.

51. See especially J. Zmijewski, *Der Stil der paulinischen 'Narrenrede': Analyse der Sprachgestaltung in 2 Kor 11,1-12,10 als Beitrag zur Methodik von Stiluntersuchungen neutestamentlicher Texte* (BBB, 52; Köln: Peter Hanstein, 1978).

authority – Paul performed 'the signs of the apostle' – and at the same time they refer not to Paul's own power, but to a transcendent source of that power: Jesus Christ or the Gospel.

Finally, after having concluded that Paul did indeed perform actions we would label 'miracles', that Paul must indeed have been a miracle worker, we must at the same time admit that we don't know anything about the exact content of these miracles. We don't know whether Paul did perform exorcisms and/or healings, but the evidence we have been discussing does suggest that such must have been the case. Having seen this, it is all the more remarkable to notice that Paul himself downplays the importance of the 'signs and wonders' he performed. He apparently did practise these activities, but at the same time he stresses that it was not through his own power that he did so. It thus appears that Paul used the paradigm of a miracle worker to present the power of the gospel and to point out that Jesus Christ actually does reign. At the same time, Paul stressed the fact that these signs and wonders were not performed by him or on his behalf, but by Jesus Christ on behalf of God.

Conclusion

In the book of Acts as well as in later apocryphal writings, the apostle Paul is presented as a miracle worker. Several second- and third-century authors consider such miracle stories as are told of Paul to be proof of the divine authority of the one who works the miracles, as well as evidence of the superior character of the Christian God and Jesus Christ. This paradigm formed the context for Pauline miracle stories, but not only for the stories – also for Paul's ministry itself. In Paul's own description, the performance of some kind of miraculous action is mentioned as proof of the power of God's or Christ's spirit. Clearly, the performance of miraculous deeds was not restricted to the realm of the literary, it also pertained to real life itself.[52] It thus appears that we have found a frame of reference that helped shape not only narrative traditions about Paul, but also Paul's ministry itself. At the same time it should be noticed that both in the writings of Paul, and in the later narrative traditions of his ministry, the emphasis is consistently on the fact that Paul did not perform his miraculous deeds through his own power, but rather through the power of Jesus Christ. Seen from this perspective, the 'miracles' performed by Paul and other early followers of Jesus Christ were an effective contribution to the spread of the new faith. They presented the miracle worker as a legitimate envoy of Christ, but, what is even more than that, by ascribing the origin of his deeds to Jesus Christ, the miracle worker referred to a transcendent source for his power and presented the gospel not only in words, but also in deeds. This is something that is all to easily forgotten in a western academic approach to early Christianity in general and Paul in particular.

---

52. This means that we cannot dismiss Paul's characterization in Acts as easily as Haenchen does. The picture of Paul as a miracle worker in Acts is the first argument for Haenchen to conclude that the image of Paul in Acts does not coincide with that of Paul's letters – see E. Haenchen, *Apostelgeschichte*, pp. 100–101.

ESCHATOLOGICAL SIGNS AND THEIR FUNCTION IN THE REVELATION OF JOHN

Beate Kowalski

'Eschatological Signs and Miracles' – this was the title of the paper I was asked to present at the EABS meeting in Copenhagen 2003. What do miracles mean in general and more precisely in the Revelation of John? According to P.-H. Menoud, miracles are 'something amazing, unusual phenomena, deeds of power, signs, inexistent, extraordinary visions in the natural course'.[1] K. Gatzweiler underlines this point of view and states that miracles are 'a direct and extraordinary intervention of divine power in the world of human beings' and 'extraordinary incidents such as miraculous healings, special historical events or unusual occurrences of natural forces'.[2]

Very important is the definition of O. Weinreich, who argues that 'every divine action can be called a miracle' and 'the border between miracle and non-miracle in ancient times is not determined/defined, human beings decide on the definition'.[3] According to A. Weiser, miracles are 'impressive occasions understood by the faithful as signs of God's salvific action (*Heilshandeln*)'.[4] And R. L. Hamblin states that 'a miracle is a marvelous occurrence taking place in human experience which could not have been exercised by human powers or by the power of any natural agency. It is an event that must be attributed to divine intervention. It is usually thought of as an act which demonstrates divine control over the laws of nature'.[5]

---

1.   P.-H. Menoud, 'Die Bedeutung des Wunders nach dem Neuen Testament', in A. Suhl (ed.), *Der Wunderbegriff im Neuen Testament* (WdF, 295; Darmstadt: WBG, 1980), pp. 279–99, 282–83.

2.   K. Gatzweiler, 'Der paulinische Wunderbegriff', in A. Suhl (ed.), *Wunderbegriff*, pp. 374–415, (376).

3.   O. Weinreich, *Antike Heilungswunder: Untersuchungen zum Wunderglauben der Griechen und Römer* (RVV, 8.1; Gießen: Töpelmann, 1909), pp. vii–viii.

4.   A. Weiser, *Was die Bibel Wunder nennt: Ein Sachbuch zu den Berichten der Evangelien* (Stuttgart: Katholisches Bibelwerk 1975), p. 20.

5.   R. L. Hamblin, 'Miracles in the Book of Acts', *SWJT* 17 (1974), pp. 19–34 (20).

1. Introduction

Interpreters of the Revelation of John easily run the risk of misinterpreting this final book of the Bible in certain respects. Church history and current times give enough examples of fundamentalistic readings and *eisegesis*. Often Revelation is misused for prophecies or to prove historical incidents.

But for many people the book of Revelation remains a book of seven seals, with bizarre images of aggression and violence, hope and admonition. Its content touches the great issues of theology:

1. The question of God and his justice on earth (theodicy): How can one speak about justice in the face of the violent events of which Revelation tells us?

2. Closely connected with this problem is the idea of revenge (*Vergeltungsdenken*), which characterizes great parts of Revelation. What is the right approach for Christians, who know of Jesus' command to love their enemies, when they read pericopes in Revelation that demonize enemies and emphasize the idea of revenge? Is it possible to connect both ideas together to a unit? And how?

3. Furthermore, the fundamental questions of the deeper meaning of evil and how to overcome any form of crisis are indirectly concerned.

4. The final but key topic is the problem of predestination, which supposes a plan made by God concerning the fate of all mankind and the world: Does this idea not restrict the freedom of human beings? Or what else could this mean for people suffering persecution and tribulation?

What do we do with this list of questions and problems? Could the solution be to simply avoid the book of Revelation or even exclude it from the canonical writings, from the Christian liturgy and from pastoral work without further discussion and attempts to understand this book? This can hardly be a fitting response to all the problems mentioned. It would seem better to use different exegetical methods to explain this last book for pastoral practice.

To avoid the danger of *eisegesis* instead of an interpretation of the text, it is necessary to first analyse the historical situation of its recipients[6] in order to distinguish between *story* and *history*,[7] and then to discern the correlation[8] and interaction between both levels of the narrative. This is the only way to define the theological message of Revelation and can, in any case, only be demonstrated by examples. In what follows we will have a look at the eschatological signs that

---

6.   'Es ist durchaus denkbar, dass der Autor dabei auf Anfragen der Gemeinde nach dem Grund von aktuellen Repressalien reagiert': P. Busch, *Der gefallene Drache: Mythenexegese am Beispiel von Apokalypse 12* (TANZ, 19; Tübingen: Francke, 1996), p. 189.

7.   Cf. the narrative approach of J. L. Ska, *Our Fathers Have Told Us: Introduction to the Analysis of Hebrew Narratives* (SubB, 13; Rome: Pontificio Istituto Biblico, 1990), p. 6, who distinguishes between story and discourse: 'Discourse' means 'the concrete narrative, in its actual shape, that the reader has before his eyes'; 'story', 'an abstract reconstruction in which the reader (re)places the elements of the "discourse" according to a logical and chronological order and supplies what is missing'.

8.   Cf. B. Kowalski, 'Das Verhältnis von Theologie und Zeitgeschichte in den Sendschreiben der Johannes-Offenbarung', in K. Backhaus (ed.), *Theologie als Vision: Studien zur Johannes-Offenbarung* (SBS, 191; Stuttgart: Katholisches Bibelwerk, 2001), pp. 54–76.

appear in the central texts of Revelation. They have a socio-historical background and literary functions. In conjunction with the analysis of the *story* we will have to ask: What narrative functions do they have in the course of the story? In which parts are they mentioned? What are the implications? With what connotations? What is their Old Testament background? What are the effects of the signs? How are the actors described? The analysis of the *history* has to look at the socio-historical background of the signs. What are the actual socio-historical events they reflect on?

It is the aim of this article to work with examples, so that the method can be used for other texts and issues. To reach this target we have to make the different steps of interpretation and the methodological approach as transparent as possible. A first step of analysis will introduce the world of ideas and mentality of the book of Revelation, the situation of its author and his recipients. The second step follows an overview of all references and pericopes in which eschatological signs appear. The third step systematizes these references. The fact that the chosen pericopes are more fantastic and mythological than other texts in the book of Revelation underlies the choice of these particular texts. A last part summarizes the results of our analysis and tries to formulate the relevance of this topic for the present. If exegesis is not only to be understood as a purely linguistical and historical science, we have to pay attention to the intention of Revelation mentioned by the author himself at the beginning of his book in the form of a makarism: 'Happy are those, who read these prophetic words and hear them, and fulfill what is written; since the time is close' (1.3). According to this makarism, it is not only important to proclaim and hear the words of Revelation, but also to accept its message for the daily life. The necessity of scientific exegesis is to build a bridge between exegetical details and theological questions.

2. The Situation of the Recipients and the Author of the Book of Revelation

The historical background of Revelation belongs to the less doubtful aspects of exegesis. One can discern the situation from the call narrative of John (1.9-20) and furthermore from the praise and accusation, admonition and promise John directs within his letters to the different Christian groups in the church of Asia Minor (chs. 2–3). Allusions and comments in the main apocalyptic body of the book confirm the results, especially the call for patient endurance addressed to the ideal reader, exhorting him or her to keep the commandments of God and to hold fast to faith in Jesus.

The main problem to which John tries to find a solution are the dangers for Christians posed by Gentile cults, especially the practices of the Roman Emperor Cult. The relation of the Christians towards the state/government and a more or less polytheistic and syncretistic society is charged because of the required participation in common feasts of food sacrificed to idols as a condition for commerce and trade. To avoid these Gentile cultic feasts meant isolation from society and trade. For a long time exegetes and historians assumed that there had been a persecution of Christians under Domitian (81–96 CE), who lived at the time Revelation was written. Nowadays this hypothesis has been corrected: it is better to speak about an 'open situation',[9] with possible but not systematically organized persecutions, accusations and martyrdoms. The dangers for Christians were more subtle and therefore more dangerous than a systematical persecution, since they meant a slow process of assimilation into Gentile society forced by reprisals. That could easily lead to abandoning/renouncing the Christian faith.

The dangers described above are reflected upon theologically in the seven letters. They show all possible nuances of reactions to this situation between the two extreme positions of complete assimilation into Gentile society and convinced confession of Christian faith. Thus, one can distinguish between three main types of Christians in the churches:

1. Faithful Christians with a clear confession of faith in Christ without any fear of social reprisals, isolation, economic poverty and martyrdom.[10]
2. Christians who compromise, and worship both Christ and pagan gods at the same time.
3. The group of Christians who are totally assimilated into Gentile Roman society and who have attained wealth and reputation. John strongly differentiates within his descriptions and presents a specific profile of each of the churches.

He introduces himself in 1.9 as ὁ ἀδελφὸς ὑμῶν καὶ συγκοινωνὸς ἐν τῇ θλίψει καὶ βασιλείᾳ καὶ ὑπομονῇ ἐν Ἰησοῦ. That means that he shares the same situation with the seven churches as it is described with θλῖψις, βασιλεία, and ὑπομονή. But the author of Revelation does not only speak about the difficulties of the situation in Asia Minor (θλῖψις), he also mentions the positive aspects (βασιλεία and ὑπομονή), Christian faith and hope given by Christ (1.5b, 6; 5.9, 10; 7.14; 12.11; 14.3-4; 20.6).[11]

It is the aim of Revelation to present a solution to the readers who are confronted with the conflicting demands of their Christian faith and the requirements of the surrounding Gentile society with its cults. According to John, the only solution is an unwavering profession of Christian faith, even if it entails social reprisals. The energy[12] needed to prevail in this difficult situation (2.7, 11, 17, 26; 3.5, 12, 21; 6.2; 15.2; 21.7) is given by the presence of God's salvation, his love (1.5; 3.9; 20.9), Christ's death at the cross (αἷμα: 1.5; 5.9; 7.14; 12.11; 19.13) and his resurrection (1.5, 9-20; 5.6, 9-10, 12; 6.9-11; 11.7-11; 20.4-6; 21.4). Ultimate victory

9.   Cf. especially H.-J. Klauck, 'Das Sendschreiben nach Pergamum und der Kaiserkult in der Johannesoffenbarung', *Bib* 73 (1992), pp. 153–82. G. K. Beale's commentary, *The Book of Revelation: A Commentary on the Greek Text* (NIGT; Grand Rapids: Eerdmans Carlisle: Paternoster Press, 1999) is an exception to the rule (p. 27).

10.   Cf. H. Roose, '*Das Zeugnis Jesu': Seine Bedeutung für die Christologie, Eschatologie, und Prophetie in der Offenbarung des Johannes* (TANZ, 32; Tübingen: Francke, 2000).

11.   The solution is provided by Jesus' blood: αἷμα 1.5; 5.9; 7.14; 12.11, and ransom ἀγοράζω 5.9; 14.3, 4.

12.   Νικάω means to hold onto God and Christ; cf. H. Giesen, *Die Offenbarung des Johannes* (RNT; Regensburg: Pustet, 1997), p. 342.

comes from bearing afflictions and giving a testimony with one's word and life (6.9; 12.11), by fulfilling God's commandments (12.17), bearing witness to his words (1.2; 6.9; 20.4), holding fast to his name (2.13) and the testimony of Jesus (1.2, 9; 12.17; 17.6; 19.10; 20.4), and last but not least, by patient endurance and faith (2.13, 19; 13.10; 14.12).

3. References of Eschatological Signs in Revelation

After describing the historical background of Revelation we will present all pericopes in which eschatological signs (σημεῖον) occur.[13] It is no coincidence that there are seven references (12.1, 3; 13.13-14; 15.1; 16.14; 19.20). Seven is a number with symbolic meaning and importance for the structure of Revelation, describing abundance and completeness. Eschatological signs always occur in the narrative when the tension dramatically increases towards the climax and final solution.[14] Somehow eschatological signs are heralds of the happy end. They want to give confidence to Christians who are suffering from a situation of great danger and who no longer expect God's salvation. Eschatological signs appear for the first time around the dramatic climax of Revelation and in the final chapters. The first signs appear within the only myth in Revelation. The fifth sign within the last series of plagues solicits comparison with the two previous series of plagues. Therefore one can infer a connection between eschatological signs and the dramatically increased narrative.

The signs are further described by adjectives: the positive signs are characterized as great (σημεῖον μέγα, 12.1) or as great and wonderful (μέγα καὶ θαυμαστόν, 15.1)[15], while the negatives are only called 'another' sign (ἄλλο σημεῖον, 12.3) or introduced without any further characterization. Three of the signs appear in heaven (ἐν τῷ οὐρανῷ): the woman (12.1), the dragon (12.3) and the angels with the seven bowls of God's wrath (15.1).

These three belong to a series of unusual figures of the last days of the world that are called 'signs': a woman, a dragon, a beast, seven angels with bowls of God's wrath, three foul spirits like frogs coming from the mouth of the dragon and of the beast and from the false prophet, and at least one false prophet. It is no coincidence that these figures form a double series of seven, there are all together fourteen figures. The symbolic number seven also occurs in the eschatological signs of the seven angels. This list makes it obvious that the typical dualism of good and evil, God and his opponents, is also to be found among the eschatological signs. The eschatological figures introduced as signs are not described in all aspects as individuals, but as models. Thus, they reflect the connection between God and the world.

---

13. Τέρας does not occur in Revelation (cf. Mt. 24.24; Mk 13.22; Jn 4.48; Acts 2.19, 22, 43; 4.30; 5.12; 6.8; 7.36; 14.3; 15.12; Rom. 15.19; 2 Cor. 12.12; 2 Thess 2.9; Heb. 2.4), δύναμις is not used with the meaning 'miracle'.

14. J. Roloff, *Die Offenbarung des Johannes* (ZBKNT, 18; Zürich: Theologischer Verlag, 2nd edn, 1987), p. 121. Rev. 12.1–19.10 asks the question of evil. All eschatological signs are to be found in this context. They are necessary when evil gets out of hand.

15. Θαύμαστος and μέγας occur only in Rev. 15.1, 3.

Three of the seven signs are combined with the verb ὁράω (12.1, 3; 15.1), the first two are interpreted with the passive form ὤφθη[16] (in the synoptic tradition ὤφθη occurs in the context of Jesus' resurrection or the appearance of an angel) as appearances in heaven clearly visible for everybody, the active verb introduces the third sign as a vision of John.[17] The four other references to σημεῖον are connected with ποιέω (13.13-14; 16.14; 19.20). 'Making' is only to be found in connection with the negative signs, while the passive occurrence of signs – with one exception: the dragon – have positive connotations.

In the remainder of this article we will proceed as follows: we will interpret all seven signs without discussing all the exegetical problems at stake, and we will especially focus on ch. 12 and its background.

4. Interpretation of the Eschatological Signs in Their Context
a. The Woman of Light and the Dragon

The background of the composition of ch. 12[18] is an Egyptian and Ugaritian myth, which emphasizes the dramatic action.[19] The woman of light and the dragon occur within this chapter as the first signs in heaven. They are composed antithetically, therefore both signs are easily compared with each other.[20] In the following narrative analysis we will have a look at the clothing of both figures, which has the function of reflecting/mirroring their nature (*Wesen*), deeds and state (*Ergehen*). It soon becomes obvious that the descriptions are models (*Typisierungen*), open enough to different interpretations; identification with a historical figure is not automatically possible.[21] Metaphors are not only open to further interpretations but reflect reality on a higher and reflected level – they are instruments for conquering a crisis.[22]

---

16. The form ὤφθη occurs in the context of Jesus' resurrection (Mt. 17.3; Mk 9.4; Lk. 24.43; Acts 13.31; 1 Cor. 15.5-8) or the appearance of an angel (Lk. 1.11; 22.43; Acts 7.2, 26, 30; 1 Tim. 3.16). In Revelation the ark of the covenant appears in heaven (Rev. 11.19).

17. The connection between Rev. 12.1, 3 and 15.1 is not logical according to J. Roloff, *Offenbarung*, p. 157.

18. Cf. U. B. Müller, *Die Offenbarung des Johannes* (ÖTK, 19; Gütersloh: Gütersloher Verlagshaus; Würzburg: Echter, 2nd. edn, 1995), pp. 241–45, who discusses the mythological background of 12.7-12.

19. Cf. J. Roloff, *Offenbarung*, pp. 123–25, and extensively P. Busch, *Drache*.

20. Cf. the narrative analysis according to P. Busch, *Drache*, pp. 36–44, and D. E. Aune, *Revelation 6-16* (WBC, 52B; Dallas, TX: Word Books Publisher, 1998), pp. 675–76, who speaks about *dramatis personae*.

21. J. Roloff, *Offenbarung*, p. 126, interprets the woman as 'Bild der endzeitlichen Heilsgemeinde, Symbol der Kirche. Diese ist Erbin der Verheißungen des alttestamentlichen Gottesvolkes: darauf deutet die Zwölfzahl der Sterne (vgl. 1. Mose 37,9) hin, die das heilige Zwölfstämmevolk in seiner endzeitlichen Fülle und Vollendung symbolisiert (vgl. 7,4-8; 14,1). Gegen die Möglichkeit, dass mit der Himmelsfrau das Gottesvolk des Alten Bundes, aus dem der Messias geboren wurde, gemeint sei, spricht neben dem Fortgang der Erzählung (v.13-17) ganz allgemein der Umstand, dass die Apk. nirgends die Frage nach dem Verhältnis Israels zur Kirche theologisch thematisiert. Ihr genügt die Gewissheit, dass die Kirche ihre Wurzeln in Israel hat, und dass sie nunmehr in die Rechte Israels eingetreten ist.'

22. 'Die Verschlüsselung ist zugleich auch eine sehr klare und beredte Symbolisierung, mit

The woman is the first great portent that occurs in heaven in Revelation.[23] She is a σημεῖον since she refers to another reality: God's acting through her. He protects and cares for her, but also deprives the mighty of their power.[24] The woman's clothing is described according to the scheme 'garment – feet – head'. That is typical for the literary context of Revelation.[25] The decoration and the clothes of the woman are the sun, the moon and the stars.[26] They give her a radiant, majestic, and victorious charisma. The garment of the sun is a sign of her special election, the stars express her δόξα.[27] Furthermore it is said that, crying out in birth pangs, she gives birth to a son,[28] who is to rule all the nations with a rod of iron and who was taken up to God and his throne (12.5).[29] This underlines the majestic character of his mother, her close relationship with Christ or God and his works of creation. It is part of the woman's character that she gives birth to new life that brings blessings to many.[30] But her child is associated with suffering and pain from the very start. Only a few of the woman's deeds are mentioned: she cries out in birth pangs and escapes from her opponent to the desert (v. 6),[31] or she receives the two wings of a great eagle[32] to fly into the wilderness (v. 14).[33]

---

der Johannes Rom die Maske seiner hohen Ansprüche herunterreißt und sein mörderisches Gesicht zeigt. Darüber hinaus hebt die Symbolisierung den Konflikt mit Rom auf eine höhere Ebene und entscheidet ihn dort in der Überwindung durch Gott und seinen Messias'; K. Wengst, *Pax Romana: Anspruch und Wirklichkeit. Erfahrungen und Wahrnehmungen des Friedens bei Jesus und im Urchristentum* (München: Kaiser, 1986), p. 163.

23. Cf. G. K. Beale, *Revelation*, p. 631, who argues for Isa. 7.10, 14 as the pre-text of Rev. 12.1-2.

24. H. Giesen, *Offenbarung*, p. 276: 'Als Zeichen weist die Frau auf eine andere Wirklichkeit hin'.

25. Cf. P. Busch, *Drache*, pp. 50, 53–55, who refers to Dan. 10.5-6; Jdt. 10.3; *Jos. Asen.* 3.6 and parallels in Revelation. The parallel between angel and whore is conspicuous.

26. J. Roloff, *Offenbarung*, p. 126, argues for a 'allgemein wahrnehmbare außergewöhnliche Erscheinung am Himmel'. 'Es liegt nahe, hier an eine bestimmte Gestirnkonstellation zu denken: Wenn die Sonne ins Zeichen der Jungfrau tritt, das von den Alten mehrfach mit Isis gleichgesetzt wurde, dann steht am Nachthimmel der Vollmond zu ihren Füßen. Dieses allen sichtbare Himmelsphänomen wird nun als "Zeichen" gedeutet, d.h. als ankündigender Hinweis auf Ereignisse der Endzeit'.

27. 'Das himmlische Licht, das sie verbreitet, ist Bild für die Herrlichkeit Gottes und für alle, die zu ihm gehören', H. Giesen, *Offenbarung*, p. 277.

28. 'The idea of persecution is also highlighted by the fact that βασανίζω is not attested anywhere in biblical or extrabiblical literature with reference to a woman suffering birth pains', G. K. Beale, *Revelation*, p. 629.

29. The child is described with elements from Ps. 2.9; cf. P. Busch, *Drache*, pp. 86–93.

30. P. Busch, *Drache*, pp. 56–61, does not interpret the pangs of birth eschatologically, but on the basis of 1QH 3.3-18 in the context of the ecclesiastical situation.

31. The wilderness is a place of emigration and protection, cf. J. Roloff, *Offenbarung*, p. 128. 'Johannes zeigt in 12,6.14 mit Hilfe dieses positiven Wüstenmotivs, dass die Frau, die das wahre Volk Gottes repräsentiert, in der Geborgenheit und im Schutz Gottes lebt. Sie genießt seinen Schutz, und er garantiert ihren Bestand'; H. Giesen, *Offenbarung*, p. 284.

32. The wings of the great eagle remind the reader of Exod. 19.4; Deut. 32.11; Isa. 40.30-31, and of a mythical eagle, 'der als Bote und Werkzeug Gottes der Rettung der Frau zu dienen hat'; U. B. Müller, *Offenbarung*, p. 239.

33. The escape of the women into the wilderness in v. 6 and v. 14 have supported the discussion of a doublet; cf. P. Busch, *Drache*, pp. 164–66.

Related to the few deeds of the woman are the many and powerful deeds of God towards the woman. God prepares her escape, nourishes her[34] and protects her from her opponent, the dragon. Three different identifications of the woman are to be found in modern exegesis:

1. The individual interpretation as the virgin Mary that was very common among Catholic exegetes; the detail in the text about her other children detracts from this interpretation.
2. A collective interpretation as God's people, the Christian Church.
3. God's people in the entirety of the old and new covenants.[35] Surely, this last interpretation can be accepted best, so that Jews and Christians at any time are enabled to identify themselves with her and recognize in her figure God's special care for those who are faithful to him.

Nowadays the feminist approach criticizes the stereotypes of female figures in Revelation as bride, whore, mother and widow, and the passive attitude of the woman of light who is 'only' giving birth to a child.[36] But this is only one aspect of the text, the other one is God's visible care for the woman. Furthermore, conquering difficult situations with faithfulness and belief is also a form of activity.[37]

The dragon is introduced as a figure of contrast to the woman of light, and as a second, but not great, sign. He is called a dragon, but also an accuser (12.10),[38] devil (12.12)[39] and serpent (12.15).[40] His apppearance with the red colour and seven heads is ugly and life-destroying, his nature is full of evil and characterized by death-bringing power (v. 3). He is the enemy of the woman, her child and the rest of her children; between him and the powerful child a dangerous competition develops.[41] In oriental symbolism the dragon symbolizes God's enemy and the power of chaos (Job 7.12; Isa. 27.1; 51.9; Ps. 74.13-14).[42] Many deeds charac-

---

34. Cf. the manna in Exod. 16.1-36 and the eucharistic meaning in Rev. 2.17.

35. Cf. H. Giesen, *Offenbarung*, pp. 270–75.

36. Cf. M. J. Selvidge, 'Powerful and Powerless Women in the Apocalypse', *Neot* 26 (1992), pp. 157–67, and B. Kowalski, 'Vrouwenfiguren in de Openbaring van Johannes', *TvT* 42 (2002), pp. 378–89.

37. P. Busch, *Drache*, pp. 169–75.

38. ὁ κατήγωρ is a *hapax legomenon*.

39. The identification of the dragon with the devil is well known in contemporary literature, cf. P. Busch, *Drache*, p. 118.

40. U.B. Müller, *Offenbarung*, p. 239, points to the description of the dragon as a huge creature of the sea (cf. Ps. 74.13; *T. Ash.* 7.3). The identification of snake and dragon occurs often in ancient times (cf. P. Busch, *Drache*, p. 116). The attribute ἀρξαῖος is the identification with the snake in Gen. 3. Cf. especially J. Ellul, *Apokalypse: Die Offenbarung des Johannes – Enthüllung der Wirklichkeit* (Neukirchen-Vluyn: Neukirchener Verlag, 1981), p. 76. J. Roloff, *Offenbarung*, p. 127, thinks of an appearance in heaven. Cf. also P. Busch, *Drache*, pp. 125–28.

41. Cf. J. Roloff, *Offenbarung*, p. 128: 'Das Kind ist sein Konkurrent, weil es seinen Anspruch auf die Weltherrschaft in Frage stellt!'

42. Cf. U. B. Müller, *Offenbarung*, p. 233. Dan. 7.7 is the OT pre-text.

terize him: he contests with everybody; the dragon makes war against the stars
(Rev. 12.4), the woman (12.4, 13, 15-17), the Christians (12.9-10, 13, 17),
against Michael and his angels (12.7), and against the whole world. These activities are related to his state: he is thrown down to the earth (vv. 12-13) and his
power is minimized (v. 12). He precipitates his own destruction with the same
abandon with which he makes war.

The dragon's identity is connected with the Roman Emperor Cult. The way he
is presented displays the typical demonizising of enemies, as K. Wengst suggests:
'Die Hoffnung auf den Untergang Roms ist nicht frei von Rachegelüsten' ('The
hope of Rome's destruction is not clear of the appetite for revenge'). This points
to the desire for twofold revenge, as shown in the passages that speak of 'pools
of fire and brimstone'. 'Das zeigt etwa der Wunsch nach doppelter Vergeltung; das
zeigen auch die Stellen, die vom "Pfuhl von Feuer und Schwefel" sprechen.' And
furthermore: 'Genau dagegen [die verübten Untaten] aber bleiben die Vergeltungs-
und Gerichtswünsche der Apokalypse ein unüberhörbarer Protest'.[43]

The message of this chapter is that only actions and combat against everybody
finally destroy human power. The behaviour of the woman of light is characterized
by a passive and calm attitude; she bears daily life with all its pain and suffering,
gives birth to new life in the meanwhile and is assured of God's protection.[44] One
can observe a clear *Leserlenkung* to convey the essence of the woman's nature and
her trust in God's protection to the reader. The hymn 12.10b-12, placed in the
centre of Revelation 12,[45] in an anticipatory interpretation of the narrative,[46]
confirms this way of reading. It twice mentions the ideal recipients, viz. Christians
who have conquered the dragon by the word and life of their testimony (12.11).[47]
Furthermore, the rest of the woman's children, the Christians, are characterized
by keeping the commandments of God and holding the testimony of Jesus (12.17).

43.   K. Wengst, *Pax Romana*, pp. 157–58: 'Nicht die gewalttätigen Sieger der Geschichte
haben Zukunft, sondern gerade ihre Opfer. Die Bilder der Apokalypse vom Sieg des Lammes
widersprechen der erfahrenen Wirklichkeit, in der die Lämmer gerade nicht siegen, sondern
geschlachtet werden. Sie bilden daher ein Widerstandspotential, dieser Wirklichkeit in wider-
sprechendem Leiden standzuhalten und damit Zeugnis zu geben für eine Wirklichkeit, eine
Gegenwirklichkeit von Frieden und Gerechtigkeit, die stärker ist. In der Gewißheit, dass dafür
Christus als dem geschlachteten Lamm Gottes selbst einsteht, zeichnet Johannes nicht nur den
kommenden Untergang Roms, sondern entwirft auch positive Hoffnungsbilder' (pp. 159–60).

44.   Cf. U. B. Müller, *Offenbarung*, p. 239.

45.   Cf. J. Roloff, *Offenbarung*, p. 130.

46.   U. B. Müller, *Offenbarung*, p. 275, speaks about anticipation within the hymn.

47.   J. A. Du Rand, '"Now the Salvation of our God has Come...": A Narrative Perspective
on the Hymns in Revelation 12–15', *Neot* 27 (1993), pp. 313–50 argues: 'The hymn in 12:10-
12 can be viewed as an interpretative commentary on 12:1 9 ... It is also meaningful to note that
this hymn functions as a narrative expression of heavenly worship stressing the spatial dimension
of things to come' (323). And further: 'The innertextual appropriation of a textual tradition from
Exodus 15 plays an important role in the narrative. The enemies and oppressors of the faithful
are labelled as Pharaoh-types. The faithful are placed within the context of an ideological
struggle by these hymns. That is why the victorious singers of this song of the Lamb praise God

b. Angels with Bowls of Wrath

The seven angels with the bowls of wrath form the third and last series of plagues in Revelation, which builds a bridge between Revelation 12–14 and 17–18.[48] They are not easily interpreted since they raise the problem of God's justice. How can it be possible that God not only permits pain and suffering but also initiates it? For the correct interpretation of the text it is necessary to analyse not only the effect of each plague, but also its addressees and intention. Every action is an interpersonal act, therefore the actor and his addressees, the motivation and results have to be recognized.

The prelude in heaven in 15.1-8 and the series of plagues in 16.1-21 are closely connected with the seven angels as eschatological signs.[49] Thus, to interpret them we have to take a look at their context. The seven angels with the bowls of wrath[50] are a great and wonderful sign in heaven. In this way, they are characterisized as the climax of all seven signs.[51] They provoke plagues, which affect the four elements[52] and the power of the beast, the Roman Empire. The Egyptian plagues (Exod. 7–10) seem to be the Old Testament background.[53]

Usually these specific kinds of plagues should generate an extensive impact, but its real addressees are limited. They are exclusively addressed to the followers of the Roman Emperor Cult (Rev. 16.2, 4-6, 12-16, 19), who on the one hand worship the emperor as God and on the other hand do harm to faithful Christians.[54] The book of Revelation does not think about natural disasters that harm both the guilty and innocent equally. This discrepancy between text and reality, and the annotated hymn[55] indicate that the bowls of God's wrath have a literary function: they proclaim God's salvation[56] and

for what he is and for what he has done. The scene is set for the appearance of the seven angels with the final plagues. The battle in heaven has been won and God is unfolding salvation as well as judgement on earth. The faithful need not fear or become anxious because God's acts in the past have been convincing and victorious' (329).

48. Cf. J. Roloff, *Offenbarung*, p. 161.

49. Cf. U. B. Müller, *Offenbarung*, p. 273; H. Giesen, *Offenbarung*, p. 341.

50. 'Die Schalenvisionen sind Teil des Gerichtsgeschehens, das durch die siebte Posaune in Gang gesetzt wird (11.15ff.), sowie Teil des dritten Wehe (11.14)'; U. B. Müller, *Offenbarung*, p. 271. 'Den Schalenvisionen ist, ähnlich wie schon den Posaunenvisionen (vgl. 8,2-5), ein himmlisches Vorspiel vorangestellt, das den Deuteschlüssel für das Folgende liefern soll'; J. Roloff, *Offenbarung*, pp. 156-57.

51. Cf. U. B. Müller, *Offenbarung*, p. 273; H. Giesen, *Offenbarung*, p. 342.

52. The eschatological signs for the Roman Empire are destroyed, God's signs remain.

53. Cf. U. B. Müller, *Offenbarung*, p. 279.

54. U. B. Müller, *Offenbarung*, p. 278, argues: 'Wichtig ist die Beobachtung, daß die Plagen die treuen Christen aussparen'. (H. Giesen, *Offenbarung*, p. 179: 'Gott setzt sich durch').

55. Cf. K.-P. Jörns, *Das hymnische Evangelium: Untersuchungen zu Aufbau, Funktion und Herkunft der hymnischen Stücke in der Johannesoffenbarung* (SNT, 5; Gütersloh: Mohn, 1971).

56. H. Giesen, *Offenbarung*, p. 342: 'Wie in den übrigen Lobliedern der Offb lässt der Seher seine Adressaten wissen, dass die zu berichtenden Gerichtsgeschehen für die Glaubenden Heil bedeuten.' For the political dimension of the holiness see T. Söding, 'Heilig, heilig, heilig: Zur politischen Theologie der Johannes-Apokalypse', *ZTK* 96 (1999), pp. 49–76.

revenge,[57] his judgement and justice towards the faithful Christians (see the 'doxology of judgment', 16.5-7). The plagues (16.9, 11, 21), and the hardness of the addressee's heart,[58] have the parenetical and pedagogic aim, to convert[59] the followers of the Roman Emperor Cult from idolatry (16.11, 21) and to encourage Christians not to join this group.[60] At least, the plagues' intention is to make preparation for the final eschatological battle at the day of judgement (16.12).

Now we can return to the problems with God's theodicy mentioned at the beginning. The bowls of God's wrath are an answer to the faithfulness and stability of Christians. Whilst they punish the followers of the Roman Emperor Cult they are a reward for the believers. Justice is therefore not a static term, but a dynamic expression of appropriateness, which articulates God's solidarity with his people. The author of Revelation can only imagine justice if God takes the destruction of the adversaries literally. The destruction of the godless correlates with the justice the believers are given. God implements his salvation.

The text affects the various recipients differently and creates either consolation, horror or anxiety. John's strict dualism[61] is contrary to our way of thinking. It is typical of the apocalyptic genre and the author's perspective. He expresses his opinion on the Roman Emperor Cult against the backdrop of oppression, as is made visible by diverse indicators. The dualism replies to the question of the martyrs in 6.10: 'Sovereign Lord, holy and true, how long will it be before you judge and avenge our blood on the inhabitants of the earth?'

---

57. Cf. 2.22-23; see J. Roloff, *Offenbarung*, p. 162.

58. Cf. H. Giesen, *Offenbarung*, p. 348.

59. The OT motif of pilgrimage of peoples to Jerusalem occurs in 15.4; cf. H. Giesen, *Offenbarung*, p. 345.

60. Cf. H. Giesen, *Offenbarung*, p. 180.

61. U. B. Müller, *Offenbarung*, p. 283: 'Fragt man nach dem Wirklichkeitsverständnis, das die Plagenreihe prägt, so ist vor einer bloß metaphorischen Auslegung zu warnen (Günther, U.B. Müller). Gerade die wiederholte Formel "und es wurde" zeigt an, dass der Verfasser z.B. eine wunderbare Verwandlung von Wasser zu Blut für real hält (Vers 3f.). Es geht um wirkliche Geschwüre (Vers 2). Dementsprechend hat man auch die Plagen, die die letzten drei Schalenengel auslösen, so wörtlich wie möglich zu nehmen. Bei 16,10f. handelt es sich um eine tatsächliche Verfinsterung im Reich des Tieres, nicht um ein Symbol für die Zweifel und Ängste, die die Menschen jenes Reiches ergreifen (Caird). Gleiches gilt für die in der letzten Plage beschriebenen Einzelereignisse: das Erdbeben, der Zerfall der großen Stadt in drei Teile, der Einsturz der übrigen Städte, das Verschwinden von Inseln und Bergen. Hier nur Metaphern für die umfassende Vernichtung der Macht des Römischen Reiches zu sehen (Caird), übersieht das gegenständliche Denken des apokalyptischen Autors, der die sichtbaren Ereignisse nicht nur als äußere Form für einen Gedanken oder eine Idee betrachtet. Die Engel, die die Schalen ausgießen, lösen auf wunderhaft-magische Weise reale Geschehen aus, die für den Verfasser so wirklich sind wie sonstige Wundertaten für den antiken Wunderglauben.'

5. The Signs That are Done: σημεῖον + ποιέω

a. Revelation 13.13-14: The Signs of the Beast That Rose from the Earth

Among the four references to signs in Revelation, those in Rev. 13.13-14 are the first connected with the beast from the earth. Both the eschatological character of the beast and its repercussion within verses 11-17 are dealt with here in detail.

Beside the three foul spirits in 16.13, the origin of this beast alone is mentioned. It rises out of the earth (v. 11) and is introduced as 'another beast' after the dragon and the beast from the sea. The motif of the land could identify the beast as Behemoth (Leviathan lives in the abyss of the sea). Its two horns recall the appearance of the lamb, its manner of speaking is reminiscent of the dragon. It has the power of the first beast (v. 12), its name is identical with the number of its name and of a human being: 666 (vv. 18-19).[62] In the later chapters of Revelation it is equated with the 'false prophet' (16.13; 19.20; 20.10) for its deeds, and the execution of signs.

The beast from the earth performs great signs (ποιεῖ σημεῖα μεγάλα) and makes fire come down from heaven. It is the sign of Elia, which has ambivalent meaning in Revelation, because it is also used as a plague of God.

1. When the first angel blew his trumpet in 8.7 fire falls on earth as God's plague (καὶ ἐγένετο χάλαζα καὶ πῦρ μεμιγμένα ἐν αἵματι καὶ ἐβλήθη εἰς τὴν γῆν).
2. Fire comes out of the mouths of the horses as the sixth angel blows his trumpet (ἐκ τοῦ πυρὸς καὶ τοῦ καπνοῦ καὶ τοῦ θείου τοῦ ἐκπορευομένου ἐκ τῶν στομάτων αὐτῶν, 9.18).
3. The fourth angel with the bowl causes the sun to scorch men with its fire (καὶ ἐδόθη αὐτῷ καυματίσαι τοὺς ἀνθρώπους ἐν πυρί, 16.8)
4. Finally fire comes down from heaven while judgement is passed on Satan (20.9). The sign of the beast from earth has a pseudo-religious character that wants to convince men of the divine character of the Emperor Cult.

When God himself also uses fire from heaven in Revelation it has another meaning:

1. A plague warning the followers of the Emperor Cult (cf. 8.7 within the context of 9.4)
2. An educational method to turn men from idolatry (cf. 9.18 within the context of 9.20 and 16.8 within the context of 16.9)
3. The way of destroying God's opponents (20.9)

Thus, fire falling from heaven has an ambivalent meaning and is not easily interpreted. It is thus necessary to differentiate. On the one hand, fire caused by God does not lead to the temptation (cf. 20.14) to admire the works of creation or

62. Different interpretations of the number 666 exist among scholars; cf. H. Giesen, *Offenbarung*, pp. 316–19.

power, but urges conversion to God. On the other hand, it wants to protect the faithful Christians from their opponents by destroying their antagonists. The same sign has two different meanings and effects. It can only be evaluated correctly by taking its context into account.

Essentially, the beast from the earth has an impact in four different ways: three of them are closely connected with idolatry, all four with the Roman Emperor Cult. So the beast instructs men to make an image of the first beast (13.14), gives breath to it (v. 15), so that the image of the beast should even speak, and it causes those who would not worship the image of the beast to be slain (v. 15). Furthermore, it effectuates a mark on the right hand or the forehead[63] so that no one can buy or sell without this mark (vv. 16-17). All effects and tasks are connected with the propaganda mechanisms of the cult. The beast lures people into worshipping the Roman Emperor as a divine person (2.20; 12.9; 13.14; 20.10: πλανάω) like the false prophetess Jezebel (2.20). There is a close connection between the beast from the earth and the false prophetess by the verb πλανάω and the identification with it in 16.13; 19.20; 20.10. This shows that one can surmise that early Christian and apocalyptic experience of false prophets, appearing in the last days and trying to test Christians' faith by signs, is the background of the text (cf. Mt. 7.15; 24.11, 24; Mk 13.22 – strangely, Luke does not speak about false prophets within the context of his apocalyptic sections).[64] This happens by glorifying propagandistic proclamation of the first beast and confusing signs (ποιεῖ σημεῖα μεγάλα).

The historical identity of the beast from the earth is disputed. One suggestion says that it was a priest with state-approved authorization, who achieved his goal – the Emperor Cult – with propagandistic tricks in Asia Minor.[65] More convincing is the thesis that a separate group propagated the Roman Emperor Cult.[66] The beast is not completely identical with the Roman Emperor, 'it appears as antichrist time and time again in the powers and rulers of history, who resist Christ and his community'.[67]

The beast from the earth can be understood as a minister of propaganda, its signs as 'Schauwunder mit propagandistischem Effekt, dazu bestimmt, die Menschen zu blenden und unter die Macht zu versklaven'.[68] J. Roloff compares the beast's signs with those of the two witnesses, who also throw fire from heaven. But the beast's intention is different: it wants to establish a reign that is already deprived of power by God and that has no future. We cannot be certain whether and to what extent John is alluding to historical events of his day, since the interpretation is determined by traditional *topoi* such as demonic imitation of God's signs (cf. Exod. 7.11).[69]

---

63. The mark could mean a tattoo, cf. H. Giesen, *Offenbarung*, p. 314. J. Roloff, *Offenbarung*, p. 255 argues for a metaphorical meaning.
64. J. Roloff, *Offenbarung*, p. 139.
65. J. Roloff, *Offenbarung*, p. 140.
66. Cf. H. Giesen, *Offenbarung*, p. 311.
67. H. Giesen, *Offenbarung*, p. 427.
68. J. Roloff, *Offenbarung*, p. 141.
69. J. Roloff, *Offenbarung*, p. 141.

b. Revelation 16.13-14: The Signs of the Three Foul Spirits
The three foul spirits are the penultimate eschatological signs in the book of
Revelation. They coincide with the climax of all the signs, the plague of the sixth
of the seven angels with bowls, who prepares the way for the kings and assembles
them for battle on the great day of God. The foul spirits do not become victims
of the plagues, but instead they cause them;[70] that means: God uses his opponents
to initiate a battle against themselves.

The origin of the three foul spirits like frogs[71] is described in the same way as
the beast from the earth. They come from the mouth of the dragon, the beast and
false prophet (v. 13). This origin is reminiscent of their nature as opponents of God
and Christians. Three different actions are connected with them:

1. Performing signs (v. 14)
2. Going abroad to the kings of the whole world (v. 14)
3. Assembling them for the last battle (vv. 14, 16) in Harmagedon (v. 16)

The foul spirits unleash the last battle on the great day of God. That means that
they precipitate their own destruction by gathering all inferior earthly powers to
battle against God.

The consequence of the sixth plague of the bowls of wrath is that the water of
the Euphrates dries up. Afterwards three foul spirits like frogs appear (v. 13), from
the mouth of the dragon and from the mouth of the beast and from the mouth
of the false prophet, and perform signs. Another function is that they go abroad
to the kings of the whole earth, to gather them for the last day (v. 14) – in
Hebrew, Harmagedon (v. 16). Just as the dragon and the beast from the sea, the
foul spirits assemble for battle (v. 14: εἰς τὸν πόλεμον / πολεμέω; cf. the dragon:
12.7[3],17; the beast from the sea: 13.4, 7).

c. Revelation 19.20: The Signs of the False Prophet
Revelation 19.19-20 speaks about the eschatological battle that is prepared and
announced in 16.13-14. The beast and the kings of the earth have gathered with
their armies for battle. The beast and false prophet, who is responsible for the signs
of temptation, are thrown alive into the lake of fire that burns with sulphur.[72]

This last occurrence of signs in Revelation speaks only of the beast and false
prophet. The verse consists of three parts: twice the destruction of the beast and
false prophet is mentioned within an *inclusio*. This event is introduced by a
passivum divinum of πιάζω (v. 20a) and further refined by the description of the
fact that the two evil characters are thrown alive into the lake of fire that burns

70. J. Roloff, *Offenbarung*, p. 163.
71. Βάτραχος is a *hapax legomenon*; the image of the frogs is used to depict impure demons;
cf. H. Giesen, *Offenbarung*, p. 357. It is an allusion to Exod. 7.26–8.11 (cf. also Pss. 78.45;
105.30; Wis. 19.10).
72. Cf. H. Giesen, *Offenbarung*, p. 427, who argues for Sodom and Gomorrah (Gen. 19.24)
as the OT pre-text.

with sulphur (βάλλω). Two reasons are mentioned for their destruction: the causing of signs and the tempting of those who are marked.

ἐπιάσθη τὸ θηρίον καὶ μετ' αὐτοῦ ὁ ψευδοπροφήτης
    ὁ ποιήσας τὰ σημεῖα ἐνώπιον αὐτοῦ
    ἐν οἷς ἐπλάνησεν τοὺς λαβόντας τὸ χάραγμα τοῦ θηρίου καὶ τοὺς
    προσκυνοῦντας τῇ εἰκόνι αὐτοῦ
    ζῶντες ἐβλήθησαν οἱ δύο εἰς τὴν λίμνην τοῦ πυρὸς τῆς καιομένης ἐν θείῳ

                                                                    (19.20)

The temptation by the false prophet to accept the mark of the Emperor Cult is limited in time. All eschatological figures responsible for signs of temptation are destroyed by God, by his plagues and by the last eschatological battle. With that, God's signs are proved to be great (12.1) and wonderful (15.1). They are not propaganda, that influences and tempts men, but visible and effective signs for everybody (12.1, 3 – ὤφθη) or rather on John's behalf (15.1 – εἶδον).

The climax of God's signs are the seven angels with bowls, who pour out the last plague, God's wrath, on earth. Moreover, one of these angels shows the holy city Jerusalem to the Lamb's bride. The plagues caused by the angels renew the sight of God's presence again. The closed temple in 15.8 – the temple was filled with smoke from the glory of God and from his power, and no one could enter the temple until the seven plagues of the seven angels were ended – becomes accessible again, but with a difference: In the holy city Jerusalem a temple is no longer necessary because the Lord God the Almighty and the Lamb are its temple (21.22). The signs connected with the Emperor Cult and the temptation of men are finally destroyed. God's signs receive his protection (woman of light) or reveal – as the seventh angel with the bowl – the bride of the Lamb (21.9).

All four signs are closely connected with the Emperor Cult. The following excursus analyses this aspect, especially its linguistical expression and OT background.

6. Excursus: Old Testament Polemic Against Idols as Background for the Book of Revelation

Repeatedly we have argued for the Emperor Cult and Gentile religions as the historical background of the book of Revelation. Within the following excursus we will analyse the language and the expressions John uses to describe these two phenomena of Gentile society. Furthermore, we will ask for the OT pre-texts.[73] It is obvious that the Old Testament has shaped John's Apocalypse, so that we can suppose the same background for the interpretation of the socio-ecclesiastical problems John is responding to.

References to the Roman Emperor Cult and its threat for the Christians can be recognized in *metaphorical* descriptions of certain figures: Dragon, Devil, Satan, throne of Satan, snake, the beast and its number, the false prophet, demon,

---

73. Cf. A. van Schaik, 'De Apocalyps als tekstmozaïek', *Schrift* 114 (1987), pp. 231–34.

Babylon. They are also discernible in John's polemical descriptions of the cult and its practices, such as idolatry, blasphemy and immorality, adoration of the beast and its image, and the mark on the forehead of its followers.

John does not describe the Emperor Cult in sober, objective terms, but in metaphorical–polemical language. The metaphors stigmatize the figures, who are connected with the Emperor Cult – the Emperor or his 'propaganda minister' – with negative metaphors and the identification as false prophets, that received their power from the dragon described as the evil, devil or snake. Demonic and satanic powers are ascribed to him. The practices of the Emperor Cult are polemically characterized by the semantic domains of idols and blasphemy. Its followers, the opponents of the Christians, are polemically named as worshippers of idols, liars, wizards, Nicolaitans, supporters of Balaam and Jezebel.

With that a clear evaluation is given, which describes the cultic veneration and adoration of God in positive terms, but uses negative words for the divine veneration and adoration of the Emperor. The linguistic expression shows a polemic against idols, perfected by accentuating God's good qualities and his conduct towards the faithful Christians. For the moment, the followers of the Roman Emperor Cult have social advantages, since they are not isolated. They are enabled to do a great deal during the sacrificial feasts. That is why they get rich and acquire a good social reputation. However, the faithful Christians have to live in poverty (cf. πτωχεία, 2.9; πτωχός, 3.17; 13.16). Conspicuously John speaks more about the short-lived richness of the followers of the Roman Emperor Cult than about the poverty of the Christians. Rather, the images of salvation are also characterized by richness. Richness occurs within a limited time frame (πλουτέω, 3.17-18; 18.3, 15, 19; πλοῦτος, 18.17). It will be destroyed (cf. Rev. 18, especially vv. 9-17 and the verbs στρηνιάω 18.7, 9; ἀγοράζω, referring to salvation, 13.17; 18.11;[74] πλουτέω, to the list of products in vv. 12-14, 16) and the social situation will be reversed.

The Roman Emperor Cult is clearly observable in the statements about God, his reign and exclusive holiness. The climax of John's theology – beside the accentuation in 4.11: ὁ κύριος καὶ ὁ θεὸς ἡμῶν[75] – is to be found in 15.4: ὅτι μόνος ὅσιος. The climax is placed within the only hymn characterized as the song of Moses and the lamb (15.3: τὴν ᾠδὴν Μωυσέως τοῦ δούλου τοῦ θεοῦ καὶ τὴν ᾠδὴν τοῦ ἀρνίου) and thus as the song of liberation, that reminds of the double exodus:

1. The exodus from Egypt and the salvation from sins
2. The death of Jesus Christ. μόνος ὅσιος understood as the culmination of God's creation in Revelation

The only appropriate answer is for all peoples to adore God. Cultic–liturgical vocabulary (incense, prayers, priests, altar, temple, throne, cf. also the numerous

---

74. Cf. Rev. 3.18; 5.9; 14.3-4.
75. Cf. H. Giesen, *Offenbarung*, 26: God is quite the opposite of the Roman Emperor.

hymns) and God's description as 'him who is and who was and who is to come', or 'the Alpha and the Omega,' – cf. the christological titles 'I am the first and I am the last' and the 'the beginning of God's creation' – and 'the almighty' are closely connected with the semantic domains of omnipotence and exclusive adoration of God.

Therefore John's concern is to prove God's singular power. Thus, his writing is beholden to the semantic domains of power, war, reign and battle, in which God's power has the first and last word, both at the beginning and at the end of the book (1.4-5; 22.13). Furthermore, John pays attention to God's exclusive holiness and his adoration. His writing pleads for monotheism. One can describe the book of Revelation tentatively as a kind of apocalyptic midrash on Deut. 5. 6-16, the first commandments of the decalogue, that deals with the service for YHWH.

John uses prophetic literature many times throughout his writing, especially from the prophets Daniel, Isaiah and Ezekiel. His idioms in connection with the Roman Imperial Cult originate in the OT polemic against idols, in particular in Deutero-Isaiah ('idol', cf. Isa. 42.17; 44.9, 19; 45.20). He tries to prove that idols are nothing (cf. Isa. 41.24, 29; 44.9) and stigmatizes their worshippers. Idols are not in the position to predict the future (cf. Isa. 41.23; 42.8 – they do not hold the plan, cf. Rev. 5) and, as such, do not have an effect in the world (Isa. 57.13). But God has a plan for mankind, that is known only to him and the lamb. Idols cannot achieve salvation and resurrection by their blood, quite the reverse! They are responsible for the death and martyrdom of Christians, but are unable to liberate mankind. This contrasts with the many allusions to theological themes from Genesis and Exodus in Revelation.

7. The Relevance of the Texts

Definition:[76] At the end of our analysis we can define the meaning of eschatological signs in Revelation. They are signs, good or bad, coming from God or his opponents, that occur within a dramatic time or crisis of faith. They are revealed to the believers or their opponents and bring about the last events.[77] They want to give hope and courage to those who suffer in the crisis. One can recognize God's action in them,[78] reflect on his protection and care for the faithful Christians, but

---

76. Cf. D. E. Aune, *Revelation*, vol. II, p. 679: '(1) *a characteristic mark by which something is known or recognized* (Gen 1:14; Exod 12:13; Josh 2:12; Matt 16:3; 26:48); (2) *a monument that is a reminder of a past event* (Gen 9:12, 17; 17:11; Exod 13:9; Deut 6:8; 11:18); (3) *an omen or indication of something to come* (2 Kgs 19:29; Isa 7:14; Ezek 4:3; Matt 24:3; Luke 21:11; 25; Acts 2:19); (4) *a miracle*, which may be either genuine (Exod 7:3; Josh 24:17; Ps 77:43; Mark 16:20; John 2:11; 4:48; 6:30; 1 Cor 14:22) or a lie (Mark 13:22 = Matt 24:24; 2 Thess 2:9-10; Rev. 13:13-14; 16:14); or (5) *a constellation*, for in Greco-Roman astrological lore the Greek term σημεῖον could mean "constellation".'

77. Cf. U. B. Müller, *Offenbarung*, p. 231.

78. According to R. Rengstorff, σημεῖον, in *TWNT* 7 (1964), pp. 199–268 (202, 205): σημεῖον means an 'optisches Zeichen, an dem man jemand oder etwas erkennt', 'im übertr. Sinn; Erkenntnis und Entschluß in einer auf den einzelnen zugespitzten und ihm nicht abzunehmenden Weise'. A

also on his accusation and revenge towards the unbelievers. The characters representing the Roman Emperor Cult who produce signs are destroyed at the end, but the effect of God's signs last. The Gentile cults, and among them especially the Roman Emperor Cult, form the socio-religious background of the crisis that makes the Christians suffer.

Literary function: The eschatological signs have different literary functions depending on their position in the macro-text of Revelation. They are to be found around the literary climax in Revelation. The dramatic tension is emphasized by the use of mythical material (esp. chs. 12–13) and the declaration, just before the last series of plagues, that no one can enter God's temple until the last plagues are ended (15.8).[79] The actual order of the seven signs has a special meaning. It appears to be the biblical principle of hope that signs of God's salvation appear before any evil occurs. Another aspect of the relation between the two signs in heaven, the woman of light and the dragon, is that they are antitypes who reflect the battle between Good and Evil, between God's people and its opponents. Chapters 12 and 16 of Revelation emphasize two different aspects that belong together just like two sides of the same coin. Revelation 12 underlines God's protection and care for the Christians,[80] while the bowls of God's wrath in Revelation 16 speak about the destruction of the opponents of God and his people. Both perspectives reveal one picture. They emphasize God's omnipotence and justice.[81] God's judgements demand that he alone be worshipped (15.48).[82] Thus, the biblical connotation of justice is obvious. It is not a static but a dynamic term of relation. In our context the relation between God and man is considered. The biblical meaning of justice asks mankind to decide in favour of God.

σημεῖον is an object of sensual detection (p. 209) 'und dient als Mittel der Vergewisserung' (p. 211). 'Wenn im AT von Gottes Zeichen und Wundern die Rede ist, dann fast immer in Bezug auf den Exodus'. Rengstorff again: 'Dabei ist wesentlich, dass die Vorgänge selbst stumm sind und dass Israel seinerseits zunächst – und dies darf nicht übersehen werden – das wortlose Objekt dieses Geschehens ist. Alles Gewicht liegt in der Wendung "Zeichen und Wunder" also von Haus aus bei dem Geschehen als solchem in seiner Eigenschaft als göttliches Wirken' (p. 214).

79. 'Gerade durch diesen letzten Hinweis wird deutlich, dass es der Offb als ein erklärtes Hauptziel um die alleinige Anerkennung und anbetende Verehrung Gottes geht (erstes Gebot! – "Ihr Gott duldet keinen anderen neben sich. Er fordert den Menschen ganz; er ist aber auch ganz für den Menschen da")'; H. Giesen, *Offenbarung*, p. 28. See also B. Kowalski, '"sie werden Priester Gottes und des Messias sein; und sie werden König sein mit ihm – tausend Jahre lang" (Offb 20,6): Martyrium und Auferstehung in der Offenbarung des Johannes', *SNTU.A* 26 (2001), pp. 139–63.

80. Cf. U. B. Müller, *Offenbarung*, p. 272.

81. Cf. J. Roloff, *Offenbarung*, p. 121.

82. U. B. Müller, *Offenbarung*, p. 272, who interprets 15.3-4 as the salvation of the Christians. The admission to God is refused in 15:8, and heaven is not opened up before 19.11 (parallel to 4.1).

Theological meaning: It is clear in the eschatological signs described in Revelation that every evil of the world will be destroyed by God. Thus, the signs are closely related to theodicy, but also to creation and liberation theology. The signs, woman of light, dragon and angels with bowls of wrath, are coupled with terms of creation theology, so that they can be understood as works of a new creation.[83] A second OT background is the exodus tradition, that interpretes eschatological events as acts of liberation.

Actual meaning: Finally, we will take a look at the topical relevance of this subject. Surely, it is not easily possible to draw direct lines between Revelation and our situation, since our problem as Christians is not the Roman Emperor Cult. But Revelation confronts us with the question of how we can encounter the indifference of modern societies, how seriously we take our own decisions as Christians, and what kind of gods/idols we worship beside the Holy Trinity. We have to pay attention not to identify the wars and dramatic world events as eschatological signs of the final events. All biblical writings have one thing in common: we do not know the date of the last day, but what is given instead is the commandment to stay on the alert for the signs of the time and God's way of revelation.

---

83. The description of the woman and the dragon, with the cosmic imagery used, clearly refers to Gen. 1–3. For this reason, the eschatological sign they reflect should be interpreted as a sign of the new creation. Creation theology is also present in the references to God as 'creator' (Rev. 1.8; 4.8; 11.17; 15.3; 16.7, 14; 19.6, 15; 21.22), the election of the creatures (3.14; 13.8; 17.8), and the act of creation itself (4,11; 10.6; 14.7). The second OT tradition that influenced this scene in Revelation is that of Exodus. It is present in the description of the woman's fleeing to the desert and her maintenance there, as well as the fact that the earth comes to the rescue of the woman (12.16). For this point, see J. Dochhorn, 'Und die Erde tat ihren Mund auf: Ein Exodusmotiv in Apc 12,16', *ZNW* 88 (1997), pp. 140–42; G. S. Adamsen, *Exodusmotiver i Johannes's Åbenbaring* (Aarhus: Århus, Teol-tryk, 1992). H. Giesen, *Offenbarung*, p. 342, considers 15.2 to be reminiscent of Exod. 7.1–11.10. Cf. also G. K. Beale, *Revelation*, p. 633 (and his Excursus pp. 643–45), who points at 11.6, 8; 12.13-17; 13.1-3; 15.2-4.

PART III

CANNIBALS, MYRMIDONIANS, SINOPEANS OR JEWS? THE FIVE VERSIONS OF *THE ACTS OF ANDREW AND MATTHIAS* AND THEIR SOURCE(S)

Lautaro Roig Lanzillotta

In spite of the abundant scholarly literature on the *Acts of Andrew* (*AA*) that has appeared in recent years, the question of whether or not the story of the *Acts of Andrew and Matthias in the City of Cannibals* (*AAM*) belongs to the primitive textual core is still a matter of controversy today.[1] As early as 1883, R. A. Lipsius claimed not only that *AAM* belonged to the ancient *Acts*, but also that it allowed us to recognize the unquestionable gnostic nature of the primitive text.[2] Admittedly, Lipsius' criteria for stating the Gnosticism of *AAM* are no longer tenable,[3] but the problem concerning its textual relationship with *AA* is still an open matter. In point of fact, the last two textual reconstructions of the ancient *Acts*, by J. M. Prieur and D. R. MacDonald, come to different conclusions, since they exclude and include, respectively, the story of the man-eaters from their editions of the *Acts of Andrew*.[4] This disagreement is nothing new, since both hypotheses have had their supporters throughout the twentieth century.[5]

---

1. References to *AAM* follow M. Bonnet's edition in *Acta Apostolorum Apocrypha* II-1 (Leipzig: Mendelssohn, 1898), pp. 65–127.

2. R. A. Lipsius, *Die apokryphen Apostelgeschichten und Apostellegenden: Ein Beitrag zur altchristlichen Literaturgeschichte* I (Braunschweig: Schwetschke, 1883), p. 590.

3. Among the gnostic traces, he mentions Christ's manifestation as a child in *AAM* 18 (87.3ff), as light and voice in *AAM* 3 (67.6ff) and 4 (68.12ff), 22 (94.9-97.9), as a pilot in *AAM* 5 (69.14-71.3), the fantastic journey in *AAM* 3ff and Andrew's invisibility (99.13-101.10). R. A. Lipsius also recognizes traces of gnostic theology in *AAM* 6 (71.4-72.11) and 10 (76.9-77.10). Also, the narration about the sphinx in *AAM* 12-15 (78.9ff) betrays, in his view, gnostic traces. J. D. Kaestli, 'Les principales orientations de la recherche sur les Actes apocryphes des Apôtres', in F. Bovon *et al.*, *Les Actes apocryphes des Apôtres: Christianisme et monde païen* (Publications de la Faculté de Théologie de l'Université de Genève, 4; Geneva: Labor et Fides, 1981), pp. 49–67 (49), and J. M. Prieur, *Acta Andreae* (Turnhout: Brepols, 1989), p. 137, have rightly remarked that Lipsius' criteria are outdated. The Gnosticism of the primitive *Acts of Andrew* has also been claimed by other authors and on more consistent basis, see our *The Apocryphal Acts of Andrew: A New Approach to the Character, Thought and Meaning of the Primitive Text* (Diss. University of Groningen, 2004), pp. 56–57; see also our conclusions in pp. 343–47.

4. J. M. Prieur, *Acta*; D. R. MacDonald, *The Acts of Andrew in the City of the Cannibals* (SBLTT, 33; Christian apocrypha series, 1; Atlanta: Scholars Press, 1990).

5. For the inclusion of *AAM* in the primitive *Acts*, see R. A. Lipsius, *Die apokryphen*

The purpose of the present contribution is certainly not to reopen this old controversy, since a definitive answer to the problem appears to be unviable on the basis of the textual material available today. Rather, it intends to draw attention to some aspects that, although very relevant to the discussion about the textual relationship between *AA* and *AAM*, are usually neglected by most discussions on the issue. A reconsideration of these aspects will allow us, if not to reach a definitive solution, at least to show that, as is usually the case, the truth of the matter may not be on either side, but somewhere in the middle.

1. Different Versions of the Story of Andrew and Matthias

The text of *AAM* presents the longest and most developed version of the adventures of the apostle Andrew when rescuing his friend Matthias from prison. This text was very popular throughout the Middle Ages and, owing to numerous versions in different languages,[6] is the best-known among scholars today. Consequently, both supporters and detractors of the story belonging to the ancient *Acts of Andrew* tend to consider *AAM* as the 'original' account of the episode.

As a matter of fact, however, in addition to *AAM* we have at our disposal four other texts that include a version of the story, namely the *Liber de miraculis Andreae apostoli* by Gregory of Tours (*Epitome*),[7] the anonymous so-called *Narratio*,[8] the *Acta Andreae apostoli cum laudatione contexta* (*Laudatio*)[9] and the *Vita Andreae*

Apostelgeschichten; O. Bardenhewer, *Geschichte der altchristlichen Literatur: 1 Vom Ausgang des apostolischen Zeitalters bis zum Ende des zweiten Jahrhunderts* (Darmstadt: WBG, 1962 [Repr. of Freiburg im Breisgau: Herder, 2nd edn, 1913]) 568–74; T. Schermann, 'Review Flamion', *TRu* 10 (1912), pp. 300–303; R. Söder, *Die apokryphen Apostelgeschichten und die romanhafte Literatur der Antike* (Darmstadt: WBG, repr. 1969), p. 14; M. Blumenthal, *Formen und Motive in apokryphen Apostelgeschichten* (TU, 48.1; Leipzig: Hinrichs, 1933), pp. 38–57; D. R. MacDonald, *The Acts of Andrew*. For its exclusion, see J. Flamion, *Les Actes Apocryphes de l'Apôtre André: Les Actes d'André et de Matthias, de Pierre et d'André et les textes apparentés* (Recueil de travaux, 33; Louvain: Bureau du Recueil, 1911), pp. 302ff; M. R. James, *The Apocryphal New Testament, being the Apocryphal Gospels, Acts, Epistles, and Apocalypses with Other Narrations and Fragments Newly Translated* (Oxford: Clarendon, 1924), F. Dvornik, *The Idea of Apostolicity in Byzantium and the Legend of the Apostle Andrew* (DOS, 4; Cambridge: Harvard University Press, 1958); M. Erbetta, *Gli Apocrifi del Nuovo Testamento* II: *Atti e leggende: versione e commento* (Casale: Marietti, 1966), pp. 393–449; L. Moraldi, *Apocrifi del Nuovo Testamento* II (Torino: Unione tipogr., 1971), pp. 1351–429 and, especially, J. M. Prieur, *Acta*.

6.   The story's popularity is obvious from the large number of translations, résumés and recasts of *AAM* not only in numerous oriental languages, but also in occidental ones. For the different ancient versions in Latin, Coptic, Armenian, Ethiopic, Syriac and Arabic, see below notes 12–17 and our *The Apocryphal Acts of Andrew: A New Approach to the Character, Thought and Meaning of the Primitive Text*, 1–3.

7.   M. Bonnet, 'Georgii Florentii Gregorii Episcopi Turonensis liber de miraculis Beati Andreae Apostoli', in B. Krusch (ed), *Monumenta Germaniae historica: Scriptores rerum merovingicarum* I.2 (Hannover: Hahn, 1969) pp. 371–96 [Reprint of Hannover: Hahn, 1885].

8.   M. Bonnet, 'Martyrium sancti apostoli Andreae', *ABo* 13 (1894) 353–72. Bonnet first called it 'martyrium', but see his *praefatio* to *AAA* II.1, XIV.

9.   M. Bonnet, 'Acta Andreae apostoli cum laudatione contexta', *ABo* 13 (1894) 309–52.

by Epiphanius the Monk (*Vita*).[10] These versions are generally believed to depend upon *AAM* in the scholarly literature, although as far as we know, not a single study has ever established such a relationship of dependence on the basis of a serious textual comparative analysis of the versions. In what follows we offer a detailed analysis of the different accounts that may allow us to, firstly, to highlight convergences and divergences between the versions in order to determine, secondly, the textual relationship between them.

a. The Acts of Andrew and Matthias in the City of Cannibals
This text was originally written in Greek, and was published by M. Bonnet on the basis of numerous manuscripts dating from the ninth to the sixteenth centuries.[11] The lengthy, incomplete text ends abruptly and none of the later versions in Latin,[12] Coptic,[13] Armenian,[14] Ethiopic,[15] Syriac[16] and Arabic[17] help us to

10.   A. Dressel, 'Epiphanii monachi et presbyteri de vita et actibus et morte sancti, et plane laudandi, et primi vocati inter alios apostolos Andreae', in *Epiphanii monachi et presbyteri edita et inedita* (Paris: Avenarius; Leipzig: Brockhaus, 1843) pp. 45–82 [*PG* 120, cols. 216–60].

11.   M. Bonnet, *AAA* II.1, 65–127.

12.   F. Blatt, *Die lateinischen Bearbeitungen der 'Acta Andreae et Matthiae apud Anthropophagos'* (BZNW, 12; Giessen: Töpelmann, 1930), pp. 32–95 (recensio Casanatensis) and pp. 96–148 (recensio Vaticana).

13.   Several Coptic fragments have been preserved: 1) Coptic Fayyumic fragments 6–9 in ms Copt. Tischendorfianus VI, see O. von Lemm, 'Koptische apokryphe Apostelacten', *BASStP* N.S. 1 (33) (1890), pp. 558–76; 2) Coptic Sahidic fragment in ms Vindobonensis K 9576, f. 75, first edited by C. Wessely, *SPP* 18 (1917), pp. 72–73. Reprinted and translated by E. Lucchesi and J. M. Prieur, 'Fragments coptes des Actes d'André et Matthias et d'André et Barthélemy', *ABo* 96 (1978) 339–50; 3) Coptic fragment in Papyrus Copt. Amherst-Morgan 14 published and translated by W. E. Crum, *Theological Texts from Coptic Papyri* (Anecdota Oxoniensia, II; Semitic Series 1.12; Oxford: Clarendon Press, 1913), pp. 64–65. Further, E. Lucchesi and J. M. Prieur, 'Fragments Coptes', pp. 348–49.

14.   There are two independent versions of *AAM*, a long and a short, which were edited by C. Tchékarian, *Ankanon Girk' arak'elakank' [Non-Canonical Apostolic Writings. Armenian Treasury of Ancient and Recent Texts 3]* (Venice, 1904), pp. 146–67, 168–73, respectively. Translated into French by L. Leloir, *Écrits Apocryphes sur les Apôtres. Traduction de l'édition arménienne de Venise* I: *Pierre, Paul, André, Jacques, Jean* (Turnhout: Brepols, 1986), pp. 205–27.

15.   There are two versions in Ethiopic as well. The long version was edited by E. A. W. Budge on the basis of two mss under the title 'The Acts of Saints Matthias and Andrew', in E. A. W. Budge, *The Contendings of the Apostles* I: *Ethiopic Texts* (London: Henry Frowde, 1899), pp. 307–35. Translated into English by E. A. W. Budge under the title 'The Preaching of Saint Matthias', in E. A. W. Budge, *The Contendings of the Apostles* II. *The English Translations* (London: Henry Frowde, 1901), pp. 370–403. The short version was published by Budge under the title 'The Preaching of Saint Matthew (sic)', in E. A. W. Budge, *Contendings* I, 225–42. Translated into English by E. A. W. Budge under the title 'The Preaching of Saint Matthias in the City of Cannibals', in E. A. W. Budge, *Contendings* II, pp. 267–88.

16.   W. Wright, *Apocryphal Acts of the Apostles* I (London: Williams and Norgate, 1871), pp. 102–26. English translation, W. Wright, 'The History of Mar Matthew and Mar Andrew, the Blessed Apostles, when they converted the City of Dogs, the inhabitants of which were cannibals', in *Apocryphal Acts of the Apostles* II: *English Translations* (London: Williams and Norgate, 1871), pp. 93–115.

17.   A. Smith Lewis, 'Acta mythologica apostolorum', *HorSem* 3 (1904), pp. 109–18. English translation, idem, 'The Mythological Acts of the Apostles', *HorSem* 4 (1904), pp. 126–36.

complete the development of certain events that in *AAM* do not find a proper solution.[18] Its date of composition is uncertain, although Flamion at the beginning of the twentieth century suggested that it was written before the end of the fourth century.[19]

The *Acts of Andrew and Matthias* begins with the casting of lots and with Matthias' departure for his field of activity (1). On his arrival in the city of the cannibals, Matthias is imprisoned, but the cannibals, after gouging out his eyes and giving him a magical drug, delay his sacrifice for thirty days in order to fatten him up (2). While Matthias is praying, a light shines and Matthias gets back his sight. Jesus announces to Matthias that after twenty-seven days he will be released by Andrew (3). Consequently, three days before his captors will have Matthias for dinner, Jesus appears to Andrew and compels him to go to rescue his friend (4), which he does after a miraculous trip in a ship piloted by Jesus himself in disguise. Without knowing the real identity of his interlocutor, Andrew has a long conversation with Jesus (5-15), which includes the long excursus with the episode of the talking sphinxes (13-15).[20]

After this lengthy conversation, Andrew falls asleep and Jesus orders his angels to transport the apostle and his disciples ashore (16). Next morning, when they awake, they first marvel at the miraculous trip, but also immediately understand the true identity of the pilot (17). They all rejoice and Andrew says a prayer inviting Jesus to appear to him again. Jesus fulfils the apostle's wish and orders him to go now to the city prison in order to free Matthias and the rest of the prisoners. He also encourages Andrew to endure his coming sufferings (18).

Here begins the story about the cannibals proper. Invisible to its inhabitants, Andrew and his disciples enter the city of the cannibals. They arrive at the prison and, after a silent prayer by the apostle, its seven guardians drop down dead; Andrew marks the gate with the sign of the cross and it opens of its own accord. Once inside, Andrew salutes his friend Matthias (19) and sees the other prisoners behaving like animals. The apostle pronounces some words in which he accuses Satan of being responsible for the conduct of the cannibals (20). These words prelude the devil's active part in the story in the next chapters.[21] Having restored their sight and understanding, Andrew orders the 270 men and 49 women to wait for him under a fig tree in the lower parts of the city. Andrew then commands a cloud to take Matthias and his own disciples to the mountain where Peter was teaching (21).

18. Thus, for example, Andrew plans to join Peter, Matthias and the liberated prisoners later (*AAM* 93.6-10), but he never does so. The same happens with the order Andrew receives from Jesus to rescue those who have died in the abyss (*AAM* 116.3-4).

19. J. Flamion, *L'Apôtre*, pp. 302ff.

20. This episode was the main argument adduced by J. Flamion, *L'Apôtre*, pp. 310ff, to claim the Egyptian origin of *AAM*, but as F. Dvornik, *Apostolicity*, p. 202, has already pointed out, this theory has its weakness since sphinxes were well known in antiquity in a variety of geographical regions. In addition, the absence of this episode in the other four versions of the story seems to indicate that the writer of *AAM* added it to the primitive account.

21. See *AAM* 91.14-92.15; 99.13-101.10; 103.17-104.2; 104.4-107.2.

As Andrew has freed not only Matthias but also all the other prisoners, the cannibals, confronted with a lack of victims, have to resort to their own people to meet their needs. They will begin with the seven dead guards and continue by killing seven men each day until they get new prisoners. Andrew's intervention frustrates the first part of their plan by turning their hands into stone (22). Becoming hungry, the cannibals proceed to the second part of their plan. When they seize seven old men, one of them gives his two children in exchange for his life. Andrew's intervention, however, once again frustrates the intentions of the executioners (23).

It is at this point that the devil appears to the cannibals in disguise telling them that Andrew is responsible for what is happening and encouraging them to kill him. When the voice of the invisible Andrew rebukes him, the devil renews his invective against the apostle and orders everyone to find him (24). When they fail to do so, however, Andrew follows Jesus' orders and shows himself to them. The cannibals apprehend the apostle, fasten a rope around his neck and drag him through the streets and lanes of the city. Even though his flesh sticks to the ground and his blood flows, the apostle endures the torture and his captors put him into prison (25). Next morning they repeat the same procedure. When, in the evening, they bring the apostle back to prison, the devil and seven demons are waiting for him (26). They try to kill Andrew, but after they fail they mock and humiliate him (27). When the next day they drag the apostle around the city for the third time, Andrew invokes Jesus and complains that his flesh and hair is sticking to the ground. Jesus then tells him to look behind and Andrew sees great trees springing up from his flesh and hair. Again he is put back in prison (28).

Jesus then appears to Andrew in prison and restores him. In the middle of the prison (εἰς μέσον τῆς φυλακῆς) is an alabaster statue standing on a pillar and the apostle compels it to spew an acid flood from its mouth (29).[22] He then asks Jesus to send the Archangel Michael in a cloud of fire and to put a wall around the city so that no one may escape from it, which he does. Seeing that they cannot escape, the cannibals beg Andrew to stop the deadly waters. The apostle, convinced by the repentance of the survivors, commands the statue to stop spewing (30). The old man who had given up his children asks for pity, but Andrew rebukes him. At his prayer the earth opens and the abyss swallows the waters, the fourteen executioners and the old man (31). Andrew then reanimates the victims of the deadly waters, builds a church and baptizes them. The cannibals pray for him to stay, but he does not comply with their request and leaves the city with the intention of joining his disciples (32). However, Jesus orders him to remain in the city for seven more days until the faith of its inhabitants has been confirmed, and to bring up those who remain in the abyss (33).

22. M. Bonnet, *AAM* 110.7-8, καὶ ὑψώθη τὸ ὕδωρ ἐπὶ τὴν γῆν, καὶ ἦν ἁλμυρὸν σφόδρα κατεσθίον σάρκας ἀνθρώπων.

b. The Liber de miraculis Andreae apostoli *of Gregory of Tours*
The Bishop of Tours wrote his abridgement of *AA* at the end of the sixth century.
Throughout the twentieth century numerous scholars have claimed that Gregory's
text preserves the most trustworthy outline of *AA*,[23] although a closer examination
raises serious doubts about this.[24] When his version can be checked against other
texts, it becomes obvious that Gregory freely transforms and significantly abridges
his sources.[25]

The *Epitome* includes a very short version of the story about Andrew and
Matthias in the first chapter of its abridgement of *AA*. On arrival in Myrmidon,[26]
Matthew is captured by its inhabitants.[27] They put out his eyes, load him with
chains, put him in prison and plan to kill him within a few days.[28] But an angel
of the Lord informs Andrew of Matthew's imprisonment and orders him to free
his friend. As Andrew declares that he neither knows the way nor has the means
to get there, the angel tells him that the apostle will find a boat on the seashore
and that he will lead him to that city.[29]

When Andrew arrives in Myrmidon, after entering through the gates he goes
directly to the prison. At the sight of Matthew he begins to cry and to pray; a great
light shines then and Matthew receives his sight back, the chains break and all the

23. See J. Flamion, *L'Apôtre*; M. R. James, *Apocryphal NT*, p. 260; G. Quispel, 'An
Unknown Fragment of the Acts of Andrew', *VC* 10 (1956), pp. 129–48; F. Dvornik, *Apostolicity*,
pp. 192–93; L. Moraldi, *Apocrifi*, pp. 1351–429 and J. M. Prieur, *Acta*, pp. 40–45; M. Hornschuh
and E. Plümacher with reservations (see note 24 below).
24. Already E. Hennecke, *Handbuch zu den neutestamentlichen Apokryphen* (Tübingen:
Mohr, 1904), pp. 544–62 (545–46), expressed his doubts about Gregory's reliability.
M. Hornschuh, 'Andreasakten', in E. Hennecke, W. Schneemelcher, *Neutestamentliche
Apokryphen* II (Tübingen: Mohr Siebeck, 1964), pp. 270–96 (277–80), followed by E. Plümacher,
'Apokryphe Apostelakten', PRES, 15, pp. 11–70: *AA* at 30–34, only retains issues from the
Epitome when they are supported by other testimonies as well. The most critical attitude against
the view that Gregory's *Epitome* is a trustworthy, if abridged, testimony for the reconstruction
of *AA*'s primitive account is in L. Van Kampen, *Apostelverhalen: Doel en Compositie van de
oudste apocriefe Handelingen der apostelen* (Diss. Utrecht, 1990), pp. 160–61; see also his
'Acta Andreae and Gregory's *de miraculis Andreae*', *VC* 45 (1991), pp. 18–26.
25. See, for example, the works by M. Hornschuh and L. Van Kampen quoted in note 24
above.
26. Even though *AAM* does not name the city (see, however, M. Bonnet's *app. ad* 1-2 for the
readings of mss A, 9th century, and N, a. 1307, which mention Sinope in their titles), the Latin
transmission and other later reworkings introduce the variants Myrmidonia, Mermedonia,
Myrmidona, Mermidona. Among the Greek testimonies, the *Martyrium Matthaei* (M. Bonnet,
AAA, 217-61) mentions the name Μύρνη (*MM* 4, 9) and Nicephorus (*HE* 2.41) Μυρμήνη, the
forms which A. von Gutschmid (*Kleine Schriften 2: Schriften zur Geschichte und Literatur der
semitischen Völker und zur älteren Kirchengeschichte* [ed. F. Rühl; Leipzig: Teubner, 1890],
p. 383) traces back to Μυρμηκίων. See S. Reinach, 'Les apôtres chez anthropophages', *RHLR*
9 (1904), pp. 305–20; F. Blatt, *Bearbeitungen*, pp. 6–7. See also n. 38.
27. For the alternation between the forms Matthias/ Matthew, see F. Blatt, *Bearbeitungen*,
p. 6.
28. M. Bonnet, *Epitome* 377.21-28.
29. M. Bonnet, *Epitome* 377.28-33.

captives are set free. Everyone leaves the city, but Andrew remains there to preach the word of God.[30] As the inhabitants know that the apostle is responsible for the liberation of the prisoners, they seize him, fasten a rope around his feet and drag him through the streets of the city; his hair falls out and his blood flows. As Andrew prays God to forgive his captors, the latter in awe release the apostle and beg him to forgive them. Andrew preaches and baptizes them.[31]

c. The Narratio

This text was written in the eighth or ninth century[32] and is the oldest of the comprehensive accounts of Andrew's life and activities.[33] Its anonymous author refers to the use of local traditions and other written sources, as the *Laudatio* and the *Vita* also do.[34] The *Narratio* was first edited by Bonnet from four manuscripts of the tenth to eleventh centuries.[35]

As far as the account provided by the so-called *Narratio* is concerned, it presents a much shorter version of the story than *AAM* but is longer than the *Epitome*. After the first three chapters, which include an account of the apostle Andrew that relies on New Testament tradition,[36] from chapter 4 onwards its anonymous writer describes Andrew's peregrinations. Its version of Andrew's rescue of Matthias occurs in chapters 5–7.[37]

Having visited different sea ports on the Black Sea, Andrew finally arrives in Sinope,[38] the inhabitants of which are a barbarous and bloodthirsty (αἱμοβόροι) people, who behave harshly towards all strangers and have captured, tortured and imprisoned Matthias.[39] When Andrew arrives in that city, he hears that Matthias is being kept captive and goes to the prison with some of his disciples. By means of a prayer he kills the guardians, opens the doors, and frees his friend and the rest of the prisoners.[40]

---

30. M. Bonnet, *Epitome* 377.33–378.11.

31. M. Bonnet, *Epitome* 378.12-24.

32. For the former date, see F. Dvornik, *Apostolicity*, pp. 172–73; for the latter, J. M. Prieur, *Acta*, p. 121, see our *Apocryphal Acts of Andrew*, pp. 5, 81–82, n. 72.

33. Unlike the martyrdom texts that focus exclusively on Andrew's death, *Narratio, Laudatio* and *Vita* provide comprehensive accounts of Andrew's life and activities, which include both his peregrinations and martyrdom in Patras. This peculiarity has been frequently explained as a result of *collatio* of sources, although this hypothesis cannot be proved on the basis of the available material.

34. *Narratio* 356.8 and 356.24-25; 357.1, respectively.

35. See above n. 8.

36. See M. Bonnet, *Narratio* 354–356, *app. ad* Chapters 1–3.

37. M. Bonnet, *Narratio* 356.19–358.6.

38. Unlike *AAM* and the *Epitome*, the *Narratio* locates the city of the cannibals in Sinope, as the *Laudatio*, the *Vita* (see below n. 46) and two mss of *AAM* (see above n. 26) also do. Sinope as the name of the city of the cannibals already appears in a work by Theodosius written around 550 (see *Itinera Hierosolymitana*, CSEL, 39.144, as quoted by F. Dvornik) and, later on, in Theophanes Cerameus, *Hom.* 50.146 Scorsi.

39. M. Bonnet, *Narratio* 356.19-28.

40. M. Bonnet, *Narratio* 357.1-5.

When the inhabitants of the city find out what has happened, they capture the apostle and drag him around the city, after which they put him in prison with the intention of killing him. However, Andrew compels a stone statue outside the prison to produce a flow of water, not so much to punish as to convert the inhabitants by means of the miracle.[41] Andrew's intentions are achieved, since the people run to the prison, beg him to stop the water and to give them the light of the faith. Seeing that they are repenting sincerely, Andrew orders the statue to stop, forgives the people, teaches them and builds a church, after which he remains seven more days before leaving the city.

d. The Laudatio *and the* Vita

The most peculiar version of the story, however, appears in the *Laudatio* and the *Vita*.[42] Both texts present so similar an account that they can be considered to depend upon a common source, to which they add some individual transformations.[43] Given that their differences are irrelevant for our present inquiry, we shall base our analysis on the *Laudatio*'s account and confine the *Vita*'s variations to the footnotes.

The most interesting aspect of the *Laudatio* and *Vita* version is that it splits the story into two parts which are separated from each other by many chapters.[44] The first part describes Andrew's arrival in Sinope, a city in which 'there was a multitude of gentiles and Jews of different beliefs and religions, who due to their wild character and barbarous customs were called cannibals'.[45] Having visited Antioch of Syria, Tyana of Cappadocia and Anchyra of Galatia, Andrew, Peter, Matthias and other apostles and disciples go to an island close to Sinope.[46] One day, however, Matthias goes to Sinope and is captured by the Jews, who put him in prison planning to kill him the next day.[47] In the meantime Andrew arrives in

41. M. Bonnet, *Narratio* 357.6-20. For the Greek text see n. 97.

42. A. Dressel's edition of the *Vita* relies on a deficient ms, Vat. gr. 824, 11th cent., ff. 105v-128r. The other two versions of the story in mss Paris BN 1510, 11th cent., ff. 1-19v (henceforth, *VitaParis*) and Escorial y II 6 (gr. 341), 12th cent., ff. 226v-246r (henceforth, *VitaEsc*) were already known to R. A. Lipsius (*Apostelgeschichten* I, 575) and M. Bonnet (see *Laudatio* 310, although he wrongly calls the former, cod. Par. 1540), but they remain thus far unpublished.

43. R. A. Lipsius, *Apostelgeschichten* I, 574, and M. Bonnet, *Supplementum codicis apocryphi* (Paris: Klincksieck, 1895), p. XI, stated that *Laudatio* and *Vita* relied on a common source, although F. Diekamp, *Hippolytos von Theben: Texte und Untersuchungen* (Münster: Aschendorff, 1898), pp. 143–45, suggested that *Laudatio* also used *Vita*. Drawing on F. Diekamp, J. Flamion, *L'Apôtre*, 205–12, surmised that *Laudatio* depended exclusively upon *Vita*. Since then, this opinion has been widely echoed. However, the analysis of Flamion's arguments raises serious doubts about his view; see our *Apocryphal Acts of Andrew*, p. 17 n. 160.

44. *VitaParis* and *VitaEsc* do not include the first part of the account, because their beginning is truncated. The former begins at *Vita* 224D 5; the latter, in its turn, at *Vita* 224A 10. The first part of the story about Andrew and Matthias appears in *Vita* 220A–221A.

45. M. Bonnet, *Laudatio* 317.13-20.

46. M. Bonnet, *Laudatio* 316.17–317.12.

47. According to *Laudatio* 'next day'; according to *Vita* the 'fourth day' after his imprisonment, see below n. 68.

the city, goes to the prison, the door of which opens of its own accord, and frees his friend Matthias together with the rest of the prisoners. They all convert to Christianity. Andrew hides them for seven days in a cave outside the city, beside which there is a wood of fig trees, and baptizes his followers at the seashore.[48] Finally, Andrew, Matthias and other disciples continue their travels towards the Eastern parts.[49]

In the second part of the story, Andrew has just returned to Sinope, where he meets some of the new disciples he baptized during his earlier sojourn in that city.[50] Hearing that he was responsible for the liberation of the prisoners, the Jews become angry and attempt to set his house alight. They seize Andrew and drag him through the streets of the city, beating him with stones and biting his body like wild dogs. The fiercest of them takes the apostle's hand and bites one of his fingers off.[51] At this point the author once again gives an aetiological (and ironical?) explanation: 'this is the reason why still today the Sinopeans are called by some *daktylophagoi* ("finger-eaters")'.[52] After the Sinopeans throw him out of the city, Jesus appears to Andrew, restores his finger and orders him to go back to the city. Andrew obeys, returns to Sinope, where he converts its inhabitants to Christianity and heals the sick.[53]

2. The Versions of Andrew and Matthias's Story Compared
As we have seen in the previous section, the stories included in these texts are not as similar as one might expect of texts that are considered to depend upon each other. All five texts apparently include the same basic story, but the fact is that they present important differences, both general and particular. Let us first review their similarities.

a. Similarities Between the Accounts
For comparative purposes the story can be reduced to three basic segments: 1) Matthias's imprisonment; 2) Andrew's liberation of Matthias; 3) Andrew is captured but finally Christianizes the people of the city. Whereas the beginning and the end of the story present important divergences in the different accounts, they all present a similar version of the central section.

---

48. M. Bonnet, *Laudatio* 318.14-27.

49. For this section we have to rely exclusively on Dressel's edition of *Vita*, because the other two mss lack their beginnings.

50. M. Bonnet, *Laudatio* 330.20–331.25. Compare *Vita* 240C–241B: given that *Vita* omits the name of the city due to a lacuna, the story's relationship with Andrew's first sojourn in Sinope remains concealed in this text. In this section Dressel's version can be checked against *VitaParis* and *VitaEsc*, which include the section as well: see *VitaEsc* 239v, col. 1, 30 and *VitaParis* 12v, col. 2, 20 mention Sinope after referring, some lines above, to Amastra.

51. M. Bonnet, *Laudatio* 330.20–331.3.

52. M. Bonnet, *Laudatio* 331.3-4, οὗ χάριν παρά τισιν οἱ Σινωπεῖς μέχρι τῆς σήμερον δακτυλοφάγοι κατονομάζονται.

53. M. Bonnet, *Laudatio* 331.4-18; A. Dressel, *Vita* 240D–241A.

As far as the first part is concerned, common to all versions is the fact that Matthias is captured and imprisoned.[54] In addition, the texts also coincide in mentioning that he is not alone but accompanied by many other prisoners.[55] In all five versions, Andrew is acquainted with his friend's imprisonment and goes to rescue him, but, as we shall see below, the texts notably disagree both as to how Andrew comes by the information and how he arrives in the city to rescue Matthias.[56]

With regard to the second section, all versions present an equivalent account of Andrew's arrival in the city and how he goes to liberate his friend. Of course, the versions present divergences of detail, but, in general, convergences are far more numerous. For example, some versions mention the gates of the city and others omit them, but all versions, with the exception of the *Epitome*, connect Andrew's entering the prison with one or more miraculous action by him: according to some texts, the guardians fall down dead at his prayer and the doors open of their own accord;[57] other versions are silent about the guardians, but mention the door that opens at his prayer or at the sign of the cross.[58] Once inside the prison, he finds his friend together with a number of other prisoners. Andrew achieves his goal without important obstacles and liberates both Matthias and his fellow prisoners, in whom, however, not all texts show the same interest.[59]

Concerning the third part, the versions do agree in letting the apostle be captured and tortured by the inhabitants, but they disagree both in explaining why and how he is captured and in specifying the means and the duration of the torture.[60] Andrew endures the torture and is eventually released by his torturers: all versions agree on this, but again they disagree in explaining why they changed their minds. The apostle finally converts everyone to Christianity.

b. Differences Between the Versions

Despite these similarities, however, the texts present important divergences. As already stated, the first section narrating Matthias's imprisonment is notably different in the versions: according to *AAM*, for example, after the casting of lots Matthias leaves for his allotted field of activity, apparently 'the land' (χώρα) but in fact 'the city of the cannibals'.[61] When he arrives in that city, which in *AAM*

---

54. M. Bonnet, *AAM* 66.7-12; *Epitome* 377.25-28; *Narratio* 356.24-28; *Laudatio* 318.14-16; A. Dressel, *Vita* 220D 4-7.

55. M. Bonnet, *AAM* 91.8ff; *Epitome* 378.1-2; *Narratio* 357.1-2; *Laudatio* 318.19-20; A. Dressel, *Vita* 221A 1ff.

56. See below notes 69–76.

57. M. Bonnet, *AAM* 90.1.6, *Narratio* 357.3-4.

58. M. Bonnet, *Laudatio* 318.17-18; A. Dressel, *Vita* 220D 8-9.

59. Whereas *AAM* (91.8-94.8), *Laudatio* (318.19-27) and *Vita* (221A 1-B 7) show especial interest in the prisoners, not so *Epitome* (378.8-11) and *Narratio* (357.4-5), which only include some brief references.

60. M. Bonnet, *AAM* 101.11-109.2, *Epitome* 378.12-16, *Narratio* 357.6-11, *Laudatio* 330.24-331.4, *Vita* 240C 14–241A 1.

61. Even though the text reading of the references to Matthias's field of activity preserved by

remains unnamed,[62] he is imprisoned, blinded and drugged, since the cannibals intend to sacrifice him a month later after fattening him up. Matthias then prays and a light shines in the prison: he receives back his sight and a voice assures him that Andrew will come to liberate him within 27 days.[63] None of these numerous details appears in any of the other versions, which, in general, simply mention that Matthias was imprisoned. In the *Epitome*'s version, for instance, Matthew's field of activity is not the land of the cannibals but Myrmidon.[64] The inhabitants of this city capture, blind and imprison the apostle, whom they plan to kill within a few days, not because they are cannibals but because they are reluctant to hear his message.[65] At the same time, instead of recovering his sight after his prayer, as in *AAM*, in this version Matthew remains blind until Andrew arrives and prays for him.[66] A third version of the location of the events appears in the *Narratio*. Unlike *AAM* and the *Epitome*, the *Narratio* begins its account with Andrew's arrival in Sinope, where Matthias happens to be being held captive together with his disciples by its barbarous and bloodthirsty inhabitants, who are inimical and aggressive not only against foreigners but also against each other.[67] The *Laudatio* and the *Vita* coincide with the *Narratio* in locating the story in Sinope, although they disagree in describing how Matthias is imprisoned: Andrew and Matthias happen to be travelling together; they sojourn on an island in front of Sinope and one day when Matthias goes to the city he is apprehended and put in prison by the Jews of the city, who plan to kill him the next day (*Laudatio*), or four days

---

M. Bonnet (and supported by the majority of the mss) is usually πόλις, family Ω (see M. Bonnet *app. ad*) tends to replace it by χώρα, probably in an attempt to homogenise the references (see M. Bonnet's index, s.v. χώρα).

62. See, however, n. 26 above.

63. *AAM* shows a clear predilection for figures and tends to be precise in specifying the numbers of days, prisoners, victims, demons, etc. See, e.g., *AAM* 67.13, 68.12.16, 94.1-2, 95.10, 97.10, 105.4, 107.1-2, etc.

64. M. Bonnet, *Epitome* 377.24-25, *Matheus autem apostolus, qui et euangelista, Mermidonae urbi verbum salutis adnuntiavit.* For the variants of the name of the city, see M. Bonnet, *Epitome* 377.45.

65. M. Bonnet, *Epitome* 377.25-28, *Sed incolae civitatis dure, indignae ferentes quae de Redemptoris nostri virtutibus audiebant ac sua nolentes destruere templa, adpraehensum beatum apostolum, erutis oculis, circumdatum catenis, in carcere detruserunt, ut, interpositis paucis diebus, interficerent.*

66. Cf. M. Bonnet, *Epitome* 378.6-7.

67. M. Bonnet, *Narratio* 356.19-357.2, Καταλαβὼν δὲ καὶ τὸν Εὔξεινον πόντον, ἐν μιᾷ τῶν πόλεων Σινώπη καλουμένη εἰσελθών, ἐν ᾗ οἱ ταύτην οἰκοῦντες αἱμοβόροι τινὲς καὶ ἀνήμεροι καὶ θηρίων ἀγριωδέστερον τῇ γνώμῃ διέκειντο οὐ μόνον πρὸς ἀλλήλους ἀλλὰ καὶ πρὸς πάντας τοὺς ἔξωθεν ἐπεισερχομένους ἐπήλυδάς τε καὶ νεήλυδας, τούτοις ἀσπλαγχνίᾳ κεχρημένοι καὶ ἀνημέρῳ τρόπῳ μετερχόμενοι, ὡς καὶ τὸν μακάριον ἀπόστολον Ματθίαν, καθὰ λόγος κεκράτηκεν, χάριν τοῦ κηρύγματος Χριστοῦ τοῦ ἀληθινοῦ θεοῦ ἡμῶν παρ' αὐτοῖς γενόμενον κατασχεῖν καὶ ἀνηλεῶς αἰκίσασθαι καὶ κατάκλειστον ἐν φρουρᾷ ποιῆσαι ὡς μετὰ ταῦτα τοῦτον σφοδρότερον τιμωρησόμενοι, παραγενόμενος τοίνυν ὁ ἁγιώτατος καὶ πρωτόκλητος ἀπόστολων ᾿Ανδρέας, καθὰ δεδήλωται, ἐν τῇ τοιαύτῃ πόλει, καὶ γνοὺς τὸν ἀπόστολον Ματθίαν ἐνφρούριον ὑπάρχειν μετὰ καὶ ἑτέρων πιστῶν ... κτλ.

later (*Vita*).[68] In their accounts there are neither chains nor drugs, nor any reference to disciples of the apostle.

It is easy to see, consequently, that all five versions present rather diverging accounts of Matthias's imprisonment. They disagree about how Matthias arrives there, about the name of the city, about the nature of its inhabitants and their motivation in apprehending the apostle, and, finally, about the tortures they inflict on him.

As far as the central section is concerned, the texts appear to present a somewhat more homogeneous version, although differences are nevertheless numerous. Their most important disagreement is, perhaps, in the manner in which Andrew is acquainted with his friend's imprisonment: in *AAM* Jesus appears to Andrew in order to inform him about the imprisonment of his friend, after which he orders the apostle to go to rescue him;[69] according to the *Epitome*, however, an 'angel of the Lord' (*angelus Domini*) announces Matthew's capture and compels his friend to go to free him.[70] Unlike in these two versions, in the *Narratio* Andrew knows about Matthias fortuitously, since he arrives in the city where Matthias happens to be imprisoned; according to the *Laudatio* and the *Vita*, finally, Andrew and Matthias are travelling together and Andrew knows about his imprisonment when his friend does not return from the city.

Another disagreement concerns the description of Andrew's arrival in the city: according to *AAM*, Andrew is invisible and therefore easily enters the city.[71] When he arrives at the prison *AAM* describes how the guards drop dead and how at Andrew's sign of the cross the doors open.[72] The *Epitome*, in turn, mentions Andrew's entering the gates of the city, but not his invisibility.[73] The *Narratio* omits any reference to the apostle's arrival and entering the city, but mentions the killing by prayer and the miraculous opening of the prison doors.[74] According to the *Laudatio*, Andrew opens both the gates of the city and the doors of the prison;[75] the *Vita* only mentions the latter.[76]

With regard to the narration of how Andrew rescues Matthias, *AAM* offers a very poor account. As a matter of fact, it only mentions Mathias and his liber-

68. See M. Bonnet, *Laudatio* 318.14-16; A. Dressel, *Vita* 220D 4-7.

69. M. Bonnet, *AAM* 68.13-16, ἐφάνη ὁ κύριος ἐν τῇ χώρᾳ ᾗ ἦν διδάσκων ὁ Ἀνδρέας, καὶ εἶπεν αὐτῷ· Ἀνάστηθι καὶ πορεύθητι μετὰ τῶν μαθητῶν σου ἐν τῇ χώρᾳ τῶν ἀνθρωποφάγων καὶ ἐξάγαγε Ματθείαν ἐκ τοῦ τόπου ἐκείνου.

70. M. Bonnet, *Epitome* 377.28.

71. M. Bonnet, *AAM* 89.17-18, Ἀνδρέας δὲ ἀναστὰς εἰσῆλθεν ἐν τῇ πόλει σὺν τοῖς μαθηταῖς αὐτοῦ, καὶ οὐδεὶς αὐτὸν ἐθεάσατο.

72. M. Bonnet, *AAM* 90.1-6.

73. M. Bonnet, *Epitome* 377.33-378.1, *prospere navigavit* [Andrew] *ad urbem, ingressusque portam civitatis, venit ad carcerem*.

74. M. Bonnet, *Narratio* 357.3-4, διὰ προσευχῆς ἀπενέκρωσεν τοὺς φύλακας καὶ τὰς θύρας τῆς φυλακῆς ἀνοίξας ἐξήνεγκεν αὐτόν τε τὸν ἀπόστολον κτλ.

75. M. Bonnet, *Laudatio* 318.16-18, ὁ φερώνυμος Ἀνδρέας κατελθὼν ἀπὸ τοῦ ὄρους διὰ νυκτός, τῶν πυλῶν τῆς πόλεως καὶ τοῦ δεσμωτηρίου αὐτοματὶ διανοιγμένων αὐτῷ, κτλ.

76. A. Dressel, *Vita* 220D 8-9, ἡ δὲ πύλη τῆς φυλακῆς αὐτομάτως ἐνοίχθη αὐτῷ.

ation by the apostle: Andrew cannot heal him, since in this text Jesus has already healed him in the first chapters.[77] In *AAM*, consequently, Andrew's healing mainly concerns Matthias's fellow prisoners (below). Unlike *AAM*, the *Epitome* mainly focuses on Matthew's condition and healing: horrified at the sight of his friend, Andrew begins a prayer, after which Matthew gets back his sight.[78] The *Narratio* omits every detail about the liberation and simply says that everyone was set free.[79] The *Laudatio* and the *Vita* only describe that Andrew liberates Matthias and all his fellow prisoners by means of his word.[80]

With regard to Matthias's fellow prisoners, *AAM* provides many details. When the apostle arrives there, they are behaving like animals, since the cannibals' drug is affecting their minds. Andrew restores their sight and understanding, liberates them and invites them to wait for him under a fig tree in the lower parts of the city until he returns to them.[81] The *Epitome* and the *Narratio* omit every detail and simply mention that they were set free.[82] The *Laudatio* and the *Vita* only mention their liberation, although later on they include the most developed version of the events following the liberation: the apostle converts them and hides them for seven days in a cave *beside* a wood of fig trees; finally, he baptizes them at the seashore and, on the eighth day, he departs.[83] In addition, the *Laudatio* and the *Vita* are the only texts to mention Andrew's return to the city and his visit to these new believers.[84]

The most important disagreements, however, appear in the third section of the story, namely the part narrating the reaction of the inhabitants of the city. The *Acts of Andrew and Matthias* presents the lengthiest account. Immediately following the liberation of the prisoners, an excursus narrates how Andrew frustrates the cannibals' attempts to resort to their own citizens to get food.[85] In addition, *AAM* gives the devil an important role in the action, since he incites the cannibals against the apostle.[86] None of the other versions include the slightest trace of either issue. In *AAM*, when the cannibals seize the apostle they fasten a rope around his neck and drag him around the city on three consecutive days.[87] In the *Epitome*, however, the inhabitants of the city capture Andrew once they know he is responsible for the liberation of their prisoners and not because of the devil's interference.

---

77. M. Bonnet, *AAM* 67.6-9.

78. M. Bonnet, *Epitome* 378.1-7, *Videns autem Matheum apostolum ... amarissime flevit, et facta oratione simul, ... et statim locus ille contremuit, et lux magna refulsit in carcere, et oculi beati apostoli restaurati sunt,* etc.

79. M. Bonnet, *Narratio* 357.4-5.

80. M. Bonnet, *Laudatio* 318.19-20, τοὺς πεπεδημένους καὶ συνδεδεμένους ἅμα τῷ θείῳ Ματθία λόγῳ μόνῳ λύσας ἐξήγαγεν.

81. M. Bonnet, *AAM* 93.1-13.

82. M. Bonnet, *Epitome* 378.7-11; for *Narratio* see above n. 67.

83. M. Bonnet, *Laudatio* 318.20-27; A. Dressel, *Vita* 221A 1-8.

84. See above n. 50.

85. M.Bonnet, *AAM* 94.9–99.12.

86. M. Bonnet, *AAM* 100.1–101.10.

87. M. Bonnet, *AAM* 101.11–109.2.

Unlike in *AAM*, they fasten the rope around the apostle's feet and drag him through the city only once.[88] The *Narratio* agrees with the *Epitome* in letting the Sinopeans apprehend Andrew in order to punish him once they realize he is responsible for the liberation of the prisoners, although it does not include any reference to the rope. The *Laudatio* and the *Vita* present a quite different account, since after freeing Matthias and his companions Andrew just walks away and leaves the city.[89] It is not until his second sojourn in Sinope that the Jews, having heard that Andrew was responsible, get angry and seize him.[90] Even though both texts mention that the apostle was dragged around the city, they omit the reference to the rope, as does the *Narratio*. In turn, the *Laudatio* and the *Vita* include some additional details: while dragging the apostle, the Jews beat him with stones and bite the apostle like dogs; the fiercest of them bites one of his fingers off.[91]

With regard to Andrew's torment, all the versions coincide in describing his endurance. In *AAM*, however, when Andrew sees that his flesh and blood is sticking to the ground, he invokes Jesus and, quoting Matt. 21:18, he complains that his hair is falling out; a voice then orders him to look back and as he does so he sees trees growing from it.[92] The *Epitome* only mentions Andrew's endurance and adds that his hair fell out and his blood flowed.[93] The *Narratio*, the *Laudatio* and the *Vita* do not mention anything about this.

The *Acts of Andrew and Mathias* and the *Narratio* agree in reporting that after being dragged through the city Andrew was put back in prison. However, whereas in the *Narratio* the Sinopeans bring the apostle back to prison just once, according to *AAM* the cannibals do it on three consecutive nights.[94] The second time he is back in prison, the devil and seven demons are waiting for him in order to kill him, but, as they fail, they mock and humiliate him.[95] On the third night Jesus raises him up whole and Andrew proceeds to severely punish the cannibals by means of the statue flowing with acid, the Archangel Michael in a cloud of fire, and the abyss that opens at his prayer.[96] Nothing of this appears in any of the other versions, since *AAM* is the only text that refers to Andrew's vengeance on the people of the city. The *Narratio* does mention a statue, which is not *in* the prison but outside and does not flow with acid but water, although its flow is not intended as a punishment but as a miracle to convert the Sinopeans.[97]

88. M. Bonnet, *Epitome* 378.12-13, *Cognoscentes autem homines illi de carceris vinctis quae facta fuerant, adprehensum Andream, ligatis pedibus, trahebant per plateas civitatis.*
89. M. Bonnet, *Laudatio* 318.28ff.
90. See n. 50.
91. See above n. 51.
92. M. Bonnet, *AAM* 107.3–108.13.
93. M. Bonnet, *Epitome* 378.13-14.
94. See above n. 87.
95. M. Bonnet, *AAM* 104.4–107.2.
96. M. Bonnet, *AAM* 109.3–114.4.
97. M. Bonnet, *Narratio* 357.14-20, καὶ προσσχὼν ἀνδριάντι τινὶ λιθίνῳ ἑστῶτι ἀντικρὺς

As far as the attitude of the inhabitants is concerned, in *AAM* the cannibals beg for mercy when they are confronted with the effects of the deadly waters;[98] in the *Epitome*, however, all the elements that in *AAM* provoke the cannibals' repentance have disappeared: the statue flowing with acid, and Andrew's prayer to God not to pardon his captors but to augment their punishment by sending Michael and the cloud of fire. The citizens of Myrmidon are simply so impressed by his endurance and perseverance that they release the apostle and beg for forgiveness;[99] in the *Narratio* Andrew converts the people with the miraculous flood;[100] the *Laudatio* and the *Vita* omit these events altogether.[101]

The closing section also presents important divergences. According to *AAM*, Andrew baptizes the cannibals and builds a church in their city, but when they pray for him to remain some days with them, he rejects their invitation and leaves.[102] However, Jesus orders him to return to the city, to remain there for seven days and to rescue those in the abyss.[103] The *Epitome* does not mention anything about all this. Gregory simply reports that Andrew preaches and baptizes them.[104] The *Narratio*, differently, reports that Andrew forgives his captors, instructs them, builds a church and remains in Sinope for seven more days, but without referring to Jesus' orders.[105] According to the *Laudatio* and the *Vita*, finally, when the Jews of Sinope throw him out of the city, Jesus appears to Andrew, restores his finger and orders him to go back the city. Andrew obeys, converts the Jews and heals the sick.[106]

3. The Alleged Dependence of the Other Accounts upon the *Acts of Andrew and Matthias*

The above textual-comparative study of the five versions shows that they are in one way or another related with each other. However, their textual convergences are not enough to clearly establish their textual relationships with a view to determining whether one of them served as a source for the others. The far more numerous general and particular divergences pose an important obstacle in our efforts to find out what is primitive and what secondary.

Given these profound divergences and given that no study of the five texts has ever established a textual dependence of the *Epitome*, the *Narratio*, the *Laudatio*

τῆς φυλακῆς, ἐκτείνας τὴν χεῖρα καὶ σφραγίσας εἶπεν· σοὶ λέγω τῷ ἀνδριάντι, φοβήτι τὸ σημεῖον τοῦ σταυροῦ καὶ ἐξάγαγε ὕδωρ, ὅπως ἰδόντες οἱ ταύτην τὴν πόλιν κατοικοῦντες ἀπηνέστατοι ἄνθρωποι παιδευθῶσιν καὶ ἐπιστρέψωσιν εἰς ἐπίγνωσιν καὶ πίστιν τοῦ ἀληθινοῦ θεοῦ, ... κτλ.

98. M. Bonnet, *AAM* 111.2–112.10.
99. M. Bonnet, *Epitome* 378.16-20.
100. M. Bonnet, *Narratio* 357.21-27.
101. M. Bonnet, *Laudatio* 330.25–331.5; A. Dressel, *Vita* 240C 14–241A 2.
102. M. Bonnet, *AAM* 114.9–115.5.
103. M. Bonnet, *AAM* 115.6–116.15.
104. M. Bonnet, *Epitome* 378.20-24.
105. M. Bonnet, *Narratio* 358.3-6.
106. M. Bonnet, *Laudatio* 331.5-25; A. Dressel, *Vita* 241A 2-B 6.

and the *Vita* upon *AAM* on the basis of an exhaustive scrutiny of their convergences and divergences, it is to say the very least surprising that this alleged relationship is accepted by the scholarly literature without further inquiry. In this section, therefore, we shall compare *AAM* with the different versions, in order to evaluate whether the textual evidence can sustain the hypothesis about such a relationship of dependence.

a. General Divergences Between the Acts of Andrew and Matthias *and the Other Versions*
Despite apparent similarities, a closer scrutiny of *AAM* and the other versions reveals both that they present profound divergences with regard to their literary character, content and intention, and that they also have important structural dissimilarities.

From the point of view of their literary character, the texts can clearly be divided into two groups: on the one hand there is *AAM*, and, on the other, the remaining versions of the story. Whereas *AAM* shows a clear interest in fantastic issues and includes abundant digressions, the other four versions, even though not completely excluding fantastic elements, are far more sober and present a straightforward account.

With regard to content, the texts allow the same division: whereas *AAM* narrates the adventures of the apostle Andrew in the land of the cannibals, the other four stories simply narrate Andrew's liberation of his friend Matthias, who appears to be imprisoned by the harsh inhabitants of one of the stations of his travels. In point of fact, *AAM* is the only text to mention the cannibals as such, and the other four texts either lack any reference to the anthropophagites or include only the vaguest of references.[107]

However, the best proof for asserting the different nature of *AAM* from the other versions is their radically different intention. A good indication of this is the different status Andrew has in the accounts: in *AAM* the real protagonist is not the apostle but Jesus; it is Jesus' role that occupies the main focus of the story, while Andrew appears as a simple mediator.[108] In the other four versions, however, the real protagonist of the story is Andrew and, although his role always remains that of an apostle, his activities in general arise from his own determination. The *Acts of Andrew and Matthias*, due to its fantastic character and secondary, fabulous digressions appears to the reader mainly as an adventure story, in which Andrew

107. Whereas the *Epitome*, for example, does not include any reference to the cannibals, the *Narratio* mentions 'bloodthirsty people', while the *Laudatio* and the *Vita*, in their first part, say that the inhabitants were called by some 'cannibals' owing to their cruel and barbarous nature, in the second part, they include a curious story about *daktylophagoi* or 'finger-eaters'. It is plausible to think that these references found their way into the text as a result of the influence of the very widespread story preserved in *AAM*.

108. In contrast to the other versions, Jesus has a central role in *AAM*. This can be seen in his frequent intervention in the action. See *AAM* 67.6ff; 68.12ff; 69.14-89.16; *passim*, 101.7ff; 108.7ff; 109.3ff; 115.6ff.

is the first hero owing to the divine support he receives at every moment. In the other versions, on the other hand, the story retains the classic line of an apostle narrative, since the story about Andrew rescuing Matthias appears integrated into the account of the apostle's deeds in his missionary enterprise. Divine manifestations, God's or Jesus' intervention in the action and divine support are not as prominent in these stories as in *AAM*. In these texts Andrew is not the invincible legendary hero we see in *AAM*, but rather an apostle who fulfils his duty and solves the problems he encounters during his apostolic activities.

But the most important reason for rejecting the theory about a textual dependence of the other texts upon *AAM* is their structural dissimilarity: whereas the other four versions include a well-structured account consisting of three visible parts, *AAM*'s version of the story lacks any proportions whatsoever: whereas the introduction and conclusion are disproportionately developed, the central section, which should narrate the main event of the story, is strikingly brief. *AAM*'s introductory section occupies approximately 50 per cent of Bonnet's edition[109] and is notably omitted by the other versions of the story: the *Epitome* narrates Matthias's imprisonment in thirteen lines,[110] the *Narratio* in ten, the *Laudatio* in three lines.[111] As far as the central section is concerned, Matthias's liberation itself, in *AAM* it occupies less than 10 per cent of Bonnet's edition. In addition, it is surprising that, although this part (*AAM* 19–21) should focus on Matthias's rescue, nothing substantial is narrated about this. The section offers little more than repetitions,[112] a dialogue between Matthias and Andrew and a diatribe by Andrew against the devil, neither of which, due to the abundant scriptural references, seems to be primitive.[113] In contrast, *AAM* pays much more attention to Matthias's fellow prisoners: a whole chapter is dedicated to describing how Andrew gives them back their sight and understanding and provides them with a place to hide until he returns to them.[114] Unlike *AAM*, the *Epitome* mainly focuses on Matthias's liberation, but also includes, in the ten lines dedicated to this section, a reference to the other prisoners;[115] the *Narratio* gives all the essential information concerning the liberation of Matthias and his fellow prisoners in six lines and the *Laudatio* in twelve.[116]

As far as the third section is concerned, *AAM* includes a very lengthy last section occupying the last twelve chapters, i.e. approximately 30 per cent of Bonnet's edition or 337 lines. Many elements in *AAM*'s account are missing in all other versions, such as Andrew's three-day-long torture, the central role played

---

109. Of the 810 lines of Greek text of Bonnet's edition, 395 are occupied by this section.

110. M. Bonnet, *Epitome* 377.21-33.

111. M. Bonnet, *Laudatio* 318.14-16. Similarly, *Vita* 220D 4-7.

112. See M. Bonnet, *AAM* 90.10-11, compare 67.6–68.18, especially 68.16-18; see also 91.1-5, compare 67.13-16 and 68.12.

113. See M. Bonnet's *app. ad AAM* chapters 19–20.

114. M. Bonnet, *AAM* 93.1–94.8.

115. M. Bonnet, *Epitome* 378.1-11.

116. M. Bonnet, *Narratio* 356.28–357.5; *Laudatio* 318.16-27; cf. *Vita* 220D 7–221A 8.

by the devil, all details about the cannibals' eating customs, etc. The other texts include a much shorter version of Andrew's works among the inhabitants of the city: in the *Epitome* it occupies just fourteen lines; in the *Narratio* and the *Laudatio*, however, this part is somewhat more developed, since it occupies thirty and twenty-three lines, respectively.[117]

b. Particular Comparison of the Acts of Andrew and Matthias *with the Versions*
1. The *Epitome*
As we have clearly seen in the previous pages, in spite of a couple of common elements, the *Epitome* and *AAM* present rather divergent accounts of the episode. In the first place, the *Epitome*'s version is quite brief and lacks the numerous excursuses of *AAM*. However, more important is the fact that numerous elements are simply different: the name of the city where Matthew is imprisoned, the nature of the inhabitants, Matthew's healing and liberation, the reference to Matthew's fellow prisoners, Andrew's capture by the citizens, the character and the duration of his torment, their repentance, Andrew's release and his conversion of the people are radically different in both accounts.

In explaining the obvious differences between the *Epitome* and *AAM*, scholars normally suggest that they arise from Gregory's tendency to eliminate all fantastic or exaggerated issues in order to keep to the basic account of the story. Admittedly, it is known that Gregory abridged and reworked his sources profoundly and on occasion extremely.[118] However, if one affirms that *AAM* was his source, one must also admit that Gregory's omissions have been in this case far more extensive; in fact, he only retains a couple of details of the alleged source, to wit that Matthias has been captured and that Andrew comes to rescue him. All other aspects of the story, both general and particular, have been either transformed or eliminated. As already mentioned, Gregory does not even mention that the inhabitants of Myrmidon were cannibals. Consequently, in the *Epitome* there is no such a thing as a version of the story of 'Andrew and Matthias in the City of the Cannibals', but a simple narration about how Andrew goes to Myrmidon to free his friend Matthias.

2. The *Narratio*
When compared with *AAM*, the *Narratio* not only appears to present a much shorter version of the story, but also shows numerous divergences from *AAM*. The dissimilarities are obvious already in its first part: the name of the city, the nature of its inhabitants, Matthias's imprisonment, Andrew's knowledge of it and his intervention to free Matthias are all quite different in both accounts. In addition, there are no apparitions, marvellous sea trips, or conversations between Jesus and Andrew, no talking sphinxes, nor fantastic transportation ashore by angels. The

---

117. M. Bonnet, *Narratio* 357.6–358.6, and *Laudatio* 330.22–331.13, provided that we exclude the section *Laudatio* 331.13-25, which almost certainly is an amplification.

118. See the references included in above n. 24.

second and third parts of the *Narratio*'s account present important divergences as well. The action is not only reduced to a minimum and many personages eliminated, but also many events or their intent are considerably changed. For example, when the Sinopeans capture and torture the apostle, he compels a statue to flow with water, but this is not intended as a punishment, as is clearly the case in *AAM*, but simply to provoke the awe of the citizens with a view to converting them.[119] As already stated, moreover, the statue spews water and not acid, as in *AAM*, and the cloud of fire and the abyss are missing as well. Finally, as Andrew does not intend to depart right away, Jesus' intervention and order to the apostle to remain seven more days among the people is missing.

In addition, the *Narratio* also presents important structural dissimilarities. Unlike *AAM*, the anonymous writer presents a balanced and well-structured narration, since he organises the material into three sections with an equal number of lines. Chapter 5 includes the preliminary events, Andrew's arrival and Matthias's liberation; chapter 6 narrates Andrew's capture and torture and his stratagem to turn the people to the faith; chapter 7, finally, focuses on the repentance and final conversion of the Sinopeans.

3. The *Laudatio*

This version is highly different from *AAM*. Among the numerous divergences, which we have already commented upon, the most striking is perhaps that Matthias is neither apprehended by the cannibals or the Sinopeans in general, but by the Jews of Sinope.[120] This reference is certainly interesting: in antiquity the Jews were frequently accused of ritual human sacrifices,[121] but the indictment of anthropophagy is a later development.[122] The writer does not seem to give credence to the accusation, since he suggests that the Jews were called 'cannibals' due to their wild nature and barbarous customs, an example of which he will introduce later on.[123]

However, the most important issue is that the *Laudatio* gives a rather divergent

---

119. See above n. 97.

120. See above p. 231.

121. Apion accused the Jews of sacrificing a Greek every year, Josephus, *Apion*. 2.92-96, for which see E. Bickerman, 'Ritualmord und Eselskult, I: Tempelopfer', *MGWJ* 71 (1927), pp. 171–87 (= *Studies in Jewish and Christian History* II [AGAJU, 9; Leiden: Brill, 1980], pp. 225–55); see also J. Rives, 'Human Sacrifice among Pagan and Christians', *JRS* 85 (1995), pp. 65–85 (70–72).

122. As far as we know, this is the first documentation of the accusation of anthopophagy levelled against the Jews, which would reach its climax between the twelfth and fifteenth centuries. On the extension of the accusation against the Jews, see our forthcoming article 'The Early Christians and Human Sacrifice' (in J. N. Bremmer [ed.]). In general, R. P. Hsia, *The Myth of Ritual Murder. Jews and Magic in Reformation Germany* (New Haven and London: Yale University Press, 1988).

123. See above p. 229.

version of how Andrew is informed of Matthias's capture. The *Laudatio* neither attributes this to divine commission, like *AAM* or the *Epitome*, nor to chance, like the *Narratio*, since in its account Andrew and Matthias appear to be travelling together. In addition, the narration lacks many details, such as the death of the guardians of the prison, the blindness of Matthias and, logically, his regaining his sight. On the other hand, it includes a reference to the door opening of its own accord as all other versions do, with the exception of the *Epitome*, it mentions the liberation of the other prisoners and includes, with important transformations, the mention of the wood of fig trees.

c. Conclusions from the Comparative Study of the Acts of Andrew and Matthias *and the Other Versions*
As *AAM* is customarily seen as the original text, the other four versions of the story of Andrew and Matthias are dealt with as if they were later versions depending on a common source, to wit *AAM*. However, such a theory does not survive a comparative, closer examination of all five accounts. The scrutiny above shows that there too many textual divergences to support the dependence of the *Epitome*, the *Narratio*, the *Laudatio* and the *Vita* upon *AAM*. These divergences concern not only general issues, such as literary character, content and intention, which, it might be argued, could arise from the changing scopes of the writers of the different texts. They also concern innumerable particular issues of the story, which affect both the sequence of the narration itself and the nature and intention of numerous characters and events.

As far as we can judge on the basis of the textual evidence available today, the most obvious conclusion is that the other four versions of the story do not depend upon *AAM*.

4. The Source of the Story of Andrew's Liberation of Matthias
Given that *AAM* was not the source for the other versions, the question arises whether any of the other stories could have served as a source for the remaining ones. This study, however, has sufficiently shown not only that the versions present divergences when compared with *AAM*, but also that they reveal important disagreements among themselves as well: in general each text gives *its own* version both of the story in general and of its parts and details in particular. The textual evidence, consequently, seems to indicate that we are faced with four different versions of the story – *AAM*, the *Epitome*, the *Narratio*, the *Laudatio/Vita* – four of which adapted it and transformed it to suit their own literary purposes.

a. Original Elements in the Versions and Character of the Primitive Account
On the basis of the comparative study above, we now possess enough material to hypothesize what the source of these five versions might have looked like.

As regards the first part, the story plausibly did not include the lengthy introduction occupying 50 per cent of *AAM*'s text. The other four versions do not present the slightest trace of the abundant fantastic and legendary elements included in this section of *AAM*, such as the description of the cannibals' customs, the magical drug they give their prisoners, Jesus' apparitions, the miraculous trip in a ship piloted by Jesus, the talking sphinxes, or the angels transporting Andrew and his disciples ashore. The only exception is, perhaps, the *Epitome*'s brief account of how an angel commissions Andrew and leads him by boat to Myrmidon.

Despite the relative coincidence of *AAM*'s and the *Epitome*'s account, it is very difficult to determine how the primitive account described Andrew's arrival in the city, since we have up to three different versions thereof: the narration of *AAM* and the *Epitome*, that of the *Narratio* and that of the *Laudatio* and the *Vita*. The same holds true for the text's explanation of how Andrew learns about the imprisonment of his friend: Jesus or an angel in *AAM* and the *Epitome*, chance in the *Narratio* and direct acquaintance in the *Laudatio* and the *Vita*. These differences between the accounts seem to indicate that their source did not include a clear reference to either issue, and that, consequently, each version attempted to fill the gap in its own way, as a result of which their accounts differ from one another; however, it could also be that the versions simply adapted what they found to their own literary purposes.

With regard to the central section, coincidences are more numerous. As pointed out above, it is interesting that, with the exception of the *Epitome*, all versions refer to one or several miraculous activities by the apostle when he enters the city and the prison. The liberation of Matthias and his fellow prisoners is common to all versions of the story, although Matthias's blindness might not be a primitive detail, since it appears in *AAM* and in the *Epitome*, but is ignored by the remaining accounts. With regard to the other prisoners, it is difficult to ascertain whether they originally occupied a prominent place in this part of the story since the versions do not pay equal attention to them. It might be that, in this case, *AAM* preserves the best account of the issue, since it occupies a middle point between the *Epitome*, which ignores them almost completely, and the *Laudatio* and the *Vita*, which include a very developed account with additional information which does not appear in any of the other versions.

As regards the third section of the episode, the source story almost certainly included Andrew's capture by the inhabitants of the city and his being dragged through the city's streets and squares. All five versions agree on this, even though they present differences in detail: *AAM*'s three-day-long torment, the role played in it by the devil and his seven demons, and the trees growing from Andrew's flesh and hair are almost certainly secondary developments of the original account. This might also be the case with the punishment of the cannibals by Andrew, which, even though present in *AAM,* is missing in all other versions. It should be noted that the only other text that mentions the miracle of the statue, the *Narratio*, does not present it as a punishment of the Sinopeans but as means for their conversion.[124] On the other hand, the question of whether the story of the statue spewing water was included in the original account is difficult to answer. However,

---

124. See above n. 97.

despite the fact that three texts omit it, the *Narratio*'s support of *AAM* seems to lend some plausibility to the primitive character of the story.

Be that as it may, Andrew's torturers eventually repent and release the apostle. The primitive account probably described how Andrew preached, taught and converted them to Christianity, since all the versions agree, with minor divergences, on this: according to the *Epitome* and the *Narratio*, Andrew does not depart immediately, but remains in the city; according to *AAM*, the *Laudatio* and the *Vita*, Andrew leaves, or is thrown out of the city, but Jesus appears to him ordering him to return there.

b. Does the Episode about Andrew and Matthias Belong to the Primitive Acts of Andrew?

As we mentioned at the start of this contribution, the question of whether or not the Andrew and Matthias episode belongs to the primitive *AA* is still today a matter of controversy. Strikingly, however, supporters and detractors of the story belonging to the primitive *AA* exclusively base their acceptance or rejection on an analysis of *AAM*, as if this text were the only and most primitive account of the story of Andrew's liberation of Matthias. On the one hand, D. R. MacDonald has collected abundant literature and arguments in different works to sustain including *AAM* in his textual reconstruction of *AA*.[125] On the other, ever since Flamion suggested that *AAM* should be dated to the end of the fourth century,[126] those who reject the story belonging to *AA* exclusively focus on *AAM* in order to accept Flamion's hypothesis or to provide additional support for it.

Our previous comparative study of the five versions of the story has shown that *AAM* cannot have been the source of the other four versions, a conclusion that seems to be further supported by previous studies on *AAM* that claim its later composition. On the basis of his study of *AAM* and its comparison with the *Acts of Peter and Andrew*, the *Martyrdom of Matthew* and later versions of the *Acts of Peter* and the *Acts of Thomas*, Flamion suggested that these texts belong to the later apostolic romance, which was influenced by Orthodox thought and, consequently, was free from the doctrinal peculiarities of the oldest *Acts of the Apostles*.[127] More recently Hilhorst and Lalleman have provided more solid philological arguments to definitively rule out the possibility of considering that *AAM* and *AA* could ever have belonged to the same text.[128]

Our study has also shown that the numerous divergences between the accounts indicate, as M. Blumenthal already suggested,[129] that it is rather unlikely that any of them could serve as a source for the other versions. Rather, their dissimilar

125. D. R. MacDonald, *Cannibals*, pp. 6–47.

126. J. Flamion, *L'Apôtre*, pp. 269–300.

127. J. Flamion, *L'Apôtre*, pp. 269–300; F. Dvornik, *Apostolicity*, p. 203.

128. A. Hilhorst, P. Lalleman, 'The Acts of Andrew and Matthias: Is it Part of the Original Acts of Andrew?', in J. N. Bremmer (ed.), *The Apocryphal Acts of Andrew* (Studies on the Apocryphal Acts of the Apostles, 5; Leuven: Peeters, 2000), pp. 1–14.

129. M. Blumenthal, *Formen*, pp. 40–45.

accounts seem to prove that all five texts are versions of a common source that they rework and adapt to their own textual framework.

The obvious conclusion is that neither hypothesis concerning the story belonging to the primitive *AA* is correct, or, positively formulated, that both have attained a certain degree of truth. As far as the former is concerned, if *AAM* is in fact a later version of an earlier source containing the episode of Andrew and Matthias, it seems clear that *AAM*, as we know it today, was not included in the primitive *AA*, although it is right in assuming that the story as such might have appeared in it. As regards the second theory, it errs in denying that story in whatever form belonged to the primitive *Acts*, but is right in affirming that *AAM* presents enough traces to be dated to a later period.

Given that, according to the results of our own survey, *AAM* could not be the source of the other versions of the story, it follows that all five accounts must rely on a previous source. As long as there is no other text including Andrew's activities and as long as the majority of the apostle's peregrinations included in the primitive *AA* are unknown to us, it seems logical to assume that the origin of the different versions of the story about Andrew and Matthias should be searched for in the primitive *Acts*. The original version of the story in a simpler and shorter form might very well have been one of *AA*'s numerous episodes.

IMAGES OF HOPE:
TOWARDS AN UNDERSTANDING OF NEW TESTAMENT
MIRACLE STORIES

Bernd Kollmann

1. Introduction

For more than three hundred years, the understanding of the New Testament
miracle stories has posed one of the most difficult problems for research into the
Bible. In a narrower sense, a miracle is an event which runs against the established
laws of nature. From the beginnings of Christianity, church tradition used to
interpret miracles in supernatural terms as interventions by God in the course of
nature. Within Christian doctrine, the biblical miracles acquired a key position
since they took the burden of proof for the truth of the revealed religious system.
Since the time of the Enlightenment, more and more people came to think that
believing in a divine supernatural intervention in space and time was incompatible
with modern science. Rational thinking viewed the concept of miracle as an
outmoded idea that had become untenable to the educated and was to be
abandoned. While in the period of rationalism efforts were made to explain the
miracles of Jesus as natural events, soon afterwards the mythical explanation was
seen as the key to an understanding of the miracle stories as non-historical fiction.
Later on, comparative religion, with its view of the Jewish and Hellenistic parallels,
showed that the New Testament miracle stories were not unique with regard to
their form, content and motifs. Thus, the programme of demythologization
completed the devaluation of the miracle stories, interpreting them as an
ambiguous and dispensable cloak of the message of faith. All that seemed to
remain of the biblical miracles were myths and symbols. In this situation, an understanding of miracles as documents of hope provided new perspectives. In present
research, psychological and feminist approaches to the Bible discover the miracle
stories as documents of liberation. This essay will give an overview of the
continuing debate on miracles and try to show that biblical miracle narratives are
best interpreted as images of hope.

2. The Rationalistic Approach to Miracles

The modern controversy about miracles started at the time of the Enlightenment.
The supernatural view that the power of God is able to interrupt the course of
nature by miracles did not remain undisputed and was rejected. From the philosophical perspective, the main objection against the miracle was its contradiction

to reason. In the seventeenth century, the radical Dutch thinker Baruch de Spinoza (1634–77) endeavoured to replace the traditional concept of God with a religion of humanity that left no room for miracles. In his *Theological-Political Treatise*, he argued that nothing happened contrary to nature and concluded that God's existence could not be known through miracles but instead through rational thinking. For whatever is contrary to nature is contrary to reason, and should therefore be rejected. The common people preferred to remain in ignorance of natural causes partly for reasons of piety, partly for the sake of opposing reason. They staunchly adhered to the belief in supernatural powers, even when new scientific knowledge enabled them to explain the miracles on a natural basis. The numerous miraculous events in the Bible were due to the narrators' purpose of appealing to fantasy and imagination instead of convincing people on rational grounds.

> Therefore, to interpret Scriptural miracles and to understand from their accounts how they really took place, one must know the beliefs of those who originally related them and left us written records of them, and one must distinguish between these beliefs and what could have been presented to their senses. Otherwise we shall confuse their beliefs and judgments with the miracle as it really happened. And awareness of their beliefs is of further importance in avoiding confusion between what really happened and what was imagined and was no more than prophetic symbolism. For many things are related in Scripture as real, and were also believed to be real, but were nevertheless merely symbolical and imaginary.[1]

During the eighteenth century, the rational criticism on the subject of the miracles flourished. Hermann Samuel Reimarus (1694–1768), a professor of oriental languages, condemned blind faith in miracles from the position of naturalistic deism and attacked the foundations of Christianity.[2] He demanded a natural religion based upon reason. The essential truths of this universal religion were the existence of God, the immortality of the soul, and morality. The belief in miracles, mysteries and revelations was rejected. Although it might be admitted that Jesus effected cures, which in the eyes of his contemporaries were miraculous, the biblical miracle stories were based on superstition, ignorance, and fraud. In the eyes of Reimarus, they were as false as the religious system for whose purposes they were invented. The gospel miracles aimed to prove Jesus to be the expected Messiah. Jesus himself did not actually perform miraculous works. Had he only performed a single miracle publicly, convincingly, and undeniably, such was human nature that people at once would have flocked to his movement instead of demanding his crucifixion.

---

1.   B. Spinoza, *Theological-Political Treatise* (trans. S. Shirley; Indianapolis and Cambridge: Hackett Publishing Company, 1998), p. 83.
2.   H. S. Reimarus, *Apologie oder Schutzschrift für die vernünftigen Verehrer Gottes* (2 vols.; ed. G. Alexander; Frankfurt a. M.: Insel-Verlag, 1972), vol. 2, pp. 371–91. Reimarus himself did not dare to publish this work during his lifetime. After his death, Gottfried Ephraim Lessing began to publish the most important portions of it, cf. A. Schweitzer, *The Quest of the Historical Jesus: A Critical Study of its Progress from Reimarus to Wrede* (trans. W. Montgomery; London: Black, 2nd edn, 1911), pp. 13–26.

David Hume (1711–76) strictly defined miracles as transgressions of the law of nature. In a more philosophical way, he discussed existing evidence for miraculous events outside our experience.[3] His interest focused on the principles for the rational acceptance of testimony, i.e. on the rules that ought to govern our either believing or not believing what we are told. For the miracles of the Gospels we had to rely upon the testimonies of the past. Those miracles did not meet the investigations of reason directly but only through the medium of human witnesses. According to sound judgement, it was likely, in general, that the testimony of a miracle was incorrect and unreliable since natural laws had been observed to function on countless occasions. Experience and observation proved that human witnesses tended to be unreliable or mistaken. 'A wise man proportions his belief to the evidence.' Weighing the alternatives, the evidence for the rational explanation of an event was always regarded as stronger than the evidence for a miraculous interpretation.

> When anyone tells me, that he saw a dead man restored to life, I immediately consider with myself, whether it be more probable, that this person should either deceive or be deceived, or that the fact, which he relates, should really have happened. I weigh the one miracle against the other; and according to the superiority, which I discover, I pronounce my decision, and always reject the greater miracle.[4]

Hume did not generally deny the possibility of miracles but endeavoured to show that we never had good reason to believe they had happened. Therefore, miracles could not be the foundation for any system of religion.

While philosophical rationalism waged a stubborn battle against belief in miracles and the foundations of Christianity, a completely different answer to the question of miracle was given by rationalist theologians of the late eighteenth and early nineteenth centuries. They also were influenced by the Enlightenment and tried to deal with the biblical miracles on the grounds of reason. While Reimarus and Hume claimed that the miracles had not taken place or could at least not be proven, they attempted to defend the historicity of the miracles by applying non-supernatural interpretations. The main representatives of rationalist exegesis were Carl Friedrich Bahrdt (1741–92), Carl Heinrich Venturini (1768–1849), and Heinrich Gottlieb Paulus (1761–1851). In providing natural explanations, the theological rationalism attempted to smooth away the contradiction between miracles and natural law.

Bahrdt was the first to give a natural interpretation of the miraculous events in his *Explanation of the Plans and Aims of Jesus*, addressed to 'readers who seek

3.   D. Hume, 'An Inquiry Concerning Human Understanding: Section X. Of Miracles', in Hume, *Essays: Moral, Political, and Literary* (2 vols.; eds. T. H. Green, T.H. Grose; reprint Aalen: Scientia-Verlag, 1964) vol. 2, pp. 88–108. Cf. J. L. Mackie, 'Miracles and Testimony – Hume's Argument', in R. Swinburne (ed.), *Miracles* (New York: Macmillan, 1989), pp. 85–96.
4.   D. Hume, *Miracles*, p. 94.

the truth'.[5] In all cases of healings he claimed the process to have been natural. The apostle Luke, with his medical skills, called Jesus' attention not only to the sick, but also to remarkable cases of apparently dead people who were restored. The explanation of the feeding of the five thousand lay in a secret cave where a great quantity of bread was stored and distributed to the multitude. With reference to the walking on the water, Bahrdt thought it reasonable that Jesus walked over the surface of a floating raft while the disciples, unable to see the wooden raft, supposed this event to have been a miracle. Venturini, who wrote a popular *Natural History of the Great Prophet of Nazareth*, was convinced that for modern medical science, the healing miracles were by no means miraculous.[6] In his eyes, Jesus always carried a portable medicine chest with him and never healed without applying medication or surgical skills. The raisings from the dead were cases of people in coma diagnosed and restored by Jesus. The nature miracles rested on error and obvious misunderstandings. With regard to the stilling of the storm, Venturini asserted that Jesus made an intelligent observation of the state of the weather and had an exalted courage in the presence of real peril. In the case of the feeding of the multitude he proposed that Jesus convinced the rich to share their supplies with the poor, thus providing enough food for everyone. The walking on the water was explained as an optical illusion. While Jesus was walking along the shore, the disciples believed him to be walking on the water.

Paulus, representative of a fully developed rationalism, put forth in his *Life of Jesus*, perfected the natural explanation of miracles.[7] He consistently tried to look beneath the surface of the miracles in order to illuminate the real events. In the case of the exorcisms and healings, Jesus influenced and improved the nervous system of the sufferers with his spiritual power. Discussing the raisings from the dead, Paulus shared the common rationalistic explanation, supposing deliverances of apparently dead people from premature burial. The explanation of the nature miracles is almost identical to that in the theories of Venturini, since both scholars influenced one another on this point. Thus the rationalistic theologians looked for intermediate causes not mentioned in the biblical narratives that could provide them with the knowledge necessary to render the miraculous events compatible

5. C. F. Bahrdt, *Ausführung des Plans und Zweks Jesu: In Briefen an Wahrheit suchende Leser* (11 vols.; Berlin: August Mylius, 1784–92). Cf. A. Schweitzer, *Quest of the Historical Jesus*, pp. 38–44; E. Keller, M.-L. Keller, *Miracles in Dispute: A Continuing Debate* (trans. M. Kohl; London: SCM Press, 1969), pp. 67–79.

6. C. H. Venturini, *Natuerliche Geschichte des großen Propheten von Nazareth* (4 vols.; "Bethlehem" = Kopenhagen: Schubothe, 1800–1802). Cf. A. Schweitzer, *Quest of the Historical Jesus*, pp. 44–47; B. Kollmann, *Jesus und die Christen als Wundertäter: Studien zu Magie, Medizin und Schamanismus in Antike und Christentum* (FRLANT, 170; Göttingen: Vandenhoeck & Ruprecht, 1996), pp. 19–20.

7. H. E. G. Paulus, *Das Leben Jesu als Grundlage einer reinen Geschichte des Urchristentums* (2 vols.; Heidelberg: C. F. Winter, 1828). Cf. A. Schweitzer, *Quest of the Historical Jesus*, pp. 48–57.

with reason and sound judgement. Under the spell of the supernatural, the biblical narrators were assumed not to have been capable of perceiving the intervening causes. According to the rationalist theologians, miracles really happened but did by no means break the laws of nature.

3. Miracle and Myth

In his groundbreaking work *The Life of Jesus*, David Friedrich Strauss (1808–74) marked a new approach to miracles. He provided a consistent application of mythological explanations to the New Testament and used the term 'myth' to develop his understanding of the miraculous events.[8] According to this view, the miracle stories were unhistorical narratives designed to express the notion of Jesus as the expected Jewish Messiah. In summing up previous attempts to explain miracles, Strauss rejected both the supernatural and the naturalistic interpretations, which he found unsatisfying. Instead, he consistently adhered to the mythical pattern of thought. The miraculous incidents, as narrated by the evangelists, had to be regarded as supernatural events that never happened. They were due to the messianic faith and to be understood mythically. During the time of Jesus, the Messiah was not only generally expected to work miracles, according to the Old Testament types and declarations, even the particular miracles he was to perform were fixed. The signs and wonders performed by Moses, the first redeemer, were expected from the Messiah as the last redeemer. Another important source of the gospel miracles might be found in the traditions of Elijah and Elisha. Among the prophecies, Isa. 35.5-6 was especially influential in forming the miraculous portion of the messianic idea. According to Strauss, Jesus as portrayed by the Gospels, more than satisfied this demand his contemporaries made on the Messiah. The Christians wished to adorn their Messiah with greater powers than the prophets and miracle workers of the Old Testament possessed. To prove this theory, Strauss started with an investigation into the exorcisms, the therapies, and the resuscitations of the dead. With regard to these types of miracles, he observed an evident climax in the marvellous and a gradation in inconceivability.

> We have indeed been able to represent to ourselves how a mental derangement, in which none of the bodily organs were attacked beyond the nervous system, which is immediately connected with mental action, might have been removed, even in a purely psychical manner, by the mere word, look, and influence of Jesus: but the more deeply the malady appeared to have penetrated into the entire corporeal system, the more inconceivable to us was a cure of this kind. Where in insane persons the brain was disturbed to the extent of raging madness, or where in nervous patients the disorder was so confirmed as to manifest itself in periodical epilepsy; there we could scarcely imagine how permanent benefit could be conferred by that mental influence; and this was yet more difficult where the disease had no immediate connection with the mind, as in leprosy, blindness, lameness, etc. And yet, up to this point, there was always something present, to which the miraculous power of Jesus

---

8.   D. F. Strauss, *The Life of Jesus Critically Examined* (ed. P.C. Hodgson; trans. G. Eliot; London: SCM Press, 1973), pp. 413–534. Cf. A. Schweitzer, *Quest of the Historical Jesus*, pp. 78–96; E. Keller, M.-L. Keller, *Miracles in Dispute*, pp. 80–91.

could apply itself; there was still a consciousness in the objects, on which to make an impression – a nervous life to be stimulated. Not so with the dead. The corpse from which life and consciousness have flown has lost the last fulcrum for the power of the miracle worker; it perceives him no longer – receives no impression from him; for the very capability of receiving impressions must be conferred on him anew. But to confer this, that is, to give life in the proper sense, is a creative act, and to think of this as being exercised by a man, we must confess to be beyond our power.[9]

Following from these considerations, Strauss provided a mythical derivation of the miraculous healings. Some of the healings might have been historical, but not in the form tradition had preserved them. The cures of leprosy, blindness, and lameness, as well as the resuscitations of the dead, were included in the Jewish idea of the Messiah. The Christians, who believed the Messiah to have actually appeared in the person of Jesus, glorified his history with such traits taken from the Mosaic tradition and prophetic legend. In the Gospels, Jesus appeared as the one who surpassed the miracles of the prophets and fulfilled Isaiah's promise of the dawn of the messianic kingdom that would provide the end of all human misery. With regard to the nature miracles, the messianic faith of the early Church was the presupposition of the gospel narratives to an even higher degree. To Strauss it was unimaginable that Jesus determined and mitigated the motions of irrational and even of inanimate objects such as water or bread. The stilling of the storm originated in the desire to attribute to Jesus a similar command over the wind and the sea as Moses had in his partition of the Red Sea. The feeding of the multitude in the desert was part of the messianic expectations at the time of Jesus and also had its prototypes in the Old Testament. Here, striking similarities to the Mosaic narratives of the manna miracle appeared even in details. The prophetic traditions of Elijah and Elisha continued to develop this type of miraculous supply of nourishment. Thus, 2 Kgs 2.42-44 provided the closest example to Jesus' food miracle.

Although Strauss overestimated the importance of the Old Testament with regard to the development of the New Testament legend, his mythical view was a milestone in the study of the biblical miracles. The radical criticism of the supernatural and the rationalistic explanations, combined with a consequent mythological interpretation of the gospel narratives, was groundbreaking. As a result of the mythological concept, the question of the miracle increasingly lost its importance. Strauss marked the beginning of the period of a non-miraculous view of the life of Jesus, as well as the exclusion of the miracle from the centre of Christian faith.

4. The Theory of Demythologization
In his epoch-making approach to miracles, Rudolf Bultmann (1884–1976) was deeply influenced by the mythological view. He developed a demythologizing programme in the interest of an existentialist theology and adopted a new way

---

9.   D. F. Strauss, *Life of Jesus*, p. 486.

of interpreting the miracles in the tradition of form criticism and comparative religion. Bultmann found much to agree with in the mythological understanding of the miracles as established by Strauss. While Strauss interpreted the miracle tradition against the background of the prophetic and messianic traditions of Israel, Bultmann rejected the Old Testament as a source of influence. Instead, the Hellenistic parallels to the New Testament miracle stories moved to the centre of interest. In his *History of the Synoptic Tradition*, which first appeared in 1921, Bultmann provided a large collection of motifs and parallels the New Testament miracle stories shared with pagan miracle stories of antiquity.[10] Here, Bultmann was influenced by classical philologists, such as Richard Reitzenstein and Otto Weinreich, who investigated the Hellenistic miracle traditions. Both scholars encountered considerable material resembling the New Testament miracle stories in form and content.[11] With regard to the Hellenistic material, Bultmann saw the possibility that not only single motifs but entire miracle stories had been transferred from the Hellenistic world into the synoptic tradition. 'Moreover the Hellenistic origin of the miracle stories may be taken to be overwhelmingly probable.'[12] To be sure, the doubts in the historical value of the miracles of Jesus drove Bultmann into scepticism with regard to the belief in miracles. More importantly, his scepticism was founded in the fear of objectifying God. He rejected the idea that miracles could function as objective proof upon which Christians might base their faith.[13] Even if all miracles in the Gospels were historically verified, they were entirely open to critical investigation. As the deeds of a man in the past they did not directly concern us.[14] For this reason, Bultmann made a distinction between miracle and wonder. There is only one wonder, he argued, which is the wonder of the revelation of God's grace to the godless, the revelation of forgiveness. In contradiction to the world process, God by this wonder destroyed our understanding of ourselves as achievers and provided freedom through forgiveness. In contrast to the wonder of grace and forgiveness, the deeds of Jesus were miracles that revealed the ambiguity of the Christian preaching. According to Bultmann, they represent an outmoded idea of miracle that has become untenable and must be abandoned. Christian faith should have no interest at all in proving the possibility or reality of the miracles of Jesus. Since the biblical writers, who used the

10. R. Bultmann, *The History of the Synoptic Tradition* (trans. J. Marsh; New York: Harper & Row, 1963), pp. 218–38.

11. R. Reitzenstein, *Hellenistische Wundererzählungen* (Stuttgart: B. G. Teubner, 1906); O. Weinreich, *Antike Heilungswunder: Untersuchungen zum Wunderglauben der Griechen und Römer* (RVV, 8.1; Gießen: A. Töpelmann, 1909).

12. R. Bultmann, *History of the Synoptic Tradition*, p. 240.

13. Cf. R. Bultmann, 'Bultmann Replies to His Critics', in H. W. Bartsch (ed.), *Kerygma and Myth: A Theological Debate* (New York: Harper & Row, 1961), pp. 191–211 (199): 'The conception of miracles as ascertainable processes is incompatible with the hidden character of God's activity. It surrenders the acts of God to objective observation, and thus makes belief in miracles (or rather superstition) susceptible to the justifiable criticisms of science.'

14. R. Bultmann, 'The Question of Wonder', in R. Bultmann, *Faith and Understanding* I (ed. R. W. Funk; trans. L. P. Smith; New York and Evanston: Harper & Row, 1969), pp. 247–61 (260).

miracles in accordance with the ancient world-view, had not fully apprehended the idea of miracle and its implications, Bultmann did not consider the authority of Scripture abandoned when the idea of miracle was relinquished.

This radical approach to the New Testament miracle stories was completed by the theory of demythologization. Bultmann strove to demythologize the early Christian perspective on the miracles of Jesus in order to provide a better understanding of miracle stories in modern times. The primitive Church expressed the revelatory kerygma, the message of faith, in the mythological way of its time. In antiquity, people used the mythical view of the universe to explain the divine or supernatural in human terms. The miracles were a central part of the biblical mythology, like the virgin birth or the reference to Jesus as a pre-existent being. Since modern mankind had scientific presuppositions that did not fit the mythological thinking of the New Testament, it was impossible for any modern person to intellectually accept the mythical views of the first century and to believe the events described in the biblical miracle stories.

> It is impossible to use electric light and the wireless and to avail ourselves of modern medical and surgical discoveries, and at the same time to believe in the New Testament world of spirits and miracles. We may think we can manage it in our own lives, but to expect others to do so is to make the Christian faith unintelligible and unacceptable to the modern world.[15]

Therefore, demythologization can be defined as an interpretation of the New Testament enabling people today to grasp the message of the myths without abandoning their scientific knowledge of modern times. Bultmann did not try to eliminate or remove the myths from the Bible, an act which he believed to be the error of liberalism. Instead, he tried to unwrap the revelatory kerygma hidden in the mythological veil of the miracles. He considered the cosmology and world-view of the Bible to be excess baggage representing an obstacle to believing in the message of faith today. The process of demythologization implied a translation of the New Testament into modern times. The core of the miracle stories was to be interpreted in terms of existentialist hermeneutics. He argued that it was pointless speaking of miracles in general and discussing the possibility of their occurrence. Considering an act of God without speaking simultaneously of our own existence was impossible. Therefore, Bultmann was convinced that the demythologized biblical traditions provided opportunities of human existence waiting to be grasped through faith.

The tradition of demythologization formed a consensus stating that the miracle stories themselves were not important. Rather the hidden message of faith was essential. The biblical narratives only appeared to report remarkable events in the life of Jesus. In truth they proclaimed what God did through Jesus as the Christ,

---

15. R. Bultmann, 'New Testament and Mythology', in H. W. Bartsch (ed.), *Kerygma and Myth*, pp. 1–44 (5).

through the crucified and risen Lord, to the Church and what he willed to do to the world.[16] In consequence, the miracle stories should be regarded as witnesses of the kerygma veiled in the cloaks of myth. They told how people were shaken in their old existence in meeting with Christ and how they were led to a new existence that saved them from fear and desperation.

5. Miracles as Images of Hope

The concept of demythologisation reduced the miracles to an ambiguous and dispensable cover of the message of faith. Within these limits, redaction criticism in the first place attempted to show how the belief in miracles was critically revised by the evangelists to convey their message.[17] Modern theologians tended to project their problems with the miracles onto the Gospels. They refused to see that a positive attitude of the evangelists towards the miracles also existed. Surprisingly it was the merit of a Marxist philosopher, Ernst Bloch, to remind theology of the indispensable value of the belief in miracles. In the nineteenth century, Ludwig Feuerbach had regarded religion as the opiate of the people and saw the biblical miracles as illusions that provided the imaginary fulfilment of wishes in fantasy.[18] The power of the miracle was seen as sorcery of the imagination which satisfied, without contradiction, all the wishes of the heart and lacked any positive element. The infantile belief in miracles allegedly prevented mankind from growing up and working towards a better world. In his *Principle of Hope* (1957), Bloch, however, pointed out that daydreams, visions, myths, and miracles all provided the material for a critique of the present situation and the impetus for revolution.[19] The belief in miracles was more than childish superstition. It contained the concept of the leap, which stemmed from explosive religion. According to Bloch, the miracle is

---

16. W. Schmithals, *Wunder und Glaube* (BSt, 59; Neukirchen-Vluyn: Neukirchener Verlag, 1970), pp. 25–26. Cf. also G. Klein, 'Wunderglaube und Neues Testament', in G. Klein, *Ärgernisse* (München: Kaiser, 1970), pp. 13–57. In his commentary on Mark, Schmithals provides a detailed kerygmatic interpretation of the miracle stories. He rejects the theory of an oral tradition and denies the historical value of the Markan miracle stories. The author of the pre-Markan miracle stories is seen as an excellent theologian who developed the Pauline message of faith in narratives. For instance, Mk 3:1-6, according to this theory, proclaims the freedom of man from the Mosaic law, whereas Mk 5.1-20 is a narrative display of Rom. 7.24, cf. W. Schmithals, *Das Evangelium nach Markus* (ÖTbK, 2.1-2; 2 vols.; Gütersloh: Gütersloher Verlagshaus; Würzburg: Echter, 1979) vol. 1, pp. 28, 198.

17. Cf. G. Theissen, A. Merz, *The Historical Jesus:. A Comprehensive Guide* (trans. J. Bowden; London: SCM Press, 1998), pp. 288–89; B. Kollmann, *Neutestamentliche Wundergeschichten: Biblisch-theologische Zugänge und Impulse für die Praxis* (UT, 477; Stuttgart: Kohlhammer, 2002), pp. 117–36.

18. L. Feuerbach, 'Über das Wunder', in L. Feuerbach, *Kleinere Schriften* I *(1835-1839)* (Collected Works, 8; Berlin: Akademie-Verlag, 2nd edn, 1982), pp. 293–339. Cf. H.-J. Klimkeit, *Das Wunderverständnis Ludwig Feuerbachs in religionsphänomenologischer Sicht* (UARG NF, 5; Bonn: Rörscheid, 1965).

19. E. Bloch, *The Principle of Hope Part V* (trans. N. Plaice, S. Plaice, P. Knight; Oxford: Blackwell, 1986), pp. 1303–11.

both characterized by a formal point of interruption of the accustomed status quo and by the material part of its absolutely good content. In the light of the miracles with their vision of a better world, reality was confronted with a counterpart that unmasked the insufficiency of the contemporary world. Miracles provided a view of the unrealized opportunities of human existence and intended palpable change of an external kind within the frame of humanity's utopian desires.

This concept rendered an entirely new view of the biblical miracles and influenced Gerd Theissen in his understanding of the miracle stories as collective symbolic actions of lower social classes. Unlike the programme of demythologization, he stood up for a rehabilitation of the belief in miracles and provided a functional investigation into the synoptic miracle tradition.[20] Theissen proposed that the biblical miracle stories should be read not only kerygmatically 'from above' but also as the expression of human protest 'from below'. Although in general ancient miracle stories did not originate in the lower classes, a certain degree of class correlation could hardly be denied. In the simplicity of their theology and, above all, in their subject matter, the miracle stories presented themselves as an expression of the lower classes. Ordinary people gained courage in the face of concrete emergencies by telling miracle stories. The biblical belief in miracles focused on specific situations of distress, such as demonic possession, disease or hunger. Those were remote experiences to the upper classes. Theissen argues that in miracles the desires of mankind stand up against reality. He proposes that miracle stories, more clearly than other traditions, focus on the crossing of boundaries and the transcending of human logic. Even the most impossible things simply appear possible. Therefore, the belief in miracles would rather deny the truth of all human experience than give up the claim that human distress must be overcome.

> The miracles of Jesus were initially meant to bring concrete, material, healing help. They contain a protest against human distress. They deny all previous experience its validity rather than denying the right for human distress to be removed. Wherever these stories are related, people are not content that there is too little bread for many, that there is no healing for many who are sick, and that there is no home in our world for many who are hurt. Wherever these miracles are related, people do not turn away from those who are hopelessly ill. The miracle stories need always to be read 'from below' as a protest against human suffering.[21]

Seen against the background of the community which recounted them, the miracle stories were collective symbolic actions. In the eyes of Theissen, they remedied distress and offered people the strength to combat despair in their ordinary lives through actions that were not merely symbolic. The miracle stories did not only enable the primitive Christian communities to meet fears such as illness and hunger. They also assured people in need and distress that they would not be

---

20. G. Theissen, *The Miracle Stories of the Early Christian Tradition* (ed. J. Riches; trans. F. McDonagh; Edinburgh: T&T Clark, 1983), pp. 231–302.
21. Theissen, Merz, *Historical Jesus*, p. 313.

abandoned by others. According to this concept, the belief in miracles and myths was an important step back to a world of childish experience in which the boundaries of reality were transgressed. It provided the image of a better world and, at the same time, demanded visible change to the present world. Reality was opposed and radically transcended. The miracle stories were seen as narratives against distress and despair as they contained timeless images of hope.

6. The Psychological Interpretation of the Miracles

Eugen Drewermann's concept of depth psychology as a tool for the interpretation of religious traditions marked the beginning of a new debate on miracles.[22] The starting point was the depth psychology of Carl Gustav Jung, who developed the theory of archetypes as the mode of expression of the collective subconscious.[23] Jung discovered the preconscious psychic disposition in the depth of the soul that enables individuals to react in a human manner. These archetypes or patterns at the unconscious level exist in every culture and in every period of human history. As the universal or collective subconscious, they are rooted in the common development of the human species and are shared by all humans. The subconscious archetypes manifest themselves in archaic symbols such as dreams, religious beliefs, myths and fairy tales. Since the archetypes are not consciously controlled, humans may tend to fear them and deny their existence by way of suppression. Jung distinguishes between anima, animus and shadow as parts of the archetypes. The anima and the animus are hidden opposite genders in each individual. While the animus is the more rationalistic male part of the female soul, the anima is the more emotional female part of the male soul. The search into the subconscious also involves confronting the shadow, the dark side of the soul that humans deny in themselves and project onto others. A disharmony of animus and anima, as well as the hidden shadow archetype, causes illness of the soul. Healing is a process of individuation by which a person becomes a psychological unity. In this therapeutic process whose desired goal is harmony between conscious and subconscious, the archetypical symbols may be helpful. They include inherited patterns of behaviour that enable people to deal with crises and to integrate the dark sides of the soul through recognition and acceptance. At the end of the process of individuation stands wholeness and integration. The opposites of the animus and the anima are joined in harmony, while the shadow is integrated into the self.

This concept forms the basis of Eugen Drewermann's approach to the miracles. In his deep psychological hermeneutics he aims at recovering the healing power

22. E. Drewermann, *Tiefenpsychologie und Exegese* (2 vols.; Olten: Walter-Verlag, 3rd edn, 1992), vol 2, pp. 43–309. See also E. Drewermann, *Das Markusevangelium* (2 vols.; Olten: Walter-Verlag, 1987); E. Drewermann, *Das Matthäusevangelium* (3 vols.; Olten: Walter-Verlag, 4th edn, 1990).

23. C. G. Jung, *The Archetypes of the Collective Unconscious* (Collected Works, 9.1; Princeton: University Press, 2nd edn, 1968). Cf. R. Robertson, *C. G. Jung and the Archetypes of the Collective Unconscious* (New York: Peter Lang, 1987), pp. 75–176.

of religious symbols in the Bible. He argues that the biblical miracle stories, as well as other miraculous traditions, essentially function as a remedy for the broken soul. With regard to primitive societies, he develops an understanding of illness as mental disharmony. The situation today is characterized by people's experience of existential psychological anxieties. Psychological rather than physical reasons primarily cause illness. A disturbed or even hostile human relationship with the invisible world of the subconscious forms the basis of illness and mental disharmony. The close connection between guilt and illness is of great importance, as implied in miracle stories such as Mk 2.1-12. Humans who unlearn to dream lose the belief in themselves. Thus they develop feelings of guilt and become sick. The suffering of the body is thought to be the reflected image of the broken soul that has lost its centre. According to this point of view, illness in the biblical miracle stories in general is psychosomatic. The human body reacts with leprosy, fever, blindness or lameness to the disruption of the soul. This concept portrays Jesus as a shaman whose healings of a remarkable number of sick persons are completely acceptable from the psychological point of view. To Drewermann the biblical miracles do not substantially differ from those of figures such as Orpheus, Pythagoras, Empedocles or Black Elk, a modern medicine man of the Sioux.[24] Like these miracle workers, Jesus is seen as a shaman in a primitive society whose mirac-ulous healings caused harmony of body and soul, effecting a reintegration of man into the unity of the universe. Shamanism is thought to be the pure and true form of religion that needs to be rediscovered in order to displace rationalistic theology and to heal the psychosomatic desperation of our times.

> Thus paradoxical is the situation: the historical critical approach to the Bible as a belated bastard of modern rationalism and secularism stumbles into one embarrassment after the other. Just one view of the life of a true miraculous healer beyond European civilization is apt to demonstrate the way the miracle of healing should be understood. More importantly, it shows the power credited to an unadulterated form of religiousness.[25]

Thus miracle stories have to be read as answers to the timeless experience of anxiety and desperation. According to Drewermann, the situation of modern humans is characterized by the morbid obsession to gain recognition and power. For instance, the illness of Peter's mother-in-law should be seen as a symbol of our everyday life that is nothing more than a 'crazy fever'.[26] The paralysed man who had to be lowered to Jesus through a torn-up roof (Mk 2.1-12) also suffers from an illness we all more or less share in our lives. Again and again humans gain the experience of bodily lameness that is caused by paralysis of the soul, derived from hopelessness, resignation, and feelings of guilt.[27] Drewermann proposes that in the

---

24. E. Drewermann, *Tiefenpsychologie und Exegese*, vol 2, pp. 79–141. For information on Black Elk, see J. G. Neihardt, *Black Elk Speaks: Being the Life Story of a Holy Man of the Oglala Sioux* (Lincoln, NB: University of Nebraska Press, 1961).

25. E. Drewermann, *Tiefenpsychologie und Exegese*, vol. 2, p. 123.

26. E. Drewermann, *Markusevangelium*, vol 1, p. 206.

27. E. Drewermann, *Tiefenpsychologie und Exegese*, vol 2, p. 223.

depth of the miracle stories, archetypical patterns of behaviour may be found which provide healing. As in biblical times, the encounter with the healing Jesus provokes a therapeutic process that leads to wholeness and integration.

7. The Significance of the Miracles in Feminist Theology

Feminist theologians offer quite a different approach to miracle stories. It is commonly acknowledged that the biblical world is a patriarchal world. Men led the oral tradition of the biblical stories, as well as the process of writing. The male authors of the Bible were men of their times who unconsciously or deliberately obscured the role of women. Thus a significant part of the biblical tradition promotes the suppression of women, and claims their inferiority to men with regard to theological and spiritual matters. Feminist theology sees the necessity both to describe the story of women in the Bible, and to systematically uncover tendencies hostile to women. The patriarchal shell of Scripture needs to be broken in order to unwrap a kernel of biblical traditions that show the equality of the sexes.[28] Research has observed that women often are more present in miracle stories and make themselves better heard than in other genres of religious writing, such as doctrinal or liturgical texts.[29] The primary focus of investigation on what miracle stories can tell about female action and theology should be the remarkable presence of women as acting characters in many narratives.

In the Old Testament, the resuscitation narratives 1 Kgs 17.17-24 and 2 Kgs 4. 8-37 are the most outstanding examples of female action in miracles. In both stories, women act in an uncommonly independent way.[30] In the narrative of Elijah and the widow of Zarephath, a non-Israelite woman surprisingly expresses the legitimation of the prophet (1 Kgs 17.24). While Ahab, the king of Israel, adheres to idolatry and worships Baal, the Gentile widow gives an exuberant testimony of the trustworthiness of the word of God. In the story of Elisha and the great woman of Shunem, the father of the child plays no role at all. He remains nameless and is defined only in relation to his wife. While she receives the title of a great woman, he is only known as her husband. When the child becomes ill, the man shifts the responsibility to his wife. She informs him neither about the death of the boy nor about the reasons of her trip to Elisha. With regard to the prophet, the woman of Shunem continues to stand out as the active person throughout the story. The power of the man of God is subverted by that of the great woman.[31]

28. Cf. E. Schuessler Fiorenza, *In Memory of Her: A Feminist Theological Reconstruction of Christian Origins* (New York, NY: Crossroad, 1984); L. Schottroff, S. Schroer, M.-T. Wacker, *The Bible in Women's Perspective* (Augsburg: Fortress, 1998); L. Schottroff, M.-T. Wacker (eds), *Kompendium Feministische Bibelauslegung* (Gütersloh: Gütersloher Verlagshaus, 1998).

29. A.-M. Korte (ed.), *Women and Miracle Stories: A Multidisciplinary Exploration* (SHR, 88; Leiden: E. J. Brill, 2001).

30. Cf. J. Siebert-Hommes, 'The Widow of Zarephath and the Great Woman of Shunem: A Comparative Analysis of Two Stories', in B. Becking, M. Dijkstra (eds), *On Reading Prophetic Texts: Gender-Specific and Related Studies in Memory of Fokkelien van Dijk-Hemmes* (Leiden: E. J. Brill, 1996), pp. 231–50.

31. Cf. M. E. Shields, 'Subverting a Man of God, Elevating a Woman: Role and Power

Elisha apparently experiences difficulties with his prophetic calling. Instead of personally restoring the boy to life, he sends his servant Gehazi, who fails to perform the miracle. Gehazi's failure is also Elisha's failure. The woman's insistence on Elisha's presence marks the turning point of the story. Referring to Elisha's calling by Elijah, she appeals to the prophet's responsibility and reminds him of his prophetic tasks as a man of God.[32] The prophet acts in response to the woman's initiative. Thanks to her persistence and actions, Elisha brings the child back to life and proves to be Elijah's true successor. While the ostensible power lies in the hands of the prophet, the real power rests with the woman.

In the New Testament, Mk 7.24-30 reports the most remarkable presence and religious action of a woman in a miracle story. The exorcism story tells the encounter of a teaching woman and a learning Jesus. The heart of the narrative is the dialogue between Jesus and the woman, who is begging for her afflicted daughter to be healed. Jesus not only refuses to perform the exorcism but also addresses the petitioner with harsh and insulting language, applying the term 'dog' to the Gentiles. The Syrophoenician woman is not silenced by Jesus' insult but starts struggling and contending with him. In her reply she refers to the words of Jesus and teaches him that the mercies of God are not limited to ethnic Israel. While the story confirms Israel's privileges, it claims the grace of God also for Gentiles. The persistence of the non-Jewish woman overcomes her rejection by Jesus. In the view of feminist or feminist-orientated theology, the encounter with the Syrophoenician woman is seen as a turning point in the mission of Jesus. Thus Jesus, the 'Messiah of the women' or 'the first new man', is thought to have been cured by the woman of patriarchal thinking, enabling him to open to female forms of spirituality.[33]

The woman suffering from a permanent menstrual flow (Mk 5.24-34) also initiates her healing in an unusual way. She believes she physically has to touch Jesus in order to be healed. Thus, she draws near Jesus in the crowd, touches his cloak, and is immediately cured of her illness that was a constant source of ritual impurity according to the laws of Leviticus.[34] Considering the woman's social

Reversals in 2 Kings 4', *JSOT* 58 (1993), pp. 59–69; F. van Dijk-Hemmes, 'The Great Woman of Shunem and the Man of God: A Dual Interpretation of 2 Kings 4.8-37', in A. Brenner (ed.), *A Feminist Companion to Samuel and Kings* (Sheffield: Sheffield Academic Press, 1994), pp. 218–30.

32. The woman's oath in 2 Kgs 4.30 is identical to the one used by Elisha in 2 Kgs 2.4. Elisha's response to the woman's declaration ('So he rose up and followed her') is a direct repetition of his response to Elijah's call (1 Kgs 19.21). These parallels strongly indicate that Elisha is not simply acceding to the request of a distraught woman. Rather, he is following the lead of the one in charge, cf. W. J. Bergen, *Elisha and the End of Prophetism* (JSOTSup, 286; Sheffield: Sheffield Academic Press, 1999), p. 101.

33. Cf. C. Mulack, *Jesus der Gesalbte der Frauen* (Stuttgart: Kreuz-Verlag, 1987), pp. 80–90; F. Alt, *Jesus – der erste neue Mann* (München: Piper, 1989), pp. 70–71.

34. Lev. 15.19-30; 18.19; 20.18. See also U. Metternich, '*Sie sagte ihm die ganze Wahrheit*': *Die Erzählung von der 'Blutflüssigen' – feministisch gedeutet* (Mainz: Grünewald, 2000), pp. 78–132.

stigma, it is remarkable that she is the central figure of the story and becomes the model of true faith. The healing involves social reinstatement and demonstrates the liberation women experience in the Bible.

The case of the bent woman in Lk. 13.10-17 also 'has become a paradigm for the oppression and liberation which Christian women experience in biblical religion'.[35] The woman was bound both by an evil spirit and by the powers of patriarchy. She had suffered from a demon for eighteen years and was unable to stand up straight. Jesus laid his hands on the afflicted woman and freed her from her chains, thus violating the Sabbath law. Consequently, the cure led to a controversy over the Sabbath. The adversary in the story is a synagogue ruler who protests against the healing. From the feminist point of view, he is a representative of the male authorities that hinder women in their struggle to overcome the inferiority imposed by patriarchy. The narrative is influenced by the idea of an equality of the sexes, proclaiming the message that both women and men are children of Abraham. The healing of the bent woman is a sign of courage and hope for women to be freed and empowered to stand upright.

In the narrative of the raising of Lazarus (Jn 11.1-44), the role of Lazarus is entirely passive. Since his hometown Bethany is defined as the town of his sisters Mary and Martha, these women are the important characters. They set the story in motion. While Mary's activity is characterized by mourning, the story portrays Martha as the theologian.[36] Her conversation with Jesus forms the hermeneutics through which we are to understand the raising of Lazarus.[37] The encounter between Martha and Jesus leads to a theological discourse resulting in his self-revelation and her confession. Martha's representational value is not different from Peter's. Like him, she is portrayed as a faithful disciple and true confessor of Jesus. Her words surpass an inadequate faith based on signs and mark the fullest confession of Jesus as demanded by the fourth gospel (Jn 20.31). To the readers of John, Martha represents an exemplary role model to be followed.[38] Thus, from a feminist perspective, Jn 11.1-44 is another outstanding example that miracle stories with female characters should be read as documents of emancipation apt to empower women.

35. E. Schuessler Fiorenza, *But She Said: Feminist Practices of Biblical Interpretation* (Boston, MA: Beacon Press, 1992), pp. 195–217 (199).

36. S. van Tilborg, 'The Women in John: On Gender and Gender Bending', in J. W. van Henten, A. Brenner (eds.), *Families and Family Relations as Represented in Early Judaisms and Early Christianities: Texts and Fictions* (STAR, 2; Leiden: Deo Publishing, 2000), pp. 192–212, (199).

37. C. M. Conway, *Men and Women in the Fourth Gospel: Gender and Johannine Characterization* (SBLDS, 167; Atlanta, GA: Scholars Press, 1999), p. 151.

38. The phenomenon of John's giving a quasi-apostolic role to Martha as an intimate disciple of Jesus demonstrates the importance of women in the Johannine community, cf. R. E. Brown, 'Roles of Women in the Fourth Gospel', in R. E. Brown, *The Community of the Beloved Disciple* (London: Geoffrey Chapman, 1979), pp. 183–97. According to M. R. D'Angelo, 'Women Partners in the New Testament', in *JFSR* 6 (1990), pp. 65–86 (77–81), Jn 11.1-44 provides evidence that Martha and Mary were a well known missionary couple in the early Church.

8. The Hermeneutics of Alienation

The approach offered by the hermeneutics of alienation[39] is not related to a particular concept of understanding of miracle stories. It can be integrated into any model of interpretation and focuses renewed attention on the old miracle traditions. The hermeneutics of alienation are inspired by Bertolt Brecht and his alienation theory. Employing the estrangement effect *(Verfremdungseffekt)*, Brecht intended to provoke his audience to taking a fresh look at the message of a play.

> The estrangement effect turns a common, known, and present object into a peculiar, extraordinary, and unexpected object. An object that is taken for granted is rendered incomprehensible in a way. However, this happens only to render it even more comprehensible. An object has to leave its inconspicuous existence in order to be not merely known but perceived. The habitual assumption that an object requires no explanation has to be discarded. However manifold, humble or popular it may be, from now on it will be labelled unusual.[40]

Biblical texts can be alienated literarily or in visual ways. A variation of the form, such as the conversion of a miracle story into a poem, is one of the most important techniques of literary alienation. In a similar way, a different temporal or geographical setting of a narrative, as well as the introduction of new acting characters, causes estrangement. Visual alienation is effected by introducing paintings, photographs, sculptures or caricatures of biblical motifs. The hermeneutics of alienation are apt to close the deep gap between the historical setting of the text and the different situations of its addressees. Alienation provokes an intense discussion of the well-known documents of Christianity and brings new life into the old stories many readers are overly familiar with. An alienated reproduction of familiar narratives produces astonishment, curiosity, and contradiction, opening a new perspective on biblical traditions. Thus Rudolf Otto Wiemer's poem on the healing of the blind Bartimaeus provides a provocative view of Jesus' crucifixion and the sense of human suffering.

Bartimaeus

I am the one who he
made see.

What I saw? The cross
and him, executed,

him, more helpless than I was,
him, the helper, tortured.

---

39. Cf. H. K. Berg, *Ein Wort wie Feuer: Wege lebendiger Bibelauslegung* (München: Kösel; Stuttgart: Calwer Verlag, 1991), pp. 366–85.
40. B. Brecht, *Schriften zum Theater* 1 (Collected Works, 15; Frankfurt am Main: Suhrkamp, 1973), p. 355.

I asked, did I need
to lose my blindness
to see this?[41]

Erich Fried offers a new perspective on the exorcism in Mk 5.1-20. After the
healing, the biblical story concludes with the former demoniac begging to be with
Jesus, whereas Jesus surprisingly refuses the man's request and sends him home
to his people. This experience of rejection is the starting point for a literary alienation of the biblical story. From the perspective of the healed man, Jesus is
portrayed as a self-complacent miracle worker who does not care for the consequences of his deeds. The provocative poem appeals to human compassion and
evokes critical reflections on a faith in Christ primarily based on miracles.

The Healed Gadarene

The one who drove away the legions of my devils
does not want to take me along since the swineherds drive him away
('Work your miracles elsewhere
and not at the expense of our pigs.')

The one who loved me enough to save me,
does he not love me enough to have me with him?
Never did I have enough love.
It was in the empty caves
of unbelovedness within me
the devils were able to sit
(just as I found refuge in empty graves).

'God is love' he says
but whom does he love?
Does he love just his miracles
and the glory that is his part?
Does he love humankind and not the individual person?
Does he love only the thought of his love?

Or does he care equally for all humans
and just hates their devils?
Do I mean nothing to him, like the drowned pigs
and the herdsmen living on the pigs?

Perhaps his love is not really from here?
Does he love only his father and his mission?

41. R. O. Wiemer, 'Bartimäus', in S. Berg, H. K. Berg, *Himmel auf Erden: Wunder und
Gleichnisse* (München: Kösel; Stuttgart: Verlag, 1989), p. 43.

I go and call out his miracles
as he told me.
I want to love him,
him who saved me.
But what is this love like
that leaves me all alone?[42]

In her alienated retelling of the narrative of the bent woman in Lk. 13.10-17, the
artist Mary Lou Sleevi tells the story of contemporary women held in chains by
the powers of sexism and patriarchy.

A Stooped Woman

Healing is in process.
She is empowered
to stand straight and free.
A small, bony woman,
bent over double with her eyes to the ground,
had shuffled around
the house of worship for years. [...]

When he saw the double outcast,
Jesus called her to him.
That was her first surprise,
She had the backbone to come
as fast as she could. [...]

A question mark – ? –
is the shape of sexism
on the back of society today. The answer,
an exclamation point – ! –
is making its way. [...]

Both are body signs of church
called to repentance and healing
even on Sunday.

Ever since Jesus,
woman has been backbone of church.
Shortly thereafter,
she was returned to the background.

She has always been where church is,
her head bowed not only in prayer.
Schooled in retreat,
she was put on a pedestal
where movement is strictly limited. [...]

---

42. E. Fried, 'Der besessene Gadarener', in S. Berg, H. K. Berg, *Himmel auf Erden*, pp. 56–57.

Out of experience and prayer.
she is talking back and walking
ahead.
She is beyond the reach
of a pat on the head.
It deprives her; circumscribes her.
Exclusion disables, inclusion enables.
Behind the screen of golden rhetoric,
who knows better? It is her back!

She's a Crossing Point,
a shunned world
the church fears to touch
for fear it will touch back.
It will.

Raised by Jesus
to a lonely vantage point
in an obscure house of worship
in an unnamed town,
an anonymous woman
is a sign of Good News!

Here is a very little story,
seldom told on Sunday.

We are witnessing a new miracle
of empowering one another.
We glorify God
in stretching our backs![43]

The photo-project *I.N.R.I.*, by Serge Bramly und Bettina Rheims,[44] is one of the most fascinating attempts of visual alienation of biblical traditions. The photographs depicting the gospel narratives resemble pictures from a fashion journal or a lifestyle magazine. Models play the roles of Jesus, Mary and the apostles in contemporary settings like a railway station, a garage or a ghetto. The images carry a provocative appeal. The photographic alienation of the miraculous feeding (Mk 6.30-44) shows a happy young couple, wearing white clothes, on a yellow stubble field. The child in front of the couple appears a symbol of life. In the background, dozens of fish fly around an enormous tree. The photograph impresses the viewer with its atmosphere of peace and harmony. The artists' fascinating vision conveys an interpretation of the biblical miracle as an image of hope that provides a counterpoint to a world of distress and despair.

43. M. L. Sleevi, 'The Stooped Woman', cited in a condensed version according to Schuessler Fiorenza, *But She Said*, pp. 203–5.
44. S. Bramly, B. Rheims, *I.N.R.I.* (München: Kehayoff-Verlag, 1998).

9. Conclusion

The history of the research into the miracles of Jesus has proven to be a history of the evolution of ever new perspectives. There is more than one way of dealing with the miracles. As a consequence of the Enlightenment, a naïve understanding of the biblical miracles as supernatural events has become untenable. Although we should trust more in the historical value of at least Jesus' exorcisms and therapies than a majority of the scholars in the nineteenth and twentieth centuries did, comparative religion has shown that the miracles of Jesus as told by the gospel narratives are by no means unique. Thus we need to look out for a truth of the miracles that lies beyond the question of their historicity. The solution offered by the programme of demythologization led to an inadequate devaluation of the miracles. In contrast, Bloch's 'principle of hope' demonstrated the indispensable value of the belief in miracles. In addition, psychological and feminist exegesis discovered important patterns of wholeness and emancipation hidden in the miracle stories. The hermeneutics of alienation provided new perspectives of the outmoded and overly familiar narratives, thus provoking curiosity. The problem of the miracles remains an open question that will always lead to new answers. At present the concept of hope surely is the most proper key for an adequate understanding of the biblical miracle stories.[45]

45.   I am grateful to my wife Christine Wyatt for revising the style of this article and for translating the poems of Rudolf Otto Wiemer and Erich Fried.

Index of References

Bible

Old Testament

Genesis
1   1
1.31   123
2.2-3   119
3   207
5.1-32   3
11.10-32   3
11.26-28   8
11.27-32   3, 6
11.28   8
11.29-30   7
11.29   8
11.30   7
12.4   3
12.7   3
12.10-20   7
13   9
15.1-6   10
15.2-3   3
15.4   3
15.5   3
15.18   3
16.1-4   10–11
16.1-2   3–4
16.2   11
16.4-14   11
16.4   4
16.15-16   10–11
17   4
17.1   4
17.2-6   4
17.4-14   4
17.15-16   4
17.17   12
17.19   15
17.23-27   4
18.1-15   4, 13–15
18.16-19.38 4

19.24   213
20.1-18   7
21.1-7   4, 16–17
21.1-3   4
21.1   5
21.2   18
21.5-7   18
50.25-26   58

Exodus
1-11   56
7.1-11.10   218
7-10   209
7.3   196
7.5   32
7.9   32, 196
7.11   212
7.26–8.11   213
8.18   32
8.19   32
11.9   196
11.10   196
13.19   58
16.1-36   207
17.8-16   64
19   1
19.4   206
31.13-16   119
33.1   187
33.18-20   137
35.2   119

Leviticus
13–14   117
15.19-30   257
18.19   257
20.18   257
21.18   119, 234
23   119
26.14-16   117
26.16   109

Numbers
5.21   112
5.27   112

Deuteronomy
4.34   196
5.6-16   216
5.12-15   119
6.22   196
7.19   196
11.3   196
13.2-3   196
15.21   119
28.22   109
29.15   117
29.21-22   117
32.11   206

Joshua
14.6   187
24.32   58

Judges
6.22-23   137
13.22-23   137
16.17   110

1 Samuel
5.3   183
5.6   183
7.13   183

1 Kings
12.22   187
12.24   187
13.1-5   187
17.17-24   46, 173, 256
17.24   256
18.46   183
19.21   257

2 Kings
2.4   257
2.42-44   249
4.8-37   256
4.9   110
4.19-37   173
4.21-25   187
4.27   187
4.30   257
4.34   186
4.40   187
4.42   187
5.1-14   46
5.8   119

Ezra
7.6   183

Nehemiah
13.15-22   119

Job
7.12   207
9.27   119
17.7   120

Psalms
2.1-2   167
2.9   206
74.13-14   207
78.45   213
90.8-9   117
105.30   213
106.16   110
107.17-20   117

Proverbs
10.20 (A)   120

Ezekiel
2.1-2 (LXX) 121
3.14   183

Isaiah
1.5   123
6.5-7   137
7.10   206
7.14   206
8.18   197
11.6-9   33
20.3   197
25.8   110

27.1   207
33.23   117
35.3   117
35.5-6   248
35.6   117
38.17   117
40.30-31   206
41.23   216
41.24   216
41.29   216
42.8   216
42.17   216
44.9   216, 216
44.19   216
45.20   216
51.9   207
57.13   216
61.1   46
66.1   169

Jeremiah
39.20-21   197

Daniel
7.7   207
10.5-6   206

Joel
2.28 (LXX)   156, 173
3.1-5   164

Apocrypha
Judith
10.3   206

Wisdom of Solomon
19.10   213

Ben Sira
12.11   119
19.26 (LXX) 119

Baruch
2.11   196

1 Maccabees
1.41-44   119
2.29-38   119

2 Maccabees
6.6   119
9.4-10   175

New Testament

Matthew
2.2-9   38
2.12   29
4.18-22   136
4.24   116
7.15   212
8.1-4   93
8.6   116
8.23-27   45
9.1-8   93
9.2   116
9.6   116
9.18-26   93
9.20   45
9.22-23   46
9.22   45
9.32-34   93
11.5   46, 116–17
12.9-14   118
12.22-26   93
12.38-39   32
14.24-27   45
15.28   46
15.29-31   93
15.30-31   116, 118
15.30   115, 119
17.3   205
18.8   116, 118
21.14   116–17, 119
22.16   118
23.15   118
24.11   212
24.24   204, 212
28.16-20   134

Mark
1.11-13   97
1.13   110
1.15   109–10, 123
1.16-20   136
1.17   142
1.21-28   97–98, 109, 118
1.23-28   98, 109
1.22   109
1.27   109, 111, 186
1.29-31   97, 109–10
1.29   109, 111
1.30   105, 111
1.31   110
1.32-34   109

1.32	109
1.34	100, 109
1.35-38	109
1.40-45	93
1.41	46
2.1-3.6	97–98, 117
2.1-12	93, 105, 115, 117–18, 122, 173, 255
2.1-4	121
2.3-4	116
2.4	115
2.5	116–17
2.9-11	110, 116
2.10	117
2.11	46, 118, 149
2.12	149
2.17	100
2.31	116
3.1-6	97, 115–18, 123
3.1	115
3.3	110
3.4	118
3.5-6	98
3.5	46, 118, 120
3.6	118
3.10-12	109
3.10	149
3.12	111
3.22-27	98, 109
3.22-26	93
3.28-29	117
4-8	96–97
4.6	118
4.35-41	45
4.39	111
5.1-20	98, 109, 260
5.21-43	93
5.21-24	173
5.24-34	257
5.27-29	45
5.29	118
5.30	45
5.35-43	46, 173
5.40-41	149, 173
5.41	110
6.7	90
6.34-44	96
6.45-52	45
6.52	98, 120
6.55-56	149

6.56	45
7.22	117
7.24-30	109, 257
7.32-36	122
7.31-37	93, 122
7.34	110
7.37	123
8.1-9	96
8.11	32
8.15 *v.l.*	118
8.17-21	98
8.17	120
8.22-26	93, 96, 119, 122
8.23-35	122
8.23	45
8.30	111
8.32-33	111
8.33	98
9.4	205
9.14-29	98, 109, 121
9.14-27	122
9.18	118
9.25	111
9.27	110
9.28-29	122
9.29	110
9.38-39	93
9.38	120
9.43	118
10.13	111
10.46-52	96, 98
10.48	111
10.49	110
10.52	46
11.12-15	96
11.16-20	96
11.20-21	118
11.21-25	96
12.13	118
13.22	204, 212
14.64	117
15.29	117
16.9	131
16.17-18	68

Luke
1.1	159
1.4	114
1.11	205
2.32	120
3.6	120
3.10	165

4.16-30	111
4.18	46
4.23	100
4.25-27	46
4.34	110
4.36	111
4.38-39	111, 114
4.38	105, 149
5	139, 141
5.1-11	128–29, 130, 136–39, 141–42
5.1	137-138
5.2	138
5.3	138
5.4	138
5.5	138
5.6	138, 139
5.7	138
5.8	129, 137–39
5.10	137
5.11	139
5.12-16	93
5.15	114
5.17-26	93
5.23-25	149
6.18	114
6.19	45, 149
7.7	46
7.15	149
7.22	115, 117, 119
8.22-25	45
8.40-56	93
8.46	149
9.1-6	114
9.2	44, 166
9.6	166
9.49-50	93
9.49	120
10.1-16	114
10.8	166
10.17	120
10.18	111
10.19	68
11.14-15	93
11.17-18	93
11.29	32
13.10(11)-17	115, 117–19, 258, 261
13.12	46, 118
13.17	120
14.1-6	121

14.13	115–16, 119–20	5.8	46	18-20	140
14.15-24	120	5.10-18	118	18.10	134
14.21	115–16, 119–20	5.14	93, 117, 134	18.15-18	137
		5.16-18	126	18.15	134
17.11-19	93	6	127, 135–37, 144	18.18	135
17.14	46			18.25-27	137
21.28	119	6.1-15	135	18.25	134
22.3-6	167	6.1	134–36	19.26-27	134
22.3	159	6.11	134–35	19.26	135
22.43	205	6.15	136	19.38	134
23.31	118	6.16-21	45	20.1	131
24	162–64	6.16	136	20.2-10	134
24.1	131	6.21	138	20.2	135
24.13-35	136, 139	6.30-44	262	20.5-8	132
24.16	139	6.44	136, 144	20.6	134
24.22	131	6.68	134, 137	20.12	144
24.30	135, 139	6.69	110	20.14	131, 139
24.31	139	7.1	134	20.19-29	127
24.32	178	7.4	134	20.19-23	133
24.43	205	7.33	134	20.19	137
24.44-49	163	8.14	134	20.21-23	127
		8.21-22	134	20.24-29	133
John		8.25	134, 139	20.24-28	135
1-20	127–28, 130–31, 133, 137, 140	9.1-7	93	20.24	134
		9.1	115	20.26	137
		9.3	134	20.29	127
		9.6	45	20.30-31	127
1-2	128	10.11	135	20.30	127
1.18	137	11.1-44	258	20.31	144, 258
1.19	134, 139	11.11	134	21	127–28, 130–31, 135–36, 138, 140–43
1.31	134	11.16	134–35		
1.35-51	135	11.41-42	110		
1.42	134	11.47-53	126	21.1-23	130
1.45-49	134	11.50	135	21.1-14	127–30, 134–35, 137, 140–42, 144
2-11	126	12.32	136, 144		
2.1-11	132	13.1-20	135		
2.1	134	13.7	134	21.1-2	140
2.11	132, 134	13.9	134	21.1	131, 135–36
3.21	134	13.23-26	134–35	21.2-4	141
3.22	134	13.24	134	21.2	137
4	111	13.33	134	21.3-4	141
4.10	134, 139	13.36	134	21.3	136, 138
4.35-38	144	14.4	134	21.4	128, 131, 134, 137, 139–40
4.42	134	14.5	135		
4.46-54	46	14.26	144	21.5	140
4.48	204	14.28	134	21.6	134, 136, 138, 141
5.1-9	93	15.6	118		
5.1	134	15.13	135	21.7	131–32, 134, 137–40
5.2-9	118	16.5	134		
5.3	115, 119	16.10	134	21.8	139, 141
5.5	115	16.17	134	21.9	140
5.7	116	17.6	134	21.10-11	141

21.11	134, 136, 139, 141	2.47	156	5.11	160, 165, 168
21.12-14	140	3.1-5.16	152	5.12-16	150, 160, 168
21.12	134, 139	3.1-16	155	5.12	155–56, 168, 204
21.13	134–36	3.1-10	120–21, 150, 152–53, 156, 160, 166	5.13-14	175
21.14	131			5.13	148, 155, 168
21.15-17	137	3.2-10	183	5.14-15	168
21.15-19	132, 135	3.2-6	116	5.14	157
21.24-25	144	3.2	115–16, 148, 183	5.15-16	114, 149
				5.15	148, 155–56
Acts		3.6-7	120	5.16	148, 155–56, 159
1-15	152	3.6	149, 184, 195		
1-12	146–79	3.9-10	148	5.17-42	152, 160, 168–70
1.1-12	160	3.10	149		
1.1-11	162–64	3.11-26	160, 183	5.17-25	155
1.1-9	157	3.12	166	5.17-21	156–57, 175
1.3	163	3.13-22	166, 175	5.23	168
1.4-11	163	3.13-15	166	5.25	175
1.7-8	164	3.16	166, 195	5.26	168
1.10-11	157	3.17	165	5.28	150
1.10	154	3.21	158, 163	5.29	158–59
1.13-14	160	4–5	153	5.33	168
1.15-26	153, 160	4.1-22	160	5.34-39	169
1.16-26	158	4.1-3	150	5.36	169
1.16	157	4.2	166	5.38-39	158
1.18-19	156	4.4	166	5.40-42	169
1.24-26	156	4.5	150	6–7	153
2.1-47	152	4.7	120, 195	6.1-8.4	152
2.1-13	160, 164–66	4.8	157	6.1-7	160
2.1-12	157	4.10	120, 184, 195	6.1-6	153, 169
2.2-6	155	4.12	158, 195	6.2	169
2.2	165	4.13	150, 166	6.3	157
2.13-15	155	4.17-18	195	6.5	157
2.14-41	160	4.22	115, 120	6.7	169, 175
2.17	156, 164, 173	4.23–5.16	167	6.8-10	160
2.18-19	165	4.24-30	167	6.8	155–56, 169, 196, 204
2.19-20	165	4.25-31	160		
2.19	204	4.29-30	167	6.10–7.1	160
2.21	164–65	4.30	121, 195, 204	6.10	157
2.22	121, 156, 196, 204	4.31	152, 155, 157, 167	6.11	117
				6.13-14	169
2.23	165, 175	4.32-37	160	6.15	157
2.36	183	4.33	167	7.2-53	160
2.38	165, 195	4.36-37	153, 167	7.2	205
2.40	165	5.1-11	148, 152–53, 155–57, 167–68	7.26	205
2.41	164			7.30	205
2.42-47	160	5.1-10	160	7.35-44	169
2.42-43	165	5.3	159, 167	7.36	204
2.42	165	5.5	157	7.48	169
2.43	120, 148, 155, 156, 168, 204	5.6	168	7.49-50	169
		5.9	157	7.51	157
2.46	168			7.53	169

7.54-60	157, 160	9.27	195	11.17	157
7.55-56	165, 173	9.29–11.18	152	11.18	174
7.55	157	9.29-30	172	11.19-30	152
8.1-3	160, 169	9.31-32	120	11.19-26	161, 174
8.1	170	9.31	157, 161, 170,	11.19-20	174
8.2	164		172	11.21	156–57
8.4-25	170–71	9.32-43	152–53,	11.24	157, 174
8.4-8	160		171–73	11.26	153
8.6-8	155	9.32-35	156	11.27-30	158, 161, 174
8.6-7	148, 156	9.32-33	161	12	153
8.7	115–16, 148,	9.33-35	155	12.1-24	152
	159	9.33-34	149	12.1-23	174–76
8.5-40	152	9.33	115, 148	12.1-11	152
8.9-13	160, 183	9.34	120, 161	12.1-4	161
8.10	170	9.35-41	161	12.2	175
8.12	170	9.35	157, 173	12.3-17	156–58
8.13	155–56	9.36-40	148	12.3-4	175
8.14-25	155, 183	9.36-42	155–56	12.3	175
8.14-24	148	9.36	149	12.4-17	178
8.14-17	157, 160	9.40-41	149	12.5-11	155, 161
8.18-24	160	9.40	110, 149	12.6-11	175
8.18-20	167	9.42	157, 161, 173	12.9	155
8.25	160, 171	9.43	161	12.11	175
8.26-39	152	10.1-11.18	172–74	12.12-17	161, 175
8.26-40	153, 171	10.1-8	158, 173	12.12-15	155
8.26	157, 161, 171	10.1-4	161	12.15	157
8.27-28	161	10.2	174	12.17	175
8.29-38	161	10.5-8	161	12.18-23	161
8.29	157–58, 171	10.9-16	157–58, 161,	12.19-23	158
8.39-40	158, 161, 171		173	12.20-23	175
8.39	152, 155	10.11	165	12.23	155
9.1-19	171–72	10.17-23	157–58, 161,	12.24	161, 175
9.3-19	171		173	12.25	161
9.1-9	158	10.19	157	13-15	152
9.1-5	161	10.23-33	161	13	80
9.3	165	10.24	173	13.6-12	148, 182–83
9.6-9	161	10.25-26	148	13.10	159
9.6	158	10.28	159	13.11	121
9.8-9	155–56	10.30-33	173	13.31	205
9.10-19	156	10.34-43	161	13.46-47	175
9.10-16	158, 161, 172	10.34-35	173	13.47	120
9.15-16	195	10.38	114, 159	14.3	204
9.16	158	10.40-41	164	14.4	182
9.17-19	158, 161, 172	10.44-48	158, 161, 171,	14.9-10	44
9.17-18	155		173	14.8-12	182–83
9.17	157	11.1-18	161	14.8-10	121, 148
9.19-30	161	11.1-3	173	14.10	118
9.19-25	172	11.4-10	173	14.8	115, 121
9.21	195	11.11-12	173	14.9	121
9.26-28	172	11.12	157	14.11-13	113
9.26-27	172	11.13-14	173	14.11-12	44
9.27-28	120	11.15-17	173	14.14	44, 182

14.14-17	183	28.9-10	148	2.4	196, 204
14.15-18	121	28.9	114, 148	3.8	120
14.15-17	113			3.13	120
14.15	44, 148	*Romans*		3.15	120
14.18	44, 113, 115	1.16	196	4.7	120
14.19	44	15.19	195–97, 204	11.29	118
15	120–21, 150				
15.8	156	*1 Corinthians*		*James*	
15.10	169	1.17	195	1.11	118
15.12	177, 204	2.1-5	195	5.13-15	122
16.16-24	182, 184	2.1	195	5.14-18	110
16.16-18	148	2.4	195, 197	5.15-16	117
16.18	120, 184	4.20	196		
16.23-24	184	5.4	120	*1 Peter*	
16.25	110, 184	6.11	120	1.24	118
19	189	9.1	197		
19.2	148	9.5	90, 109	*1 John*	
19.11-20	182, 184–86	11.29-30	117	2.1	131
19.11-17	184, 194	12.7	196	2.12	131
19.11-12	114	15.1-11	91	2.14	131
19.11	148	15.5-8	205	2.28	131
19.13-19	148	15.32	188–89		
19.15	148	15.55	110	*Revelation*	
19.21	111			1.2	204
20	189	*2 Corinthians*		1.3	202
20.7-12	178, 182, 186–87	12.10	198	1.4-5	216
		12.11	198	1.5	203
20.7-8	186	12.12	195–97, 204	1.6	203
20.7	178			1.8	218
20.9-10	178	*Galatians*		1.9-20	202–203
20.9	148, 186	2	150	1.9	203–204
20.10	186			2-3	202
20.11-12	186	*Ephesians*		2.7	203
20.29-30	179	5.20	120	2.9	215
22	171			2.11	203
22.3-16	171	*Philippians*		2.13	204
22.12	172	2.10	120	2.17	207
26	171			2.19	204
26.9-18	171	*Colossians*		2.20	212
26.19	155	3.17	120	2.22-23	210
27-28	111			2.26	203
27.37	111	*1 Thessalonians*		3.5	203
27.43	111	1.5	195	3.9	203
28.1-10	111			3.12	203
28.2	113	*2 Thessalonians*		3.14	218
28.3-6	68, 112	2.9	196, 204	3.17-18	215
28.4	113	3.6	120	3.17	215
28.6	113–14			3.18	215
28.7	113	*1 Timothy*		3.21	203
28.8	108, 110, 112–13, 121, 148	3.16	205	4.8	218
				4.11	215, 218
		Hebrews		5	216

5.6	203	13.16-17	212		213–14
5.9-10	203	13.16	215	20.4-6	203
5.9	203, 215	13.17	215	20.4	204
5.10	203	14.3-4	203, 215	20.6	203
5.12	503	14.7	218	20.9	203, 211
6.2	203	14.12	204	20.10	211–12
6.9-11	203	14.15	118	20.14	211
6.9	204	15.1-8	209	21.4	110, 203
6.10	209	15.1	204–205, 214	21.7	203
7.14	203	15.2-4	218	21.9	214
8.7	211	15.2	203, 218	21.22	214, 218
9.4	211	15.3	204, 218	22.13	216
9.18	211	15.4	210, 215		
9.20	211	15.8	217	OTHER ANCIENT REFERENCES	
10.6	218	15.48	217		
11.6	218	16	217	PSEUDEPIGRAPHA	
11.8	218	16.1-21	209	*Jubilees*	
11.7-11	203	16.2	209	2.16-20	119
11.17	218	16.4-6	209	2.20	8
11.19	205	16.5-7	210	2.30	119
12-14	209	16.7	218	11.9-10	8
12-13	217	16.8	211	11.12-14	8
12	205, 208, 217	16.9	210–11	11.14–12.15	6
12.1	204–205, 214	16.11	117, 210–11	12.9-11	6–9
12.3	204–205, 214	16.12-16	209	12.9	7
12.4	208	16.12	118, 210–11	12.11	8
12.5	206	16.13-14	213	12.30	9–10
12.6	206	16.13	211–12	13	9
12.7	213	16.14	204–205, 218	13.13-15	7
12.9-10	208	16.16	213	13.17	9
12.9	212	16.18-19	211	13.18	9–10
12.10-12	208	16.19	209	14.1-6	10
12.10	207	16.21	117, 210	14.1	18
12.11	203–204, 208	17–18	209	14.10	18
12.12	207–208	17.6	204	14.18	18
12.13-17	218	17.8	218	14.21-24	10–11
12.13	208	18	215	15.1-5	18
12.14	206	18.3	215	15.15-22	11–13
12.15-17	208	18.7	215	15.16-17	12
12.15	207	18.9	215	15.19	18
12.16	218	18.11	215	15.21	18
12.17	204, 208, 213	18.12-14	215	16.1-4	13–16
13.1-3	218	18.15	215	16.3-4	15
13.4	213	18.16	215	16.11-31	16–18
13.6	117	18.17	215	16.12-13	17
13.7	213	18.19	215	16.13	18
13.8	218	19.6	218	16.14	18
13.10	204	19.10	204, 212	16.15-19	17–18
13.11-17	211	19.13	203	16.17-18	18
13.13-14	204–205, 211–12	19.15	218	22.1-9	18
13.14	212	19.19-20	213		
13.15	212	19.20	204–205, 211,		

Liber Antiquitatum
Biblicarum
3.10   110
23.4   8

Testamenta XII Patriarcharum
T. Ash.
7.3   207

T. Sim.
2.12   118
8.3-4   58

1 Enoch
5.8-9   110
25.6-7   110
91.15-17   110
96.3   110

2 Baruch
73.1-3, 7   110

4 Ezra
7.7   110
7.21-34   110
8.52-54   110

Sibylline Oracles
III 367-80   110

Testament of Solomon
7.6-7   107

Joseph & Aseneth
3.6   206
8.9   119
22.13   119

QUMRAN
1QGenAp
20.29   112

1QH
3.3-18   206

4Q560
1.4   107

CD
11.4.13-14   119
12.3-6   119
16.1-4   1

Philo
De Exsecrationibus
143   106, 109

De Opificio Mundi
125   109

De Specialibus Legibus
2.193   116
3.100-03   76

Quod Omnis Probus Liber Sit
74   76

De Vita Mosis
2.22   119

JOSEPHUS
Antiquitates Iudaicarum
1.151   8
2.205   79
3.271   112
6.3   112
10.20-23   70
10.220-28   70
13.398   105
17.168-170   106
19.343-50   174
20.50-53   174
20.101   174

Contra Apionem
1.144   70
2.23   119
2.92-96   239

De Bello Iudaico
1.106   105
1.656-660   106
2.189-191   73
7.180-185   73

MISHNAH
Berakhot
5.1   67
5.5   67

Rosh Ha-Shannah
3.8   57, 64

Ta'anit
3.8   66

Yevamot
16.6   59

Nedarim
3.2   57

Sotah
1.9   59
9   56
9.15   63, 67–68

Sanhedrin
10.2   64

Shevu'ot
3.8   57

Avot
5.5   60
5.6   57
5.19   64

TOSEFTA
Berakhot
3.3   67
3.20   67–68

Shabbat
13.9   60

Yoma
2.4   60

Ta'anit
2.13/3.1   66

Yevamot
14.6   52
14.7   59

Nedarim
2.1   57

Sotah
4.7   54, 58
4.19   64
8-15   56
10.4   56
13.3-6   59

13.7-8   60–61
15.5   67

Gittin
7.8   57

Qiddushim
5.17   64

Sanhedrin
8.3   60
11.5   62

Hullin
2.22-23   63
2.24
          62

TALMUD YERUSHALMI
Berakhot
5.1   67
5.5 (9d)   67–68
9.3 (13d)   62

Shevi'it
9.1 (38d)   62

Demai
1.2 (22a)   63
1.3 (21d-22a)   62
1.3 (22a)   63, 67

Shabbat
16.7 (15d)   60

Sheqalim
5.2 (48d)   63

Yoma
8.5 (45d)   60

Ta'anit
3.9 (66d-67a)
              66–67
3.10 (67a)   66

Mo'ed Qatan
3.1 (81cd)   52, 62
3.1 (81d)   66

Hagigah
2.1 (77b)   62

Yevamot
16.4 (15d)   52

Nedarim
4.9 (38d)   60

Sanhedrin
7.19 (25d)   62

TALMUD BAVLI
Berakhot
19a   66
33a   67
34b   67–68
60a   52

Shabbat
34a   62
53b   56
121a   60

Ta'anit
2ab   65
23a   66–67
23ab   66
24b-25a   62–63, 67

Megillah
14a   8

Yevamot
121b   52, 63
121b *bar.* 67

Nedarim
41a   117

Bava Qamma
50a   63, 67

Bava Metsi'a
59b   52, 62
86b   65

Sanhedrin
68a   62
69b   8
113a   65

Hullin
43a   52

Me'ilah
17b   62

TARGUMIC TEXTS
Fragmentary Targum (TFrag.)
on Gen. 30.22 65

Targum Neofiti (TNeoI.)
on Gen. 30.22 65

Targum Pseudo-Jonathan (Tg. Ps-J.)
on Gen. 11.29 8

OTHER RABBINIC TEXTS
Avot of Rabbi Nathan (ARN)
A 22.1   67
B 32   67

Bereshit Rabba (BerR. = Genesis Rabba)
13.7   67
38.14   8
79.8   62

Megillat Ta'anit
Scholion 20./22. Adar
          67

Mekilta (MekhY)
'Amalek 1 (Exod. 17.9)
          64
'Amalek 1 (Exod. 17.11)
          57, 64
Bahodesh 1 (Exod. 19.2)
          64
Beshallah 1 (Exod. 13.19)
          54, 58
Beshallah 2f. (Exod. 14,9)
          64
Kaspa 3 (Exod. 23.7)
          60
Wayassa' 3 (Exod. 16.4)
          56
Wayassa' 6 (Exod. 16.32)
          57
Shabbeta (Exod. 31.13)
          119

Midrash Tehillim (MTeh.)
78.5   65
126.1   66
126.2   66

Pesiqta Rabbati (PesR.)
42.7   65

Qohelet Rabbah
7.8.1   62

Rut Rabbah
6.4   62

Shemot Rabba
3.12   67

Sifre Devarim (SifDev)
32   56
250   64
343   64
355   57
357   64

Sifre Bamidbar (SifBam)
42   56
157   64

Sifra Emor Pereq
9.5   60

Tanhuma (Tan.)
וארא 4   67

Tanhuma (Buber) (TanB.)
וארא 22   67

Early Christian Literature

Acts of John
108   100

The Acts of Andrew and
Matthias
*Acts of Andrew and Matthias
among the Cannibals (AAM)*
66.7-12   230
67.6-68.18   237
67.6ff   221, 236
67.6-9   233
67.13-16   237
67.13   231

68.12ff   221, 236
68.12   231, 237
68.13-16   232
68.16-18   237
68.16   231
69.14–89.16 236
69.14–71.3 221
71.4–72.11 221
76.9–77.10 221
78.9ff   221
87.3ff   221
89.17-18   232
90.1.6   230, 232
90.10-11   237
91.8ff   230
91.8–94.8 230
91.14–92.15 224
93.1–94.8 237
93.1-13   233
93.6-10   224
94.1-2   231
94.9–99.12 233
94.9–97.9 221
95.10   231
97.10   231
99.13–101.10 221, 224
100.1–101.10 233
101.7ff   236
101.11–109.2 230, 233
103.17–104.2 224
104.4–107.2 224, 234
105.4   231
107.1-2   231
107.3–108.13 234
108.7ff   236
109.3–114.4 234
109.3ff   236
110.7-8   224
111.2–112.10 235
114.9–115.5 235
115.6–116.15 235
115.6ff   236
116.3-4   224

Epitome
377.21-33   237
377.24-25   231
377.25-28   230-231
377.28   232
377.33–378.1 232
378.1-11   237
378.1-7   233

378.1-2   230
378.6-7   231
378.7-11   233
378.8-11   230
378.12-16   230
378.12-13   234
378.13-14   234
378.16-20   235
378.20-24   235

Narratio
354–356   227
356.8   227
356.19–358.6 227
356.19–357.2 231
356.24-28   230
356.24-25   227
356.28–357.5 237
357.1-2   230
357.1   227
357.3-4   230, 232
357.4-5   230, 233
357.6–358.6 238
357.6-20   228
357.6-11   230
357.14-20   234
357.21-27   235
358.3-6   235

Laudatio
316.17–317.12 228
317.13-20   228
318.14-27   229
318.14-16   230, 232, 237
318.16-27   237
318.16-18   232
318.17-18   230
318.19-27   230
318.19-20   230, 233
318.20-27   233
318.28ff   234
330.20–331.25 229
330.20–331.3 229
330.22–331.13 238
330.24–331.4 230
331.3-4   229
331.4-18   229
331.5-25   235
331.13-25   238

Vita
220A–221A 228

220D 4-7   230, 232, 237
220D 7–221A 8 237
220D 8-9   230, 232
221A 1-B 7 230
221A 1-8   233
221A 1ff   230
224A 10   228
224D 5   228
240C–241B 229
240C 14–241A 1 230
240D–241A 229
240C 14–241A 2 235
241A 2-B 6 235

Apostolic Constitutions
2.24.6   156

Augustine
De Civitate Dei
10.16   46
22.8   190

Christian Papyri
P. Egerton
2b (35-47) 93

Cyprianus
Confessiones
7   107

Ad Demetrianum
15   190

Eusebius
Against Hierocles
35   75

Ecclesiastical History (Hist. Eccl.)
1.8.9   106
6.43.11   194

Hermas
Mandata
4.3.4   156

Ignatius
Letter to the Ephesians
7.2   100
20.2   100

The Infancy Gospel of Thomas (Inf. Gosp. Th.)
2.1–3.3   47
4.1   45
4.2   45
5.1   45
10.1-2   47

Irenaeus
Adversus Haereses
2.32.4   192

Itinera Hierosolymitana
39.144 (CSEL)

Jerome
Commentarius in Matthaeum
12.13   116, 123

John Chrysostom
De mutatione nominum homiliae quattuor
PG 51.117

Justin Martyr
2 Apology
6.4-6   191

Dialogue with Trypho
30.23   190
49.8   190
76.6   190
85.2   191

Minucius Felix
Octavius
27.1   192
27.5-7   192

Origen
Commentarius in Mattheum
13.6   122

Contra Celsum
1.6   193
1.46   45
1.67   45
2.55   45
6.4   79

The Protoevangelium of James (Prot. Jas.)
18   45

Pseudo-Clementines
Homilies
6.11   119
10.13.2   156

Tertullian
Apologia
23   190
27   190
32   190
37   190

Theophilus
Ad Autolycum
2.35   118

CLASSICAL LITERATURE
Alexander Aphrodisiensis
De Febribus
1.81-106   104
1.93   105

Alexander Tralleis
De Febribus
1.407   107

Ammianus Marcellinus
24.3.7   106

Anonymus Londinensis
Iatrika
7.25   100

Anthologia Graeca
7.290   112
9.269   112

Antigonos Paradox.
Historiarum mirabilium collectio
112a, 1-2   119

Apollonius
Epistulae
16   79
17   79
26   78, 81
65–67   78, 81

Aretaios of Cappadocia
2.4   105
2.4.4   108
3.7   115
3.7.9   116
3.13.16   112
4.9   100, 112

Aristotle
Nicomachean Ethic (Eth. Nic.)
1102b   116

Fragments
191 Rose (DK 14,7)
               68

Historia Animalium
572a   119
585b   119

Athenaeus Mechanicus
De machinis
18.10   119
22.6.8   119

Caelius Aurelianus
De tardis passionibus
Praef. 2   112
1.150   108
2.2   115
2.15   104, 116
2.40   118
2.43   118
2.47   118
2.59   116

Caesar
De bello Gallico
6.26-28   73

Cassius Dio
Roman History
41.46.3   37
66.8.1   42
67.18   79
77.18.4   79

Celsus
De medicina
1.1   104
3.1   115

3.1.27   115
3.3-17   103
3.3   105
3.3.1   110
3.4   105
3.7.2   105
3.8   106
3.22   103, 118
3.22.8   115
3.23.1   106
3.27   116
4.29-31   116

Cicero
Catilina
13.1   106

De Divinatione
1.39-64   117
1.55   117

De Natura Deorum
3.63-64   108

Corpus Hippocraticum
Aphorismi
2.20   118
5.9   115
6.3   112

Coa praesagia
193.2   116
307   116
431   115

De articulis
15.6   118
37.37   118

De fracturis
23.10   118

De glandulis
11   115

De locis in homine
10   115

De morbis popularibus
7.1.8   116
7.1.11   118

De morbo sacro
6   115

De mulierum affectibus
2.110   104
217.7   118

De semestri partu
5.2   119

De superfetatione
19.7   118

Prorrheticon
1.118   116
2.22   112

Vectiarius
36.8   118

Cyranides
1.1.110   116
3.9.12   116

Diodorus Siculus
8.12.14   116
18.31.4   116
20.72.2   116
36.13.3   106

Digesta
21.1.4   106
42.1.60   106

Diogenes Laertios
1.114   76
6.68-70   76
8.3   76
9.34   76
9.49   103

Dioscorides
De materia medica
1.16.2   116
1.22.1   112
1.42.1   112
1.64.4   112
1.70.1   112
1.73.3   112
1.74.1   112
1.82.1   112
1.97.1-2   112

1.100.3   112
1.106.1   112
3.78.2   116
3.81.1   116
4.176.2   116
4.183.2   116
5.18.3   116

Euporista vel De simplicibus
medicinis
1.226.1   116

Epictetus
Dissertationes
1.19.6   108
1.28.9   119
2.21.22   112
4.8.28-29 119

Euripides
Electra
239   118

Galen
Ars medica
1.387.18   118

De compositione
medicamentorum
13.1045   116

De differentiis febrium
17.273-77 105
17.275   105

De libris propriis
19.18   30

De locis affectis
8.322.17   118

De marcore liber
7.666.1   118

De methodo medendi
10.161   118
10.438-40 118
10.442   118

In Hippocratis aphorismi et
Galeni in eos commentarii
28   115

In Hippocratis Epidemiarum
Librum VI Commentaria
1.29   104
4.8   21

Herodotus
4.2.7-10   73
5.45   118

Hippocrates
Epidemics
1.3   105
1.12   105

Historia Augusta Vita
Hadriani
24.9   43, 105
25.3-4   105

Homer
Iliad
2.718-25   112

Horace
Ars Poetica
343-344   178

Iamblichus
De Vita Pythagorica
36   133

Julian
Contra Galilaeos
Fr 57   30

Juvenal
Satirae
12.106-07 34
14.96-106 119

Livy
2.36.1-8   117

Lucian
Alexander
5   76, 79

Philopseudes
9   107
11-12   117
18-20   107
25   105, 108

Scytha
2   107

Toxaris
24   118

Martial
Epigrammata
1.6   34
1.14   35
1.14.6   35
1.104.11   35
1.104.21-2 35
4.2   36
4.30   36
8.15.2   35
8.21   34
8.21.11   34
9.16   26
9.31   36

Book of Spectacles
16b.3   35
17   33-34
30.1-4   33

Oribasius
Collectiones Medicae
45.30.1-2 107
45.30.10-14 107

Philostratos
Epistulae
8   76
72   74

Gymnasticus
1   76

Heroicus
25.10   73

Vita Apollonii Tyanensis
1.2   76
1.3   71, 78
1.6   73
1.7-12   78
1.9-11   79
1.9   77
1.26   76
1.31-32   73
1.31   77

2.4	76
2.7	73
3.12	74
3.14	74
3.17	74
3.28	73
3.34	77
3.38-39	115
3.38	74, 76
3.39	74, 76
3.41	78
4.4	76
4.10	76, 107
4.12	74
4.16	74
4.20	76
4.25	76
4.44	75
4.45	76
5.12	76
5.19	79
6.27	76
6.39	77
6.40	73
6.42	76
7.34	74-75
7.38	75
7.39	76
8.3	75
8.5	75
8.7-8	76
8.12	75
8.13	75
8.25-26	75
8.26	80
8.30	77
8.31	77, 79

Vitae sophistarum

490	76
494	76
523	75
590	75
607	74

Plato
Politeia

2.381e	117

Plinius maior
Historia Naturalis

2.3.15-16	108
2.16	107
2.28	38
2.94	39
7.166	105
8.119	107
21.166	107
22.38	107
22.60	107
28-32	103
28.41	107
28.48	107
28.72	107
28.86	107
28.121	107
29.79	107
30.30	107
30.95-96	107
30.98-99	107
32.113	107
36.64	115
36.100	115
37.54	107

Plinius minor
Panegyricus

22.3	43

Plutarch
Brutus

20	108

Caesar

38.5	37

Coniugalia praecepta

141b	106

Cicero

20.1-2	177

Coriolanus

24.1-3	117
38.4-5	177

Pelopidas

3.8.4	119

Pericles

6	106
15.1	100

Pompeius

21	106

Quaestionum convivialium libri ix

732e	100

Quomodo adolescens poetas audire debeat

35c	119

Sulla

37	80

Polybius
Histories

8.4.2	116
11.14.6	116
20.10.9	116
32.8.1	116

Porphyrius
De Vita Pythagorica

25	133

Scriptores Historiae Augustae
Hadrian

24.8	43
25.1-4	43

Sophocles
Philoctetus

254-74	112

Strabo
Geographica

5.3.11	100

Suetonius
Augustus

6	43
94	39

Tiberius

14	39

Claudius

2.1	39
44.2	40

Nero

6.4	39

Galba
1   42
4   39
4.2   40
4.3   40

Vitellius
3.2   40

Vespasian
1.1   39
5   39
7.1   40
7.2   41
23.4   42

Suidas
3.210   118

Valerius Maximus
2.5.6   108

Tacitus
Annales
4.64.3
4.81.1   41
4.81.3   41
6.20-21   80
14.22   38

Historiae
1.22   80
4.81   41
5.4-5   119

Theocritus
Idyllia
24.86-87   33

Thucydides
1.109   118

Virgil
Catalepton
2.3   106

Xenophon
Anabasis
3.4.19   119
3.4.21   119

PAPYRI
Cod Paris.
2316 fol. 433 r 107

PGM
13.15-17   107

P. Oxy.
6.924.6   105
1381   107

INSCRIPTIONS

CIL I^2
278 (Philocal. 354) 47

Epidaurian Inscriptions
A1   24
A3   24, 118
A8   24
A11   23
A12   23
A13   24
A15   118
B3 (23)   25
B12 (32)   24
B15 (35)   118
C 14 (57)   118
C 21 (64)   118

I.Cret
1: xvii 8   27
1: xvii 9   27
1: xvii 17   28

IG
IV/1^2
121–24   23
126   23
127   27

IGUR
148   28

I.Perg.
246

OGIS
332, 8-9

SIG^3
1169,123   112
1239-40   107

INDEX OF AUTHORS

Achtemeier, P. J. 146, 162, 165
Adamsen, G. S. 218
Aland, B. 112, 120
Aland, K. 112, 120
Aleshire, S. B. 23, 29
Alexander, P. S. 2, 49
Alkier, S. vii, 125, 147, 180
Alt, F. 257
Anderson, G. 71, 74, 76, 78–79
Arnold, C. E. 196
Avalos, H. 102
Avery-Peck, J. 61
Aune, D. E. 89, 205, 216

Bahrdt, C. F. 246–47
Barb, A. A. 114
Bardenhewer, O. 222
Barnard, L. W. 191
Barrett, C. K. 132, 170, 186
Bauer, B. 149
Bauer, W. 112, 120
Bauernfeind, O. 152
Baumgarten, A. I. 52
Baumgartner, W. 53
Baur, F. C. 150
Beale, G. K. 203, 218
Becker, H.-J. 57
Becker, J. 119, 126, 140–41
Becker, M. vii, 49–54, 57–59, 61–66, 68, 80
Bee-Schroedter, H. 125
Ben-Amos, D. 55
Benedum, J. 115
Bengtson, H. 37
Berg, H. K. 259
Bergen, W. J. 257
Berger, K. 43, 120
Berman, D. 63
Beschorner, A. 71
Betz, H.-D. 44, 46
Betz, O. 65–66
Bickerman, E. 239

Bieler, L. 72, 114
Bietenhard, H. 59
Billault, A. 77
Billerbeck, P. 115, 119
Blaskovic, G. 128, 130, 135, 140
Blatt, F. 223, 226
Blau, L. 49
Blidstein, G. J. 48
Bloch, E. 252, 263
Bloch, R. 49
Blum, E. 3
Blumenthal, M. 222, 242
Bodenhofer-Langer, G. 52
Böcher, O. 109–110
Bogaert, P. M. 2
Bokser, B. M. 68
Bonnet, M. 221–23, 225–35, 237–38
Borg, M. 88–89, 95
Bovon, F. 111, 129, 137, 142, 146
Bowersock, G.W. 71
Bowie, E. L. 71–72, 76, 78–79
Bramly, S. 262
Brecht, B. 259
Breytenbach, C. 113, 142
Bron, B. 125
Brown, R. E. 128–29, 134, 140, 258
Brox, N. 193
Bruce, F. F. 182
Buchanan, G. W. 49
Bucheit, V. 33
Budge, E. A. W. 223
Büchler, A. 63, 68
Bühner, J. A. 64
Büjükkolanci, M. 31
Bultmann, R. 126, 249–51
Burchard, C. 172
Busch, P. 201, 206–207
Byrskog, S. 141

Calvin, J. 4
Citroni, M. 35
Clauss, M. 43–44, 123

Coats, G. W. 3
Conway, C. M. 258
Conzelmann, H. 113–14
Cook, J. G. 106–109
Cosgrove, C. H. 158–59
Cotter, W. vii, 89, 181, 198
Craffert, P. F. 90
Crombie, F. 194
Crossan, J. D. 89–94
Crum, W. E. 223

D'Angelo, M. R. 258
Dalman, G. 131
Davenport, G. L. vii
De Lannoy, L. 70–71
De Vries, S. J. 5
De Wette, W. M. L. 147–49
Dibelius, M. 55, 153, 173–74
Diekamp, F. 228
Dietzfelbinger, C. 119
Dillon, M. P. J. 26
Dochhorn, J. 218
Dölger, F. J. 36, 113
Doering, L. 9
Dörnemann, M. 100
Donahue, J. R. 104
Downing, F. G. 125
Dressel, A. 223, 228–30, 232–33, 235
Drewermann, E. 254–55
Dschulnigg, P. 134
Dunderberg, I. 129
Du Rand, J. A. 208
Dvornik, F. 222, 224, 226–27, 242
Dzielska, M. 71, 76–77, 79–82

Edelstein, E. J. & L. 20, 23, 27, 30
Egger, R. 107
Eisenhut, W. 117
Ellenburg, B. D. 97
Elliott, J. K. 187–89
Ellul, J. 207
Engelmann, H. 31
Esser, D. 71–72
Evans, C. A. 49
Eve, E. 50

Fabry, H.-J. 53
Falls, T. B. 190–91
Fauth, W. 133
Feneberg, R. 96
Feuerbach, L. 252
Fichtner, G. 100

Fiebig, P. 48–49
Fitzmyer, J. A. 129, 142
Flamion, J. 222, 224, 226, 228, 242
Flinterman, J.-J. 70–71, 74–75, 77–78, 81
Fornaro, S. 125
Fortna, R. T. 129, 141
Francis, J. A. 73
Freedman, D. N. 2
Frey, J. 129
Freyne, S. 68, 80
Fried, E. 261
Friedländer, L. 33, 37
Fusco, V. 184

García Martínez, F. 1
Gasque, W. 147, 150–51
Gatzweiler, K. 200
Gerth K. 70
Gesché, A. 88
Giesen, H. 203, 206–207, 209–13, 215, 217–18
Gilat, Y. D. 62
Ginzberg, L. 49
Girone, M. 21, 27
Gispen, W. H. 3
Glover, T. R. 192
Gnilka, J. 81
Goldberg, A. 55, 60
Goldin, J. 66
Gow, A. S. F. 33
Grässer, E. 146, 153
Graf, F. 78–79, 82
Grant, R. M. 193
Green, W. S. 51, 54, 61, 65
Grmek, M. D. 102
Grundmann, W. 38–39, 196
Guarducci, M. 27
Güdemann, M. 59
Gulkowitsch, L. 63
Guttmann, A. 48, 52, 59

Habicht, C. 22
Haenchen, E. 153, 164, 166–68, 170–71, 173, 174, 177, 182, 199
Hahn, P. T. 20
Halpern-Amaru, B. 7–9
Halton, T. P. 190
Hamblin, R. L. 200
Hamm, D. 166
Hardon, J. A. 149, 155, 162
(von) Harnack, A. 112, 115–16, 119–20, 150–52, 167

Harrington, D. J. 104
Hasitschka, M. 127
Heekerens, H.-P. 141
Heinemann, I. 48, 53
Heller, B. 59
Hemer, C. J. 154
Hennecke, E. 226
Hengel, M. 110, 115, 154, 181
Hengel, R. 110, 115
Herzog, R. 23, 118
Hezser, C. 50, 61
Hilhorst, A. 242
Hiller von Gaertringen, F. 20, 23
Hobart, W. K. 112, 119
Holladay, C. R. 197
Holtzmann, H. J. 149
Holzberg, N. 37
Horn, H. J. 103, 105–108, 113
Hornschuh, M. 226
Horovitz, J. 59
Howell, P. 34–35, 37
Hruby, K. 48
Hsia, R. P. 239
Hübner, H. 137
Hüneburg, M. vii, 46
Hughes, J. 5
Hume, D. 246
Huttner, U. 106

Ingolfsland, D. 95
Instone Brewer, D. 49

Jackson, R. 102
Jacob, B. 4
Jacobs, L. 63
James, M. R. 222, 226
Jaubert, A. 18
Jepsen, A. 5
Jervell, J. 154, 164, 166–68, 170–71, 174, 176
Jörns, K.-P. 209
Jung, C. G. 254

Kadushin, M. 48, 53, 56
Kaestli, J. D. 221
Kahl, W. vii, 77, 89, 112
Kalinka, E. 70
Kanda, S. H. 114
Kasher, R. 48
Kee, H. C. vii, 95, 102, 125–26
Kelhoffer, J. A. 68
Keller, E. & M.-L. 125, 247–48

Kertelge, K. 95
Kienast, D. 38
Kirchschläger, W. 113
Kittel, G. 59
Klauck, H. J. 45, 72, 112–13, 170, 175, 183, 203
Klein, G. 5, 129
Koch, D.-A. 95
Koch, K. 5
Köhler, L. 53
Koester, C. R. 133–34, 136
Koet, B. J. 157, 173
Kollmann, B. vii, 32, 40, 89, 100, 109–10, 117, 125, 129, 132, 142, 247, 252
Korte, A.-M. 256
Koskenniemi, E. 71–75, 80–82, 123
Kottek, S. S. 103
Kowalski, B. 201, 207, 217
Krug, A. 103, 118
Kühn, C. G. 30
Külken, T. 104, 106
Künzl, E. 118
Kuhn, P. 59, 95
Kyrieleis, H. 38, 42

Labahn, A. 137
Labahn, M. vii, 126–29, 135–37, 142
Lalleman, P. 242
Lang, M. 129, 140
Lee, D. A. 126
Lekebusch, E. 151
Leloir, L. 223
Lessing, G. E. 245
Levine, L. 62
LiDonnici, L. R. 23–25
Lietaert Peerbolte, L. J. 181, 197
Lightstone, J. N. 61
Lipsius, R. A. 221, 228
Lohfink, G. 172
Lohmeyer, M. 64
Longrigg, J. 103, 112
Lown, J. S. 177
De Luca, G. 22
Lucchesi, E. 223
Lüdemann, G. 151, 164, 166, 167–68, 170–71, 173, 174, 181, 183, 185
Lührmann, D. 109, 117
Luz, U. 38–39, 118

MacDonald, D. R. 221–22, 242
Mackie, J. L. 246
Maisch, I. 117, 120
Malina, B. J. 127, 130, 132
Marcovich, M. 190–91
Martin, D. B. 192
Masaracchia, E. 30
McCord Adams, M. 146, 149, 155, 162, 165
McGuinty, P. 126
Meeks, W. A. 196
Meier, J. P. 72, 87–89, 92–94, 128–29
Menoud, P.-H. 200
Merz, A. 89, 92, 252–53
Metternich, U. 257
Meyer, E. 71, 78–79, 152
Moloney, F. J. 128, 132
Moraldi, L. 222, 226
Moraux, P. 30
Morenz, S. 42
Morgenstern, J. 63
Mosheim, J. L. 147
Mulack, C. 257
Müller, H. 21–22
Müller, K. 49, 61
Müller, U. B. 205–10, 216–17
Mumprecht, V. 78–79
Münscher, K. 70

Naveh, J. 107
Neihardt, J. G. 255
Neirynck, F. 95, 127–28, 136, 140, 146, 148–49, 153, 155–56
Neumann, J. 103
Neusner, J. 48–53, 55, 61–62, 65
Newmyer, T. 103
Nickelsburg, G. W. E. 1, 2
Niklas, T. 133
Nobbs, A. 179
Noy, D. 55

Oberweis, M. 133
Önnerfors, A. 107
Osborne, G. R. 128
O'Toole, R. F. 156–57
Overbeck, F. 149

Palmer, D. 177
Parsons, M. C. 49, 163, 165
Paulus, H. E. G. 246–47
Peek, W. 20, 23
Penella, R. J. 78, 81

Perrot, C. 2
Pervo, R. 158, 168, 171, 173, 175, 178
Pesch, R. 109, 140–42
Peterson, D. 161
Petzke, G. 71–72
Phillips, E. A. 2–4
Pilch, J. J. 101, 159
Plümacher, E. 177–78, 226
Porter, S. 182, 184
Potter, P. 105, 121
Prieur, J. M. 221–23, 226–27

Quispel, G. 226

Radl, W. 119, 175
Radt, W.
Räisänen, H. 96
Raynor, D. H. 76, 79
Rebell, W. 47
Reimarus, H. S. 164, 245
Reimer, A. M. vii
Reinach, S. 226
Reitzenstein, R. 71, 250
Renan, E. 148
Rendall, G. H. 192
Rengstorf, K. H. 64–65, 123, 216
Rheims, B. 262
Rhoads, D. 97–98
Riedweg, C. 126, 133
Ritter, A. M. 46
Rives, J. 239
Robert, L. 22
Robertson, R. 254
Roesch, P. 29
Rösel, M. 5, 117
Rohrbaugh, R. L. 127, 130, 132
Roloff, J. 113, 164, 167–68, 170–71, 174, 204–10, 212–13, 217
Roose, H. 203
Rosenfeld, B. Z. 62
Rottzoll, U. 8
Ruckstuhl, E. 130–31
Rüsen, J. 143
van Ruiten, J. T. A. G. M. 9, 13, 18

Sabourin, L. 48
Saffrey, H. D. 30
Safrai, S. 63, 67–68
Saldarini, A. J. 55
Sanders, E. P. 89, 92, 94
Sarfatti, G. B. A. 63
Sauter, F. 33–34, 36, 45

Schäublin, C. 117
Schaller, B. 8, 119
Schermann, T. 222
Schlatter, A. 48–49
Schmid, W. 70
Schmithals, W. 252
Schmitz, R. 103
Schnackenburg, R. 140
Schneckenburger, M. 148
Schnelle, U. 126–28, 137, 139
Schönberger, O. 70
Scholtissek, K. 64
Schottroff, L. 256
Schreiber, S. vii, 111, 113–14, 121, 180, 195
Schroer, S. 256
Schubert, C. 106
Schubert, K. 48
Schürer, E. 2
Schürmann, H. 129
Schuessler Fiorenza, E. 256, 258
Schulz, S. 158
Schulze, C. 116
Schwankl, O. 131
Schwartz, J. 146
Schweitzer, A. 245, 247–48
Scott, K. 33–35, 42
Seebass, H. 3
Segonds, A.-P. 30
Selvidge, M. J. 207
Semeria, A. 23
Semler, J. S. 147
Shaked, S. 107
Shields, M. E. 256
Siebert-Hommes, J. 256
Ska, J. L. 201
Skinner, J. 5
Sleevi, M. L. 261
Slusser, M. 190
Smith, D. M. 129
Smith, M. 46, 49
Smith Lewis, A. 223
Söder, R. 222
Söding, T. 130, 209
Söllner, P. 11
Solmsen, F. 70–71
Speyer, W. 71, 78
Spinoza, B. 245
Stemberger, G. 50–51, 55, 61
Strack, H. L. 115, 119
Strauss, D. F. 248–50
Szelest, H. 37

Talbert, C. H. 138
Tannehill, R. C. 136–37, 163–64, 171–72
Tchékarian, C. 223
Telford, W. R. 96
Theißen, G. 60, 81, 89, 92, 95, 111, 252–53
Theobald, M. 136
Thyen, H. 130
Tigchelaar, E. J. C. 1
Towner, W. S. 55
Traub, G. 115
Tuckett, C. M. 96
Turner, L. A. 2, 4
Twelftree, G. H. 89, 180, 196

Urbach, E. E. 48
Uro, R. 141

Van Bekkum, W. J. 5
Van Cangh, J.-M. 65
Van Dijk-Hemmes, F. 257
VanderKam, J. C. 1, 8, 18
Van der Loos, H. 128
Van Groningen, B. A. 74
Van Kampen, L. 226
Van Oyen, G. 88, 91
Van Schaik, A. 214
Van Seters, J. 3
Van Straten, F. T. 27–28
Van Tilborg, S. 258
Van Unnik, W. C. 177–78
Veltri, G. 49
Venturini, C. H. 246–47
Vermes, G. 2, 49, 65, 68
Von Bendemann, R. 103, 119
Von Gutschmid, A. 226
Von Lemm, O. 223
Von Staden, H. 103
Vorster, W. S. 130

Wacker, M.-T. 256
Waters, K. H. 42
Wehnert, J. 112, 114
Weinreich, O. 33–36, 37, 125, 200, 250
Weiser, A. 113, 154, 164, 200
Weiss, B. 150–51
Weiß, K. 105
Weissenrieder, A. 101–102, 104, 114, 119
Welck, C. 126, 130–31
Wells, L. 27
Wengst, K. 67, 206, 208
Werlitz, J. 133

Wessely, C. 223
Westermann, C. 3
Wetter, G. 71
Whittaker, M. 114
Wiarda, T. 130
Wiemer, R. O. 259–60
Willems, G. F. 67
Williams, B. E. 109, 120
Witherington III, B. 91, 128, 132, 134
Wohlers, M. 106
Wolter, M. 29
Wrede, W. 96, 163, 165
Wright, W. 223

Zanker, P. 39
Zeller, E. 149, 151
Ziegenaus, O. 22
Ziethen, G. 41
Zmijewski, J. 198
Zumstein, J. 127–28, 130, 133, 144